THE COMPLETE COLOUR
COOKBOOK

THE COMPLETE COLOUR
COOKBOOK

700 Recipes for Every Occasion

Edited by Norma MacMillan and Wendy James
Consultant Gill Edden

ORBIS PUBLISHING London

First published 1982 in Great Britain by
Orbis Publishing Limited, 20–22 Bedfordbury
London WC2

Reprinted 1983

ISBN 0-85613-472-4

© 1976 EDIPEM, Novara
© 1978, 1979, 1980, 1981, 1982 Orbis Publishing, London

The material in this book has previously appeared in
The Complete Cook and the *100 Recipes in Colour* series

Printed in Spain by
Printer industria gráfica sa
Sant Vicenç dels Horts   Barcelona   D.L.B. 31406-1983

Acknowledgements

Photographs were supplied by Editions Atlas, Editions Atlas/Cedus,
Editions Atlas/Zadora, Cadbury, Flour Advisory Board, Gales Honey,
Archivio IGDA, Lavinia Press Agency, Orbis GmbH, Pasta Information
Centre, Tate & Lyle Refineries Ltd., Wales Tourist Board.

Contents

Hungarian cabbage soup

Overall timing 2 hours

Freezing Suitable: add flour and soured cream when reheating.

To serve 4

8 oz	Onions	225 g
1	Garlic clove	1
3 tbsp	Oil	3x15 ml
12 oz	Stewing beef	350 g
12 oz	Canned sauerkraut	350 g
½ teasp	Fennel seeds	2.5 ml
½ teasp	Coarse salt	2.5 ml
3½ pints	Stock	2 litres
4 oz	Streaky bacon	125 g
2	Frankfurters	2
1 tbsp	Paprika	15 ml
2 tbsp	Plain flour	2x15 ml
4 tbsp	Water	4x15 ml
2 tbsp	Soured cream	2x15 ml

Peel and slice onions; peel and crush garlic. Heat 2 tbsp (2x15 ml) oil in large saucepan. Add onions and garlic and fry over moderate heat till golden. Cut beef into small cubes, add to pan and brown all over.

Add drained canned sauerkraut, fennel seeds and coarse salt to the pan. Cover with the stock (made with 2 stock cubes if necessary) and simmer gently for 1 hour or till meat is tender.

Derind and roughly chop the bacon. Fry bacon in remaining oil in a frying pan till crisp, then add the sliced frankfurters and paprika. Cook for 5 minutes, then remove and add to the saucepan.

Blend flour with cold water in a bowl till smooth, then stir into the soup mixture and cook for a further 5 minutes. Stir in the soured cream, adjust the seasoning and serve at once with slices of black bread.

Savoury dumpling soup

Overall timing 2½ hours

Freezing Suitable: add dumplings after reheating

To serve 6–8

1	Onion	1
4 oz	Carrots	125 g
3 oz	Parsnips	75 g
5	Stalks of celery	5
3 oz	Butter	75 g
2 tbsp	Plain flour	2x15 ml
3 pints	Chicken stock	1.7 litres
1 lb	Cooked chicken joints	450 g
Dumplings		
4 oz	Fresh breadcrumbs	125 g
2 oz	Streaky bacon	50 g
4 oz	Calf's liver	125 g
4 oz	Minced beef	125 g
1	Onion	1
1	Egg	1
½ teasp	Dried marjoram	2.5 ml
	Salt and pepper	
1 tbsp	Chopped parsley	15 ml

First make dumplings. Soak breadcrumbs in ½ pint (300 ml) water for 15 minutes. Derind and chop bacon and fry till crisp. Mince liver. Add beef, squeezed out breadcrumbs, chopped onion, drained bacon, egg, marjoram, seasoning and parsley. Shape into small dumplings.

Peel and chop onion, carrots and parsnips; chop celery. Melt butter, add onions and cook for 2–3 minutes. Add carrots, celery and parsnips, cover and cook till tender. Sieve vegetables and return to pan. Stir in flour then 1 pint (560 ml) stock. Simmer until thickened. Add remaining stock.

Skin, bone and chop chicken. Add to soup with dumplings and simmer for 15 minutes.

Scotch broth

Overall timing 2½ hours

Freezing Not suitable

To serve 4

4 oz	Pearl barley	125 g
2 lb	Scrag end of neck of lamb	900 g
2 oz	Butter	50 g
2	Onions	2
4	Stalks of celery	4
1 tbsp	Plain flour	15 ml
4 pints	Water	2.2 litres
1 teasp	Sugar	5 ml
	Salt and pepper	
1 lb	Potatoes	450 g
4	Carrots	4
1	Leek	1

Wash the barley and drain thoroughly. Wipe and trim the lamb and cut into pieces. Melt the butter in a saucepan or flameproof casserole. Add the lamb and fry over a high heat till browned on all sides.

Peel and chop the onions; trim and slice the celery. Add to the meat and fry till transparent. Add the barley and cook for 2 minutes. Sprinkle in the flour and cook, stirring, till flour begins to brown. Gradually add the water and bring to the boil, stirring constantly. Add the sugar, salt and pepper. Cover and simmer for about 1½ hours.

Peel and quarter the potatoes; scrape and slice the carrots. Add to the soup and simmer for a further 30 minutes.

Wash and finely chop the leek and add to the soup. Simmer for 3 minutes more. Taste and adjust the seasoning. Serve immediately with toast or granary rolls and butter.

Tregaron broth

Overall timing 1 hour

Freezing Not suitable

To serve 6

1 lb	Streaky bacon	450 g
1 lb	Shin beef	450 g
1 oz	Butter	25 g
1	Large leek	1
1 lb	Potatoes	450 g
8 oz	Carrots	225 g
8 oz	Parsnips	225 g
1	Small swede	1
3 pints	Water	1.7 litres
1	Small white cabbage	1
2 oz	Fine or medium oatmeal	50 g
	Salt and pepper	

Derind the bacon and cut into 1 inch (2.5 cm) pieces. Trim the beef and cut into chunks. Melt the butter in a large saucepan and fry the bacon and beef for 5 minutes.

Meanwhile, trim and slice the leek. Peel the potatoes, carrots, parsnips and swede. Cut into chunks. Add vegetables to pan and fry for 5 minutes. Add the water and bring to the boil.

Shred the cabbage and add to the pan with the oatmeal and seasoning. Cover and simmer for 45 minutes. Adjust the seasoning to taste before serving.

Shin of beef soup

Overall timing 4 hours

Freezing Not suitable

To serve 6–8

3 lb	Shin of beef on bone	1.4 kg
	Plain flour	
	Salt and pepper	
1	Onion	1
4	Stalks of celery	4
1	Leek	1
3	Carrots	3
2	Turnips	2
1 lb	Potatoes	450 g
1 lb	White cabbage	450 g
	Sprig of parsley	
	Sprig of thyme	
2 teasp	Powdered mustard	2x5 ml
4	Slices of toast	4

Wipe beef; slash meat through to bone several times. Make a stiff paste of flour and water and use to seal ends of bone to keep in the marrow. Place in large saucepan with 3 pints (1.7 litres) water, salt and pepper. Bring to the boil, skim off scum, cover and simmer for 3 hours.

Peel and chop onion; trim and chop celery and leek; scrape and slice carrots; peel turnips and potatoes and cut into chunks; shred cabbage.

Add vegetables to beef with herbs and cook for a further 30 minutes.

Lift out meat and cut into cubes and slices, reserving the bone. Remove vegetables with a draining spoon and place in serving dish with meat. Keep hot to serve as main course. Pour stock into a warmed soup tureen and keep hot.

Preheat grill. Scoop out marrow from bone. Mix with salt, pepper and mustard and spread on toast. Grill till bubbling, then serve with soup.

Turkish soup with meatballs

Overall timing 1¾ hours

Freezing Not suitable

To serve 4–6

1	Knuckle of veal	1
1 lb	Shin of beef	450 g
1	Large onion	1
2	Large carrots	2
1	Stalk of celery	1
	Parsley stalks	
	Salt and pepper	
2	Eggs	2
3 tbsp	Lemon juice	3x15 ml
Meatballs		
1 lb	Minced beef	450 g
4 oz	Cooked long grain rice	125 g
1	Egg	1
1 tbsp	Chopped parsley	15 ml
¼ teasp	Grated nutmeg	1.25 ml
	Salt and pepper	
1 oz	Butter	25 g
2 tbsp	Oil	2x15 ml

Chop knuckle in half lengthways. Dice beef. Peel and chop onion and carrots; chop celery. Put meat and vegetables into a saucepan with 4 pints (2.2 litres) water, parsley stalks and seasoning. Cover and simmer for 45 minutes.

Meanwhile, mix beef with rice, egg, parsley, nutmeg and seasoning to a stiff paste and shape into small balls.

Heat butter and oil in a frying pan. Add meatballs and fry till browned all over.

Strain stock, discarding meat and vegetables. Return to pan and bring back to boil. Add meatballs and simmer for 15 minutes.

Put the eggs and lemon juice into a tureen and gradually stir in soup.

Manhattan clam chowder

Overall timing 2 hours

Freezing Suitable

To serve 8

4 oz	Streaky bacon	125 g
2 tbsp	Oil	2x15 ml
3	Large onions	3
2	Large tomatoes	2
2	Leeks	2
1	Stalk of celery	1
1	Carrot	1
2	Potatoes	2
1½ pints	Fish stock	850 ml
2	Sprigs of parsley	2
1	Bay leaf	1
¼ teasp	Grated nutmeg	1.25 ml
	Salt and pepper	
¾ pint	Milk	400 ml
1 lb	Canned clams	450 g
1 oz	Butter	25 g
1 oz	Plain flour	25 g
2 teasp	Worcestershire sauce	2x5 ml
¼ teasp	Tabasco sauce	1.25 ml

Derind and dice bacon. Heat oil in a saucepan, add bacon and cook gently. Peel and slice onions and add to pan. Cook till transparent.

Blanch and peel tomatoes. Finely chop leeks and celery. Peel and finely chop carrot and potatoes. Add to pan and cook for 2–3 minutes. Add stock, parsley, bay leaf, nutmeg and seasoning. Cover and simmer for 10 minutes.

Discard parsley and bay leaf. Purée soup in blender, return to rinsed-out pan and add milk and drained clams. Simmer gently for 4 minutes.

Knead butter and flour to a paste. Stir into soup in tiny pieces. Cook for 2–3 minutes until thick. Stir in Worcestershire and Tabasco sauces and serve.

American fish chowder

Overall timing 1½ hours

Freezing Suitable

To serve 4

2 lb	Mixed white fish	900 g
2 oz	Streaky bacon	50 g
1 tbsp	Oil	15 ml
1	Large onion	1
4	Medium potatoes	4
4	Carrots	4
4	Stalks of celery	4
1 tbsp	Chopped parsley	15 ml
14 oz	Can of tomatoes	397 g
1½ pints	Fish stock or water	850 ml
2 tbsp	Tomato ketchup	2x15 ml
2 tbsp	Worcestershire sauce	2x15 ml
	Dried thyme	
	Salt and pepper	

Skin and bone fish and cut into bite-size pieces. Derind and dice bacon.

Heat oil in a saucepan and fry bacon till crisp. Remove from pan. Peel and chop onion and add to pan. Cook gently till transparent.

Peel and chop potatoes and carrots. Finely chop celery. Add to pan with chopped parsley, tomatoes and their juice, fish stock or water, tomato ketchup, Worcestershire sauce, a pinch of thyme and seasoning. Cover and simmer gently for about 45 minutes.

Add the fish pieces and bacon, cover and cook for a further 15 minutes.

Cantonese fish soup

Overall timing 35 minutes plus marination

Freezing Not suitable

To serve 6

12 oz	White fish fillets	350 g
2 tbsp	Soy sauce	2x15 ml
2 teasp	Dry sherry	2x5 ml
3 tbsp	Oil	3x15 ml
2	Medium onions	2
4	Shallots	4
2	Medium carrots	2
3	Stalks of celery	3
2½ pints	Chicken stock	1.5 litres
2 oz	Long grain rice	50 g
	Salt and pepper	

Cut across the fillets into thin strips and put into a bowl. Add the soy sauce, sherry and 1 tbsp (15 ml) of the oil. Mix well and leave to marinate in a cool place for 1 hour.

Peel and chop the onions and two of the shallots. Peel and dice the carrots. Trim and chop the celery. Heat remaining oil in a large saucepan, add prepared vegetables, cover and cook gently for 5 minutes. Add the stock and bring to the boil. Stir in rice and salt, bring back to the boil, cover and simmer for 10 minutes.

Add the fish and marinating juices and cook for a further 10 minutes. Taste and adjust seasoning. Pour into soup bowls and garnish with remaining shallots, peeled and finely chopped.

Provençal cod soup

Overall timing 1 hour

Freezing Not suitable

To serve 4

1	Large onion	1
1	Leek	1
1	Large tomato	1
2 tbsp	Oil	2x15 ml
1	Stalk of fresh fennel (optional)	1
2	Garlic cloves	2
2½ pints	Water	1.5 litres
	Bouquet garni	
	Orange rind	
¼ teasp	Saffron	1.25 ml
	Salt and pepper	
1¾ lb	Potatoes	750 g
1 lb	Cod fillets	450 g
4	Thick slices of bread	4
1 tbsp	Chopped parsley	15 ml

Peel and slice onion. Trim and finely chop leek. Blanch, peel and chop tomato. Heat oil in a large saucepan. Add onion, leek and tomato and cook, stirring, for 5 minutes.

Chop fennel, if using. Peel and crush garlic. Add water, bouquet garni, fennel, a strip of orange rind, garlic, saffron and pepper. Bring to the boil.

Peel and thickly slice potatoes. Add to pan and cook for 10 minutes. Chop cod fillets into pieces and add with seasoning. Cook for a further 15 minutes.

Remove cod and potatoes with a draining spoon and place in warmed serving dish. Put the slices of bread in a warmed soup tureen and pour the cooking juices over. Sprinkle with parsley. Serve soup and cod together or as separate courses.

Cock-a-leekie

Overall timing 2¼ hours

Freezing Suitable

To serve 6

2 lb	Leeks	900 g
1 oz	Butter	25 g
3 lb	Ovenready chicken	1.4 kg
3 pints	Stock or water	1.7 litres
	Bouquet garni	
	Salt and pepper	
4 oz	Prunes (optional)	125 g

Wash, trim and slice leeks. Melt butter in a frying pan, add leeks and fry quickly for 5 minutes. Put into a saucepan with the chicken, giblets, stock (made with cubes if necessary) or water, bouquet garni, salt and pepper. Bring to the boil, cover and simmer for 1½ hours.

Stone prunes and add to pan, if using. Cook for 30 minutes longer. Discard bouquet garni.

Remove chicken from pan. Cut the meat into strips, discarding skin and bones. Return meat to pan. Taste and adjust seasoning. Serve with baps or oatcakes.

Chicken, lemon and egg drop soup

Overall timing 2 hours 10 minutes

Freezing Suitable: add eggs after reheating

To serve 6

1 lb	Knuckle of veal	450 g
3½ pints	Water	2 litres
3 lb	Boiling chicken with giblets	1.4 kg
1	Lemon	1
2	Onions	2
2	Cloves	2
	Salt and pepper	
2	Eggs	2

Place knuckle in saucepan with the water. Bring to the boil, then cover and simmer for 1 hour.

Meanwhile, chop the chicken into joints and remove skin if liked. Wash giblets. Grate the rind of the lemon and squeeze out the juice. Reserve both. Peel onions and spike each with a clove. Add chicken, giblets, lemon rind, spiked onions and seasoning to pan. Cover and cook gently for 1 hour till chicken is tender.

Strain the stock into a clean pan. Cut meats into small pieces, discarding bones, skin, giblets and onions. Skim stock, add meats and bring to the boil. Stir in lemon juice, then taste and adjust seasoning.

Beat the eggs in a small bowl. Remove saucepan from heat and pour soup into tureen. Drizzle egg in a thin stream into soup, stirring continuously. Serve.

Chicken noodle soup

Overall timing 10 minutes

Freezing Not suitable

To serve 4

2½ pints	Chicken stock	1.5 litres
3 oz	Fine egg noodles	75 g
2 tbsp	Lemon juice	2x15 ml
	Salt and pepper	
2 tbsp	Chopped parsley	2x15 ml

Put the stock into a large saucepan. Bring to the boil and add the noodles. Boil for 3–4 minutes till tender.

Add the lemon juice and seasoning and sprinkle with chopped parsley. Serve with a side dish of grated mature Cheddar cheese.

Bacon dumpling soup

Overall timing 2¾ hours

Freezing Suitable: add dumplings to stock after thawing

To serve 4

12 oz	Stale white bread	350 g
½ pint	Milk	300 ml
2 oz	Lean bacon rashers	50 g
1 oz	Butter	25 g
1	Onion	1
1	Garlic clove	1
1 tbsp	Chopped parsley	15 ml
¼ teasp	Dried marjoram	1.25 ml
	Salt and pepper	
3	Eggs	3
4 oz	Self-raising flour	125 g
2 pints	Stock	1.1 litres

Remove crusts from bread, then soak in milk for 2 hours. Derind and chop bacon. Fry in butter till crisp.

Peel and finely chop onion. Peel and crush garlic. Put both into bowl with bread, bacon, parsley and marjoram. Season and add eggs. Mix together well. Sift in flour and stir until absorbed.

Heat the stock in a large saucepan. Make the bacon mixture into 1 inch (2.5 cm) balls and roll them in a little flour so they don't fall apart when cooking. Add the dumplings to the stock and simmer for 15 minutes. Serve hot.

Pea and bacon soup

Overall timing 2¾ hours plus overnight soaking

Freezing Suitable

To serve 6

12oz	Dried whole green peas	350g
4 pints	Water	2.3 litres
2lb	Knuckle of smoked bacon	900g
	Salt and pepper	

Put peas in a saucepan and cover with the cold water. Leave to soak overnight.

Add the bacon knuckle to the pan and bring to the boil. Skim off any scum. Cover and simmer for 1½–2 hours till the bacon and peas are tender.

Remove and drain the bacon joint. Discard the skin and bone and cut the meat into small cubes. Reserve one third of the peas. Purée the remaining peas in a blender or by pressing through a sieve. Return the puréed peas and reserved whole peas to the saucepan. Bring to the boil, stirring occasionally.

Add the diced bacon, and season to taste. Pour into a warmed tureen and serve with crispbread.

Turkey vegetable soup

Overall timing 1¼ hours

Freezing Not suitable

To serve 6

1	Large carrot	1
1	Large onion	1
1	Stalk of celery	1
2	Turkey wings	2
2½ pints	Water	1.5 litres
	Salt and pepper	
8 oz	Waxy potatoes	225 g
2	Leeks	2
4	Thick slices of bread	4
3 oz	Butter	75 g

Peel and chop carrot and onion. Trim and chop the celery. Wipe the turkey wings and put into a saucepan with the prepared vegetables, water and seasoning. Bring to the boil, skim off any scum, cover and simmer for 45 minutes.

Peel potatoes and cut into ½ inch (12.5 mm) cubes. Trim and slice leeks.

Lift turkey wings out of pan with a draining spoon and leave to cool slightly. Add potatoes and leeks to the soup and simmer for 5 minutes till vegetables are tender.

Remove the skin and bones from the turkey wings and cut the flesh into strips. Add to the soup and reheat gently.

Meanwhile, remove the crusts from bread and cut into cubes. Melt butter in a frying pan, add the bread and fry till golden all over. Drain croûtons on kitchen paper.

Taste soup and adjust seasoning. Pour into a warmed tureen and sprinkle with croûtons. Serve immediately.

Swiss cream of barley soup

Overall timing 2¾ hours

Freezing Not suitable

To serve 4–6

2	Large onions	2
3	Cloves	3
1	Calf's foot	1
4oz	Pearl barley	125g
	Bay leaf	
3 pints	Water	1.7 litres
	Salt and pepper	
12oz	Carrots	350g
4	Stalks of celery	4
2	Small leeks	2
4oz	Smoked streaky bacon rashers	125g
2oz	Lard	50g
2	Egg yolks	2
¼ pint	Carton of single cream	150ml
1 tbsp	Chopped chives	15ml

Peel one of the onions and spike with cloves. Wash calf's foot, chop in half lengthways and put into a saucepan with the barley, spiked onion and bay leaf. Add the water and seasoning, then cover and simmer for 2 hours.

Meanwhile, scrape and dice carrots. Peel and chop remaining onion. Trim and chop celery and leeks. Derind and dice bacon. Melt lard in a large saucepan. Add bacon and vegetables and fry for 10 minutes till golden.

Remove spiked onion and bay leaf from stock and discard. Lift calf's foot out of stock and remove the meat, discarding skin and bones. Add meat to stock with the vegetables. Bring to the boil and simmer for 10 minutes till vegetables are tender.

Put the egg yolks and cream into a tureen and beat together with a fork. Season the soup to taste and gradually stir into tureen. Sprinkle with chives and serve.

Spicy bortsch

Overall timing 2½ hours

Freezing Suitable

To serve 6

1	Carrot	1
1 lb	Parsnips	450 g
4	Tomatoes	4
1	Onion	1
9	Cloves	9
1 lb	Beef bones	450 g
1 lb	Stewing beef	450 g
½ teasp	Salt	2.5 ml
1 teasp	Sugar	5 ml
6	Peppercorns	6
1	Bay leaf	1
2½ pints	Cold water	1.5 litres
1½ lb	Raw beetroots	700 g
4 oz	Red or green cabbage	125 g

Peel and chop carrot and parsnips. Chop tomatoes. Peel onion and spike with cloves. Crack bones; dice beef.

Put vegetables, bones and beef into a large saucepan with salt, sugar, peppercorns, bay leaf and water. Bring to the boil, cover and simmer for 2 hours or until meat is tender. Remove bones, onion and bay leaf.

Peel and coarsely grate beetroots. Chop cabbage. Add to pan and simmer, uncovered, for a further 12–15 minutes.

Florentine minestrone

Overall timing 2¾ hours plus soaking

Freezing Suitable: add cabbage and macaroni after reheating

To serve 4

8 oz	Dried haricot beans	225 g
2	Large carrots	2
2	Stalks of celery	2
1	Garlic clove	1
2	Onions	2
4 tbsp	Oil	4x15 ml
1½ teasp	Dried mixed herbs	7.5 ml
14 oz	Can of tomatoes	397 g
8 oz	Cabbage	225 g
4 oz	Short macaroni	125 g
	Salt and pepper	

Place beans in large saucepan and cover with cold water. Bring to the boil and boil for 2 minutes. Remove from heat, cover and soak for 2 hours.

Drain beans, return to pan, cover with boiling water and simmer for 2 hours.

Peel and chop carrots; chop celery. Peel and crush garlic. Peel and slice onions. In a large saucepan, heat oil and fry vegetables until golden.

Drain beans, reserving cooking liquor. Purée half the beans. Add beans, whole and puréed, to fried vegetables with cooking liquor, herbs and tomatoes. Bring to the boil. Shred cabbage and add to boiling soup with macaroni and seasoning. Simmer for 20 minutes.

Tuscan vegetable soup

Overall timing 2 hours plus overnight soaking

Freezing Not suitable

To serve 6

8 oz	Dried beans	225 g
1¼ lb	Cabbage	600 g
1	Onion	1
1	Large leek	1
1	Stalk of celery	1
1	Carrot	1
1	Garlic clove	1
3 tbsp	Oil	3x15 ml
1	Bay leaf	1
3	Sprigs of oregano	3
	Sprig of rosemary	
	Salt and pepper	
2 tbsp	Tomato purée	2x15 ml
3 pints	Light stock	1.7 litres

Soak beans in cold water overnight. The next day, drain beans, put into a large saucepan and cover with fresh cold water. Bring to the boil and simmer for about 1½ hours till tender.

Meanwhile, shred cabbage. Peel and thinly slice onion; trim and slice leek and celery. Scrape and chop carrot. Peel and crush garlic. Heat oil in a large saucepan and fry vegetables, except cabbage, with garlic and herbs till lightly browned. Add cabbage and seasoning and fry for a further 5 minutes.

Remove herbs from pan and add the tomato purée, drained beans and stock. Bring to the boil and simmer for a further 15 minutes. Taste and adjust the seasoning and pour into warmed individual bowls.

Watercress soup

Overall timing 40 minutes

Freezing Suitable: add cream after thawing

To serve 4

1	Large onion	1
2	Large floury potatoes	2
1 oz	Butter	25 g
3	Bunches of watercress	3
1¾ pints	Chicken stock	1 litre
	Salt and pepper	
4 fl oz	Double cream	113 ml

Peel and finely chop onion. Peel and chop or grate potatoes. Melt butter in a saucepan, add onions and potatoes and turn till coated in butter. Cover and cook gently for 10 minutes.

Wash, dry and chop watercress leaves and stalks, reserving some whole leaves. Add to pan with stock and bring to boil. Cover and simmer for 15 minutes.

Rub soup through sieve or purée in blender. Return to pan, add reserved watercress leaves and reheat. Taste and adjust seasoning. Serve immediately with side dish of whipped cream, or cool, stir in cream and chill well before serving.

Rice and cabbage soup

Overall timing 45 minutes

Freezing Not suitable

To serve 6–8

1	Large onion	1
8 oz	Streaky bacon	225 g
1	Garlic clove	1
2 oz	Butter	50 g
8 oz	Long grain rice	225 g
3 pints	Light stock	1.7 litres
	Salt and pepper	
	Bouquet garni	
1 lb	Green cabbage	450 g
4 oz	Cheese	125 g

Peel and chop the onion; derind and finely dice the bacon. Peel and crush garlic. Melt the butter in a saucepan and add the onion, bacon and garlic. Fry gently for 5 minutes without browning.

Add the rice and cook, stirring, for 2 minutes till coated with butter. Add the stock, seasoning and bouquet garni. Bring to the boil and simmer for 15 minutes.

Meanwhile, coarsely shred the cabbage. Add to the pan, bring to the boil again and simmer for 5 minutes.

Remove pan from the heat and discard the bouquet garni. Grate cheese, stir into soup and adjust seasoning. Pour into a tureen and serve immediately with rye bread.

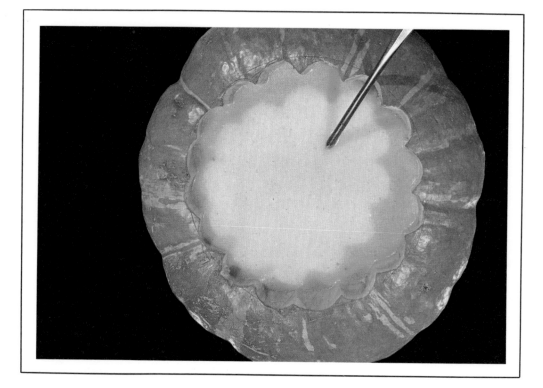

Pumpkin soup

Overall timing 50 minutes

Freezing Not suitable

To serve 6

2 lb	Pumpkin or other squash	900 g
$\frac{1}{2}$ pint	Water	300 ml
	Salt and pepper	
$1\frac{1}{2}$ pints	Milk	850 ml
1 teasp	Sugar	5 ml
$\frac{1}{4}$ teasp	Grated nutmeg	1.25 ml
1	Egg yolk	1
4 tbsp	Single cream	4x15 ml

Prepare the squash, discarding fibrous centre and seeds. Cut the flesh into chunks, put into a saucepan with the water and salt and bring to the boil. Simmer for about 30 minutes till tender, then purée in a blender or food mill. Place purée in saucepan with milk, sugar and nutmeg. Heat through gently till almost boiling, stirring occasionally.

Beat the egg yolk and cream together in a bowl and pour in a little of the hot soup, stirring constantly. Pour back into the pan and stir over a low heat for 3 minutes – do not boil. Taste and adjust seasoning, then serve immediately with toasted rye bread.

Onion soup with wine

Overall timing 45 minutes

Freezing Suitable: pour soup over bread and add cheese after reheating

To serve 4

3	Large onions	3
2 oz	Butter	50 g
1 tbsp	Plain flour	15 ml
½ teasp	Brown sugar	2.5 ml
2½ pints	Water	1.5 litres
8	Slices of French bread	8
2 tbsp	Dry white wine	2x15 ml
	Salt and pepper	
2 oz	Gruyère or Cheddar cheese	50 g

Peel and slice onions. Melt half the butter in a large saucepan and cook onions till transparent. Sprinkle onions with flour. Cook, stirring, until flour colours. Add sugar, then gradually stir in water. Simmer for 20 minutes.

Preheat the oven to 450°F (230°C) Gas 8.

Fry bread in remaining butter. Place bread slices in bottom of individual bowls or ovenproof soup tureen. Add wine and seasoning, then pour soup over bread. Grate cheese and sprinkle it into the bowls. Bake for 5–10 minutes to melt the cheese.

Mushroom soup

Overall timing 30 minutes

Freezing Not suitable

To serve 4

2	Stalks of celery	2
8 oz	Mushrooms	225 g
2 teasp	Oil	2x5 ml
12 oz	Cooked chicken meat	350 g
1 tbsp	Soy sauce	15 ml
1 tbsp	Dry sherry	15 ml
8	Water chestnuts	8
1¾ pints	Chicken stock	1 litre
4 oz	Bean sprouts	125 g
	Salt and pepper	
1	Egg	1

Finely chop celery. Thinly slice mushrooms. Heat oil in a saucepan and stir-fry vegetables for 5 minutes.

Cut chicken into small pieces and sprinkle with soy sauce and sherry. Quarter or dice water chestnuts.

Add stock to pan with water chestnuts. Bring to the boil, then add chicken and soaking juices. Simmer for 10 minutes. Add bean sprouts and cook for 2 minutes. Taste and adjust seasoning.

Beat egg. Remove pan from heat and trickle in beaten egg, stirring constantly. Divide soup between individual soup bowls and serve.

Chicken vermicelli soup

Overall timing 40 minutes

Freezing Not suitable

To serve 6

1 oz	Chinese dried mushrooms	25 g
2½ pints	Chicken stock	1.5 litres
6 oz	Cooked chicken meat	175 g
2	Lettuce leaves	2
4	Eggs	4
	Salt and pepper	
1 oz	Butter	25 g
2 oz	Chinese vermicelli	50 g
2 tbsp	Dry sherry	2x15 ml

Soak mushrooms in warm water for 30 minutes. Drain, discard woody stalks and put into saucepan with stock. Bring to the boil and simmer for 10 minutes.

Meanwhile, cut chicken into strips. Shred lettuce. Beat eggs with seasoning. Melt half butter in frying pan, add half egg mixture and make a thin omelette. Remove from pan and reserve. Use remaining butter and egg mixture to make another omelette. Roll up both omelettes and cut into thin slices.

Add noodles and chicken to saucepan and simmer for 2 minutes. Remove from heat and add sherry, omelette strips and lettuce. Serve immediately.

Pumpkin rice soup

Overall timing 1 hour

Freezing Not suitable

To serve 6

1	Large onion	1
1	Stalk of celery	1
1	Large carrot	1
2 oz	Streaky bacon rashers	50 g
2 oz	Butter	50 g
1½ lb	Pumpkin	700 g
3 pints	Chicken stock	1.7 litres
1	Garlic clove	1
	Salt and pepper	
6 oz	Long grain rice	175 g
3 tbsp	Grated Parmesan cheese	3x15 ml

Peel the onion, trim the celery and scrape the carrot. Derind the bacon. Finely chop vegetables and bacon. Melt the butter in a saucepan, add the vegetables and bacon and fry for 5 minutes, stirring occasionally.

Scrape the seeds and fibrous centre out of the pumpkin. Cut into chunks, leaving the skin on, and add to the pan. Fry, stirring, for a further 5 minutes.

Add the stock (made with cubes if necessary), peeled and crushed garlic and seasoning and bring to the boil. Simmer for 10 minutes.

Wash the rice and add to the soup. Bring to the boil and simmer for 15–20 minutes till the rice is tender.

Stir in the Parmesan and adjust the seasoning. Pour into warmed serving bowls and serve immediately with bread sticks or fresh crusty rolls and butter.

Minestrone

Overall timing 2¼ hours

Freezing Not suitable

To serve 8

2 oz	Smoked bacon	50 g
1	Onion	1
1	Small leek	1
4 tbsp	Olive oil	4×15 ml
1	Garlic clove	1
1 tbsp	Chopped parsley	15 ml
2	Sage leaves	2
3	Carrots	3
1	Courgette	1
2	Large potatoes	2
3	Stalks of celery	3
1	Large tomato	1
12 oz	Savoy cabbage	350 g
3	Basil leaves	3
3½ pints	Hot stock	1.7 litres
1 tbsp	Tomato purée	15 ml
	Salt and pepper	
14 oz	Can of white beans	397 g
4 oz	Short-cut macaroni	125 g
	Grated Parmesan cheese	

Derind and chop the bacon. Place in saucepan and fry till fat runs.

Peel and finely chop the onion; trim and chop the leek. Add oil to saucepan and heat, then add onion, leek, peeled and crushed garlic, parsley and chopped sage. Cover and sweat for 10 minutes.

Meanwhile, peel the remaining vegetables, as necessary, and chop them. Add prepared vegetables and chopped basil to pan and cook, stirring, for 5 minutes. Gradually add stock, tomato purée, salt and pepper and bring to the boil. Drain the canned beans and add. Cover tightly and cook gently for 1¼ hours.

Add macaroni and cook for 20 minutes more. Serve with Parmesan cheese.

Majorcan vegetable and bread soup

Overall timing 1½ hours

Freezing Not suitable

To serve 6

8 oz	Continental lentils	225 g
3 pints	Water	1.7 litres
4 oz	Streaky bacon rashers	125 g
1 lb	Fresh broad beans	450 g
1 lb	Fresh peas	450 g
1 lb	Cabbage	450 g
8 oz	Fresh spinach	225 g
	Salt and pepper	
18	Thin slices of brown bread	18

Wash and pick over the lentils and put into a saucepan with the water. Bring to the boil and simmer for 45 minutes.

Meanwhile, derind and dice the bacon. Shell the beans and peas. Shred the cabbage and spinach.

Rub the lentils with their cooking liquor through a sieve or purée in a blender. Return to the saucepan and add seasoning, bacon and vegetables and bring to the boil. Simmer for about 25 minutes till the vegetables are tender.

Taste and adjust the seasoning. Arrange three slices of bread in each soup bowl and pour the soup over. Serve immediately.

Irish celery soup

Overall timing 35 minutes

Freezing Suitable: add cream when reheating

To serve 4

1 lb	Celery	450 g
2	Potatoes	2
2	Onions	2
2 oz	Butter	50 g
	Salt and pepper	
1	Bay leaf	1
1	Garlic clove	1
	Grated nutmeg	
1¾ pints	Chicken stock	1 litre
¼ pint	Carton of single cream	150 ml

Cut off base of celery, then wash and chop stalks and leaves. Peel and finely chop potatoes and onions. Melt butter in saucepan over a low heat. Add celery stalks and leaves, potatoes and onions, cover and cook for 5 minutes, stirring to prevent colouring.

Sprinkle with salt and pepper, add the bay leaf, peeled and crushed garlic, pinch of nutmeg and hot stock (made with 2 cubes if necessary). Cover and simmer for 20 minutes.

Remove bay leaf. Push soup through sieve into a bowl, or liquidize, then return to saucepan and add the cream. Heat through without boiling. Adjust seasoning, then serve with croûtons (diced bread fried in oil till brown).

Gazpacho

Overall timing 20 minutes plus chilling

Freezing Suitable

To serve 6

1¼ lb	Tomatoes	600 g
½	Cucumber	½
1	Large onion	1
1	Green or red pepper	1
2	Garlic cloves	2
4 oz	Fresh white breadcrumbs	125 g
3 tbsp	Olive oil	3x15 ml
1 tbsp	Wine vinegar	15 ml
1	Sprig of parsley or mint	1
	Salt and pepper	
2 pints	Water	1.1 litres

Blanch, peel and chop the tomatoes. Peel, deseed and chop the cucumber. Peel and chop the onion. Deseed and chop the pepper; peel and chop the garlic.

Place all the vegetables in a blender with breadcrumbs, oil, vinegar, parsley or mint, salt and pepper and 1 pint (560 ml) of the water. Blend to a purée.

Place purée in a large bowl and stir in the remaining water. Cover and chill for 3 hours.

Before serving, add a few ice cubes. Serve with side dishes of chopped onion, hard-boiled eggs, tomatoes, peppers and croûtons.

Creamy cauliflower soup

Overall timing 35 minutes

Freezing Not suitable

To serve 4

1	Large cauliflower	1
1	Small onion	1
	Salt and pepper	
2 oz	Butter	50 g
2 oz	Plain flour	50 g
$\frac{3}{4}$ pint	Milk	400 ml
	Lamb seasoning salt	
$\frac{1}{2}$ teasp	Dried mixed herbs	2.5 ml
$\frac{1}{4}$ teasp	Grated nutmeg	1.25 ml
1	Egg yolk	1
4 tbsp	Single cream	4x15 ml
	Fresh dill	

Trim cauliflower, separate into florets and wash. Peel and finely chop onion. Put cauliflower and onion into pan of boiling salted water, cover and cook for 10 minutes. Drain, saving $\frac{3}{4}$ pint (400 ml) cooking liquor. Mash half cauliflower and onion.

Melt butter in a large saucepan. Stir in flour, then milk and reserved cooking liquor. Add a pinch of lamb seasoning salt, the herbs, nutmeg and pulped and whole cauliflower and onion. Simmer for 7 minutes. Taste and adjust seasoning.

Mix egg yolk and cream in warmed tureen. Pour in soup and serve garnished with dill.

Courgette and egg soup

Overall timing 30 minutes

Freezing Not suitable

To serve 4

1 lb	Courgettes	450 g
1 oz	Lard	25 g
3 tbsp	Olive oil	3x15 ml
1	Garlic clove	1
1¾ pints	Boiling water	1 litre
	Salt and pepper	
2	Eggs	2
10	Basil leaves (optional)	10
2 tbsp	Chopped parsley	2x15 ml
2 oz	White Cheshire or Wensleydale cheese	50 g
Garnish		
1 oz	White Cheshire or Wensleydale cheese	25 g
	Croûtons	

Wash courgettes, trim ends, then dice them. Heat the lard, oil and peeled, garlic clove in a saucepan or flameproof casserole. Cook over a moderate heat till the garlic turns golden, then discard it.

Add diced courgettes to pan and cook for a few minutes. Add the boiling water and a pinch of salt, cover and cook gently for about 15 minutes.

Break eggs into a warmed soup tureen and add chopped basil, parsley and salt and pepper. Grate or crumble in the cheese. Beat well with a fork.

Gradually add about a quarter of the soup and mix well, then pour in the rest. Garnish with more grated or crumbled cheese and freshly made croûtons.

Chicory soup

Overall timing 25 minutes

Freezing Suitable: add vermouth after reheating

To serve 4

4	Heads of chicory	4
2½ oz	Butter	65 g
2 teasp	Caster sugar	2x5 ml
1¾ pints	Chicken stock	1 litre
2 teasp	Plain flour	2x5 ml
3 fl oz	Dry vermouth	90 ml
	Salt and pepper	

Chop chicory. Melt 2 oz (50 g) of the butter in a saucepan and fry chicory over a gentle heat for about 5 minutes. Tilt pan, add sugar and allow to caramelize. Add stock, cover and simmer for 10 minutes.

Mix remaining butter with the flour to a smooth paste. Stir paste a little at a time into the soup. Return to the boil and simmer for 2–3 minutes.

Add vermouth and seasoning and cook, uncovered, for 1–2 minutes more. Pour into serving bowls and garnish with freshly made, hot croûtons.

Cheese soup

Overall timing 30 minutes

Freezing Not suitable

To serve 4-6

1	Onion	1
3 oz	Butter	75 g
1½ pints	Light stock	850 ml
¼ pint	Dry white wine	150 ml
4 teasp	Cornflour	4x5 ml
½ pint	Milk	300 ml
	Salt and white pepper	
4 oz	Cheddar cheese	125 g
4 oz	Parmesan cheese	125 g
	Croûtons	

Peel and finely chop the onion. Melt the butter in a saucepan, add onion and fry till transparent. Stir in the stock and wine and bring to the boil slowly.

Blend the cornflour with a little water and add to the pan, stirring constantly. Bring back to the boil, stirring, and cook for 3 minutes. Add the milk, salt, pepper and grated cheese. Stir over a very low heat till the cheese has completely melted. Taste and adjust seasoning, then pour into a warmed tureen. Serve immediately garnished with lots of croûtons.

Bean soup

Overall timing 30 minutes

Freezing Suitable: add soured cream after thawing

To serve 4

4 oz	Streaky bacon	125 g
1	Red pepper	1
1	Green pepper	1
1¾ pints	Strong beef stock	1 litre
12 oz	Can of butter beans	340 g
	Tabasco sauce	
	Salt	
4 tbsp	Soured cream	4x15 ml

Derind and chop bacon and fry it lightly in a frying pan till the fat runs. Place in a deep saucepan.

Deseed and finely chop half the red and green peppers and add to the pan with the stock (made up with 3 stock cubes if necessary) and drained beans. Bring to the boil and simmer for 20 minutes.

Add Tabasco sauce and salt to taste.

Slice remaining peppers and blanch for 5 minutes in boiling water. Drain well.

Remove soup from the heat and stir in the soured cream. Garnish with pepper slices and serve with a bowl of grated cheese and fresh wholemeal bread.

Barley and mushroom soup

Overall timing 3 hours 50 minutes

Freezing Suitable: add butter and cream after reheating

To serve 4

3 oz	Pearl barley	75 g
	Salt	
2	Carrots	2
2	Celery stalks	2
1	Leek	1
1	Onion	1
2	Bay leaves	2
10	Black peppercorns	10
1	Sprig of parsley	1
1½ oz	Dried mushrooms	40 g
2 tbsp .	Vinegar	2 x 15 ml
2 oz	Butter	50 g
¼ pint	Carton of single cream	150 ml

Wash barley, then cook in lightly salted, boiling water for 2½ hours till very soft and gelatinous.

Meanwhile, scrape and chop carrots. Wash and slice celery and leek. Peel and quarter onion. Put all vegetables into a saucepan with bay leaves, salt, peppercorns, parsley, mushrooms and 9 fl oz (250 ml) water. Cover and simmer gently for 1 hour.

Strain stock into a bowl. Reserve mushrooms and discard remaining vegetables. Slice mushrooms and return to pan with strained stock.

Drain barley and crush with a potato masher, or partly liquidize in a blender. Add barley and vinegar to stock, heat through and season.

Cut butter into small pieces and put in bottom of a warmed soup tureen. Pour in soup, stir in cream and serve.

Brussels sprout soup

Overall timing 1¼ hours

Freezing Suitable: add cream and egg yolk mixture when reheating

To serve 4

1 lb	Brussels sprouts	450 g
3 oz	Butter	75 g
1¾ pints	Hot beef stock	1 litre
	Salt	
1 oz	Plain flour	25 g
	Grated nutmeg	
6 tbsp	Single cream	6x15 ml
1	Egg yolk	1

Trim sprouts. Cut a cross in base of each. Melt 2 oz (50 g) butter in a saucepan, add sprouts and cook for 3 minutes, stirring continuously. Add stock and salt. Cover and cook for 40 minutes.

Sieve sprouts into a bowl, or liquidize.

Melt remaining butter in a pan. Add flour and cook, stirring, for 3 minutes. Remove pan from heat and gradually add sprout purée. Return to heat and cook for 10 minutes over low heat. Season with salt and pinch of nutmeg.

Mix cream with egg yolk. Off heat, stir cream mixture into soup to thicken.

Avocado soup

Overall timing 15 minutes plus chilling if serving cold

Freezing Suitable: add cream after thawing

To serve 4

1¾ pints	Chicken stock	1 litre
2	Ripe avocados	2
1 tbsp	Lemon juice	15 ml
1	Egg yolk	1
3 tbsp	Single cream	3x15 ml
	Salt and pepper	

Heat chicken stock (made up with 4 cubes if necessary) in a saucepan to boiling point.

Cut open avocados and lift out stones. If intending to serve soup cold, cut eight very thin slices, sprinkle with lemon juice to prevent discoloration and set aside. Scoop out remaining avocado flesh, place in a bowl and mash well with the egg yolk and cream.

Remove stock from heat. Gradually add the avocado mixture, whisking vigorously. Add salt and pepper to taste. Do not reheat.

Serve hot with fried croûtons. If serving cold, chill the soup for at least 1 hour, then serve garnished with reserved avocado slices.

Pipérade

Overall timing 1 hour

Freezing Not suitable

To serve 4

1 lb	Ripe tomatoes	450 g
2	Green peppers	2
2	Onions	2
1	Garlic clove	1
5 tbsp	Oil	5x15 ml
	Salt and pepper	
$\frac{1}{4}$ teasp	Dried marjoram	1.25 ml
	Tabasco sauce	
8	Eggs	8

Blanch, peel and chop tomatoes. Deseed and chop peppers. Peel and slice onions. Peel and crush garlic.

Heat oil in frying pan. Add onions and garlic and cook till golden. Add peppers and tomatoes and cook over a high heat for 5 minutes. Season with salt, pepper, marjoram and Tabasco. Reduce heat, cover and simmer for 30 minutes or until the mixture is reduced to a purée.

Lightly beat eggs in a bowl. Season and pour over vegetable purée. Cook over increased heat, stirring, for 2–3 minutes till creamy. Serve with buttered toast and a green salad.

Baked eggs in potatoes

Overall timing 2 hours

Freezing Not suitable

To serve 4

4x10oz	Potatoes	4x275g
2oz	Butter	50g
	Salt and pepper	
2oz	Cheese	50g
4	Small eggs	4
4 tbsp	Double cream	4x15ml
2 teasp	Chopped chives	2x5ml

Preheat the oven to 400°F (200°C) Gas 6.

Scrub and dry the potatoes and push a metal skewer lengthways through each one. Place on a baking tray and rub a little of the butter over the skins. Bake for 1–1¼ hours.

Remove from the oven. Increase the temperature to 450°F (230°C) Gas 8.

Cut a slice lengthways off each potato and scoop out the insides, leaving a shell about ½ inch (12.5mm) thick. Mash the scooped-out potato (plus any from the lids) in a bowl with the remaining butter and seasoning. Grate cheese and beat into potato mixture.

Press the mixture back into the potato shells, leaving a hollow in the centre large enough for an egg. Place on baking tray. Carefully break an egg into each potato. Season and spoon the cream over. Return to the oven and bake for 8–10 minutes till the eggs are lightly set. Sprinkle the chives over and serve hot.

Curried eggs

Overall timing 35 minutes

Freezing Not suitable

To serve 4

6	Eggs	6
2	Onions	2
2 oz	Butter	50 g
2 teasp	Curry powder	2x5 ml
1 pint	Chicken stock	560 ml
1 teasp	Cornflour	5 ml
4 fl oz	Carton of single cream or top of milk	120 ml
	Salt and pepper	

Place eggs in a saucepan of cold water. Bring to the boil and simmer for 8 minutes, then drain.

Peel and finely chop onions. Melt butter in a frying pan, add onions, cover and cook until golden over a low heat (about 15 minutes).

Sprinkle with curry powder and cook for 2 minutes, stirring. Pour in the stock and simmer for 10 minutes. Mix cornflour and cream or milk together well, then stir into curry mixture with seasoning. Heat gently but do not boil.

Shell eggs and cut in half lengthways. Remove yolks with a spoon and mash yolks and a little of the curry mixture together with a fork. Spoon back into egg whites. Place eggs in curry sauce and heat through without boiling. Serve with rice or hot buttered toast.

Deep-fried eggs

Overall timing 15 minutes

Freezing Not suitable

To serve 4

	Oil for frying	
8	Eggs	8
	Salt and pepper	
2	Tomatoes	2
	Sprigs of parsley	

Half-fill a shallow frying pan with oil and heat to 370°F (188°C) or until a cube of bread browns in 1 minute. Swirl fat round with a spoon. Break an egg into a cup and carefully slide into the hot oil. Cook for 1–2 minutes, basting with the hot oil all the time and turning the egg once or twice.

Remove from pan with a draining spoon and drain on kitchen paper. Sprinkle with salt and pepper. Keep hot while you fry remaining eggs in the same way. Garnish with tomato wedges and parsley sprigs and serve hot with toast.

Lettuce and egg pipérade

Overall timing 15 minutes

Freezing Not suitable

To serve 4

1	Onion	1
1	Small round lettuce	1
2 oz	Butter	50 g
1 tbsp	Chopped parsley	15 ml
4 oz	Frozen peas	125 g
4	Eggs	4
	Salt and pepper	
8 oz	Hot mashed potatoes	225 g

Peel and finely chop the onion. Wash, trim and shred lettuce.

Melt the butter in a frying pan. Add onion and cook till transparent. Add shredded lettuce, parsley and peas. Cook, stirring, for 5 minutes.

Lightly beat eggs in a bowl and season. Stir into pan, reduce heat and cook, stirring, until egg is lightly scrambled. Remove from heat and arrange on warmed serving dish.

Pipe or spoon mashed potato round the edge of the dish and serve immediately.

Egg and cheese sandwiches

Overall timing 30 minutes

Freezing Not suitable

To serve 4

1	Small onion	1
4 oz	Butter	125 g
2 oz	Mushrooms	50 g
4 tbsp	Dry white wine	4x15 ml
4 tbsp	Chicken stock	4x15 ml
	Salt and pepper	
4 oz	Cooked ham	125 g
6 oz	Cheddar cheese	175 g
8	Slices of bread	8
	Paprika	
4	Eggs	4

Peel and finely chop onion. Melt 1 oz (25 g) of the butter in a pan and cook onion till transparent. Slice mushrooms, add to pan and cook for 3 minutes. Add wine and stock and cook over a high heat until most of the liquid evaporates. Season with salt and pepper.

Preheat the oven to 400°F (200°C) Gas 6.

Cut the ham and cheese into thin slices. Butter the bread and place four slices in a shallow ovenproof dish, buttered side down. Divide cheese, ham, mushrooms and onion between them and sprinkle with a little paprika. Cover with remaining bread slices, buttered side up. Bake for 10 minutes until crisp and golden.

Meanwhile, melt remaining butter in a frying pan. Break eggs one at a time into a cup, then slide into the pan when butter is frothy. Cook for 2–3 minutes. Remove eggs from pan with an egg slice. Place on top of sandwiches, sprinkle with salt and pepper and serve.

Egg and pea scramble

Overall timing 50 minutes

Freezing Not suitable

To serve 2–4

2 lb	Fresh peas	900 g
1	Onion	1
2 oz	Streaky bacon rashers	50 g
2 oz	Butter	50 g
	Salt and pepper	
2 oz	Cheese	50 g
4	Eggs	4
2 oz	Fresh breadcrumbs	50 g

Shell peas. Peel and thinly slice the onion; derind and dice the bacon. Melt the butter in a saucepan and gently fry the onion and bacon till transparent.

Add the peas and salt and enough water to half cover them. Bring to the boil, then cover and simmer for 15–20 minutes till the peas are tender and most of the liquid has evaporated.

Grate cheese. Lightly beat the eggs in a bowl with the breadcrumbs and pepper. Pour over the peas and cook, stirring gently, till the eggs are lightly set. Serve immediately.

Eggs florentine

Overall timing 45 minutes

Freezing Not suitable

To serve 4

2 lb	Spinach	900 g
2 oz	Butter	50 g
	Salt	
$\frac{1}{4}$ teasp	Grated nutmeg	1.25 ml
$1\frac{1}{2}$ oz	Plain flour	40 g
$\frac{3}{4}$ pint	Milk	400 ml
3 oz	Cheese	75 g
	Cayenne pepper	
$\frac{1}{2}$ teasp	Made mustard	2.5 ml
8	Hard-boiled eggs	8
2 tbsp	Fresh white breadcrumbs	2x15 ml

Preheat the oven to 425°F (220°C) Gas 7.

Wash spinach well in several changes of water. Remove any coarse stalks. Put into saucepan with only the water that still clings to the spinach after washing. Cook for 5–10 minutes till tender. Stir in $\frac{1}{2}$ oz (15 g) of the butter and season with salt and grated nutmeg, then spread over the bottom of a greased ovenproof dish.

Melt remaining butter in a pan. Stir in the flour and cook for 1 minute. Gradually add the milk, bring to the boil, stirring, and cook for 2 minutes.

Grate cheese. Reserve 2 tbsp (2x15 ml) for the topping and stir the rest into the sauce with a pinch each of salt and cayenne and the mustard.

Shell eggs and arrange on top of spinach. Pour sauce over eggs. Mix reserved grated cheese and breadcrumbs and sprinkle over the top. Bake for 10 minutes till cheese is bubbly and golden. Serve immediately.

Eggs in a nest

Overall timing 50 minutes

Freezing Not suitable

To serve 4

2 lb	Potatoes	900 g
	Salt and pepper	
½ pint	Milk	300 ml
3 oz	Butter	75 g
8	Eggs	8
2 tbsp	Dried breadcrumbs	2x15 ml
	Grated nutmeg	
	Parsley	

Peel the potatoes. Put into a pan of salted water, bring to the boil and cook for 25 minutes. Drain.

Preheat the oven to 425°F (220°C) Gas 7. Grease ovenproof dish.

Add milk to the potatoes and return to low heat. Mash the potatoes and beat in 2 oz (50 g) of the butter until smooth and creamy. Season to taste.

Spread creamed potatoes in ovenproof dish. Using the back of a spoon, hollow out eight "nests" for the eggs. Break an egg into each of the "nests". Sprinkle with breadcrumbs, dot with remaining butter and season with salt, pepper and nutmeg.

Bake for 8–9 minutes or until the eggs are lightly set. Garnish with parsley.

Eggs with sausages

Overall timing 15 minutes

Freezing Not suitable

To serve 2–4

1 tbsp	Oil	15 ml
12	Chipolatas	12
1 oz	Butter	25 g
4	Eggs	4
3 tbsp	Tomato ketchup	3x15 ml
	Pepper	

Heat the oil in a frying pan. Cook the chipolatas till golden all over, then remove from the pan.

Melt butter in the pan, break in the eggs and place chipolatas over whites. Fry for 2–3 minutes, then spoon ketchup around the edge of the pan. Sprinkle with pepper and serve with toast and grilled tomatoes.

Variation

Sprinkle grated cheese over the eggs and chipolatas and grill until the cheese has melted and is golden brown.

Eggs in mushroom sauce

Overall timing 30 minutes

Freezing Not suitable

To serve 6

12 oz	Mushrooms	350 g
6	Large eggs	6
1 tbsp	Oil	15 ml
1	Garlic clove	1
14 oz	Can of tomatoes	397 g
2 teasp	Chopped parsley	2x5 ml
	Salt and pepper	
2 oz	Butter	50 g
4 oz	Cheese	125 g
1 tbsp	Plain flour	15 ml

Wipe, trim and thickly slice the mushrooms. Hard-boil the eggs for 10 minutes.

Meanwhile, heat the oil in a frying pan. Add peeled garlic and fry till golden. Discard garlic. Add the mushrooms and fry over a high heat for 3–4 minutes. Sieve canned tomatoes and their juice and add to the pan with the parsley, salt and pepper. Cook for about 10 minutes.

Cool the eggs quickly by running cold water over them. Cut eggs in half lengthways. Scoop out yolks and place in a bowl.

Soften the butter and grate the cheese. Add to the egg yolks with the flour and seasoning. Mix well with a fork. Shape the mixture into 12 balls about 1 inch (2.5 cm) in diameter, using floured hands. Place one ball in each egg half.

Add egg halves to pan and spoon a little sauce over them. Cover and cook for a further 5 minutes. Divide between warmed serving dishes. Serve immediately with crusty bread.

Flamenco eggs

Overall timing 45 minutes

Freezing Not suitable

To serve 4–6

1	Onion	1
4 oz	Back bacon	125 g
2 tbsp	Oil	2x15 ml
8 oz	Can of tomatoes	227 g
2	Potatoes	2
1	Small red pepper	1
2 oz	Runner beans	50 g
2 tbsp	Frozen peas	2x15 ml
2 tbsp	Canned asparagus tips	2x15 ml
6 oz	Chorizo or other spicy sausage	175 g
3 tbsp	Dry sherry	3x15 ml
	Salt and pepper	
6	Eggs	6

Peel and finely chop onion. Derind and dice bacon.

Heat oil in a saucepan or flameproof casserole. Add onion and bacon and cook till golden. Add tomatoes, mashing them into the onion/bacon mixture till well combined.

Peel potatoes and cut into small dice. Wash, deseed and chop pepper. Wash beans. Top and tail them and remove strings. Cut into short lengths. Add potatoes, pepper, beans and peas to pan and cook for 10 minutes.

Add asparagus tips, sliced sausage and sherry. Season and cook for a further 5 minutes.

Break eggs carefully on top of the mixture. Cook for 5 minutes more or until the eggs are lightly set.

Roe and egg toasts

Overall timing 30 minutes

Freezing Not suitable

To serve 6

12 oz	Soft herring roes	350 g
	Salt and pepper	
3 oz	Butter	75 g
2 tbsp	Plain flour	2x15 ml
½ pint	Milk	300 ml
2	Anchovy fillets	2
3	Hard-boiled eggs	3
1 tbsp	Lemon juice	15 ml
6	Slices of bread	6
6 oz	Smoked cod's roe	175 g

Poach soft roes in boiling salted water for 5 minutes. Drain and chop.

Melt 2 oz (50 g) of the butter in a saucepan, stir in the flour and cook for 1 minute. Gradually add the milk and bring to the boil, stirring.

Pound the anchovy fillets in a bowl. Shell the eggs and cut in half. Sieve the yolks and stir into the sauce with the anchovies, soft roes, lemon juice and seasoning. Heat through.

Preheat the grill. Toast the bread, spread with remaining butter and arrange on the grill pan. Spread the soft roe mixture over. Finely chop the egg whites and use to decorate the toast. Cut the smoked cod's roe into 12 thin slices and place two on each piece of toast. Grill for 2–3 minutes till bubbling and golden. Serve hot.

Egg and ham moulds

Overall timing 20 minutes

Freezing Not suitable

To serve 4

2 oz	Softened butter	50 g
6 oz	Cooked ham	175 g
8	Eggs	8
	Salt	
1	Tomato	1

Grease 8 dariole moulds with the butter. Finely chop the ham and press onto the bottoms and sides of the moulds. Carefully break an egg into each mould and sprinkle with salt.

Put moulds into heatproof dish containing a little boiling water, cover and cook for 8–10 minutes till eggs are lightly set.

Run a knife blade around the inside of each mould and invert on to a warmed serving plate. Garnish with tomato slices and serve with a green salad.

Tomatoes and eggs American style

Overall timing 20 minutes

Freezing Not suitable

To serve 4-6

8 oz	Streaky bacon rashers	225 g
6	Large tomatoes	6
½ pint	Milk	300 ml
	Salt and pepper	
6	Eggs	6

Preheat the grill. Derind the bacon and arrange on the grill pan. Grill till crisp and golden. Remove and keep hot.

Wipe the tomatoes and cut in half. Place the tomatoes cut sides down on the grill pan and brush with a little fat from the bacon. Grill about 3 inches (7.5 cm) below heat for 3-4 minutes.

Meanwhile, pour the milk into a frying pan, add a pinch of salt and heat till simmering. Break an egg on to a saucer, then slide it into the milk. Repeat with remaining eggs. Cover and poach for 3 minutes.

Turn the tomatoes over, brush with bacon fat and grill for 2 more minutes. Arrange stalk halves cut sides up in a warmed serving dish and season. Lift the eggs out of the milk with a draining spoon and drain on kitchen paper. Place one on each tomato half and cover with the remaining halves. Arrange the bacon round the tomatoes and serve immediately with plenty of hot buttered toast.

Spinach flan

Overall timing 50 minutes

Freezing Not suitable

To serve 6

12 oz	Wholemeal shortcrust pastry	350 g
2 lb	Spinach	900 g
	Salt and pepper	
½ teasp	Grated nutmeg	2.5 ml
	Bunch of marjoram	
4 oz	Streaky bacon	125 g
3 oz	Butter	75 g
1	Onion	1
1 oz	Sultanas	25 g
4 tbsp	Single cream	4x15 ml
6 oz	Mozzarella cheese	175 g

Preheat the oven to 400°F (200°C) Gas 6.

Roll out dough and line 9 inch (23 cm) flan tin. Bake blind for 30 minutes.

Meanwhile, cook spinach with salt and nutmeg for 10 minutes. Drain and chop. Chop marjoram and add to spinach.

Derind and chop bacon. Melt half butter in a frying pan and fry bacon till crisp. Scatter bacon over base of flan.

Add remaining butter to pan. Peel and finely chop onion and fry till transparent. Add spinach mixture, three-quarters of sultanas, cream and seasoning. Cook for 5 minutes. Spread in flan case.

Slice cheese and arrange on top. Sprinkle with rest of sultanas and bake for 10 minutes.

Prawn scrambled eggs

Overall timing 15 minutes

Freezing Not suitable

To serve 4

2 oz	Butter	50 g
8 oz	Shelled prawns	225 g
8	Large eggs	8
	Salt and pepper	

Melt half the butter in a saucepan, add prawns and fry gently for 3–4 minutes.

Break the eggs into a bowl, add seasoning and beat lightly with a fork. Pour on to the prawns and stir gently but evenly till the eggs are lightly set.

Remove from the heat, quickly stir in the remaining butter and season to taste. Divide between warmed serving dishes and serve immediately with hot toast.

Italian shredded omelette

Overall timing 35 minutes

Freezing Not suitable

To serve 4

1	Small onion	1
1	Garlic clove	1
1	Stalk of celery	1
1	Carrot	1
2 oz	Streaky bacon rashers	50 g
1 tbsp	Oil	15 ml
14 oz	Can of tomatoes	397 g
	Salt and pepper	
9	Eggs	9
1 teasp	Chopped fresh mint	5 ml
3 tbsp	Chopped parsley	3x15 ml
2 oz	Butter	50 g

Peel and finely chop the onion. Peel and crush the garlic. Trim and chop the celery. Scrape and thinly slice the carrot. Derind and finely chop the bacon.

Heat the oil in a saucepan, add the bacon and vegetables and fry gently for 5 minutes. Add the tomatoes and juice, garlic and seasoning, bring to the boil and simmer for 20 minutes, stirring to break up the tomatoes.

Meanwhile, lightly beat the eggs in a bowl with the mint, parsley and seasoning. Melt one-third of the butter in a frying pan. Add one-third of the egg mixture and cook over a moderate heat, drawing the liquid into the centre as the mixture begins to set. When set, slide the omelette on to a board. Make two more omelettes in the same way.

Roll the omelettes loosely and cut into strips about $\frac{1}{2}$ inch (12.5 mm) wide. Add to the tomato sauce and heat through for 3 minutes. Season to taste and pour into a warmed serving dish.

Minted cheese omelette

Overall timing 20 minutes

Freezing Not suitable

To serve 2

10	Fresh mint leaves	10
6	Eggs	6
1 oz	Fresh breadcrumbs	25 g
4 oz	Cheese	125 g
	Salt and pepper	
1 tbsp	Chopped parsley	15 ml
1 oz	Butter	25 g

Wash, dry and roughly chop the mint leaves. Lightly beat the eggs in a bowl with the breadcrumbs, grated cheese and seasoning. Stir in the parsley and mint and leave to stand for 5 minutes.

Melt the butter in a frying pan and pour in the egg mixture (or only half if making two omelettes). Tip the pan so that the bottom is coated and cook over a moderate heat until lightly set.

Using a large fish slice, carefully turn the omelette over and cook for 2 minutes more. Serve with tomato salad and wholemeal rolls.

Prawn omelette in béchamel sauce

Overall timing 40 minutes

Freezing Not suitable

To serve 2

1	Small onion	1
1	Small carrot	1
1	Stalk of celery	1
½ pint	Milk	300 ml
1	Bay leaf	1
2½ oz	Butter	65 g
2 tbsp	Plain flour	2x15 ml
6 oz	Shelled prawns	175 g
2 tbsp	Single cream	2x15 ml
	Salt and pepper	
6	Eggs	6
2 teasp	Chopped parsley	2x5 ml

Peel and roughly chop the onion and carrot. Trim and chop the celery. Put the milk into a saucepan with the bay leaf and prepared vegetables, cover and bring to the boil. Remove from heat and leave to infuse for 10 minutes.

Melt 2 oz (50 g) of the butter in a saucepan, add the flour and cook for 1 minute. Gradually add the strained milk and bring to the boil, stirring constantly. Cook, stirring, for 2 minutes. Reduce heat, stir in prawns, cream and seasoning. Heat without boiling.

Lightly beat the eggs in a bowl with a pinch of salt. Melt remaining butter in a frying pan, pour in the eggs and cook until set.

Spoon half the prawn sauce into the centre of the omelette and fold two sides over. Turn out of pan, placing join side down on warmed serving dish. Pour the remaining sauce round. Make a cut along the top of the omelette to expose the filling, sprinkle the parsley over and serve immediately with a tossed green salad.

Liver omelettes

Overall timing 15 minutes

Freezing Not suitable

To serve 4

4 oz	Chicken livers	125 g
4 oz	Butter	125 g
2	Sage leaves	2
	Salt and pepper	
3 tbsp	Marsala or sherry	3x15 ml
8	Eggs	8
	Sprigs of parsley	

Trim, wipe and finely chop the livers.

Melt 1 oz (25 g) of the butter in a saucepan and add livers. Chop sage and add to pan with seasoning. Stir-fry for 5 minutes. Pour Marsala or sherry over and cook till it has almost evaporated. Remove pan from heat.

Beat eggs in a bowl with a little seasoning. Melt a quarter of the remaining butter in an omelette or small frying pan. When it begins to foam, pour in a quarter of the egg mixture. Tilt pan so mixture runs evenly over the bottom. As the omelette begins to set underneath, place a quarter of the liver mixture along the centre and fold the sides of the omelette over the filling.

Slide omelette on to a warmed serving dish and keep hot. Make three more omelettes in the same way. Garnish with parsley and serve with sauté potatoes.

Chervil omelette

Overall timing 15 minutes

Freezing Not suitable

To serve 4

8	Eggs	8
	Salt and pepper	
3 tbsp	Chopped fresh chervil	3x15 ml
1 tbsp	Chopped parsley	15 ml
2 oz	Butter	50 g

Break the eggs into a bowl. Season with salt and pepper, add herbs and beat together lightly.

Melt one-quarter of the butter in an omelette pan over a high heat. When the butter begins to froth, pour in a quarter of the egg mixture. As the omelette starts to set, run a spatula round the edge to loosen it and tilt pan to let uncooked egg run underneath. When firm at the edges but still runny in the centre, fold omelette over and slide on to a warmed serving plate. Keep it hot while you make three more omelettes in the same way. Serve with a tomato salad.

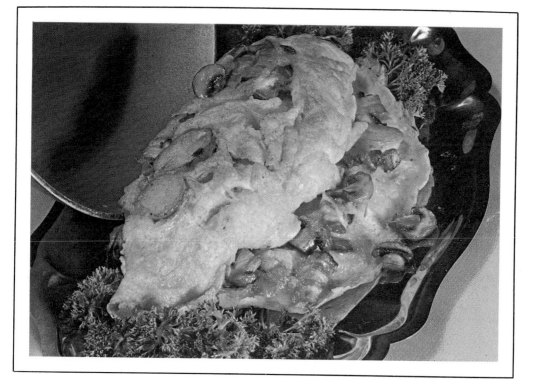

Omelette forestière

Overall timing 25 minutes

Freezing Not suitable

To serve 2

4 oz	Thick streaky bacon rashers	125 g
4 oz	Button mushrooms	125 g
2	Small potatoes	2
2 oz	Butter	50 g
4–6	Eggs	4–6
1 tbsp	Chopped parsley	15 ml
	Salt and pepper	

Derind bacon, then cut into thin strips. Thinly slice mushrooms. Peel and thinly slice potatoes. Melt the butter in a frying pan, add potatoes and bacon and fry till tender and golden all over. Add mushrooms and cook for 5 minutes more.

Meanwhile, lightly beat the eggs in a bowl with parsley and seasoning. Pour over the ingredients in the frying pan. Cook for a few minutes, lifting the edges to ensure the underneath is evenly cooked. Fold over and slide on to warmed serving plate. Serve immediately.

Devilled liver omelettes

Overall timing 20 minutes

Freezing Not suitable

To serve 2

2	Bacon rashers	2
4 oz	Chicken livers	125 g
	Salt and pepper	
1 tbsp	Plain flour	15 ml
2 oz	Mushrooms	50 g
2 oz	Butter	50 g
1 teasp	Tomato purée	5 ml
½ teasp	Worcestershire sauce	2.5 ml
½ teasp	French mustard	2.5 ml
6	Eggs	6
1 teasp	Chopped chives	5 ml

Derind and chop the bacon. Trim and chop the livers and toss in seasoned flour. Slice the mushrooms.

Melt half the butter in a saucepan, add the bacon and fry till light brown. Add the chicken livers and stir-fry till browned. Add the mushrooms, tomato purée, Worcestershire sauce, mustard and seasoning. Mix well, then cover and cook for 3 minutes.

Heat the remaining butter in an omelette pan. Lightly beat the eggs with seasoning and add to pan. Cook until almost set, then spoon the liver mixture over and sprinkle with the chives. Fold omelette, cut in half and place on two warmed plates. Serve hot with granary bread and a tomato and cucumber salad.

Cheese dishes

Anchovy brochettes

Overall timing 30 minutes

Freezing Not suitable

To serve 2

4	Large slices of white bread	4
4 oz	Mozzarella or Gouda cheese	125 g
3 oz	Butter	75 g
	Salt and pepper	
8	Anchovy fillets	8
4 tbsp	Milk	4x15 ml

Preheat the oven to 400°F (200°C) Gas 6.

Cut bread and cheese into small squares. Thread alternately on to four skewers. Arrange in an ovenproof dish so that each end of the skewer is supported by the rim.

Melt half of the butter and brush generously over the brochettes. Season with salt and pepper. Bake for about 15–20 minutes, basting occasionally with butter in dish. The brochettes should be golden brown.

Meanwhile, melt remaining butter in a saucepan. Mash anchovies and add to butter. Gradually add milk and mix well together over gentle heat. Bring to boiling point.

Pour hot anchovy sauce over brochettes and serve immediately.

Welsh rarebit

Overall timing 30 minutes

Freezing Not suitable

To serve 4

8	Slices of bread	8
3 oz	Butter	75 g
12 oz	Cheddar cheese	350 g
½ teasp	Ground mace	2.5 ml
	Pinch of powdered mustard	
5 tbsp	Beer	5x15 ml
	Pepper	

Preheat the oven to 400°F (200°C) Gas 6.

Toast the bread, and butter the slices while still hot. Place on baking tray.

Cut the cheese into small cubes and put in a saucepan with mace, mustard and beer. Cook over a low heat, stirring with a wooden spoon, until cheese melts and is thick and creamy. Spread mixture over toast. Sprinkle generously with pepper and bake for 10 minutes. Serve immediately.

Cheese flan

Overall timing 1½ hours

Freezing Suitable: reheat in 425°F (220°C) Gas 7 oven for 10–15 minutes

To serve 4–6

5 oz	Butter	150 g
¼ pint	Water	150 ml
	Salt and pepper	
8 oz	Self-raising flour	225 g
2	Medium-size onions	2
1 tbsp	Plain flour	15 ml
4 fl oz	Milk	120 ml
3	Eggs	3
¼ teasp	Grated nutmeg	1.25 ml
	Cayenne pepper	
4 oz	Cheddar cheese	125 g
4 oz	Gruyère cheese	125 g

Melt 4 oz (125 g) of the butter. Cool slightly, then stir in 3 tbsp (3x15 ml) of the water and salt. Sift self-raising flour into a bowl. Slowly add butter mixture and mix until smooth. Chill for 30 minutes.

Preheat the oven to 350°F (180°C) Gas 4.

Peel and chop onions. Melt remaining butter in a saucepan and fry onions for 10 minutes until soft. Cool.

Mix plain flour and a little of the milk in a bowl, then add the rest of the milk and the remaining water. Separate the eggs. Mix the yolks into the flour and milk mixture. Season with salt, pepper, nutmeg and a pinch of cayenne. Beat egg whites till stiff, then fold into yolk mixture.

Roll out dough and use to line a greased 9 inch (23 cm) flan tin. Spread onions over bottom of flan, then grate both sorts of cheese on top. Cover with egg and milk mixture.

Bake for 15 minutes. Reduce heat to 325°F (170°C) Gas 3 and bake for a further 45 minutes. Serve hot.

Cheeseburgers

Overall timing 30 minutes

Freezing Not suitable

To serve 4

1	Large onion	1
1 lb	Minced beef	450 g
3 tbsp	Fresh breadcrumbs	3x15 ml
4 tbsp	Milk	4x15 ml
	Salt	
	Paprika	
1 teasp	Powdered mustard	5 ml
	Oil	
4	Small tomatoes	4
4	Slices of Cheddar cheese	4
4	Buns	4

Preheat the grill.

Peel and finely chop onion. In a large bowl, mix together the onion, minced beef, breadcrumbs and milk. Season with salt, a pinch of paprika and mustard. Leave for 10 minutes.

Make 4 hamburgers from the mixture. Brush with oil. Cook for 5 minutes on each side under the grill.

Remove from heat. Top the burgers with slices of tomato and strips of cheese. Put back under the grill till the cheese melts. Serve in warm buns.

Cheese soufflé

Overall timing 45 minutes

Freezing Not suitable

To serve 4–6

3 oz	Butter	75 g
4	Eggs	4
2 oz	Cornflour	50 g
1 pint	Milk	560 ml
	Salt and pepper	
	Paprika	
	Grated nutmeg	
4 oz	Gruyère, Parmesan or mature Cheddar cheese	125 g

Preheat the oven to 400°F (200°C) Gas 6.

Grease a 7 inch (18 cm) diameter soufflé dish with 1 oz (25 g) of the butter, and tie with paper collar if liked. Separate the eggs.

Melt the remaining butter in a saucepan, stir in cornflour and cook for 1 minute. Gradually add the milk, stirring all the time until the sauce thickens. Season with salt and pepper and a pinch of both paprika and grated nutmeg. Take pan off heat and allow mixture to cool slightly.

Finely grate cheese and stir into sauce. Add egg yolks one at a time to the sauce, beating well.

In a large bowl, whisk egg whites till they hold stiff peaks, then carefully fold into the sauce with a metal spoon.

Pour soufflé mixture into prepared dish. Bake just above centre of oven for about 25 minutes or until risen and golden. Remove from oven and serve immediately with a crisp green salad, dressed with herb vinaigrette.

Cheesy tapioca fritters

Overall timing 1 hour

Freezing Not suitable

To serve 6

1	Medium-size onion	1
4 oz	Flaked tapioca	125 g
1½ pints	Milk	850 ml
1	Bay leaf	1
	Salt and pepper	
3	Eggs	3
6 oz	Cheese	175 g
½ teasp	Powdered mustard	2.5 ml
	Oil for deep frying	
	Sprigs of parsley	

Peel and finely chop the onion. Put into a saucepan with the tapioca, milk and bay leaf. Season and bring to the boil, stirring. Cook for about 30 minutes, stirring occasionally, till thick and creamy. Remove from the heat.

Separate the eggs and beat the yolks one at a time into the mixture. Grate the cheese and add to the mixture with mustard. Mix well and leave to cool.

Heat oil in a deep-fryer to 340°F (170°C).

Whisk the egg whites till stiff but not dry, then fold into the tapioca mixture with a metal spoon. Drop a few large spoonfuls of the mixture into the oil and fry for 3–4 minutes till crisp and golden. Drain on kitchen paper. Sprinkle with salt and serve hot, garnished with parsley.

Croque monsieur

Overall timing 20 minutes

Freezing Not suitable

To serve 4

8	Slices of bread	8
	Butter	
8	Slices of Gruyere or Cheddar cheese	8
4	Slices of cooked ham	4
	Extra grated cheese (optional)	

Preheat the grill.

Butter four slices of bread. Place a slice of cheese on each of the unbuttered slices of bread. Cover with the ham, then top with the rest of the sliced cheese. Place the buttered bread on top, buttered sides up.

Grill the sandwiches, buttered sides up, until golden brown. Turn and spread the other sides with butter. Continue grilling until golden. Sprinkle with a little extra grated cheese, if liked, and grill until the cheese has melted.

Variation

For a Croque milady, add sliced tomato to the sandwich and top with fried eggs.

Gnocchi

Overall timing 50 minutes plus cooling

Freezing Suitable: bake from frozen, allowing 1 hour

To serve 4

1½ pints	Milk	850 ml
6 oz	Coarse semolina	175 g
	Salt and pepper	
	Grated nutmeg	
6 oz	Grated Parmesan cheese	175 g
1	Egg yolk	1
2 tbsp	Milk	2x15 ml

Heat milk just to boiling in a saucepan, then sprinkle on semolina. Season with salt, pepper and nutmeg. Cook gently, stirring, for 4–5 minutes till mixture becomes solid. Remove pan from heat and beat in 4 oz (125 g) of the cheese. Pour into a greased Swiss roll tin. Leave in a cool place (not the refrigerator) for 45 minutes to 1 hour till cold.

Preheat the oven to 400°F (200°C) Gas 6.

Cut the cooled mixture into about 20 rounds, 2½ inches (6.5 cm) in diameter. Arrange the rounds, overlapping them, in a greased round ovenproof dish. Beat egg yolk and milk and pour over. Sprinkle with the rest of the cheese and bake for 30 minutes till golden brown. Serve immediately.

Gougère

Overall timing 1½ hours

Freezing Not suitable

To serve 6

7 fl oz	Water	200 ml
½ teasp	Salt	2.5 ml
4 oz	Butter	125 g
3½ oz	Plain flour	100 g
4	Eggs	4
8 oz	Gruyère cheese	225 g

Preheat oven to 400°F (200°C) Gas 6.

Put water and salt into a saucepan, with 3 oz (75 g) of the butter, chopped. Bring to the boil, stirring to melt the butter. Remove from heat and quickly add the flour all at once, stirring well. Return pan to heat and beat till the paste is smooth and leaves the sides of the pan cleanly. Remove from heat and allow to cool slightly.

Add three of the eggs, one at a time, beating well between additions. Grate 5 oz (150 g) of the cheese and stir into the paste.

With a large spoon, make a ring of the paste on a greased baking tray. Beat the remaining egg and brush over paste. Dice remaining cheese and place on top of the paste with tiny pieces of the remaining butter.

Bake for 20 minutes, then lower heat to 375°F (190°C) Gas 5, and bake for a further 20–25 minutes. Serve hot.

Deep-fried Mozzarella sandwiches

Overall timing 20 minutes

Freezing Not suitable

To serve 4

8	Slices of bread	8
4	Slices of Mozzarella cheese	4
	Plain flour	
1	Egg	1
	Oil for deep frying	

Remove the crusts from the bread. Make four sandwiches with the cheese and coat all over with flour. Beat the egg in a shallow dish. Dip in the sandwiches so the sides and edges are all coated.

Heat oil in a deep-fryer to 360°F (180°C). Deep fry the sandwiches until they are golden brown. Drain on kitchen paper and serve hot, with salad.

Italian deep-fried cheese

Overall timing 1¼ hours plus chilling

Freezing Not suitable

To serve 2

½	Onion	½
1 oz	Butter	25 g
2 oz	Long grain rice	50 g
4 fl oz	Chicken stock	120 ml
1 teasp	Grated Parmesan cheese	5 ml
	Pinch of grated nutmeg	
	Salt and pepper	
1 oz	Lean cooked ham	25 g
1½ oz	Mozzarella cheese	40 g
1	Egg	1
1 oz	Fine fresh breadcrumbs	25 g
	Oil for deep frying	

Peel and finely chop onion. Melt butter in a saucepan and fry onion till transparent.

Add rice and stir over a low heat for 2 minutes. Stir in stock, cover and bring to the boil. Simmer gently for 15–20 minutes till rice is tender. Remove from heat and stir in Parmesan, nutmeg and seasoning. Leave to cool completely.

Meanwhile, chop ham finely. Cut Mozzarella into four sticks about 1½ inches (4 cm) long and ½ inch (12.5 mm) thick. Break egg on to a plate and beat lightly with a fork. Spread breadcrumbs on another plate.

Beat a little egg and the ham into rice. Put 2 tbsp (2x15 ml) rice mixture in palm of one hand. Place a cheese stick on top and cover with more rice. Pat into a cylinder shape about 2½ inches (6.5 cm) long and 1 inch (2.5 cm) thick. Brush beaten egg over croquette, then coat with breadcrumbs. Shape and coat three more croquettes. Chill for 1 hour.

Heat oil in a deep-fryer to 360°F (180°C). Fry the croquettes for 5–6 minutes till golden. Drain on kitchen paper and serve hot.

Sauerkraut cheese rolls

Overall timing 1½ hours

Freezing Not suitable

To serve 6

8 oz	Plain flour	225 g
	Salt	
8 oz	Cream cheese	225 g
5 oz	Butter	150 g
2	Eggs	2
¼ pint	Carton of soured cream	150 ml
	Grated nutmeg	
1	Small onion	1
3 oz	Cheese	75 g
Filling		
4 oz	Streaky bacon	125 g
1 lb	Can of sauerkraut	454 g
1 tbsp	Sugar	15 ml
	Salt and pepper	
1	Bay leaf	1

Sift flour and salt into bowl and rub in cream cheese and 4 oz (125 g) butter. Knead till smooth, then chill for 30 minutes.

Meanwhile, for the filling, derind and chop bacon. Place in saucepan and cook till golden, then add sauerkraut, sugar, seasoning and bay leaf. Cover and cook gently for 30 minutes. Remove bay leaf. Cool.

Preheat oven to 400°F (200°C) Gas 6.

Roll out dough to rectangle 18x10 inches (45x25 cm). Spoon filling over dough, leaving border. Beginning at long edge, roll up, then cut roll into six smaller rolls. Arrange rolls in greased ovenproof dish.

Beat eggs with soured cream, salt and nutmeg. Pour over the rolls. Peel and slice onion. Grate cheese. Top rolls with onion rings, cheese and remaining butter. Bake for 40 minutes.

Three-cheese savouries

Overall timing 10 minutes plus chilling

Freezing Not suitable

To serve 6

4 oz	Danish blue cheese	125 g
3	Petits suisses cheeses	3
4 oz	Gruyère cheese	125 g
2 tbsp	Chopped fresh herbs	2x15 ml
4 oz	Dried breadcrumbs	125 g

Mash Danish blue and Petits suisses cheeses together in a bowl with a fork. Grate Gruyère and add to bowl with herbs. Mix well together.

Shape into flat cakes or cylinders and coat in breadcrumbs. Place on a plate and chill for 3 hours before serving with toast, crisp biscuits or French bread.

Variation

Use a mixture of cream, cottage and curd cheeses, and flavour with 2 cloves of crushed garlic creamed with salt. Make into shapes (use biscuit or scone cutters) and coat in breadcrumbs or finely chopped parsley. Or use prepared pepper for steak which is a combination of pepper and mustard. Chill as above before serving.

Basque cod casserole

Overall timing 1 hour

Freezing Not suitable

To serve 4–6

1 lb	Cod fillets	450 g
	Bouquet garni	
	Salt and pepper	
4	Large potatoes	4
2	Hard-boiled eggs	2
3	Tomatoes	3
3 oz	Butter	75 g
3	Garlic cloves	3
2 oz	Black olives	50 g
2 tbsp	Capers	2x15 ml
1 tbsp	Chopped parsley	15 ml
2 tbsp	Lemon juice	2x15 ml

Place cod in a saucepan and cover with water. Add bouquet garni and seasoning and bring slowly to the boil. Remove pan from heat and leave to cool.

Meanwhile, cook unpeeled potatoes in boiling salted water for 30 minutes. Drain well, then peel and slice potatoes. Shell and slice eggs. Blanch, peel and chop tomatoes.

Melt 1 oz (25 g) butter in a pan and fry tomatoes. Season with salt and pepper.

Preheat the oven to 400°F (200°C) Gas 6.

Arrange egg slices around side of greased soufflé dish and make layers of the potatoes, drained and chopped fish, and the peeled and crushed garlic. Spread tomatoes over top. Dot with remaining butter and bake for 20 minutes.

Garnish with black olives, capers and chopped parsley and sprinkle with lemon juice. Serve hot or cold.

Baked cod with rosemary

Overall timing 45 minutes

Freezing Not suitable

To serve 4–6

2½ lb	End piece of cod	1.1 kg
4 tbsp	Oil	4x15 ml
8	Anchovy fillets	8
	Fresh rosemary	
4	Basil leaves (optional)	4
2 tbsp	Dried breadcrumbs	2x15 ml
	Salt and pepper	

Ask your fishmonger to remove bones from cod, leaving two halves attached at one side. Scale fish, using a descaler or the blunt side of a knife.

Preheat the oven to 350°F (180°C) Gas 4.

Heat half the oil in a flameproof casserole, add the chopped anchovies and heat through. Mash anchovies well, then transfer to a bowl. Put a little of the mashed anchovy mixture inside the fish, together with a few sprigs of fresh rosemary and the basil leaves, if using.

Place fish in the casserole and pour the remaining anchovy mixture and oil over. Add a little more rosemary and sprinkle with breadcrumbs, salt and pepper. Bake for about 30 minutes till the fish is cooked and the top is golden. Serve with boiled potatoes and a green vegetable or salad.

Grilled cod with bacon

Overall timing 25 minutes

Freezing Not suitable

To serve 2

2	Large cod fillets	2
2 tbsp	Oil	2x15 ml
	Salt and pepper	
2 oz	Thin streaky bacon rashers	50 g
1 oz	Butter	25 g
1 tbsp	Lemon juice	15 ml
	Sprigs of parsley	
	Lemon wedges	

Preheat the grill.

Brush the cod fillets with oil and season with salt and pepper. Place under a fairly hot grill and cook for about 15 minutes, turning fillets over halfway through cooking time.

Remove rind from the bacon, then grill or fry. Drain on kitchen paper.

Melt the butter in a small saucepan, taking care not to colour it. Arrange the fish and bacon on warmed serving plates. Pour the butter over and sprinkle with lemon juice. Garnish with parsley sprigs and lemon wedges. Serve with boiled potatoes tossed in butter and sprinkled with chopped parsley, and a crisp lettuce salad.

Cod croquettes

Overall timing 45 minutes

Freezing Suitable: bake cooked croquettes from frozen in 375°F (190°C) Gas 5 oven for 30 minutes

To serve 4–6

1 lb	Cooked cod fillets	450 g
1 lb	Mashed potatoes	450 g
	Salt and pepper	
	Grated nutmeg	
1	Egg	1
	Dried breadcrumbs	
	Oil for deep frying	
	Lettuce leaves	
1	Lemon	1

Finely mince cod, then mix with potatoes in a large bowl. Season well with salt, pepper and a pinch of nutmeg. Make small round or oval shapes of the mixture.

Lightly beat egg in a bowl. Dip croquettes in egg, then breadcrumbs.

Heat oil in deep-fryer to 360°F (180°C). Add croquettes and fry for about 5 minutes till golden. Remove croquettes and drain on kitchen paper. Pile them up on a bed of lettuce with pieces of lemon between. Serve with tomato sauce (see page 19).

Cod with onions and leeks

Overall timing 35 minutes

Freezing Not suitable

To serve 4–6

1¾ lb	Cod fillets	750 g
3 tbsp	Lemon juice	3×15 ml
	Salt	
2	Large onions	2
2	Leeks	2
3 tbsp	Oil	3×15 ml
¼ pint	Dry cider	150 ml
2 tbsp	Chopped parsley	2×15 ml

Place cod fillets in a bowl with lemon juice and salt.

Peel and chop onions. Trim and chop leeks. Heat oil in a frying pan and cook onions and leeks gently till softened.

Add cod fillets, with any juices, and cider to pan and cook for 15 minutes till fish is cooked through. Sprinkle with parsley before serving with mashed potatoes.

Mustard-topped cod

Overall timing 35 minutes

Freezing Not suitable

To serve 4

1¾ lb	Cod fillets	750 g
1	Onion	1
1 tbsp	Vinegar	15 ml
1	Bay leaf	1
6	Peppercorns	6
3 oz	Butter	75 g
2 tbsp	Powdered English mustard	2x15 ml
1 teasp	Sea-salt	5 ml
	Sprigs of parsley	
	Lemon slices	

Cut cod into large pieces. Place in a saucepan and cover with water. Peel and halve the onion and add to the pan with the vinegar, bay leaf and peppercorns. Bring to the boil over a high heat, then simmer for 20 minutes.

Melt the butter with the mustard and salt in a small saucepan. Mix well and simmer for 2–3 minutes, being careful not to let mixture stick or burn.

Remove pieces of cod from the saucepan with a draining spoon and place on a warmed serving plate. Spoon a little of the mustard mixture on to each piece of fish or serve in a separate dish. Garnish with a few sprigs of parsley and lemon slices. Serve with plain boiled rice and peas.

Whiting curls

Overall timing 50 minutes

Freezing Not suitable

To serve 2

2	Small whiting	2
	Salt and pepper	
4 tbsp	Plain flour	4x15 ml
	Oil for deep frying	
1	Lemon	1
	Sprigs of parsley	

Scale and dry the whiting. Place one on its side on a board and hold it firmly by the tail. Using a sharp knife in a sawing action cut between the flesh and the back-bone to just behind the head.

Turn the fish over and repeat the action on the other side to expose the backbone. Cut off the backbone just behind the head with kitchen scissors. Repeat with the other whiting.

Curl fish, pushing tail through skin at far side of mouth to hold in place. Lightly coat each fish with seasoned flour. Shake off any excess.

Heat the oil in a deep-fryer to 340°F (170°C). Fry the whiting for about 10 minutes till tender and golden brown. Drain on kitchen paper and arrange the fish on a warmed serving dish. Garnish with parsley and lemon and serve immediately, with tartare sauce.

Hake au gratin

Overall timing 30 minutes

Freezing Not suitable

To serve 4

1	Small onion	1
2 tbsp	Chopped parsley	2x15 ml
1¾ lb	Hake steaks	750 g
	Salt and pepper	
	Grated nutmeg	
2 tbsp	Lemon juice	2x15 ml
1 oz	Butter	25 g
4 oz	Cheese	125 g
2 oz	Fresh breadcrumbs	50 g

Preheat oven to 375°F (190°C) Gas 5.

Peel and chop onion and place in a shallow ovenproof dish with half the parsley and the fish steaks. Season with salt and pepper and a pinch of nutmeg. Sprinkle the lemon juice over the fish and dot with butter. Grate the cheese and mix with the breadcrumbs and remaining parsley. Sprinkle over the fish. Bake for about 20 minutes.

Remove from oven and baste with liquid in dish. Bake for another 10 minutes until topping is golden. Serve immediately with jacket-baked potatoes.

Coley with spicy sauce

Overall timing 1 hour

Freezing Not suitable

To serve 4

4	Onions	4
4–6	Garlic cloves	4–6
1 lb	Tomatoes	450 g
1	Lemon	1
$\frac{1}{4}$ pint	Oil	150 ml
$\frac{1}{4}$ teasp	Cayenne	1.25 ml
4	Coley steaks	4
	Salt	
	Chopped parsley	

Peel and slice onions. Peel and crush garlic. Blanch, peel and chop tomatoes. Cut four thin slices from lemon and squeeze juice from remainder.

Heat oil in a saucepan. Add onions, garlic and tomatoes and cook gently for about 25 minutes.

Add cayenne and mix in well. Place coley steaks on top of mixture in pan. Sprinkle with salt and lemon juice, cover with lid and cook for a further 15 minutes, turning the fish steaks once.

Arrange coley steaks on a bed of rice on warmed serving dish. Spoon tomato mixture on top and garnish with lemon slices and chopped parsley.

Baked coley

Overall timing 1 hour

Freezing Not suitable

To serve 4

3 lb	Piece of coley	1.4 kg
1	Strip of bacon fat	1
2 oz	Butter	50 g
	Salt and pepper	
4	Smoked bacon rashers	4
1	Large can of flageolet beans	1
$\frac{1}{4}$ teasp	Dried sage	1.25 ml
$\frac{1}{4}$ pint	Chicken stock	150 ml

Preheat the oven to 425°F (220°C) Gas 7.

Roll up the coley and tie as you would a piece of beef, with the bacon fat wrapped round. Reserve a knob of butter and use most of the rest to grease a roasting tin. Place coley in it. Dot with more butter, season, then bake for 30 minutes.

Derind and chop bacon. Melt reserved knob of butter in saucepan and fry bacon till crisp. Drain can of beans and add to pan with sage and stock. Cook over a low heat for 10 minutes.

Put coley on a warmed serving plate. Arrange beans and bacon round coley and serve with parsleyed new potatoes.

Plaice and chips

Overall timing 35 minutes plus 30 minutes soaking

Freezing Not suitable

To serve 4

2 lb	Waxy potatoes	900 g
2	Whole plaice, halved and boned	2
	Salt and pepper	
4 tbsp	Plain flour	4x15 ml
	Oil for frying	
	Lemon wedges	
	Sprigs of parsley	
Coating batter		
8 oz	Plain flour	225 g
½ teasp	Salt	2.5 ml
2	Eggs	2
2 tbsp	Oil	2x15 ml
6 tbsp	Cold water	6x15 ml

Peel the potatoes and cut into chips. Soak in cold water for 30 minutes.

Wipe the fish. Season the flour and lightly coat the fish.

To make the batter, sift flour and salt into a bowl. Separate eggs. Add yolks, oil and water to flour and beat till smooth.

Heat oil in a deep-fryer to 360°F (180°C). Drain the chips and dry well. Fry, in batches, for 4–5 minutes till tender but not brown. Remove and drain on kitchen paper.

Reduce the temperature of the oil to 340°F (170°C). Whisk the egg whites till stiff but not dry and fold into the batter. Coat the plaice with batter.

Fry the plaice, one at a time if necessary, for 2–3 minutes each side till crisp and golden. Drain on kitchen paper and keep hot, uncovered.

Increase the temperature of the oil to 360°F (180°C) again, put the chips in the basket and fry till crisp and golden. Drain on kitchen paper and pile into a warmed serving dish.

Garnish plaice with lemon wedges and sprigs of parsley. Serve immediately.

Fried plaice

Overall timing 30 minutes

Freezing Not suitable

To serve 6

3 oz	Unsalted butter	75 g
2 tbsp	Chopped parsley	2x15 ml
1 tbsp	Lemon juice	15 ml
	Salt and pepper	
3 tbsp	Plain flour	3x15 ml
3	Whole plaice, halved and boned	3
2	Eggs	2
4 oz	Golden breadcrumbs	125 g
	Oil for frying	
	Lemon slices	
	Sprigs of parsley	

Mash the butter with the chopped parsley and lemon juice. Shape into a roll and chill.

Season the flour and lightly coat the plaice. Beat the eggs in a shallow dish. Spread the breadcrumbs on a plate. Dip the fish into the egg so that it covers both sides. Dip into the crumbs, pressing them on lightly till evenly coated.

Heat the oil in a large frying pan and add two or three of the coated fillets, skin side up. Fry gently for 3–5 minutes, then turn the fish carefully and cook for a further 3–5 minutes till the fish is tender and the coating crisp. Lift out of the pan with a fish slice and drain on kitchen paper. Arrange on a warmed serving dish and keep hot while the rest of the fish is cooked.

Garnish with slices of parsley butter, lemon slices and sprigs of parsley. Serve with chips or sauté potatoes.

Baked plaice au gratin

Overall timing 45 minutes

Freezing Not suitable

To serve 4

1½ lb	Plaice fillets	700 g
1	Small onion	1
2	Tomatoes	2
1 tbsp	Olive oil	15 ml
2	Bay leaves	2
	Salt and pepper	
1 tbsp	Chopped parsley	15 ml
¼ pint	Dry white wine or milk	150 ml
3 tbsp	Dried breadcrumbs	3x15 ml
1 oz	Cheese	25 g
1 oz	Butter	25 g

Preheat the oven to 350°F (180°C) Gas 4.

Remove the skin from the plaice fillets. Peel and finely chop the onion; blanch, peel and slice the tomatoes.

Sprinkle the oil into a shallow baking dish and add the chopped onion. Arrange half the plaice fillets on top with the sliced tomatoes and bay leaves. Sprinkle with salt, pepper and the chopped parsley. Cover with the remaining fish. Pour the white wine or milk over. Grate the cheese and sprinkle on top with the bread-crumbs. Dot with the butter.

Bake for about 25 minutes till golden brown on top. Serve immediately with creamed potatoes and runner beans.

Skate with capers

Overall timing 25 minutes

Freezing Not suitable

To serve 2

2x8 oz	Pieces of skate	2x225 g
	Salt and pepper	
1½ teasp	Vinegar	7.5 ml
1½ oz	Butter	40 g
1 tbsp	Capers	15 ml
1 tbsp	Chopped parsley	15 ml
1½ tbsp	Lemon juice	22.5 ml
2 tbsp	Single cream	2x15 ml

Put the skate into a saucepan. Cover with cold water and add a little salt and a few drops of vinegar. Bring to the boil, then remove from the heat, cover and leave to stand for 10 minutes.

Drain and dry the skate; remove the skin. Place on a warmed serving dish and keep hot.

Melt the butter in a small saucepan and stir in remaining vinegar, the capers, parsley, lemon juice, cream and seasoning. Cook for 2–3 minutes, without boiling, till heated through. Pour over the skate. Serve with boiled or steamed potatoes and a tossed green salad.

Grilled herrings with parsley butter

Overall timing 20 minutes

Freezing Not suitable

To serve 4

4 oz	Unsalted butter	125 g
2 tbsp	Chopped parsley	2x15 ml
1 tbsp	Lemon juice	15 ml
4	Cleaned whole herrings	4
1 tbsp	Oil	15 ml
	Salt and pepper	
1	Lemon	1
	Sprigs of parsley	

Mash butter with chopped parsley and lemon juice. Form into a roll, wrap in greaseproof paper and chill till ready to use.

Preheat the grill.

Brush herrings with oil and season. Place on grill pan and cook for 7 minutes on each side.

Arrange herrings on serving plate. Garnish with lemon, pats of chilled butter and parsley sprigs.

Fishermen's herrings

Overall timing 35 minutes plus chilling

Freezing Not suitable

To serve 6

12	Smoked herring fillets	12
1	Onion	1
4	Small gherkins	4
4 oz	Can of herring roes	113 g
1 tbsp	French mustard	15 ml
¼ pint	Oil	150 ml
	Pepper	

Put the herring fillets into a bowl, cover with boiling water and leave for 20 minutes.

Drain herring fillets, rinse and dry on kitchen paper. Peel onion and cut into thin rings. Slice gherkins.

Drain and chop the roes and put into a bowl with the mustard. Beat to a smooth paste with a wooden spoon. Gradually trickle in all but 2 tbsp (2x15 ml) of the oil, beating well after each addition. Add pepper to taste.

Spread roe sauce over bottom of a serving dish and arrange herring fillets on top. Brush with remaining oil and decorate with onion rings and gherkins. Chill for at least 30 minutes, then serve with potato and beetroot salads garnished with snipped chives.

Herrings with mustard sauce

Overall timing 20 minutes

Freezing Not suitable

To serve 4

4	Cleaned fresh whole herrings	4
2 tbsp	Oil	2x15 ml
2 tbsp	Plain flour	2x15ml
	Salt and pepper	
Sauce		
1 oz	Butter	25 g
1 tbsp	Plain flour	15 ml
½ pint	Stock	300 ml
½ teasp	Pepper	2.5 ml
1 tbsp	Prepared mustard	15 ml
2 tbsp	Single cream	2x15 ml

Preheat grill.

Wash herrings and pat dry on kitchen paper. Brush with oil and coat lightly with seasoned flour. Grill for 7 minutes on each side.

Meanwhile, make the sauce. Melt the butter in a saucepan. Stir in the flour and cook for 1 minute. Add the stock (made with a stock cube if necessary), bring to the boil and cook, stirring, for 3 minutes. Add pepper. Remove from heat and stir in mustard and cream.

Arrange herrings on warmed serving plates and spoon mustard sauce over.

Poached kippers

Overall timing 20 minutes

Freezing Not suitable

To serve 4

8	Kipper fillets	8
3 oz	Butter	75 g
2 teasp	Lemon juice	2x5 ml
½ teasp	Pepper	2.5 ml
	Sprigs of parsley	
	Lemon wedges	

Place kipper fillets in a large saucepan with the skins facing up. Cover with cold water and slowly bring to the boil.

As soon as the water boils, remove from heat, drain well and place on a warmed serving dish with the skin side down. Garnish with parsley.

Melt the butter and stir in the lemon juice and pepper. Pour over kippers at the table and serve with boiled new potatoes and lemon wedges.

Marinated kipper fillets

Overall timing 15 minutes plus marination

Freezing Not suitable

To serve 6

1	Carrot	1
2	Onions	2
1 lb	Kipper fillets	450 g
	Sprigs of thyme	
4–5	Bay leaves	4–5
4–5	Cloves	4–5
¼ pint	Oil	150 ml
4 tbsp	Wine vinegar or lemon juice	4x15 ml
Garnish		
	Hard-boiled eggs	
	Lemon slices	
	Chopped parsley	
	Capers	

Peel and slice the carrot and onions. Place kipper fillets in a glass or pottery bowl, layered with slices of carrot, onion rings, sprigs of fresh thyme, bay leaves and cloves. Pour oil and wine vinegar or lemon juice over and leave for 24 hours in a cool place.

Drain the kippers and place in a serving dish. Garnish with slices of hard-boiled egg and lemon, chopped parsley and capers. Serve with cold potato and onion salad.

Rollmops

Overall timing 30 minutes plus 48 hours soaking and 4 days standing

Freezing Not suitable

To serve 6

4	Filleted fresh herrings	4
2 pints	Water	1.1 litre
8 oz	Salt	225 g
2 tbsp	Capers	2x15 ml
2	Onions	2
1	Large gherkin	1
4 teasp	Made mustard	4x5 ml
Marinade		
½ pint	Cider vinegar	300 ml
½ pint	Water	300 ml
1	Bay leaf	1
10	Black peppercorns	10
2	Cloves	2
5	Juniper berries	5
1 teasp	Mustard seed	5 ml

Soak herrings in half water and salt for 24 hours. Drain and repeat.

Put all marinade ingredients into a pan. Bring to the boil and boil for 5 minutes. Cool.

Chop capers. Peel onions and cut into rings. Quarter gherkin lengthways. Drain and rinse herrings. Lay skin down and spread with mustard. Sprinkle with capers and onion rings. Add gherkin and roll up. Pour over marinade. Leave 4 days before eating.

Marinated sprats

Overall timing 45 minutes plus overnight marination

Freezing Not suitable

To serve 6

2 lb	Sprats	900 g
	Salt and pepper	
3 oz	Plain flour	75 g
	Oil for frying	
1	Large onion	1
8	Sage leaves	8
6 tbsp	Vinegar	6x15 ml
4 tbsp	Water	4x15 ml

Clean the fish through the gills. Rinse and drain thoroughly. Season the flour and use to coat the fish. Heat 1 inch (2.5 cm) oil in a deep frying pan and fry the floured sprats, a few at a time, for about 4 minutes till crisp and golden. Drain on kitchen paper, then put into a shallow serving dish.

Peel and slice the onion. Heat 2 tbsp (2x15 ml) oil in frying pan, add the onion and fry gently till transparent. Add the sage leaves, vinegar and water and bring to the boil. Boil for 3 minutes, then remove from the heat and season.

Pour the hot marinade over the sprats. Cover and leave to marinate in a cool place overnight. Serve cold with crusty bread and butter.

Scrowled sprats

Overall timing 30 minutes plus salting

Freezing Not suitable

To serve 4

1 lb	Fresh sprats or pilchards	450 g
	Salt	
2	Sprigs of rosemary	2
2 oz	Butter	50 g
	Lemon wedges	

Cover the sprats or pilchards with salt and leave overnight.

The next day, rinse off the salt. Cut off the heads and tails, then slit each fish along the belly and remove the insides, including the backbone. Do this under cold running water. Dry the fish with kitchen paper.

Strip the rosemary leaves from the sprig. Melt the butter. Arrange the fish on the grill rack and sprinkle with the butter and rosemary. Grill until cooked, turning once. Serve with lemon wedges.

Mackerel in mushroom sauce

Overall timing 40 minutes

Freezing Not suitable

To serve 4

8 oz	Button mushrooms	225 g
2	Onions	2
1	Garlic clove	1
12 oz	Tomatoes	350 g
5 tbsp	Oil	5x15 ml
	Salt and pepper	
2 tbsp	White wine vinegar	2x15 ml
2 lb	Mackerel fillets	900 g
2 tbsp	Plain flour	2x15 ml

Slice mushrooms. Peel and finely chop onions. Peel and crush garlic. Wash tomatoes and cut into ½ inch (12.5 mm) thick slices.

Heat 2 tbsp (2x15 ml) of the oil in a saucepan. Add onions, mushrooms and garlic and fry for 10 minutes, stirring frequently. Season. Stir in the vinegar and boil rapidly till it evaporates.

Coat fillets with seasoned flour. Heat the remaining oil in a large frying pan, add the fillets and fry for 5 minutes on each side. Drain, arrange on a warmed serving dish and keep hot.

Add tomato slices to frying pan and fry for 2 minutes. Spoon mushroom mixture over fillets. Season tomatoes and arrange on top. Serve immediately with minted peas.

Bream with mushrooms

Overall timing 1 hour

Freezing Not suitable

To serve 2

2 lb	Bream or other whole fish	900 g
4 oz	Button mushrooms	125 g
1	Small onion	1
	Salt and pepper	
4 fl oz	Water	120 ml
1 teasp	Chopped parsley	5 ml
	Pinch of dried thyme	
1 oz	Butter	25 g
1	Lemon	1

Preheat the oven to 400°F (200°C) Gas 6.

Clean fish, but don't remove head. Trim tail and fins, and wash well. Dry on kitchen paper.

Thinly slice button mushrooms. Peel and finely chop onion. Cover bottom of ovenproof dish with most of mushrooms and onion and place the fish on top. Season with salt and pepper, and pour in the water. Sprinkle fish with parsley, thyme and remaining mushrooms and onion.

Melt butter and pour over fish. Cover dish with foil or a lid and bake for 40 minutes, basting frequently with juices in dish. Turn fish over halfway through cooking time and remove foil for last 10 minutes. The fish is cooked when the flesh becomes opaque.

Garnish with lemon and serve with boiled new potatoes.

Haddock creole

Overall timing 1 hour

Freezing Not suitable

To serve 4

1	Onion	1
1	Garlic clove	1
1	Red pepper	1
1	Green pepper	1
1 oz	Butter	25 g
2 tbsp	Oil	2x15 ml
14 oz	Can of tomatoes	397 g
	Salt and pepper	
2 lb	Haddock fillets	900 g
3 tbsp	Lemon juice	3x15 ml
	Chopped parsley	

Preheat the oven to 375°F (190°C) Gas 5.

Peel and chop onion and garlic. Deseed and slice peppers. Heat the butter and oil in a pan. Add onion, garlic and peppers and fry gently for 10 minutes.

Add tomatoes and mash with a wooden spoon to break them up. Season with salt and pepper. Bring to the boil and simmer gently for 10 minutes.

Place half tomato mixture in ovenproof dish, add haddock and season with salt and pepper. Sprinkle with lemon juice and cover with remaining tomato mixture.

Cover with lid or foil and bake for about 25 minutes. Sprinkle with chopped parsley and serve with plain boiled rice.

Haddock with potatoes and onions

Overall timing 45 minutes

Freezing Not suitable

To serve 4

2	Large onions	2
4	Potatoes	4
4 oz	Butter	125 g
2 lb	Haddock fillets	900 g
2 tbsp	Plain flour	2x15 ml
	Salt and pepper	
1 tbsp	Chopped parsley	15 ml
1 tbsp	Vinegar	15 ml

Peel and thinly slice the onions and potatoes. Melt half the butter in a frying pan, add the onions and cook till transparent.

Add remaining butter and potato slices and fry for 15 minutes, turning occasionally.

Meanwhile, wipe the haddock and pat dry with kitchen paper. Cut into small pieces and coat with seasoned flour. Add to pan and cook for a further 15 minutes, stirring from time to time.

Season with salt and pepper. Add parsley and vinegar and cook over a high heat till vinegar evaporates. Serve immediately with grilled tomatoes.

Barbecued haddock

Overall timing 20 minutes plus marination

Freezing Not suitable

To serve 2

1½ tbsp	Oil	22.5 ml
1½ teasp	Lemon juice	7.5 ml
1 tbsp	Soft brown sugar	15 ml
¼ teasp	Chilli powder	1.25 ml
½ teasp	Worcestershire sauce	2.5 ml
1 teasp	Tomato purée	5 ml
1 lb	Smoked haddock	450 g

Mix together oil, lemon juice, sugar, chilli powder, Worcestershire sauce and tomato purée in a shallow dish. Add the haddock, cover and marinate in the refrigerator for 1 hour, turning fish once or twice.

Preheat the grill.

Remove fish from marinade and place on a large piece of foil on the grill pan. Grill for 5–7 minutes on each side, brushing with marinade from time to time.

Alternatively, place the fish in a fish holder and barbecue over charcoal.

Trout with almonds

Overall timing 20 minutes

Freezing Not suitable

To serve 2

2	Trout, cleaned	2
1 oz	Plain flour	25 g
2 oz	Butter	50 g
2 tbsp	Chopped parsley	2 x 15 ml
2 oz	Flaked almonds	50 g
	Salt and pepper	
2	Lemon slices	2

Dust trout with flour. Melt butter in frying pan. Add trout and cook gently on one side for 5 minutes.

Turn trout over with a fish slice. Add half the parsley, the almonds and seasoning. Cook for a further 7–8 minutes till fish is tender and almonds are golden brown (turn them as they cook).

Place fish on warmed serving plates and spoon over almonds. Garnish with lemon slices and remaining chopped parsley. Serve with boiled potatoes and a mixed salad.

Welsh trout

Overall timing 45 minutes

Freezing Not suitable

To serve 2

1 teasp	Chopped fresh sage	5 ml
1 teasp	Chopped fresh rosemary	5 ml
1 teasp	Chopped fresh thyme	5 ml
1 tbsp	Chopped parsley	15 ml
	Salt and pepper	
2 oz	Butter	50 g
2x1 lb	Trout, cleaned	2x450 g
4	Streaky bacon rashers	4

Preheat the oven to 350°F (180°C) Gas 4.

Beat the herbs and seasoning into the butter and spread half inside each fish. Derind and stretch the bacon. Wrap two rashers around each fish, securing with wooden cocktail sticks.

Place the trout in a greased ovenproof dish, cover with foil and bake for about 25 minutes till tender.

Remove the cocktail sticks, place the trout on a warmed serving dish and garnish with lemon slices and sprigs of parsley. Surround with lettuce leaves, mustard and cress and tomato wedges and serve immediately.

Salmon cakes

Overall timing 25 minutes

Freezing Suitable: fry straight from frozen

To serve 4

1 lb	Boiled potatoes	450 g
2 tbsp	Milk	2 x 15 ml
1 oz	Butter	25 g
7½ oz	Can of salmon	212 g
2	Lemons	2
	Salt and pepper	
2	Eggs	2
2 tbsp	Plain flour	2 x 15 ml
4 tbsp	Dried breadcrumbs	4 x 15 ml
¼ pint	Oil	150 ml
	Lettuce leaves	

Mash the boiled potatoes with the milk and butter. Drain canned salmon and discard skin and bones. Mash flesh and add to potatoes.

Squeeze juice from one of the lemons. Add to salmon with seasoning to taste. Mix well and bind with one of the eggs.

Lightly beat remaining egg. Spread flour and dried breadcrumbs on separate plates. Divide salmon mixture into eight and shape into flat patties. Dip first in flour, then egg, then coat lightly with dried breadcrumbs.

Heat oil in frying pan. Add patties and fry for 5 minutes on each side until crisp and golden. Remove from pan with a draining spoon and arrange on serving plate. Serve immediately, garnished with lettuce leaves and the remaining lemon, cut into wedges.

Salmon pie

Overall timing 2 hours

Freezing Not suitable

To serve 6–8

1 lb	Frozen puff pastry	450 g
12 oz	Frozen spinach	350 g
1 lb	Canned salmon	450 g
1	Egg	1
8 oz	Long grain rice	225 g
3 tbsp	Single cream	3x15 ml
2 tbsp	Lemon juice	2x15 ml
	Salt and pepper	
3	Hard-boiled eggs	3

Thaw pastry and spinach. Drain and flake salmon. Separate egg. Cook rice, then mix with egg yolk, cream, lemon juice and seasoning.

Preheat the oven to 425°F (220°C) Gas 7. Roll out dough to two rectangles, one 9x14 inches (23x36cm), the other 11x16 inches (28x41cm). Put smallest one on damp baking tray.

Spread half rice over dough, leaving a border. Cover with half spinach and the salmon. Arrange hard-boiled eggs along centre and cover with remaining spinach and rice. Brush pastry border with lightly beaten egg white.

Place remaining dough over filling, seal edges and glaze with egg white.

Bake for 20 minutes. Reduce temperature to 350°F (180°C) Gas 4 and cook for a further 20 minutes.

Fish kebabs

Overall timing 25 minutes

Freezing Not suitable

To serve 4

1½ lb	Thick firm white fish	700 g
3 tbsp	Plain flour	3x15 ml
	Salt and pepper	
2	Eggs	2
1 teasp	Curry powder	5 ml
4 tbsp	Dried breadcrumbs	4x15 ml
8	Tomatoes	8
1 tbsp	Oil	15 ml

Preheat the grill.

Cut the fish into chunks and roll in seasoned flour to coat. Beat the eggs with the curry powder. Dip the floured fish pieces in the egg, then in the breadcrumbs, pressing the crumbs on to the fish. Cut the tomatoes into quarters. Thread fish and tomato pieces alternately on to greased skewers. Brush with oil.

Cook under the grill for 7–10 minutes till the fish is tender. Turn skewers over from time to time. Serve at once.

Indonesian fish curry

Overall timing 40 minutes

Freezing Not suitable

To serve 4

1½ lb	Cod or coley fillets	700 g
	Salt and pepper	
2 tbsp	Plain flour	2x15 ml
1	Onion	1
1	Large cooking apple	1
1 tbsp	Lemon juice	15 ml
2 oz	Butter	50 g
2 tbsp	Oil	2x15 ml
2 tbsp	Curry powder	2x15 ml
1 pint	Stock	560 ml
2 tbsp	Sultanas	2x15 ml
2 tbsp	Cornflour	2x15 ml
2 oz	Split almonds	50 g

Cut fish into pieces, sprinkle with salt and coat with the flour. Peel and slice onion. Peel, core and slice apple and sprinkle with the lemon juice.

Heat the butter and oil in a flameproof casserole. Add curry powder and onion and fry for 5 minutes. Add fish and cook for a few minutes on all sides. Add apple slices and cook for 3 minutes.

Pour stock into casserole and add sultanas. Blend cornflour with a little stock or water and stir in. Bring to the boil and simmer for 10–15 minutes.

Add almonds and cook for a further 2 minutes. Taste and adjust seasoning and serve.

Fish lasagne

Overall timing 1¼ hours

Freezing Suitable: reheat from frozen in 350°F (180°C) Gas 4 oven for 1 hour

To serve 4

1½ lb	Prepared mackerel	700 g
1	Onion	1
3 fl oz	Oil	90 ml
2	Garlic cloves	2
2 tbsp	Tomato purée	2x15 ml
	Salt and pepper	
1 lb	Fresh peas	450 g
4 oz	Mushrooms	125 g
8 oz	Lasagne	225 g
2 tbsp	Grated Parmesan cheese	2x15 ml
2 tbsp	Chopped parsley	2x15 ml

Cut fish into large pieces. Peel and chop onion. Heat 3 tbsp (3x15 ml) of oil in saucepan, add onion and fry until golden. Add fish and cook for 5 minutes, turning once.

Peel and crush garlic. Stir tomato purée into ¼ pint (150 ml) of water and add to pan with half garlic and seasoning. Cover and cook gently for 10 minutes.

Shell peas. Slice mushrooms. Heat 2 tbsp (2x15 ml) of oil in another saucepan, add peas, mushrooms and other half of garlic and cook for 5 minutes. Add 3 fl oz (90 ml) of water and seasoning, cover and cook for 10 minutes.

Meanwhile, cook lasagne in boiling salted water for 10–15 minutes or till tender. Drain thoroughly.

Preheat oven to 350°F (180°C) Gas 4.

Remove fish from pan and cut into pieces, discarding bones. Return to pan with mushroom mixture. Gradually stir in Parmesan and parsley.

Line greased ovenproof dish with one-third of lasagne, cover with one-third of fish mixture and sprinkle with a little oil. Repeat layers, finishing with fish mixture. Sprinkle with oil and bake for 20 minutes.

Cheesy fish croquettes

Overall timing 40 minutes

Freezing Suitable: reheat from frozen in 375°F (190°C) Gas 5 oven for 30 minutes

To serve 2

8 oz	White fish fillets	225 g
½ pint	Milk	300 ml
1	Small onion	1
2 oz	Butter	50 g
2 oz	Plain flour	50 g
1	Hard-boiled egg	1
1 tbsp	Grated Parmesan cheese	15 ml
	Salt and pepper	
	Oil for frying	

Place the fish fillets in a large frying pan with the milk. Cover and cook over a moderate heat for about 10 minutes till fish is tender. Lift fish out of milk. Discard skin and any bones, then mash flesh. Reserve fish and milk.

Peel and finely chop the onion. Melt the butter in clean frying pan and fry onion till transparent. Add the flour and cook for 2 minutes, stirring. Gradually stir in the reserved milk and bring to the boil.

Remove pan from heat and add the reserved fish. Shell and finely chop the hard-boiled egg and add to the sauce with the Parmesan and seasoning. Spread the mixture thickly on to a plate, cover and chill till firm.

Divide the mixture into four and shape on a well floured board into round patties about ½ inch (12.5 mm) thick.

Heat oil in deep-fryer to 340°F (170°C) and fry the croquettes for 5 minutes till crisp and golden. Drain on kitchen paper and serve hot.

Baked fish steaks

Overall timing 30 minutes

Freezing Not suitable

To serve 4

4	Cod steaks	4
	Salt and pepper	
¼ pint	Dry white wine or cider	150 ml
2 oz	Butter	50 g
2 tbsp	Chopped fresh coriander (optional)	2x15 ml
2 tbsp	Lemon or lime juice	2x15 ml

Preheat the oven to 425°F (220°C) Gas 7.

Wash and dry cod steaks. Place in a greased baking dish and sprinkle well with salt and pepper. Add the wine or cider and dot with butter.

Cover dish with foil and bake in centre of oven for about 25 minutes.

Sprinkle with chopped coriander, if used, and lemon or lime juice. Serve with mashed potatoes.

Fish in piquant sauce

Overall timing 1 hour

Freezing Not suitable

To serve 6

4 oz	Streaky bacon rashers	125 g
2 lb	Centre cut steak from large firm-fleshed fish	900 g
4 teasp	Olive oil	4x5 ml
1 oz	Butter	25 g
	Salt and pepper	
½ pint	Fish or chicken stock	300 ml
2 tbsp	Tomato purée	2x15 ml
3 tbsp	Lemon juice	3x15 ml

Derind and stretch the bacon rashers then wrap them round the fish, securing with cocktail sticks.

Heat the oil and butter in a flameproof casserole, add the fish and brown all over. Add salt, pepper, stock, tomato purée and lemon juice. Bring to the boil, cover tightly and simmer gently for 40 minutes, turning fish once.

Remove the fish from the casserole and discard bacon. Cut the fish into thick slices, place on a warmed serving dish and keep hot.

Taste the cooking liquor and adjust seasoning. Thicken if liked with ½ oz (15 g) each of butter and flour mashed together, then pour over the fish.

Tuna and pea casserole

Overall timing 40 minutes

Freezing Not suitable

To serve 4

1 lb	Waxy potatoes	450 g
	Salt and pepper	
8 oz	Frozen peas	225 g
7 oz	Can of tuna	198 g
2 oz	Butter	50 g
1	Onion	1
4 tbsp	Plain flour	4x15 ml
½ pint	Chicken stock	300 ml
½ pint	Milk	300 ml
4 oz	Cheddar cheese	125 g
2 tbsp	Fresh breadcrumbs	2x15 ml

Peel and dice potatoes. Cook in boiling salted water till tender. Add the peas and cook for a further 3 minutes.

Preheat the oven to 400°F (200°C) Gas 6.

Drain the potatoes and peas and put into an ovenproof dish. Drain and flake the tuna and stir into the vegetables.

Melt the butter in a saucepan. Peel and finely chop the onion and fry in the butter till pale golden. Add the flour and cook for 1 minute. Gradually stir in the stock and milk and bring to the boil, stirring. Grate the cheese. Add 3 oz (75 g) of the cheese and seasoning to the pan and stir. Pour over tuna mixture.

Mix the remaining cheese with the breadcrumbs and sprinkle over the top. Bake for 20 minutes.

Tuna stuffed loaf

Overall timing 50 minutes

Freezing Not suitable

To serve 4

2	Small round crusty loaves	2
1	Onion	1
4 oz	Button mushrooms	125 g
2 oz	Butter	50 g
2 tbsp	Plain flour	2x15 ml
10½ oz	Can of condensed mushroom soup	298 g
2	Egg yolks	2
2 tbsp	Single cream	2x15 ml
2x7 oz	Cans of tuna	2x198 g
2 tbsp	Lemon juice	2x15 ml
	Salt and pepper	
½ teasp	Paprika	2.5 ml
2	Lemon slices	2

Preheat the oven to 400°F (200°C) Gas 6.

Hollow out each loaf with a sharp knife to leave a thick shell. Place on a baking tray.

Peel and chop the onion. Wipe and thickly slice the mushrooms. Melt the butter in a saucepan, add the onion and fry till transparent. Add the mushrooms and fry for 2 minutes. Stir in the flour and cook for 1 minute. Gradually add the mushroom soup and bring to the boil, stirring constantly. Simmer for 2 minutes, then remove from the heat and allow to cool slightly.

Beat the egg yolks and cream into the mushroom sauce. Drain and flake the tuna and add to the sauce with the lemon juice. Season to taste.

Divide the hot tuna stuffing between the loaves and sprinkle with the paprika. Bake in the centre of the oven for about 25 minutes till bubbling and golden.

Arrange the loaves on a warmed serving dish and garnish each with a slice of lemon. Serve immediately.

Prawns ravigote

Overall timing 20 minutes plus marination

Freezing Not suitable

To serve 2

1	Stalk of celery	1
$\frac{1}{2}$	Red pepper	$\frac{1}{2}$
$\frac{1}{2}$	Green pepper	$\frac{1}{2}$
8 oz	Large shelled prawns	225 g
1 teasp	Chopped fresh herbs	5 ml
$\frac{1}{2}$	Round lettuce	$\frac{1}{2}$
1	Hard-boiled egg	1
Marinade		
1 tbsp	Soured cream	15 ml
4 tbsp	Thick mayonnaise	4x15 ml
1 tbsp	Lemon juice	15 ml
1 tbsp	White wine vinegar	15 ml
$\frac{1}{2}$ teasp	Made mustard	2.5 ml
	Salt and pepper	

To make marinade, mix the soured cream and mayonnaise in a bowl. Gradually add the lemon juice and vinegar, a few drops at a time, stirring constantly. Stir in the mustard and season to taste.

Trim the celery and cut into thin strips. Deseed and thinly slice the peppers. Place the prepared vegetables in a bowl and add the chopped prawns and herbs. Pour the marinade over, toss lightly and leave to marinate for 30 minutes.

Wash and dry the lettuce and line serving dish with the leaves. Spoon the prawn salad into the centre.

Shell the egg, cut in half and remove yolk. Slice the white; press yolk through a sieve. Use to garnish the salad.

Prawns magenta

Overall timing 40 minutes

Freezing Not suitable

To serve 2

2	Stalks of celery	2
1	Large carrot	1
1	Small leek	1
2 tbsp	Olive oil	2x15 ml
8 oz	Prawns	225 g
¼ pint	Dry white wine	150 ml
8 oz	Can of tomatoes	225 g
	Salt and pepper	
3	Fresh basil leaves	3
1 oz	Butter	25 g

Trim the celery and cut into thin sticks. Peel the carrot and cut into sticks. Trim and thinly slice the leek.

Heat the oil in a saucepan, add the prepared vegetables, cover and cook over a low heat for 10 minutes to release the flavours without browning vegetables.

Shell the prawns and add to the pan with the white wine and tomatoes and juice. Season, cover and cook over a low heat for 10 minutes, shaking pan occasionally.

Add the whole basil leaves and butter, adjust the seasoning and serve hot with boiled rice.

Roast pork with stuffing balls

Overall timing 2¼ hours

Freezing Not suitable

To serve 6

2½ lb	Rolled boned hindloin of pork	1.1 kg
	Oil	
	Salt	
Stuffing balls		
1	Onion	1
2 oz	Butter	50 g
4 oz	Fresh breadcrumbs	125 g
2 teasp	Dried sage	2x5 ml
	Salt and pepper	
2	Eggs	2
1 oz	Lard	25 g

Preheat the oven to 450°F (230°C) Gas 8.

Score the skin on the joint, then rub it well with oil and sprinkle with salt. Place in a roasting tin and roast for 20 minutes. Reduce the temperature to 375°F (190°C) Gas 5, and continue roasting for 1½ hours.

Meanwhile, make the stuffing balls. Peel and chop the onion. Melt the butter in a frying pan and fry the onion till golden. Tip the onion into a bowl and add the breadcrumbs, sage and seasoning. Bind with the eggs, then shape into small balls.

About 45 minutes before the pork has finished cooking, melt the lard in an oven-proof dish in the oven. Arrange the stuffing balls in the dish and place on a shelf below the pork. Turn once during the cooking.

Transfer the pork to a warmed serving platter and surround with the stuffing balls.

Roast pork with oranges

Overall timing 2¼ hours

Freezing Not suitable

To serve 6–8

3 lb	Rolled spare rib of pork	1.4 kg
1 oz	Butter	25 g
	Salt and pepper	
5	Oranges	5
2 tbsp	Lemon juice	2x15 ml
¼ pint	Hot water	150 ml
6	Sugar lumps	6
1 tbsp	Wine vinegar	15 ml
2 teasp	Arrowroot	2x5 ml

Preheat the oven to 450°F (230°C) Gas 8.

Place pork in a roasting tin. Spread butter over lean parts and rub salt and pepper into skin. Roast for 20 minutes.

Meanwhile, squeeze juice from two oranges.

Peel remaining oranges. Cut two into slices and one into segments.

Remove pork from tin and keep warm. Pour off any fat from tin and add orange and lemon juices and water. Stir well, scraping any sediment from bottom of tin. Reduce oven temperature to 400°F (200°C) Gas 6.

Replace meat in tin and roast for a further 1½ hours, basting occasionally.

Meanwhile, put sugar lumps into a saucepan with 1 tbsp (15 ml) water. Stir till dissolved, then boil rapidly, without stirring, till golden. Remove from heat and stir in vinegar. Return to heat and stir till caramel dissolves.

Place pork on a warmed serving dish. Stir cooking liquor from tin into caramel. Blend arrowroot with 2 tbsp (2x15 ml) water and add to caramel. Bring to the boil, stirring. Add the sliced and segmented oranges. Heat through for 1–2 minutes.

Cut pork into thick slices and arrange the pieces of orange around. Serve the sauce separately in a warmed sauceboat.

Cowboy's pork and beans

Overall timing 50 minutes

Freezing Not suitable

To serve 4

1½ lb	Belly of pork rashers	700 g
1	Large onion	1
2 tbsp	Oil	2x15 ml
2	Garlic cloves	2
¼ teasp	Chilli powder	1.25 ml
2 tbsp	Black treacle	2x15 ml
1 tbsp	Vinegar	15 ml
½ teasp	Powdered mustard	2.5 ml
2 tbsp	Tomato ketchup	2x15 ml
½ pint	Chicken stock	300 ml
	Salt and pepper	
2x14 oz	Cans of haricot beans	2x397 g

Preheat the oven to 425°F (220°C) Gas 7.

Cut the pork into ½ inch (12.5 mm) pieces, discarding any bones. Place in roasting tin with no extra fat. Cook in the oven for about 20 minutes till crisp and golden.

Meanwhile, peel and finely chop the onion. Heat the oil in a flameproof casserole and fry the onion till transparent. Peel and crush the garlic and add to the pan with the chilli powder. Fry, stirring, for 2 minutes.

Stir in the treacle, vinegar, mustard, ketchup and chicken stock. Bring to the boil, season and simmer for 5 minutes.

Drain and rinse the canned beans and add to the sauce.

Remove the pork from the oven and reduce the temperature to 350°F (180°C) Gas 4. Add the pork pieces to the beans with 1 tbsp (15 ml) of the fat from the tin. Put the casserole in the oven and cook for about 15 minutes, stirring once, till liquid is reduced by half. Taste and adjust the seasoning, then serve immediately with a tomato and onion salad and crusty bread.

Country pork with parsnips

Overall timing 2¼ hours

Freezing Not suitable

To serve 4–6

2½ lb	Piece of belly pork	1.1 kg
	Salt and pepper	
1 tbsp	Oil	15 ml
2 oz	Butter	50 g
2	Onions	2
2 lb	Parsnips	900 g
½ pint	Stock	300 ml
	Bouquet garni	
1 tbsp	Plain flour	15 ml
¼ pint	Dry white wine	150 ml

Preheat the oven to 400°F (200°C) Gas 6.

Wipe the pork and score the rind with a sharp knife. Rub salt and oil into the rind. Melt the butter in a roasting tin, place the pork in it and roast in the centre of the oven for 1 hour.

Meanwhile, peel and chop the onions. Peel and slice the parsnips.

Remove the roasting tin from the oven and arrange the onions and parsnips around the pork. Pour in the stock (made with cubes if necessary), add the bouquet garni and return to the oven. Roast for a further 45 minutes, basting the parsnips occasionally.

Discard the bouquet garni. Place the pork on a warmed serving dish and arrange the parsnips around it. Keep hot.

Pour all but 2 tbsp (2x15 ml) of the juices from the roasting tin into a jug. Sprinkle the flour into the tin and cook for 1 minute, stirring. Gradually add the reserved cooking liquor and the wine and bring to the boil, stirring constantly. Taste and adjust seasoning and spoon over the parsnips.

Meatballs and spinach

Overall timing 45 minutes

Freezing Not suitable

To serve 4

1 lb	Minced pork	450 g
1 tbsp	Chopped chives	15 ml
1	Egg	1
2 tbsp	Soy sauce	2x15 ml
4 tbsp	Oil	4x15 ml
2 tbsp	Dry sherry	2x15 ml
$\frac{1}{4}$ pint	Water	150 ml
2 lb	Spinach	900 g
1 teasp	Cornflour	5 ml
	Salt and pepper	

Pound minced pork with chives, egg and half the soy sauce till mixture binds together. Shape into eight balls.

Heat half the oil in a frying pan, add the meatballs and fry over a medium heat for 10 minutes, turning till browned. Add the remaining soy sauce, the sherry and water, bring to the boil, cover and simmer for 15 minutes.

Meanwhile, shred the spinach. Heat the remaining oil in another frying pan, add the spinach and stir-fry over a high heat for 3 minutes.

Blend the cornflour with 1 tbsp (15 ml) cold water and add to the meatballs. Bring to the boil, stirring till thickened. Season to taste.

Arrange the spinach on a warmed serving dish and place the meatballs on top. Spoon the sauce over the meatballs and serve with a side dish of soy sauce.

Braised pork with plum sauce

Overall timing 1¾ hours

Freezing Not suitable

To serve 6

2 oz	Lard	50 g
	Salt and pepper	
2½ lb	Boned and rolled loin of pork	1.1 kg
½ pint	Light stock	300 ml
3	Sage leaves	3
2 lb	Small potatoes	900 g
1½ lb	Red plums	700 g
2 oz	Sugar	50 g
1 tbsp	Chopped parsley	15 ml

Preheat the oven to 400°F (200°C) Gas 6.

Melt lard in a roasting tin. Season pork and fry quickly over a high heat till browned on all sides. Pour off the fat and reserve. Add the stock and sage leaves, cover the tin with foil and braise in the oven for 45 minutes.

Meanwhile, peel potatoes. Put into a saucepan, cover with cold salted water and bring to the boil. Drain.

Remove meat from oven and strain stock into a saucepan. Add reserved fat to roasting tin with the potatoes, return to the oven and cook uncovered for a further 50 minutes, basting the meat and potatoes occasionally.

Meanwhile, wash plums. Halve 1 lb (450 g) of them and discard stones. Add to the stock with the sugar. Bring to the boil, then cover and simmer for 10–15 minutes, stirring occasionally. Poach the rest of the plums whole in a little water till tender.

Remove meat from tin, carve into thick slices and arrange on a warmed serving plate. Arrange the potatoes and whole poached plums around the meat. Sprinkle with parsley. Lightly mash remaining plums and pour into a warmed sauceboat.

Iowa skillet chops

Overall timing 1 hour

Freezing Suitable

To serve 4

8	Pork loin chops	8
	Salt and pepper	
3 tbsp	Oil	3x15 ml
1 lb 12 oz	Can of tomatoes	794 g
1 tbsp	Tomato purée	15 ml
1 tbsp	Worcestershire sauce	15 ml
1	Onion	1
11½ oz	Can of sweetcorn kernels	326 g
1 tbsp	Arrowroot (optional)	15 ml
	Sprigs of parsley	

Sprinkle chops with salt and pepper. Heat oil in a frying pan and cook chops in two batches for 2 minutes on each side. When all chops are cooked, return first batch to pan. Remove from heat.

Purée the tomatoes with juice, tomato purée and Worcestershire sauce in a blender, then pour over chops. Finely chop the onion and add with the drained corn (use some of the corn water if the mixture is too thick). Bring back to the boil and add salt and pepper.

Cover the pan and cook over moderate heat for 25 minutes. Remove lid to reduce sauce a little and cook for a further 10 minutes. Thicken with arrowroot, if you like, blended with a little hot water, and cook till clear. Garnish with parsley and serve straight from the pan.

Barbecued pork chops

Overall timing 20 minutes plus marination

Freezing Not suitable

To serve 4

4	Pork spare rib chops	4
Marinade		
1	Large onion	1
2 tbsp	Lemon juice or vinegar	2x15 ml
2 tbsp	Oil	2x15 ml
½ teasp	Powdered mustard	2.5 ml
2 teasp	Worcestershire sauce	2x5 ml
½ teasp	Salt	2.5 ml
½ teasp	Freshly ground black pepper	2.5 ml
1 teasp	Granulated sugar	5 ml
½ teasp	Paprika	2.5 ml

Place pork chops in bowl. Peel and grate the onion and place in a jug. Add rest of marinade ingredients and mix well, then pour over chops. Leave to marinate for 1 hour in a cool place, turning chops at least twice.

Preheat the grill.

Cook the chops under the grill (or on a barbecue), occasionally brushing them with the reserved marinade. Serve with mixed salad, dressed with vinaigrette flavoured with fresh dill or other herb of choice.

Chinese spare ribs

Overall timing 45 minutes

Freezing Not suitable

To serve 4

1½ lb	Pork spare ribs	700 g
2 tbsp	Oil	2x15 ml
1 tbsp	Hoisin sauce	15 ml
1 tbsp	Soy sauce	15 ml
Sauce		
½ inch	Piece of root ginger	12.5 mm
1	Green pepper	1
2	Garlic cloves	2
2 tbsp	Oil	2x15 ml
1 tbsp	Soy sauce	15 ml
2 tbsp	Dry sherry	2x15 ml
2 tbsp	Tomato purée	2x15 ml
2 tbsp	Vinegar	2x15 ml
2 tbsp	Sugar	2x15 ml
1 tbsp	Cornflour	15 ml
4 tbsp	Pineapple juice	4x15 ml
3 tbsp	Water	3x15 ml

Separate the pork into ribs. Cook in boiling water for 15 minutes, then drain and dry on kitchen paper.

Heat oil in frying pan. Add ribs and stir in hoisin and soy sauces. Cook gently for 20 minutes.

Meanwhile, prepare sauce. Shred ginger. Deseed pepper and cut into thin strips. Peel and crush garlic. Heat oil in a saucepan, add garlic, ginger and pepper and stir-fry for 2 minutes. Remove from heat and stir in soy sauce, sherry, tomato purée, vinegar and sugar. Blend cornflour with fruit juice and water and add to the pan. Bring to the boil and cook for 2 minutes, stirring constantly.

Place ribs in a warmed serving dish. Pour sauce over and serve immediately with boiled rice.

Braised pork chops

Overall timing 55 minutes

Freezing Not suitable

To serve 2

4	Pork chops	4
	Salt and pepper	
2	Cooking apples	2
2	Onions	2
1 oz	Butter	25 g
3 fl oz	Water	90 ml
2 teasp	Worcestershire sauce	2x5 ml
	Fresh parsley	

Season chops with salt and pepper. Peel and core apples and cut into wedges. Peel onions and cut into rings.

Melt butter in frying pan and brown the chops on all sides. Add water and Worcestershire sauce, cover and cook for 10 minutes.

Turn chops over. Add apples and onions. Reduce heat, cover and cook for a further 30 minutes.

Garnish with parsley and serve with creamed potatoes.

Sweetbread bake

Overall timing 50 minutes

Freezing Not suitable

To serve 2

2 oz	Button mushrooms	50 g
8 oz	Prepared lambs' sweetbreads	225 g
	Salt and pepper	
2 tbsp	Plain flour	2x15 ml
1 oz	Butter	25 g
5 tbsp	Chicken stock	5x15 ml
1	Small egg	1
5 tbsp	Plain yogurt	5x15 ml
2 oz	Cheese	50 g
	Chopped parsley	

Preheat the oven to 375°F (190°C) Gas 5.

Slice the mushrooms. Cut the sweetbreads into $\frac{1}{4}$ inch (6 mm) thick slices. Season the flour and toss the sweetbreads in it till lightly coated.

Melt butter in a frying pan, add the sweetbreads and mushrooms and fry for about 10 minutes till golden. Add the stock and seasoning and simmer for 5 minutes.

Meanwhile, beat the egg with yogurt, grated cheese and seasoning.

Arrange the sweetbreads and mushrooms in an ovenproof dish and pour the yogurt mixture over. Bake for 20 minutes till lightly set and golden. Sprinkle with parsley and serve hot.

Orange pork rolls

Overall timing 1 hour

Freezing Not suitable

To serve 6

6x4oz	Slices of lean pork	6x125g
1	Onion	1
3oz	Butter	75g
4oz	Fresh breadcrumbs	125g
2 tbsp	Chopped parsley	2x15ml
1 teasp	Dried mixed herbs	5ml
	Salt and pepper	
1	Large orange	1
1	Egg	1
2 tbsp	Plain flour	2x15ml
¼ pint	Cider	150ml
¼ pint	Chicken stock	150ml

Preheat the oven to 375°F (190°C) Gas 5.

Place slices of pork between damp grease-proof and beat till very thin. Peel and finely chop onion. Melt 1oz (25g) of the butter in a frying pan and fry onion till golden. Add breadcrumbs, parsley, herbs and seasoning. Cook for 2 minutes, then remove from the heat.

Grate orange rind into stuffing, add egg and mix well. Divide stuffing between pork slices. Roll them up carefully, turning sides in to cover stuffing, and secure with wooden cock-tail sticks.

Arrange rolls in roasting tin and dot with remaining butter. Squeeze orange and pour juice over. Cook in the oven for about 35 minutes, basting occasionally, till pork is tender.

Place pork rolls on a warmed serving dish and keep hot. Sprinkle flour into roasting tin and stir over heat for 1 minute. Gradually add cider and stock and bring to the boil, stirring. Season to taste, pour into a sauce boat and serve with the pork rolls.

Sweet and sour pork

Overall timing 40 minutes plus marination

Freezing Suitable

To serve 4

1 lb	Lean pork	450 g
2 tbsp	Dry sherry	2x15 ml
	Salt and pepper	
1	Egg	1
3 tbsp	Plain flour	3x15 ml
3 tbsp	Oil	3x15 ml
2	Carrots	2
2	Onions	2
1	Large cucumber	1
1	Garlic clove	1
4 tbsp	Tomato ketchup	4x15 ml
2 teasp	Soy sauce	2x5 ml
2 tbsp	Vinegar	2x15 ml
1 tbsp	Brown sugar	15 ml
1 tbsp	Cornflour	15 ml
½ pint	Water	300 ml

Cut meat into ½ inch (12.5 mm) cubes. Put into a bowl with sherry and seasoning and marinate for 30 minutes.

Lightly beat egg. Dip pork cubes in egg, then coat with flour. Heat oil in a large frying pan. Fry pork for 8 minutes till golden brown on all sides. Remove from pan.

Peel and chop carrots, onions and cucumber. Peel and crush garlic. Add all to frying pan and stir-fry for 5 minutes over fairly high heat. Reduce heat to moderate. Add ketchup, soy sauce, vinegar, sugar, cornflour dissolved in water and reserved marinade to the pan. Bring to the boil and cook for 3 minutes, stirring.

Return pork to pan and cook for 3 minutes more till heated through. Serve with plain boiled rice and side dishes of tomato wedges, chunks of cucumber and a little desiccated coconut for sprinkling over the finished dish.

Roast pork with turnips

Overall timing 2¼ hours

Freezing Not suitable

To serve 6

2½ lb	Rolled hindloin of pork	1.1 kg
1	Garlic clove	1
2 oz	Butter	50 g
	Salt and pepper	
2 lb	Small turnips	900 g
2 teasp	Caster sugar	2x5 ml
¾ pint	Light stock	400 ml
1 tbsp	Plain flour	15 ml
1 tbsp	Chopped parsley	15 ml

Preheat the oven to 425°F (220°C) Gas 7.

Peel the garlic clove, cut in half and rub all over the pork. Place the pork in a roasting tin and spread the butter over. Sprinkle with salt and pepper and roast in the centre of the oven for 20 minutes. Reduce the temperature to 375°F (190°C) Gas 5 and cook for a further 40 minutes.

Meanwhile, peel and halve or quarter the turnips according to size. Put into a saucepan, cover with cold salted water and bring to the boil. Drain, then dry on kitchen paper.

Arrange the turnips round the pork. Sprinkle with the sugar and add the stock (made with a cube if necessary). Cover with foil and roast for 30 minutes. Remove the foil, turn the turnips over and cook for a further 15 minutes. Test pork for doneness and cook a little longer if necessary.

Place the pork in a warmed serving dish and carve into thick slices. Arrange the turnips on the dish and keep hot.

Pour off liquid from tin and reserve. Sprinkle the flour into the tin and cook, stirring, for 1 minute. Gradually add the reserved liquid and bring to the boil, stirring constantly. Adjust seasoning. Sprinkle the parsley over the turnips and serve.

Polish-style pork with sauerkraut

Overall timing 1 hour

Freezing Not suitable

To serve 6

3 tbsp	Oil	3x15 ml
6	Pork loin chops	6
1	Large onion	1
1	Garlic clove	1
	Salt and pepper	
2 lb	Sauerkraut	900 g
1	Bay leaf	1
½ pint	Chicken stock	300 ml
1	Large dessert apple	1
1 teasp	Cumin seeds	5 ml

Heat the oil in flameproof casserole and fry the chops till browned on both sides. Remove from the pan and reserve.

Peel and finely chop the onion; peel and crush the garlic. Add both to the casserole and fry till transparent. Season, and add the drained sauerkraut and bay leaf. Arrange the chops on top. Pour the stock over, bring to the boil and simmer for 15 minutes.

Meanwhile, peel, core and dice the apple. Add to the pan with cumin seeds and stir well, then simmer for a further 15 minutes till the chops are tender.

Taste and adjust the seasoning. Discard the bay leaf. Serve with creamed potatoes, buttered carrots and thin slices of wholemeal bread.

Pork and beans

Overall timing 2¾ hours plus overnight soaking

Freezing Not suitable

To serve 4

1 lb	Dried butter beans	450 g
1	Onion	1
12	Cloves	12
2	Garlic cloves	2
2½ pints	Boiling water	1.5 litres
4 tbsp	Oil	4x15 ml
	Salt and pepper	
1 lb	Piece of smoked streaky bacon or belly of pork	450 g

Put the beans in a large saucepan of cold water and soak overnight.

The next day, bring to the boil and cook beans for 15 minutes. Drain.

Peel onion, spike with the cloves and add to pan with peeled garlic, boiling water, oil, pepper and bacon or belly pork, derinded and cut into thick rashers if easier to handle. Cover and simmer for 1½ hours. Taste and add salt, then cook for a further 30 minutes.

Remove spiked onion and garlic. Remove meat and beans from pan with a draining spoon and place in warmed serving dish. Keep hot.

Reduce cooking liquor to about ¼ pint (150 ml) by boiling fast, uncovered. Pour over beans and serve.

Frankfurter fritters

Overall timing 30 minutes

Freezing Not suitable

To serve 6

5 oz	Plain flour	150 g
	Salt and pepper	
1	Egg	1
1 tbsp	Oil	15 ml
4 fl oz	Beer	120 ml
	Oil for frying	
16	Frankfurters	16
2	Egg whites	2

Sift 4 oz (125 g) of the flour into a bowl with 1½ teasp (7.5 ml) salt and make a well in the centre. Add the whole egg and oil and mix with a wooden spoon. Gradually add the beer and mix to a smooth batter.

Heat the oil in a deep-fryer to 340°F (170°C).

Season the remaining flour. Cut the frankfurters in half and toss in flour. Whisk the egg whites till stiff but not dry and fold into the batter. Dip each frankfurter half into the batter and fry in the oil for about 3 minutes till crisp and golden. Drain on kitchen paper and serve hot.

Pork and sausage stew

Overall timing 1¾ hours

Freezing Not suitable

To serve 6

1½ lb	Onions	700 g
2 oz	Lard	50 g
6	Thin cut pork loin chops	6
1 lb	Coarse pork sausages	450 g
2 tbsp	Plain flour	2x15 ml
¾ pint	Chicken stock	400 ml
3 tbsp	Tomato purée	3x15 ml
	Salt and pepper	

Peel and thinly slice the onions. Heat the lard in a flameproof casserole, add the onions and fry gently for 10 minutes till pale golden.

Meanwhile, wipe the chops and remove the bones and any excess fat. Twist the sausages in half.

Sprinkle flour over the onions and cook for 1 minute. Gradually add the stock (made with a cube if necessary) and bring to the boil, stirring. Stir in the tomato purée.

Add the chops and sausages. Bring to the boil, cover and simmer for 1¼ hours, or cook in the centre of the oven preheated to 350°F (180°C) Gas 4 for 1¼ hours.

Adjust the seasoning to taste, then serve immediately with buttered pasta and a green salad.

Belgian pork chops

Overall timing 40 minutes

Freezing Not suitable

To serve 4

4	Pork chops	4
	Salt and pepper	
2 tbsp	Plain flour	2x15 ml
3 tbsp	Oil	3x15 ml
4	Onions	4
$\frac{1}{4}$ pint	Beer	150 ml
$\frac{1}{4}$ pint	Chicken stock	150 ml
$1\frac{1}{2}$ lb	Brussels sprouts	700 g
1 oz	Butter	25 g
2 teasp	Cornflour	2x5 ml

Coat the chops with seasoned flour. Heat oil in frying pan and cook chops for 3 minutes on each side.

Peel and thinly slice onions. Add to pan and cook for 5 minutes. Pour in beer and stock, season and simmer for 15 minutes.

Meanwhile, trim sprouts and cook in boiling water till just tender. Drain well, toss with butter and keep hot.

Remove chops from pan and place on warmed serving plate. Surround with sprouts. Mix cornflour with a little cold water and add to pan. Bring to the boil and cook for 2 minutes. Pour sauce over chops.

Porkburgers

Overall timing 25 minutes

Freezing Suitable: cook from frozen

To serve 6

1½ lb	Lean pork	700 g
	Salt and pepper	
1	Onion	1
1 teasp	Dried thyme	5 ml
1 tbsp	Oil	15 ml
	Lemon slices	

Mince the pork twice till fine and add plenty of salt and pepper. Peel and finely chop the onion and add to the pork with the dried thyme. Mix well with a wooden spoon.

Divide the meat into six portions and shape into thick burgers about 4 inches (10 cm) in diameter.

Brush a heavy-based frying pan or griddle with oil and heat well. Add the burgers and fry for about 10–15 minutes. Turn burgers carefully with a fish slice and cook for a further 5–10 minutes according to taste.

Garnish with lemon slices and serve with an endive and tomato salad or with chips.

Kidney-stuffed roast pork

Overall timing 3½ hours

Freezing Not suitable

To serve 6–8

1	Calf's kidney	1
4 lb	Boned loin of pork	1.8 kg
	Sprig of thyme	
	Salt and pepper	
6 oz	Butter	175 g
1½ lb	Cooked potatoes	700 g
3 tbsp	Oil	3×15 ml
1 lb	Button mushrooms	450 g
1 tbsp	Chopped parsley	15 ml

Preheat the oven to 375°F (190°C) Gas 5.

Prepare kidney. Spread out the pork loin and put kidney in the centre with thyme and seasoning. Roll meat tightly round kidney and tie at regular intervals with string. Place meat in roasting tin with 2 oz (50 g) of the butter. Roast for 3 hours, basting occasionally.

Meanwhile, slice cooked potatoes. Melt 2 oz (50 g) of the butter with the oil in a frying pan, add the potatoes and fry until golden.

Halve mushrooms. Melt remaining butter in another frying pan and cook the mushrooms for 5 minutes, shaking the pan from time to time.

Place meat on warmed serving plate. Surround with drained potatoes and mushrooms and garnish with chopped parsley. Serve with gravy made from roasting juices.

Pork cassoulet

Overall timing 3¼ hours plus soaking

Freezing Not suitable

To serve 6

1 lb	Dried haricot beans	450 g
1	Pig's trotter	1
4 oz	Pork rind	125 g
2	Garlic cloves	2
2	Carrots	2
2	Onions	2
	Bouquet garni	
8 oz	Italian salami	225 g
	Salt and pepper	
2 tbsp	Oil	2x15 ml
14 oz	Can of tomatoes	397 g
1 oz	Fresh breadcrumbs	25 g

Soak beans overnight.

Quarter trotter lengthways. Chop pork rind. Add to beans with peeled garlic, carrots, one onion and bouquet garni. Cover with water, cover and simmer for 1¼ hours.

Peel salami, prick and add to pan with seasoning. Cook for 15 minutes.

Chop remaining onion. Heat oil in a saucepan and fry onion till transparent. Add 1 pint (560 ml) water, tomatoes and seasoning. Simmer for 10 minutes.

Preheat the oven to 350°F (180°C) Gas 4.

Drain beans, reserving pork rind. Add sausage and trotter to other pan. Line deep ovenproof dish with pork rind. Add layers of beans and meat mixture; top with crumbs. Bake for 30 minutes.

Rib and bean stew

Overall timing 1½ hours plus soaking

Freezing Not suitable

To serve 4–6

8 oz	Dried borlotti beans	225 g
2	Carrots	2
2	Stalks of celery	2
2	Bay leaves	2
2 lb	Pork spare ribs	900 g
2	Large onions	2
4 tbsp	Oil	4x15 ml
14 oz	Can of tomatoes	397 g
4 tbsp	Tomato purée	4x15 ml
1 tbsp	Sugar	15 ml
¾ pint	Chicken stock	400 ml
	Salt and pepper	

Soak beans overnight, then drain and cover with fresh water. Slice carrots and celery and add to beans with bay leaves. Simmer for 1 hour.

Separate ribs. Peel and finely chop onions. Heat oil in saucepan and fry onions till transparent. Add ribs and brown all over. Add tomatoes, tomato purée, sugar and stock and bring to the boil.

Drain beans and add to meat. Season and simmer for 15 minutes till meat is tender and cooking liquor is thick.

Pork and treacle casserole

Overall timing 1¾ hours

Freezing Not suitable

To serve 6

1 lb	Lean boned pork	450 g
1½ lb	Thick belly of pork rashers	700 g
	Salt and pepper	
2 tbsp	Plain flour	2x15 ml
3	Large onions	3
2	Garlic cloves	2
2 oz	Lard	50 g
3 tbsp	Treacle	3x15 ml
2 tbsp	Tomato purée	2x15 ml
14 oz	Can of tomatoes	397 g
¾ pint	Beef stock	400 ml

Preheat the oven to 350°F (180°C) Gas 4.

Wipe and trim the boned pork and cut into cubes. Remove any bones from the belly of pork but leave rind on. Cut pork into 1 inch (2.5 cm) pieces. Toss in seasoned flour. Peel and slice the onions; peel and crush the garlic.

Heat the lard in a flameproof casserole, add the pork and fry over a high heat till browned all over. Remove with a draining spoon and reserve.

Add the onions to the pan and fry till transparent. Pour off any excess fat. Stir in the treacle, tomato purée and garlic. Return the pork to the pan and stir till coated. Add the canned tomatoes and juice, stock (made with a cube if necessary) and seasoning and bring to the boil, stirring to break up the tomatoes. Cover and cook in the centre of the oven for 45 minutes.

Remove the lid and stir the casserole. Cook uncovered for a further 30 minutes till the pork is tender.

Adjust seasoning to taste and serve immediately with buttered noodles.

Pork brochettes

Overall timing 30 minutes

Freezing Not suitable

To serve 4

1 lb	Lean pork	450 g
4 oz	Belly pork rashers	125 g
2	Pigs' kidneys	2
12	Bay leaves	12
	Oil	
	Salt and pepper	

Cut lean pork into 1 inch (2.5 cm) cubes. Remove rind from the belly pork rashers and chop them. Wash and dry kidneys. Cut them open, remove the fat and cut each into four.

Preheat grill.

Arrange bay leaves, meat cubes, belly pork and kidney pieces on skewers. Brush with a little oil and season liberally.

Grill for about 20 minutes, turning skewers occasionally. Serve with boiled rice and peas or a mixed salad with French dressing.

Baked pork chops

Overall timing 40 minutes

Freezing Not suitable

To serve 4

4	Pork chops	4
	Salt and pepper	
2 tbsp	Oil	2x15 ml
1 lb	Cooking apples	450 g
1 oz	Butter	25 g
1 tbsp	Chopped fresh rosemary	15 ml
$\frac{1}{4}$ pint	Stock	150 ml

Preheat the oven to 400°F (200°C) Gas 6.

Season chops with salt and pepper. Heat oil in a flameproof casserole and brown the chops for 2 minutes on each side.

Peel, core and slice apples. Arrange in casserole round the chops and dot with the butter. Sprinkle with rosemary, add stock (made with $\frac{1}{2}$ stock cube if liked) and cover casserole.

Bake in the centre of the oven for about 30 minutes, removing lid for last 10 minutes of cooking time. Serve with creamed potatoes and salad.

Pork chops with bananas

Overall timing 30 minutes

Freezing Not suitable

To serve 4

1 oz	Butter	25 g
4	Pork chops	4
3	Small, firm bananas	3
	Salt and pepper	
	Pinch of cayenne pepper	
1	Lemon	1
	Sprigs of parsley	
1 teasp	Plain flour	5 ml
¼ pint	Stock	150 ml

Melt the butter in a frying pan over medium heat. Add the chops and cook for 10–12 minutes on each side depending on thickness.

Five minutes before the chops are cooked, peel bananas and cut in half lengthways. Add to the frying pan and sprinkle with salt, pepper and cayenne.

Lift out the pork chops and bananas and arrange on a warmed serving dish. Garnish with lemon and parsley.

Stir the flour into the pan juices and add the stock gradually. Simmer for 2–3 minutes, then pour this gravy into a small serving jug.

Serve with plain boiled rice which will provide a contrast to the sweeter meat and bananas.

Pot roast pork with apples

Overall timing 1½ hours

Freezing Not suitable

To serve 4–6

2 oz	Butter	50 g
3¼ lb	Rolled pork	1.5 kg
	Salt and pepper	
2 tbsp	Cinnamon	2x15 ml
8	Granny Smith apples	8

Preheat oven to 400°F (200°C) Gas 6.

Melt 1 oz (25 g) butter in a flameproof casserole. Roll pork joint in a mixture of salt, pepper and half the cinnamon, then brown on all sides. Cover casserole and cook on the middle shelf of the oven for about 1 hour, turning joint over halfway through.

Peel and core apples and cut into quarters. Put into a saucepan with remaining butter and cinnamon. Cover and cook for about 10 minutes over a low heat, shaking the pan to prevent sticking.

Arrange the apples around the roast 15 minutes before the end of cooking time.

Remove pork from casserole; slice and place on warmed serving plate. Surround with apples. Make gravy from cooking juices and serve separately.

Russian pork chop casserole

Overall timing 30 minutes

Freezing Not suitable

To serve 4

1 lb	Potatoes	450 g
2 tbsp	Oil	2x15 ml
4	Pork rib chops	4
	Salt and pepper	
3 tbsp	Water	3x15 ml
4 oz	Button mushrooms	125 g
1 teasp	Garlic salt	5 ml
¼ pint	Carton of soured cream	150 ml
2 tbsp	Chopped parsley	2x15 ml

Peel potatoes and cut them into very small, thin pieces. Melt the oil in a flameproof casserole and fry the potatoes for 5 minutes. Remove from pan with draining spoon.

Season chops with salt and pepper. Add to casserole and cook for 1 minute on each side. Drain off excess fat. Add water, cover and cook for 10 minutes.

Slice mushrooms. Add to casserole with fried potatoes and garlic salt and cook for a further 10 minutes. Stir in soured cream and 1 tbsp (15 ml) of the chopped parsley. Heat through. Sprinkle with remaining parsley just before serving.

Scandinavian pork

Overall timing 2½ hours plus soaking

Freezing Not suitable

To serve 6–8

8 oz	Plump prunes	225 g
1	Large cooking apple	1
2 tbsp	Lemon juice	2x15 ml
3 lb	Piece of belly of pork	1.4 kg
	Salt and pepper	
1 tbsp	Oil	15 ml
½ pint	Stock	300 ml
2 tbsp	Plain flour	2x15 ml
	Sprigs of parsley	

Soak prunes in ½ pint (300 ml) hot water for 1 hour.

Preheat the oven to 375°F (190°C) Gas 5.

Drain prunes, reserving soaking water, and remove stones. Peel, core and slice apple. Toss in lemon juice to prevent browning and add to prunes.

Season pork. Place apple and prunes along the centre, then roll up lengthways and tie into a neat shape with fine string. Place in a roasting tin and rub oil into skin. Sprinkle with salt and roast for 45 minutes.

Pour prune soaking liquor and stock over pork. Reduce the temperature to 350°F (180°C) Gas 4 and roast for a further 1¼ hours.

Place the meat on a warmed serving dish, discard the string and keep hot. Drain pan juices into a small saucepan and skim off any fat. Blend flour to a smooth paste with 4 tbsp (4x15 ml) cold water. Add to meat juices and bring to the boil, stirring constantly. Simmer for 4–5 minutes. Carve pork into thick slices and garnish with sprigs of parsley. Serve with gravy.

Pork with bananas and peanuts

Overall timing 1¾ hours

Freezing Not suitable

To serve 4

12 oz	Onions	350 g
2	Garlic cloves	2
4 tbsp	Oil	4x15 ml
2 lb	Pork (top of belly)	900 g
3 oz	Rice	75 g
14 oz	Can of tomatoes	397 g
1	Chicken stock cube	1
¼ teasp	Paprika	1.25 ml
¼ teasp	Ground cinnamon	1.25 ml
8 oz	Potatoes	225 g
2	Bananas	2
2 oz	Salted peanuts	50 g
	Salt	

Peel and chop onions. Peel and crush garlic. Heat 2 tbsp (2x15 ml) of the oil in saucepan. Add onions and garlic and fry until browned.

Cut pork into cubes and add to pan with rice. Cook till rice has absorbed oil, stirring frequently to prevent sticking. Add a little water if necessary to prevent burning. Remove from heat.

Pour juice from canned tomatoes into jug. Crumble in stock cube and make up to ¾ pint (400 ml) with boiling water. Chop tomatoes and add to pan with stock mixture, paprika and cinnamon. Cover and simmer gently for 20 minutes.

Meanwhile, peel and cube potatoes. Heat remaining oil in a frying pan and fry potatoes over a low heat for about 10 minutes. Add them to the pan. Peel and slice bananas and stir into the stew with the peanuts. Cook for 10 minutes. Taste and add salt if necessary.

Pork chops with wine sauce

Overall timing 30 minutes

Freezing Not suitable

To serve 2

1 oz	Butter	25 g
2	Pork chops	2
	Salt and pepper	
1	Small onion	1
3 tbsp	Dry white wine	3x15 ml
3 tbsp	Water	3x15 ml
1½ teasp	Tomato purée	7.5 ml
4	Gherkins	4
1 teasp	Chopped parsley	5 ml
½ teasp	Made mustard	2.5 ml

Melt the butter in the frying pan and cook the pork chops gently for 10–12 minutes on each side. Season. Place on warmed serving dish and keep warm.

Peel and finely chop onion. Add to pan and fry till transparent. Stir in wine, water, tomato purée and seasoning and bring to the boil, stirring. Simmer for 3 minutes.

Remove pan from heat. Thinly slice two of the gherkins and stir into the sauce with the parsley and mustard. Pour sauce over chops. Garnish with remaining gherkins, cut into fan shapes, and serve with macaroni or noodles.

Beef

Beef pot roast

Overall timing 3 hours plus marination

Freezing Suitable: reheat, in sauce, in 400°F (200°C) Gas 6 oven for 1 hour

To serve 8–10

4 lb	Braising beef	1.8 kg
	Salt and pepper	
6 oz	Pork fat with rind	175 g
1	Large onion	1
3	Carrots	3
3	Stalks of celery	3
1	Garlic clove	1
	Sprigs of parsley	
2	Bay leaves	2
	Sprigs of thyme	
½ pint	Red or white wine	300 ml
1 oz	Butter	25 g
2 tbsp	Oil	2x15 ml
1	Pig's trotter	1
4 fl oz	Water	120 ml
1 tbsp	Tomato purée	15 ml

Season the beef. Slice the pork fat. Wrap the fat around the beef and secure with string. Peel and chop the onion and carrots. Trim and chop the celery. Peel and crush the garlic. Tie the parsley, bay leaves and thyme together with string (or use a bouquet garni).

Put the beef in a bowl and add the prepared vegetables, herbs, wine and seasoning. Marinate overnight.

The next day, drain the beef, reserving the marinade. Pat the beef dry with kitchen paper. Melt the butter with the oil in a flameproof casserole and brown the beef on all sides.

Split the trotter and add to the casserole with the marinade, water and tomato purée. Bring to the boil, then cover and simmer for 2½ hours.

Transfer the beef to a warmed serving platter and keep hot. Strain the cooking liquor, discarding the trotter and vegetables, and return to the casserole. Boil the liquor till reduced, then pour into sauceboat. Serve beef with sauce, and carrots and button onions.

Salt beef

Overall timing 3½ hours plus 2 weeks salting

Freezing Not suitable

To serve 8–10

2 lb	Coarse salt	900 g
4 oz	Sugar	125 g
1 tbsp	Saltpetre	15 ml
1 oz	Pickling spice	25 g
4	Bay leaves	4
1	Sprig of thyme	1
5 lb	Silverside or brisket of beef	2.3 kg
3	Large onions	3
5	Cloves	5
1	Stalk of celery	1
1 teasp	Black peppercorns	5 ml
1 lb	Medium carrots	450 g
2	Medium turnips	2
1 lb	Leeks	450 g

Put salt, sugar and saltpetre into a large saucepan with pickling spices tied in muslin. Add bay leaves, thyme and 8 pints (4.5 litres) water and heat gently, stirring, till sugar and salt have dissolved. Bring to the boil, then pour into bowl and cool.

Add meat to bowl, making sure that salt solution covers it. Cover with clean tea-towel and leave to soak in cold place for up to 2 weeks. Turn meat occasionally.

To cook, remove from pickle and wash under cold running water. Put into a large saucepan with one onion, peeled and spiked with cloves. Chop celery and add to pan with peppercorns. Cover with cold water and bring to the boil slowly. Skim, reduce heat, cover and simmer for 2½ hours.

Meanwhile, peel and chop carrots and turnips. Peel remaining onions and slice thickly. Chop leeks. Add vegetables to pan, bring back to the boil and simmer for 30 minutes. Use strained cooking liquor to make a sauce.

Beef and bean casserole

Overall timing 3 hours plus soaking

Freezing Suitable: reheat from frozen in 325°F (170°C) Gas 3 oven

To serve 4–6

8 oz	Dried haricot beans	225 g
2	Onions	2
2 tbsp	Oil	2x15 ml
1 lb	Stewing beef	450 g
¼ teasp	Chilli powder	1.25 ml
1 teasp	Curry powder	5 ml
2 tbsp	Plain flour	2x15 ml
½ pint	Beef stock	300 ml
14 oz	Can of tomatoes	397 g
2 tbsp	Tomato purée	2x15 ml
2 teasp	Sugar	2x5 ml
	Salt and pepper	
1	Large cooking apple	1
2 oz	Sultanas	50 g

Put beans in a large saucepan and cover with cold water. Bring to the boil. Boil for 2 minutes, then remove from the heat, cover and leave to soak for 2 hours.

Preheat the oven to 325°F (170°C) Gas 3.

Peel and chop onions. Heat oil in a flame-proof casserole and fry onions for 3 minutes. Cut beef into chunks. Add to pan and fry quickly till brown. Stir in the chilli and curry powder and flour. Fry for 2 minutes.

Gradually add stock and bring to the boil, stirring. Add the tomatoes with their juice and tomato purée. Drain beans and add to casserole with the sugar and seasoning. Cover and cook in the oven for 2 hours.

Peel, core and chop apple. Stir into casserole with sultanas and cook for a further 30 minutes. Taste and adjust seasoning. Serve with crusty bread.

Beef and mushroom stuffed tomatoes

Overall timing 1¼ hours

Freezing Not suitable

To serve 3–4

6	Large tomatoes	6
1	Onion	1
1 oz	Butter	25 g
1 lb	Lean minced beef	450 g
4 oz	Mushrooms	125 g
1 tbsp	Chopped parsley	15 ml
6 tbsp	Dry white wine	6x15 ml
	Salt and pepper	
1 oz	Fresh breadcrumbs	25 g
	Lemon wedges	

Preheat the oven to 350°F (180°C) Gas 4.

Halve the tomatoes and scoop out the flesh. Chop the flesh. Peel and chop the onion. Melt the butter in a frying pan and fry the onion till transparent. Add the beef and fry for 5 minutes.

Chop the mushrooms and add to the pan with the parsley, chopped tomato flesh, wine and seasoning. Cover and cook for 10 minutes.

Stir in the breadcrumbs. Spoon the mixture into the tomato halves. Arrange in an oven-proof dish and bake for 25–30 minutes till the tops are brown and crisp. Garnish with lemon wedges and serve with mashed potatoes.

Beef and split pea stew

Overall timing 2 hours plus soaking

Freezing Not suitable

To serve 6

12 oz	Split peas	350 g
1	Onion	1
1½ lb	Braising steak	700 g
1 oz	Butter	25 g
2 tbsp	Oil	2×15 ml
2	Large carrots	2
	Bouquet garni	
¼ teasp	Grated nutmeg	1.25 ml
1½ pints	Beef stock	850 ml
	Salt and pepper	
8 oz	Potatoes	225 g
8 oz	Fresh spinach	225 g

Wash and pick over the split peas and put into a saucepan of cold water. Bring to the boil and boil for 2 minutes. Remove from the heat, cover and leave to soak for 2 hours.

Peel and chop the onion. Cut the meat into bite-size pieces. Heat the butter and oil in a flameproof casserole and fry the onion and meat till lightly browned.

Drain the split peas and add to the meat. Scrape the carrots, slice thinly and add to the pan with the bouquet garni, grated nutmeg and stock. Add seasoning and bring to the boil. Reduce the heat, cover and simmer for 1 hour.

Peel and dice the potatoes. Chop the spinach and add both to the meat. Cook for a further 30 minutes. Taste and adjust the seasoning. Serve with creamed potatoes and a green vegetable or boiled rice, or with crusty bread for a lighter meal.

Beef and vegetable stew

Overall timing 2 hours

Freezing Suitable: simmer for 30 minutes only;
add vegetables after reheating in 350°F (180°C)
Gas 4 oven for 45 minutes

To serve 6–8

2 lb	Stewing steak	900 g
	Salt and pepper	
4 tbsp	Plain flour	4×15 ml
1 lb	Onions	450 g
3 tbsp	Oil	3×15 ml
1¼ pints	Beef stock	700 g
2 tbsp	Tomato purée	2×15 ml
	Bay leaf	
1 lb	Carrots	450 g
1 lb	Potatoes	450 g
1 lb	Parsnips	450 g
8 oz	Frozen peas	225 g

Wipe and trim the meat and cut into 1½ inch
(4 cm) cubes. Season the flour and toss the
pieces of meat in it till evenly coated. Peel and
slice the onions.

Heat the oil in a heavy-based saucepan and
fry the onions till transparent. Add the meat
and fry till browned all over, then add any remaining flour. Gradually add the stock (made
with cubes if necessary) and bring to the boil,
stirring constantly. Add the tomato purée, bay
leaf and seasoning, cover and simmer for 1
hour.

Scrape the carrots and peel the potatoes and
parsnips. Cut all into chunks and add to the
meat. Cover and simmer for a further 30
minutes. Taste and adjust seasoning.

Stir in the peas and simmer for 10 minutes,
then serve.

Beef carbonnade

Overall timing 2–2½ hours

Freezing Suitable

To serve 4

2¼ lb	Braising beef	1 kg
3 oz	Butter	75 g
8 oz	Onions	225 g
1 tbsp	Plain flour	15 ml
1 tbsp	Brown sugar	15 ml
1 tbsp	Wine vinegar	15 ml
18 fl oz	Stout	500 ml
	Salt and pepper	
1	Bouquet garni	1

Trim off any fat, then cut meat into large thin slices. Melt 2 oz (50 g) of the butter in a flameproof casserole. Add the meat and brown over a high heat. Remove beef from pan and put aside.

Peel and finely chop onions. Add onions to pan with remaining butter. Reduce heat, cover and cook for 10 minutes without burning.

Sprinkle flour into pan with the brown sugar and stir with a wooden spoon. Add vinegar, then the stout and stir until thick.

Replace beef in pan, season with salt and pepper and add bouquet garni. Cover and simmer for about 1½–2 hours over a low heat or cook in the oven at 350°F (180°C) Gas 4. Discard bouquet garni before serving, with mashed potatoes and endive salad.

Pot au feu

Overall timing 4 hours

Freezing Not suitable

To serve 6

1	Onion	1
2	Cloves	2
2	Stalks of celery	2
1 tbsp	Chopped parsley	15 ml
4 pints	Water	2.2 litres
	Salt and pepper	
1	Cow heel	1
½	Boiling chicken	½
2	Leeks	2
1	Carrot	1
2	Potatoes	2

Peel onion and spike with cloves. Chop celery. Put into a flameproof casserole with the parsley, water and seasoning. Bring to the boil, then add cow heel and chicken. Reduce heat and simmer for 3 hours, skimming occasionally.

Remove cow heel and chicken from pan. Cut meat off bones in small chunks. Trim and thinly slice leeks. Peel and slice carrot. Peel and chop potatoes.

Strain stock and return to pan. Add meat and vegetables. Bring back to the boil, then reduce heat and simmer for 30 minutes. Serve hot with toasted bread.

Boeuf en croûte

Overall timing 1½ hours plus cooling and chilling

Freezing Not suitable

To serve 6

1 lb	Frozen puff pastry	454 g
3 lb	Fillet of beef	1.4 kg
1	Garlic clove	1
1 oz	Softened butter	25 g
	Salt and pepper	
1 teasp	Dried thyme	5 ml
4 oz	Smooth liver pâté	125 g
1	Egg	1

Thaw pastry. Preheat the oven to 425°F (220°C) Gas 7.

Trim meat of all fat, then tie into a neat shape with fine string. Make tiny slits in meat with tip of a sharp knife and insert slivers of peeled garlic. Spread butter over beef, season and sprinkle with half the thyme. Place in roasting tin and roast for 10 minutes. Take meat out of tin, place on a wire rack and leave to cool completely.

Remove string from meat. Roll out dough to a large rectangle just over twice the size of the meat. Place meat on one half of dough rectangle and brush dough edges with water. Spread pâté over top of meat and sprinkle with remaining thyme. Fold dough over to enclose meat and seal edges. Trim round three sides and, if liked, make a hole in the top. Make a funnel from foil and place in hole if liked. Place on dampened baking tray.

Cut decorative shapes out of dough trimmings, dip them into beaten egg and arrange on dough. Glaze all over with egg and chill for 1 hour.

Preheat oven to 425°F (220°C) Gas 7. Bake for 35 minutes till pastry is well risen and golden. Place on a warmed serving dish, garnish with watercress and serve, cut into thick slices.

Bohemian goulash

Overall timing 2¼ hours

Freezing Suitable: add cream after reheating

To serve 4

8 oz	Boned shoulder of lamb	225 g
8 oz	Belly pork	225 g
8 oz	Chuck steak	225 g
2 oz	Butter	50 g
2	Onions	2
3	Garlic cloves	3
2 teasp	Paprika	2x5 ml
	Bouquet garni	
1 tbsp	Tomato purée	15 ml
	Salt and pepper	
¼ pint	Carton of soured cream	150 ml

Cut meats into chunks. Melt the butter in a flameproof casserole and brown the meats on all sides.

Peel and slice the onions. Peel and crush the garlic. Add both to the casserole and cook gently till golden brown. Stir in the paprika and cook for 2 minutes.

Add bouquet garni, tomato purée and seasoning. Cover with water and bring to the boil. Cover and simmer for 1½–2 hours.

Discard bouquet garni; adjust seasoning. Stir in soured cream and serve with boiled new potatoes and a crisp green salad.

Chilli con carne

Overall timing 3¼ hours plus overnight soaking

Freezing Suitable

To serve 4–6

8 oz	Dried brown or red beans	225 g
1¾ pints	Water	1 litre
2 lb	Braising steak	900 g
1	Onion	1
1 tbsp	Pork dripping or olive oil	15 ml
1 oz	Butter	25 g
	Salt and pepper	
1 teasp	Chilli powder	5 ml
1 tbsp	Sweet paprika	15 ml
8 oz	Canned tomatoes	225 g
2 teasp	Cornflour (optional)	2x5 ml

Soak beans in water overnight. The next day, place water and beans in saucepan, cover and cook gently for 1½ hours.

Cut the beef into 1 inch (2.5 cm) cubes. Peel and chop onion. Heat the dripping or oil and butter in frying pan. Add the beef. Cook till brown, then add the onion and cook till transparent.

Mix the meat and onion in with the cooked beans and season with salt, pepper, chilli powder and paprika. Cover and cook gently for 1 hour.

Add the drained tomatoes, cover and cook for 30 minutes more. Adjust seasoning. If you wish to thicken the sauce, blend the cornflour with a little water and add it to the mixture. Cook for a few minutes, then serve from the cooking pot with plain boiled rice or chunks of wholemeal bread and a crisp green salad.

Corned beef hash

Overall timing 1 hour

Freezing Not suitable

To serve 4

2	Medium-size onions	2
6 tbsp	Oil *or*	6x15 ml
2 oz	Dripping	50 g
1	Stalk of celery	1
1	Large carrot	1
1 lb	Corned beef	450 g
	Salt and pepper	
½ teasp	Powdered mustard	2.5 ml
1 lb	Potatoes	450 g
1 pint	Beef stock	560 ml

Peel and thinly slice onions. Heat oil or dripping in saucepan. Add the onions and cook gently till transparent.

Finely chop celery. Peel and grate or dice carrot. Cut corned beef into 1 inch (2.5 cm) cubes. Add all of these to onions and cook for a few minutes, then season with salt, pepper and mustard (add more if a stronger taste is preferred). Cook gently for 5 minutes.

Meanwhile, peel potatoes and cut into chunks. Add to pan with boiling stock and cook for 20 minutes. Serve in warm bowls topped with fried or poached eggs, and with lots of fresh bread to mop up the juices.

Corned beef patties

Overall timing 30 minutes

Freezing Suitable: cook from frozen

To serve 4

12 tbsp	Fresh breadcrumbs	12x15 ml
3 tbsp	Warm milk	3x15 ml
1 lb	Corned beef	450 g
2	Eggs	2
2 tbsp	Grated Parmesan cheese	2x15 ml
	Grated rind of ½ lemon	
	Plain flour	
2 oz	Butter	50 g
1 tbsp	Oil	15 ml
	Lemon wedges	
	Sprigs of parsley	

Soak 4 tbsp (4x15 ml) breadcrumbs in the milk. Cut off any excess fat from the edge of the corned beef and discard. Mash beef in a bowl with a fork, then add squeezed-out breadcrumbs, 1 egg, the cheese and lemon rind. Mix well.

With well floured hands, make patties from the mixture, then coat with flour. Lightly beat remaining egg. Using two forks, dip the patties first into beaten egg, then into remaining breadcrumbs.

Heat butter and oil in a large frying pan. Add the patties and cook over a moderate heat till brown on both sides. Remove from pan and drain on kitchen paper. Garnish with lemon wedges and parsley.

Danish meatballs

Overall timing 40 minutes

Freezing Suitable: fry meatballs after thawing, or fry from frozen, allowing 25 minutes

To serve 4

4 oz	Fresh breadcrumbs	125 g
¼ pint	Milk	150 ml
1	Small onion	1
8 oz	Minced beef	225 g
8 oz	Minced pork	225 g
	Salt and pepper	
½ teasp	Ground allspice	2.5 ml
1	Egg	1
2 tbsp	Plain flour	2x15 ml
2 oz	Butter	50 g
3 tbsp	Oil	3x15 ml
8	Lettuce leaves	8
2	Pickled beetroot	2
4 tbsp	Pickled red cabbage	4x15 ml

Put fresh breadcrumbs into a bowl with the milk and soak for 10 minutes.

Peel onion and grate into a large bowl. Add the beef and pork, squeezed out breadcrumbs, salt, pepper and allspice. Mix well and bind together with the beaten egg. Shape mixture into eight balls and coat lightly with flour.

Heat butter and oil in a frying pan. Add meatballs and fry gently for 15 minutes till brown all over and cooked through.

Meanwhile, wash and dry lettuce leaves and arrange in a shallow basket or serving dish. Drain and dice pickled beetroot.

Remove meatballs from pan with a draining spoon and drain on kitchen paper. Put one meatball on each lettuce leaf and spoon a little drained pickled cabbage and beetroot around. Serve with a lettuce, tomato and olive salad.

Flemish hotpot

Overall timing 3¾ hours

Freezing Not suitable

To serve 6

2	Pig's trotters	2
1 lb	Piece of belly of pork	450 g
1 lb	Beef flank	450 g
5 pints	Water	2.8 litres
1 tbsp	Salt	15 ml
2	Bay leaves	2
12	Peppercorns	12
3	Onions	3
4	Cloves	4
1½ lb	Potatoes	700 g
1 lb	Carrots	450 g
1 lb	Cabbage *or*	450 g
12 oz	Spinach	350 g

Split trotters lengthways, then halve each half. Cut belly of pork into 3x2 inch (7.5x5 cm) strips. Roll up beef and tie with string. Put water into a large pan and add meats with salt, bay leaves and peppercorns. Peel onions and spike one with cloves. Add it to pan and bring to the boil. Skim and simmer for 2 hours.

Remove meats from pan. Strain stock and return to pan with meats.

Peel and chop potatoes. Scrape and thickly slice carrots. Chop cabbage or spinach. Quarter remaining onions. Bring stock to the boil and add vegetables. Simmer for 20–25 minutes till vegetables are tender.

Lift meats out of stock. Remove string from beef and carve into thick slices. Strain off 1 pint (560 ml) of the stock and reserve.

Taste the soup and adjust the seasoning. Pour into a warmed tureen and serve immediately. Serve the meats after the soup with reserved stock thickened and made into gravy.

Beef with onions

Overall timing 1½ hours

Freezing Suitable

To serve 4

1½ lb	Chuck steak	700 g
12 oz	Onions	350 g
1 oz	Butter	25 g
1 tbsp	Oil	15 ml
1 tbsp	Plain flour	15 ml
½ pint	Beef stock	300 ml
1	Garlic clove	1
½ teasp	Ground cumin	2.5 ml
	Pinch of dried marjoram	
2 tbsp	Wine vinegar	2x15 ml
	Salt and pepper	

Cut meat across the grain into thin finger-length strips. Peel onions, slice crossways and separate rings. Heat the butter and oil in frying pan. Add the onion rings and cook, covered, over a low heat till transparent. Turn them over frequently so that they cook evenly but do not brown. Remove from pan.

Increase heat, put strips of meat into pan and brown them. Return onion rings. Sprinkle with flour and stir. When flour begins to colour, stir in stock, peeled and crushed garlic, cumin, marjoram, wine vinegar and seasoning. Cover and simmer for 1 hour. Serve with potatoes or rice and a crisp mixed salad.

Beef paprika

Overall timing 2¼ hours

Freezing Suitable

To serve 6

2 lb	Stewing beef	900 g
2 oz	Pork dripping	50 g
8 oz	Onions	225 g
2	Garlic cloves	2
1 tbsp	Plain flour	15 ml
1 pint	Beef stock	560 ml
½ teasp	Dried marjoram	2.5 ml
½ teasp	Caraway seed	2.5 ml
	Brown sugar	
2 teasp	Paprika	2x5 ml
	Salt and pepper	

Cube beef. Heat dripping in a large saucepan or flameproof casserole. Add beef and fry till brown on all sides. Peel and chop onions and garlic. Add to pan and cook till transparent.

Sprinkle in flour and stir into mixture. Add stock, marjoram, caraway seed, a pinch of sugar, paprika and seasoning. Cover tightly and cook gently for 1¾–2 hours.

Goulash

Overall timing 2¼ hours

Freezing Suitable

To serve 6

2 lb	Stewing beef	900 g
2 oz	Pork dripping	50 g
8 oz	Onions	225 g
2	Garlic cloves	2
1 tbsp	Plain flour	15 ml
1	Beef stock cube	1
1 pint	Boiling water	560 ml
	Salt and pepper	
½ teasp	Dried marjoram	2.5 ml
½ teasp	Caraway seed	2.5 ml
	Brown sugar	
½ teasp	Paprika	2.5 ml
8 oz	Potatoes	225 g
2	Green peppers	2
5	Tomatoes	5
¼ pint	Red wine	150 ml
¼ pint	Carton of soured cream (optional)	150 ml

Cube beef. Heat dripping in a large saucepan. Add beef and fry till meat is brown on all sides. Peel and chop onions and garlic. Add to meat and cook till transparent.

Sprinkle in flour and stir into mixture. Mix stock cube into boiling water and pour over meat. Season with salt, pepper, marjoram, caraway seed, a pinch of sugar and paprika. Cover tightly and cook gently for 1¼ hours.

Peel and roughly chop the potatoes. Deseed and slice peppers. Blanch, peel and chop tomatoes. Add all to pan, cover and cook for a further 25 minutes.

Add wine and check seasoning. Bring to simmering point and stir in soured cream, if using, or serve it separately.

Spicy meatballs

Overall timing 30 minutes

Freezing Not suitable

To serve 4–6

1	Small onion	1
1	Garlic clove	1
1½ lb	Lean minced beef	700 g
1	Egg	1
1 oz	Fresh white breadcrumbs	25 g
	Salt and pepper	
½ teasp	Ground allspice	2.5 ml
	Oil for frying	

Peel and finely chop the onion; peel and crush the garlic. Put with rest of ingredients (except for the oil) into a bowl and mix well together. Shape mixture into walnut-sized balls.

Fry the meatballs in shallow oil for about 15 minutes, turning once. Arrange on a warmed serving plate and serve with rice or pasta, and a tomato sauce or gravy.

Beef and carrot fry-up

Overall timing 45 minutes

Freezing Suitable

To serve 4

1 lb	Carrots	450 g
2	Leeks	2
2 oz	Butter	50 g
9 fl oz	White wine or beef stock	250 ml
	Salt and pepper	
1 lb	Minced beef	450 g
½ teasp	Worcestershire sauce	2.5 ml

Scrape carrots and chop into 1 inch (2.5 cm) pieces. Trim, wash and chop leeks into ½ inch (1.25 cm) slices. Melt half the butter in a frying pan or saucepan and fry chopped carrots for 3 minutes. Pour in white wine or stock, cover and cook over a low heat for 20 minutes.

Add the leeks, season with salt and pepper and cook for a further 15 minutes, or until tender.

Meanwhile, put mince in bowl and mix in salt and pepper with a fork. Roughly shape mince into 1 inch (2.5 cm) pieces. Melt remaining butter in another frying pan and fry meat for about 15 minutes until lightly browned and no longer pink in the middle. Stir from time to time.

Reduce any excess liquid in vegetable pan by boiling rapidly for a minute or two. Add meat and sprinkle with Worcestershire sauce. Serve from the pan, with creamy mashed potatoes and a green vegetable.

Mustardy beef rissoles

Overall timing 25 minutes

Freezing Suitable: fry from frozen for 15 minutes

To serve 4

2	Large onions	2
1	Carrot	1
1 lb	Minced beef	450 g
1 tbsp	Chopped parsley	15 ml
1	Egg	1
2 teasp	Mustard seeds	2x5 ml
	Salt and pepper	
3 tbsp	Plain flour	3x15 ml
4 tbsp	Oil	4x15 ml
	Sprigs of parsley	

Peel and finely chop the onions. Peel and finely grate the carrot. Put into a bowl with the minced beef, parsley and egg.

Roughly grind the mustard seed in a mortar or pepper mill and add to the beef with plenty of salt and pepper. Mix with a fork till the ingredients are well blended. Shape into 12 balls and coat with seasoned flour.

Heat the oil in a frying pan and fry the meatballs for about 10 minutes till crisp and golden on all sides. Drain on kitchen paper and arrange on a warmed serving plate. Garnish with sprigs of parsley.

Hamburgers

Overall timing 10 minutes

Freezing Suitable: cook after thawing

To serve 4

1 lb	Finely minced beef	450 g
2	Onions	2
	Salt and pepper	
3 tbsp	Oil	3 x 15 ml
4	Rolls or buns	4
2 oz	Butter	50 g
1 tbsp	French mustard	15 ml

Put the mince into a large bowl. Peel and finely chop one of the onions and add to the beef with plenty of seasoning. Mix. Divide into four portions and shape each into a thick burger.

Preheat a frying pan or griddle and brush lightly with 1 tbsp (15 ml) oil. Fry the burgers for about 5 minutes, then turn carefully and cook for a further 3–5 minutes.

While the hamburgers are cooking, peel and slice the second onion into rings. Heat the remaining oil in another frying pan and cook the onion till golden.

Meanwhile, halve and lightly toast the rolls, then spread cut sides with the butter mixed with the French mustard.

Place a hamburger in each roll and top with fried onions. Serve immediately.

Hamburgers with eggs

Overall timing 10 minutes

Freezing Not suitable

To serve 2

2	Onions	2
8 oz	Finely minced beef	225 g
	Salt and pepper	
2 teasp	Oil	2x5 ml
2	Tomatoes	2
2 oz	Butter	50 g
2	Eggs	2
	Cayenne	
	Watercress	

Peel the onions. Finely chop half of one and cut the other half and the second onion into rings. Mix the chopped onion with the beef and season. Divide in half and shape into burgers.

Heat the oil in a frying pan and fry the burgers for about 5 minutes on each side. Add the tomatoes halfway through the cooking.

Meanwhile, melt 1 oz (25 g) butter in another frying pan and fry the onion rings till crisp. Remove from the pan and keep hot.

Add the eggs to the pan with the remaining butter and fry till set.

Top each burger with an egg and arrange on warmed plates with the onions and tomatoes. Sprinkle a little cayenne over the eggs. Keep hot.

Put the watercress into the pan with the butter and fry quickly. Use to garnish the burgers.

Neapolitan beef

Overall timing 2½ hours

Freezing Not suitable

To serve 4

2 oz	Back bacon	50 g
2 oz	Belly pork fat	50 g
1 tbsp	Chopped parsley	15 ml
1 tbsp	Seedless raisins	15 ml
	Salt and pepper	
1 lb	Top rump of beef	450 g
1	Onion	1
1	Garlic clove	1
2 tbsp	Oil	2x15 ml
14 oz	Can of tomatoes	397 g
½ pint	Beef stock	300 ml
12 oz	Rigatoni	350 g
2 tbsp	Grated Parmesan cheese	2x15 ml

Chop or finely mince bacon and pork fat and mix with parsley to form a smooth paste. Work in raisins and seasoning. With a larding needle, make several deep holes in meat and firmly stuff paste into them. Tie meat into a neat roll with string.

Peel and finely chop onion. Peel and crush garlic. Heat oil in flameproof casserole, add onion and garlic and fry till transparent. Add the meat roll and fry, turning frequently, to seal. Press tomatoes and their juice through a sieve and add to casserole with the stock and seasoning. Mix well, cover and simmer for 1½ hours or till tender.

Meanwhile, cook rigatoni in boiling salted water till tender. Drain and keep hot.

Lift meat out of casserole, remove string and slice. Arrange on a warmed serving dish and arrange rigatoni round meat. Taste sauce and adjust seasoning. Spoon sauce over meat and rigatoni. Sprinkle with Parmesan. Serve immediately.

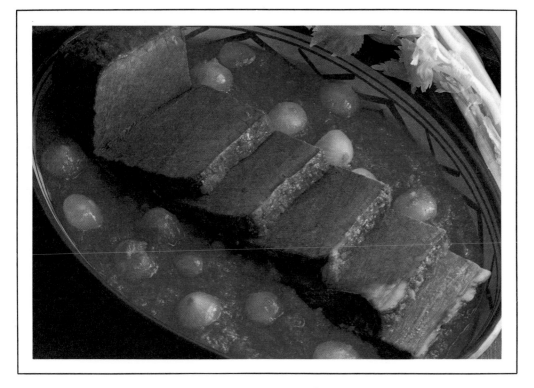

Pot roast beef with milk

Overall timing 3 hours plus overnight marination

Freezing Not suitable

To serve 6–8

3 lb	Silverside of beef	1.4 kg
1	Large onion	1
1	Large carrot	1
4	Stalks of celery	4
4	Fresh basil leaves	4
	Salt and pepper	
¾ pint	Milk	400 ml
2 tbsp	Brandy (optional)	2x15 ml
14 oz	Can of tomatoes	397 g
2 tbsp	Tomato purée	2x15 ml
8 oz	Pickling onions	225 g
1 oz	Butter	25 g

Tie the meat into a neat shape. Put into a flame-proof casserole. Peel and chop the onion and carrot. Wash, trim and chop the celery. Add to the meat with the basil leaves, salt, pepper, milk and brandy (if used), cover and marinate in a cool place overnight.

The next day, preheat the oven to 325°F (170°C) Gas 3. Stir the tomatoes with juice and tomato purée into the casserole. Cover and cook in oven for 2 hours.

Meanwhile, peel the small onions and blanch in boiling water for 5 minutes. Melt butter in a frying pan and fry onions till golden. Add to casserole and cook for further 30 minutes.

Remove the meat from the casserole and discard the string. Place the meat on a warmed serving dish and keep hot.

Purée the cooking liquor in a blender or rub through a sieve, setting aside the button onions. Put purée and onions into saucepan and reheat. Meanwhile, cut the meat into slices. Taste and adjust the seasoning of the sauce and pour around the meat.

Hungarian beef

Overall timing 2½ hours

Freezing Suitable: reheat in 325°F (170°C) Gas 3 oven for 20 minutes, then add vegetables

To serve 4

1½ lb	Braising steak	700 g
2 oz	Lard	50 g
2	Onions	2
1 tbsp	Paprika	15 ml
½ teasp	Caraway seeds	2.5 ml
¾ pint	Beef stock	400 ml
	Salt and pepper	
2	Green peppers	2
8 oz	Tomatoes	225 g
1 lb	Potatoes	450 g

Preheat the oven to 325°F (170°C) Gas 3.

Cut steak into four equal-size pieces. Melt half the lard in a flameproof casserole, add the steaks and brown quickly on both sides. Remove from casserole and reserve.

Peel and chop the onions. Add remaining lard to casserole and fry onions gently for about 10 minutes till golden, stirring frequently. Remove casserole from the heat and stir in the paprika, mixing well. Add the caraway seeds, one-third of the stock, the steak and seasoning. Cover and cook in the oven for 1½ hours.

Meanwhile, deseed and slice peppers. Blanch, peel and chop tomatoes. Peel and thinly slice potatoes. Remove casserole from oven and stir in remaining stock, peppers, tomatoes and potatoes. Cover and cook for a further 30 minutes till potatoes are tender. Taste and adjust seasoning.

Lift out meat and place in individual deep serving plates. Spoon vegetables and sauce over.

Steak and eggs

Overall timing 10 minutes

Freezing Not suitable

To serve 4

3 oz	Butter	75 g
4	Thick steaks	4
4	Eggs	4
	Salt and pepper	
	Sprigs of parsley	

Melt 2 oz (50 g) of the butter in a frying pan. Add the steaks and fry for about 3 minutes on each side or until browned and cooked to your taste.

Meanwhile, melt the remaining butter in another frying pan and fry the eggs until just set. Use buttered poaching rings to make the eggs the same shape as the steaks, if possible.

Place the steaks on a warmed serving plate and top with the eggs. Pour the steak cooking juices over and season. Garnish with parsley.

Yugoslav kebabs

Overall timing 25 minutes plus marination

Freezing Suitable: reheat in 400°F (200°C) Gas 6 oven for 25 minutes

To serve 6

1	Onion	1
1½ lb	Finely minced beef	700 g
4 tbsp	Red wine	4 x 15 ml
	Salt and pepper	
1	Egg	1
2 tbsp	Oil	2 x 15 ml
Garnish		
	Lemons	
	Tomato slices	
	Onion rings	

Peel and finely chop the onion and add to the mince with the red wine and plenty of seasoning. Mix well and leave to marinate for 1 hour.

Preheat the grill. Add the egg to the mince and mix together. Divide the mixture into 18 portions and shape each into a croquette. Thread three on to each of six skewers.

Grill the kebabs for 10–15 minutes, turning and basting with oil.

Arrange the kebabs on a warmed serving dish and serve with lemons cut into halves or wedges, tomato slices, onion rings and jacket baked potatoes.

Steamed steak and kidney pudding

Overall timing 5¾ hours

Freezing Suitable: steam from frozen for 2½–3 hours

To serve 6

1½ lb	Chuck or blade steak	700 g
8 oz	Ox kidney	225 g
1	Large onion	1
	Salt and pepper	
3 tbsp	Plain flour	3x15 ml
12 oz	Self-raising flour	350 g
6 oz	Shredded suet	175 g
½ pint	Cold beef stock	300 ml

Cut the meat into 1½ inch (4 cm) cubes. Trim the kidney, removing any core, and cut into 1 inch (2.5 cm) cubes. Peel and thinly slice the onion. Season plain flour and use to coat the steak, kidney and onion.

Sift the self-raising flour and 1½ teasp (7.5 ml) salt into a bowl and stir in the suet and enough cold water to mix to a soft but not sticky dough. Knead lightly till smooth.

Roll out on a floured surface to a round, big enough to line a 3 pint (1.7 litre) pudding basin (about 14 inches/35 cm in diameter). Cut out one-quarter of the dough round and reserve. Lift the large piece and place it in the basin, curving it so it fits neatly, and sealing the edges together. Place the meat mixture in the basin and add the cold stock to come half-way up the meat.

Roll out the reserved dough to a round slightly larger than the top of the basin. Brush the top edge of the dough lining with water and cover with the dough lid. Seal the edges well.

Cover with greased, pleated greaseproof paper and pleated foil, or a pudding cloth and secure with string. Steam for 5 hours, topping up with boiling water as required.

Texan stew

Overall timing 2¼ hours

Freezing Suitable

To serve 4

1½ lb	Braising beef	700 g
1 oz	Butter	25 g
1 tbsp	Oil	15 ml
1 pint	Stock	560 ml
2	Green peppers	2
4	Tomatoes	4
11½ oz	Can of sweetcorn kernels	326 g
10 oz	Can of peas and carrots	280 g
	Salt and pepper	
2 teasp	Cornflour	2x5 ml

Chop meat into 1 inch (2.5cm) cubes. Heat butter and oil in saucepan, add meat and cook for 10 minutes till brown all over. Pour in stock (made with 2 stock cubes if necessary) and cook, covered, for 1½ hours over a gentle heat.

Wash, deseed and cut green peppers into strips. Blanch, peel and chop tomatoes. Drain corn and peas and carrots. Add vegetables to meat and season well with salt and pepper. Cook, covered, for 15 minutes over a moderate heat.

Blend cornflour with a little water in a cup. Stir into saucepan, then bring to boil again, stirring until thickened. Serve stew in warmed bowls.

Beef and horseradish loaf

Overall timing 1 hour

Freezing Suitable: reheat in 375°F (190°C)
Gas 5 oven for 30 minutes

To serve 4

¼ pint	Strong beef stock	150 ml
4 oz	Fresh breadcrumbs	125 g
1 lb	Minced beef	450 g
1	Large onion	1
1 tbsp	Grated horseradish	15 ml
3	Eggs	3
2 tbsp	Sweet sherry	2x15 ml
	Salt and pepper	

Preheat the oven to 350°F (180°C) Gas 4.

Put the stock (made with a double quantity of cubes if necessary) in a saucepan and bring to the boil. Sprinkle in the breadcrumbs and stir till the crumbs have absorbed all the stock.

Put minced beef into a bowl with the breadcrumb mixture. Peel and finely chop onion and add to meat with the grated horseradish, eggs, sherry and seasoning. Mix well with a wooden spoon until all ingredients are well blended.

Grease ovenproof dish and press in the mixture. Smooth the top and bake in the centre of the oven for 45 minutes. Serve hot with boiled potatoes and buttered carrots.

Tripe and onions French style

Overall timing 1 hour 50 minutes

Freezing Not suitable

To serve 4

1	Large carrot	1
1½ lb	Onions	700 g
2	Stalks of celery	2
3 pints	Cold water	1.7 litres
	Bay leaf	
6	Peppercorns	6
1 tbsp	Lemon juice	15 ml
1½ lb	Dressed tripe	700 g
3 oz	Butter	75 g
	Salt and pepper	
2 tbsp	Chopped parsley	2x15 ml
2 tbsp	White wine vinegar	2x15 ml

Peel and chop carrot and one of the onions. Trim and chop celery. Put into a saucepan with water, bay leaf, peppercorns and lemon juice. Bring to the boil and simmer for 30 minutes. Strain and return to pan.

Cut tripe into pieces. Place in pan with stock and bring to the boil. Skim off any scum, cover and simmer for 1½ hours till tender.

Peel and slice remaining onions. Melt butter in a frying pan, add the onions and fry gently till golden.

Drain the tripe thoroughly, discarding the stock, and cut into thin strips. Add to the onions with plenty of seasoning and fry over a moderate heat for 10 minutes, stirring frequently. Add the parsley and vinegar and mix lightly. Season to taste and pour into a warmed serving dish. Serve immediately with crusty bread.

Italian-style tripe

Overall timing 2½ hours plus soaking

Freezing Not suitable

To serve 6

4 oz	Dried broad beans	125 g
1½ lb	Blanket tripe	700 g
8 oz	Honeycomb tripe	225 g
2 oz	Streaky bacon	50 g
1	Sprig of sage	1
1 lb	Ripe tomatoes	450 g
1	Onion	1
1	Carrot	1
1	Stalk of celery	1
2 oz	Butter	50 g
	Salt and pepper	
¾ pint	Stock	400 ml
4 tbsp	Grated Parmesan cheese	4x15 ml

Soak beans in cold water overnight.

The next day, wash and drain both types of tripe. Shred the blanket tripe and cut the honeycomb tripe into squares. Derind and finely chop the bacon. Wash the sage. Blanch, peel and deseed the tomatoes and cut into small pieces. Peel and finely chop the onion and carrot. Wash and slice the celery.

Melt the butter in a saucepan and fry the bacon and onion till just golden. Add the celery, carrot and sage and fry for 5 minutes longer.

Add the two types of tripe and the tomatoes. Season. Add the stock (made with cubes if necessary) and bring to the boil. Cover the saucepan and simmer over a low heat for about 1 hour, stirring frequently to prevent the sauce from sticking to the saucepan.

Drain beans, rinse and add to the pan. Cover and simmer for 1 hour more.

Taste and adjust seasoning and sprinkle with the grated Parmesan.

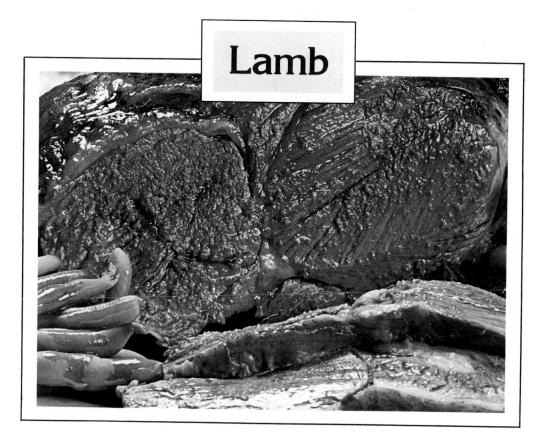

Lamb

Roast lamb with garlic

Overall timing 2 hours

Freezing Not suitable

To serve 6

2–3	Garlic cloves	2–3
3½ lb	Leg of lamb	1.6 kg
1 oz	Butter or dripping	25 g
	Salt and pepper	

Preheat the oven to 350°F (180°C) Gas 4.

Peel the garlic cloves and cut each into thin slivers. Place lamb in roasting tin with the thickest fat uppermost. Using a sharp, thin bladed knife, make incisions about 1 inch (2.5 cm) deep in the meat. Insert a sliver of garlic into each incision, pressing it down so it is level with the surface of the meat.

Spread the softened butter or dripping over the lamb and season well. Roast for 1¾ hours or until the juices run clear when a skewer is inserted into the thickest part of the meat.

Transfer meat to warmed serving plate and make the gravy in the usual way. Serve with green beans and tomatoes.

New Zealand roast lamb

Overall timing 3–3½ hours

Freezing Not suitable

To serve 4–6

4 lb	Leg of lamb	1.8 kg
2 tbsp	Oil	2x15 ml
	Fresh rosemary *or*	
2 teasp	Dried rosemary	2x5 ml
	Salt and pepper	
¼ pint	Water	150 ml
2 lb	Potatoes	900 g

Preheat oven to 350°F (180°C) Gas 4.

Place lamb in roasting tin, then rub the oil into the skin. Either make small slits in the meat and insert fresh rosemary leaves, or sprinkle surface with dried rosemary, then season well. Add water to the tin and cook for 3–3½ hours – the meat should almost be falling off the bone.

Meanwhile, peel, parboil and dry the potatoes. Add them to the roasting tin 1½ hours before end of cooking time and turn them till coated in fat. Turn again once during roasting.

Beanpot with lamb

Overall timing 2 hours 50 minutes plus
overnight soaking

Freezing Not suitable

To serve 4

8 oz	Dried haricot beans	225 g
½ teasp	Salt	2.5 ml
1 oz	Dripping	25 g
1 lb	Chump lamb chops	450 g
1	Onion	1
4 tbsp	Tomato purée	4x15 ml
½ teasp	Ground cumin	2.5 ml
1	Bay leaf	1
½ teasp	Dried rosemary	2.5 ml
½ teasp	Garlic salt	2.5 ml
	Brown sugar	
½ teasp	Vinegar	2.5 ml
1 tbsp	Chopped chives	15 ml

Soak beans in 2½ pints (1.5 litres) water
overnight. Next day, transfer beans and
water to a saucepan, add salt and cook for 1
hour.

Melt dripping in a flameproof casserole
and brown chops well on all sides. Peel and
chop onion and add to casserole. Cook till
transparent. Add beans and water, tomato
purée, cumin, bay leaf, rosemary and garlic
salt. Cover and cook for 1 hour.

Uncover and cook for a further 20 minutes
till meat is tender.

Just before serving, stir in a pinch of sugar
and the vinegar and sprinkle with chopped
chives.

Minted lamb meatballs

Overall timing 30 minutes

Freezing Suitable: fry after thawing

To serve 4

1¼ lb	Minced lamb	600 g
4	Garlic cloves	4
2 tbsp	Chopped fresh mint	2x15 ml
1	Egg	1
	Salt and pepper	
1 teasp	Ground coriander	5 ml
	Plain flour	
2 tbsp	Oil	2x15 ml
	Mint or coriander leaves	

Place the lamb in a bowl with the peeled and finely chopped garlic, chopped mint, egg, salt, pepper and coriander and mix with a wooden spoon till well combined. Make little balls of the mixture, flouring your hands so it doesn't stick, and roll the balls in the flour to coat.

Heat oil in a frying pan, add meat balls and cook over a moderate heat for 8–10 minutes on each side till well browned. Drain on kitchen paper, then garnish with mint or coriander leaves and serve with rice.

Lamb curry

Overall timing 1½ hours

Freezing Suitable

To serve 2

1 lb	Boned lamb	450 g
1	Onion	1
1 oz	Butter	25 g
1 tbsp	Oil	15 ml
1 teasp	Curry powder	5 ml
	Salt and pepper	
1½ tbsp	Plain flour	22.5 ml
8 fl oz	Stock	220 ml
½ teasp	Tomato purée	2.5 ml
	Bouquet garni	
1	Tomato	1
½	Green pepper	½
2 oz	Button mushrooms	50 g
6 oz	New potatoes	175 g

Cut meat into cubes. Peel and chop onion. Heat butter and oil in a frying pan and fry onion till transparent.

Add curry powder and cook, stirring, for 2 minutes. Add meat and cook till golden on all sides. Season with salt and pepper, sprinkle with flour and stir over a high heat for a few minutes.

Reduce heat and stir in stock and tomato purée. Add bouquet garni and bring to the boil, stirring. Cover and cook gently for 40 minutes, stirring occasionally.

Chop tomato; deseed and slice pepper; halve or slice larger mushrooms. Scrub potatoes but don't peel; cut into chunks.

Add prepared vegetables to pan and cook for a further 20 minutes. Discard bouquet garni before serving, with plain boiled rice.

Casseroled lamb

Overall timing 2 hours

Freezing Not suitable

To serve 6

1	Carrot	1
1	Onion	1
1	Stalk of celery	1
4	Spring onions	4
3 oz	Streaky bacon	75 g
1	Garlic clove	1
2 tbsp	Oil	2x15 ml
3 tbsp	Chopped parsley	3x15 ml
2½ lb	Boned shoulder of lamb	1.1 kg
2 oz	Mushrooms	50 g
½ pint	Dry cider	300 ml
¼ pint	Stock	150 ml
	Salt and pepper	
1 lb	Potatoes	450 g

Peel and chop carrot and onion. Trim and chop celery and spring onions. Derind and chop bacon. Peel and crush garlic. Heat oil in flameproof casserole, add bacon, onion, spring onions, celery, carrot, garlic and parsley and fry till lightly browned.

Tie meat into shape, if necessary, add to casserole and brown on all sides over high heat. Chop mushrooms. Add to casserole with cider, stock and seasoning. Cover and cook for 1 hour over low heat.

Meanwhile, peel and quarter potatoes. Add to casserole and cook, covered, for a further 30 minutes. Taste and adjust seasoning then serve with broccoli.

Stuffed shoulder of lamb

Overall timing 2 hours

Freezing Not suitable

To serve 6

2	Onions	2
3 oz	Butter	75 g
12 oz	Sausagemeat	350 g
2 tbsp	Chopped parsley	2x15 ml
	Salt and pepper	
2½ lb	Boned shoulder of lamb	1.1 kg
7 fl oz	Dry white wine	200 ml
7 fl oz	Stock	200 ml
	Bouquet garni	
2½ lb	New potatoes	1.1 kg
2	Tomatoes	2

Peel and chop onions. Melt 1 oz (25 g) of butter in a frying pan, add onions and fry until golden.

Add to the sausagemeat with the parsley and seasoning.

Spread the lamb out, skin side down, on a board and season. Shape stuffing mixture into a large ball and place on lamb. Fold meat around stuffing to make a ball and tie firmly with string.

Melt 1 oz (25 g) of butter in a flameproof casserole and brown meat all over. Add wine, stock (made with cubes if necessary), bouquet garni, salt and pepper. Cover and cook slowly for 1 hour.

Meanwhile, scrape potatoes. Melt remaining butter in a frying pan, add potatoes and fry until golden brown. Arrange around the meat and cook uncovered for 20 minutes.

Blanch and peel tomatoes. Add to casserole and cook for 10 minutes more.

Remove bouquet garni. Place meat on warmed serving dish and remove string. Arrange potatoes and tomatoes around. Keep hot.

Transfer cooking liquor to a saucepan. Thicken with ½ oz (15 g) each of butter and flour mashed together. Serve this gravy separately.

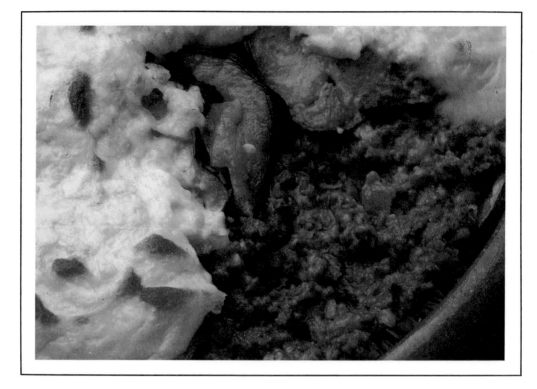

Moussaka

Overall timing 2¼ hours

Freezing Suitable: bake from frozen in 375°F (190°C) Gas 5 oven for 1½ hours; add cheese sauce and bake 30 minutes more

To serve 6

1 lb	Onions	450 g
4	Garlic cloves	4
¼ pint	Oil	150 ml
1 tbsp	Chopped parsley	15 ml
2 lb	Minced lamb	900 g
4	Tomatoes	4
2 tbsp	Tomato purée	2x15 ml
	Salt and pepper	
¼ pint	Stock	150 ml
2 oz	Fresh breadcrumbs	50 g
2 lb	Aubergines	900 g
1 oz	Plain flour	25 g
2	Egg yolks	2
¾ pint	Thick white sauce	400 ml
4 oz	Strong cheese	125 g

Peel and chop onions; peel and crush garlic. Heat 1 tbsp (15 ml) oil in saucepan and fry onions, parsley, garlic and lamb till browned. Peel and quarter tomatoes and add to pan with tomato purée, seasoning and stock. Cover and simmer for 45 minutes. Remove from heat and stir in breadcrumbs.

Preheat oven to 350°F (180°C) Gas 4.

Thinly slice aubergines. Dust lightly with flour. Heat remaining oil in frying pan and brown aubergines. Drain on kitchen paper.

Arrange two-thirds of aubergines to cover bottom and sides of greased casserole. Add meat mixture, then top with remaining aubergines. Stir beaten egg yolks into sauce with half cheese, grated. Pour sauce over aubergines. Cover with rest of grated cheese. Put casserole in a roasting tin containing a little water. Bake for 1 hour.

Lamb kebabs with prunes

Overall timing 50 minutes

Freezing Not suitable

To serve 4

12	Prunes	12
¼ pint	Red wine	150 ml
1 lb	Lean lamb cut from the leg	450 g
3 tbsp	Oil	3x15 ml
	Salt and pepper	
½ teasp	Dried thyme	2.5 ml
2	Firm tomatoes	2
1	Medium onion	1
3	Thick rashers of streaky bacon	3

Put the prunes into a saucepan, add the red wine and bring to the boil. Remove from the heat and leave to soak for 30 minutes.

Cut lamb into 12 large cubes. Place in bowl with oil, seasoning and thyme. Cover and leave for 30 minutes.

Meanwhile, quarter the tomatoes. Peel the onion and cut through the root into eight wedges. Derind bacon and cut each rasher into four. Preheat the grill.

Drain the prunes, reserving the wine. Make a slit in each prune and remove the stone. Thread the lamb, prunes, tomatoes, bacon and onion on to four skewers. Brush the kebabs with the lamb marinade and the wine from the prunes, then sprinkle with salt and pepper. Grill for about 15 minutes, turning occasionally, till the lamb is tender. Arrange on a warmed serving dish and serve with boiled rice.

Lamb steaks with beans

Overall timing 45 minutes

Freezing Not suitable

To serve 4

1½ lb	Green beans	700 g
2 oz	Butter	50 g
	Salt and pepper	
4 fl oz	Meat stock	120 ml
5 tbsp	Oil	5x15 ml
2	Slices of white bread	2
¼ teasp	Garlic salt	1.25 ml
4	Lamb steaks	4
1 teasp	Mustard seed	5 ml
2 tbsp	Chopped parsley	2x15 ml
2	Tomatoes	2
	Sprigs of parsley	

Top and tail beans and remove strings. Break or cut into short lengths. Melt the butter in a saucepan. Add the beans and cook for a few minutes. Season with salt and pour in the stock. Cook for 10–15 minutes till just tender.

Meanwhile, heat half the oil in a frying pan. Halve the slices of bread and lightly brown them on both sides in the oil. Remove from pan and keep warm.

Add rest of oil to pan and heat. Sprinkle garlic salt over the lamb steaks. Cook the steaks for 5 minutes on each side. Sprinkle with salt, then with pepper mixed with ground mustard seed.

Mix chopped parsley into beans and spread over bottom of warmed serving dish. Put the lamb steaks on the bread and place on top of the beans. Garnish with tomatoes, cut into eighths, and a few parsley sprigs.

Mutton casserole

Overall timing 2 hours

Freezing Not suitable

To serve 4

2 lb	Lean mutton or lamb	900 g
1	Onion	1
1 oz	Butter	25 g
2 tbsp	Oil	2x15 ml
5 tbsp	Dry white wine or sherry	5x15 ml
	Salt and pepper	
4 oz	Streaky bacon	125 g
1	Garlic clove	1
3 tbsp	Chopped parsley	3x15 ml
$\frac{1}{4}$ pint	Light stock	150 ml

Wipe and trim the meat and cut into neat pieces. Peel and finely chop the onion. Heat the butter and oil in a flameproof casserole, add the onion and fry for 5 minutes, stirring.

Add the meat and fry till browned on all sides. Add the white wine or sherry, salt and pepper.

Derind and finely chop the bacon. Add to the mutton with the peeled and crushed garlic, 2 tbsp (2x15 ml) of parsley and the stock (made with a cube if necessary). Stir, then cover and simmer for about 1½ hours till the mutton is tender.

Taste and adjust the seasoning. Sprinkle with the remaining parsley and serve immediately with boiled potatoes and buttered carrots.

Braised lamb with green beans

Overall timing 1¾ hours

Freezing Suitable: cook for only 1 hour; reheat from frozen in 400°F (200°C) Gas 6 oven for 1½ hours

To serve 4

1½ lb	Green beans	700 g
2 tbsp	Oil	2x15 ml
2 lb	Scrag end of lamb chops	900 g
2	Large onions	2
14 oz	Can of tomatoes	397 g
	Salt and pepper	
¼ teasp	Ground allspice	1.25 ml
¼ teasp	Grated nutmeg	1.25 ml
2	Red peppers	2

Preheat oven to 350°F (180°C) Gas 4.

Wash, top and tail beans and, if necessary, remove strings. Cut into 2 inch (5 cm) lengths. Spread over the bottom of large ovenproof dish.

Heat oil in a large frying pan. Trim lamb, removing excess fat. Fry in oil until brown on all sides. Drain and arrange on top of beans in casserole.

Peel onions and cut into wedges. Fry in oil until golden. With a spoon, break up the tomatoes in their juice. Add to onions with salt, pepper, allspice and nutmeg, stir well and cook for 5 minutes.

Deseed and slice peppers and add to casserole with tomato mixture. Cover tightly and cook in oven for 1½ hours. Serve with boiled rice.

Navarin

Overall timing 1¾ hours

Freezing Not suitable

To serve 6

2 oz	Butter	50 g
2½ lb	Middle neck of lamb	1.1 kg
4	Small onions	4
1 tbsp	Plain flour	15 ml
¾ pint	Stock	400 ml
3 tbsp	Tomato purée	3 x 15 ml
	Bouquet garni	
	Salt and pepper	
1 lb	Carrots	450 g
1 lb	Turnips	450 g
1 lb	Potatoes	450 g
8 oz	Frozen peas	225 g
1 tbsp	Chopped parsley	15 ml

Melt butter in flameproof casserole, add lamb and brown on all sides. Peel and quarter the onions. Add to casserole and fry gently for 5 minutes.

Sprinkle flour over and cook, stirring, for 2 minutes. Gradually stir in the stock, then add tomato purée, bouquet garni and seasoning and bring to the boil. Cover and simmer gently for 45 minutes.

Scrape and chop carrots. Peel turnips and cut into cubes. Add to casserole and cook for 15 minutes.

Meanwhile, peel potatoes and cut into chunks. Add to casserole and cook, covered, for 20 minutes. Add peas and cook for a further 10 minutes. Remove bouquet garni and adjust seasoning. Garnish with parsley and serve hot.

Summer casserole of lamb

Overall timing 1 hour

Freezing Suitable: add potatoes, beans and peas after reheating

To serve 6

8 oz	Button onions	225 g
1 oz	Butter	25 g
1 tbsp	Oil	15 ml
2½ lb	Middle neck lamb chops	1.1 kg
6	New carrots	6
2	Garlic cloves	2
1 tbsp	Plain flour	15 ml
4	Tomatoes	4
2 tbsp	Tomato purée	2x15 ml
¾ pint	Stock	400 ml
	Bouquet garni	
	Salt and pepper	
1 lb	New potatoes	450 g
2 oz	Green beans	50 g
2 oz	Peas	50 g

Peel button onions. Heat butter and oil in flameproof casserole and fry onions for 5 minutes. Remove from pan and reserve. Add chops and brown on all sides over a high heat.

Scrape carrots and halve if liked. Add to pan with peeled and crushed garlic and cook for 5 minutes. Sprinkle flour over and cook, stirring, for 3 minutes.

Blanch, peel and chop tomatoes. Add to the pan with tomato purée, stock, bouquet garni and seasoning. Cover and simmer for 30 minutes.

Scrape potatoes and add to the casserole. Cook for a further 10 minutes. Top and tail beans and cut into short lengths. Add to pan with peas and reserved onions. Cover and cook for a further 10 minutes. Taste and adjust seasoning if necessary. Discard bouquet garni and serve.

Dolma kara

Overall timing 1¾ hours

Freezing Not suitable

To serve 6

2 tbsp	Oil	2x15 ml
2	Onions	2
1 lb	Boned lamb	450 g
4 oz	Canned chickpeas	125 g
½ pint	Stock	300 ml
	Salt and pepper	
2 tbsp	Tomato purée	2x15 ml
8 oz	Minced cooked lamb	225 g
2 oz	Cooked rice	50 g
1	Egg	1
1 teasp	Lemon juice	5 ml
2 tbsp	Chopped parsley	2x15 ml
	Ground cinnamon	
1 lb	Courgettes	450 g

Heat oil in a saucepan. Peel and chop one of the onions and fry till tender. Cut the lamb into small pieces and add to the pan. Cook for 5–10 minutes.

Add the drained chickpeas, stock, salt, pepper and tomato purée. Cover and simmer for 30 minutes.

Preheat the oven to 375°F (190°C) Gas 5.

Mix the cooked lamb with the cooked rice, remaining onion, peeled and finely chopped, egg, lemon juice, half the parsley, seasoning and a pinch of cinnamon.

Trim courgettes, then cut them in half lengthways. Scoop out the seeds with a teaspoon. Blanch courgettes in boiling salted water for 5 minutes. Drain, then stuff the courgettes with the rice and lamb mixture.

Put the lamb and chickpea stew in an oven-proof dish and place stuffed courgettes on top. Cover with foil and bake for 40 minutes. Serve hot sprinkled with remaining parsley.

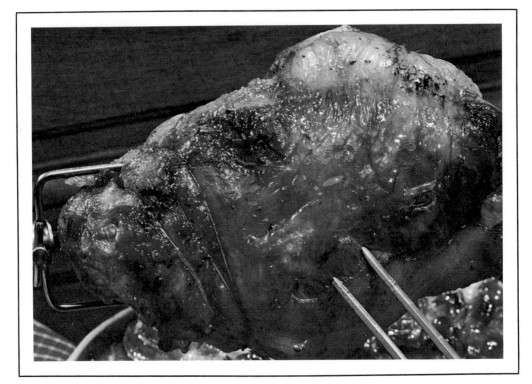

Brittany roast lamb

Overall timing 2½ hours

Freezing Not suitable

To serve 6

3	Garlic cloves	3
4 lb	Leg of lamb	1.8 kg
4 oz	Butter	125 g
	Salt and pepper	
3 lb	Waxy potatoes	1.4 kg
1 teasp	Dried thyme	5 ml

Preheat the oven to 375°F (190°C) Gas 5.

Peel the garlic cloves and slice very thinly. Make incisions through the skin of the lamb and push the garlic into them. Rub half the butter over the lamb and season well.

Grease ovenproof dish with 1 oz (25 g) butter. Peel potatoes and cut into slices about ⅛ inch (3 mm) thick. Arrange half over bottom of dish. Sprinkle with half the thyme and seasoning and dot with half the remaining butter. Repeat layer.

Place dish centrally on shelf below centre of the oven. Place the lamb directly on to the oven shelf above the potatoes so the juices will run on to the potatoes. Roast for 1¾–2 hours till the juices are only slightly pink when thickest part of meat is pierced with a fine skewer.

Place the lamb on a warmed serving dish and carve. Serve the potatoes from the oven-proof dish with a separate dish of cauliflower and whole green beans.

Lamb with broad beans and potatoes

Overall timing 1½ hours

Freezing Not suitable

To serve 6

4	Tomatoes	4
4 oz	Streaky bacon rashers	125 g
2	Onions	2
2	Garlic cloves	2
2 tbsp	Oil	2x15 ml
6	Lamb blade chops	6
½ pint	Stock	300 ml
1 tbsp	Lemon juice	15 ml
½ teasp	Dried thyme	2.5 ml
	Salt and pepper	
1½ lb	Shelled broad beans	700 g
1½ lb	Potatoes	700 g

Blanch, peel and chop tomatoes. Derind and chop bacon. Peel and slice onions. Peel and crush garlic. Heat oil in a flameproof casserole and fry onion and garlic till transparent. Add the chops and bacon and brown on all sides.

Add tomatoes, stock, lemon juice, thyme and seasoning. Cover and simmer for 30 minutes.

Blanch beans in boiling water for 5 minutes, then drain. Peel and slice the potatoes. Add potatoes to casserole and cook for 10 minutes. Add beans and cook for a further 15 minutes. Serve immediately.

Italian-style roast lamb

Overall timing 1½ hours

Freezing Not suitable

To serve 4

2 lb	Chump end of loin of lamb	900 g
	Sprigs of rosemary	
2 lb	Potatoes	900 g
2 tbsp	Oil	2x15 ml
3 oz	Butter	75 g
1	Garlic clove	1
	Salt and pepper	

Preheat the oven to 350°F (180°C) Gas 4.

Slash through the chops, leaving the loin joined at the bottom. Place sprigs of rosemary in the slashes. Peel potatoes and cut into chunks.

Heat oil and butter in roasting tin. Add the meat and arrange potatoes around it. Peel and crush garlic and add to the lamb and potatoes with salt and pepper. Roast for 45 minutes–1 hour, basting occasionally and turning potatoes halfway through cooking. Serve with a mixed salad or a seasonal green vegetable and gravy.

Sweet sour lamb riblets

Overall timing $1\frac{1}{4}$ hours plus overnight marination

Freezing Not suitable

To serve 4

1	Onion	1
2	Garlic cloves	2
2 tbsp	Honey	2x15 ml
1 tbsp	Oil	15 ml
4 tbsp	Soy sauce	4x15 ml
$\frac{1}{4}$ pint	Dry sherry	150 ml
1 teasp	Ground ginger	5 ml
2 oz	Caster sugar	50 g
1 teasp	Ground allspice	5 ml
$2\frac{1}{2}$ lb	Breast of lamb riblets	1.1 kg

Peel and slice onion. Peel and crush garlic. Put into a bowl with the honey, oil, soy sauce, sherry, ginger, sugar and allspice. Add the breast riblets, cover and marinate overnight in the refrigerator, turning occasionally.

The next day, preheat the oven to 375°F (190°C) Gas 5.

Put the meat into a roasting tin and spoon the marinade over. Bake for 1 hour, basting frequently with the marinade. Serve with plain boiled rice.

Turkish lamb stew

Overall timing 2¾ hours plus overnight soaking

Freezing Not suitable

To serve 6

12 oz	Dried chickpeas	350 g
	Bouquet garni	
2 lb	Boned shoulder of lamb	900 g
1	Onion	1
1	Garlic clove	1
2 oz	Butter	50 g
3 tbsp	Oil	3x15 ml
1 teasp	Ground cumin	5 ml
1 teasp	Ground cinnamon	5 ml
	Sprig of rosemary	
1	Bay leaf	1
	Salt and pepper	
14 oz	Can of tomatoes	397 g
2 tbsp	Lemon juice	2x15 ml
1 tbsp	Chopped parsley	15 ml

Soak chickpeas in water to cover overnight. The next day, drain chickpeas and put into saucepan. Cover with boiling water and add bouquet garni. Cover and simmer for 1 hour.

Cut the lamb into large pieces. Peel and chop the onion. Peel and crush garlic. Heat the butter and oil in flameproof casserole and fry the onion, garlic, cumin and cinnamon for 5 minutes. Add meat pieces to pan and brown on all sides.

Drain chickpeas and add to casserole with the rosemary, bay leaf, seasoning and tomatoes. Cover and cook gently for 1½ hours. Adjust seasoning and sprinkle with lemon juice and parsley just before serving.

Lamb with cauliflower

Overall timing 1½ hours

Freezing Not suitable

To serve 6

1	Small cauliflower	1
½ pint	Water	300 ml
	Salt and pepper	
8 oz	Tomatoes	225 g
1	Large onion	1
2	Garlic cloves	2
2 tbsp	Oil	2x15 ml
2 lb	Breast of lamb riblets	900 g
¼ pint	Tomato juice	150 ml

Trim cauliflower and divide into florets. Bring water and ½ teasp (2.5 ml) salt to the boil in a saucepan, add cauliflower and cook for 5 minutes. Drain, reserving cooking liquor.

Blanch, peel and chop tomatoes. Peel and chop onion. Peel and crush garlic. Heat the oil and garlic in a saucepan, add onion and cook till transparent. Season meat, add to pan and brown quickly on all sides over a high heat, turning frequently to prevent the riblets burning.

Add tomatoes to pan with reserved cooking liquor and tomato juice. Bring to the boil. Add pepper and cook, covered, for 1 hour.

Add cauliflower and cook for a further 15 minutes. Adjust seasoning, then serve with boiled potatoes.

French lamb hot-pot

Overall timing 1¾ hours

Freezing Not suitable

To serve 4

4 oz	Streaky bacon	125 g
2	Onions	2
1 oz	Butter	25 g
2 tbsp	Oil	2x15 ml
2½ lb	Neck of lamb chops	1.1 kg
1 tbsp	Plain flour	15 ml
¾ pint	Light stock	400 ml
1 lb	Turnips	450 g
1 lb	Potatoes	450 g
2	Garlic cloves	2
1 teasp	Caster sugar	5 ml
	Bouquet garni	
	Salt and pepper	
4	Large tomatoes	4

Derind the bacon and cut into strips. Peel onions and slice into thin rings. Heat the butter and oil in a saucepan and fry the bacon and onions. Add lamb and fry over a high heat till browned on both sides. Sprinkle in the flour and cook, stirring, till it browns. Gradually add the stock and bring to the boil.

Peel the turnips and potatoes and cut into quarters. Add to the pan with the peeled and crushed garlic, sugar, bouquet garni and seasoning. Cover and simmer for 1¼ hours.

Remove bouquet garni. Add the tomatoes and cook for a further 15 minutes. Taste and adjust the seasoning. Arrange the meat and vegetables on a warmed serving dish and spoon the cooking liquor over. Serve immediately.

Shepherds' pie

Overall timing 1 hour

Freezing Not suitable

To serve 4

2 lb	Potatoes	900 g
	Salt and pepper	
1	Large onion	1
3 tbsp	Oil	3x15 ml
1	Garlic clove	1
1 lb	Minced cooked lamb	450 g
2 oz	Butter	50 g
¼ pint	Milk	150 ml
3 oz	Cheese	75 g

Peel and halve potatoes. Cook in boiling salted water for 25–30 minutes.

Peel and finely chop onion. Heat oil in a frying pan, add onion and cook for about 10 minutes. Peel and crush garlic. Add garlic and meat to pan and cook for about 5 minutes, stirring.

Preheat the oven to 425°F (220°C) Gas 7.

Drain potatoes and mash with half the butter and the milk. Season to taste. Cover bottom of ovenproof dish with half of the mashed potato, cover with the meat, then spread or pipe the remaining potato on top.

Grate cheese. Sprinkle over potato, dot with remaining butter and bake for about 15 minutes till the top is browned. Serve with green salad.

Lamb stew

Overall timing 2 hours

Freezing Suitable: add potatoes after reheating

To serve 4

2 oz	Butter	50 g
1 tbsp	Oil	15 ml
2½ lb	Middle neck lamb chops	1.1 kg
2 tbsp	Plain flour	2x15 ml
½ pint	Stock or water	300 ml
8 oz	Turnips	225 g
2	Onions	2
8 oz	Carrots	225 g
1	Stalk of celery	1
	Bouquet garni	
	Salt and pepper	
1 lb	Potatoes	450 g

Heat the butter and oil in a flameproof casserole, add the chops and brown well on all sides. Sprinkle flour over and cook, stirring, for 3 minutes. Gradually stir in stock or water.

Peel and chop turnips and onions. Peel carrots and cut into pieces lengthways. Add to casserole with celery stalk, bouquet garni and seasoning. Cover and cook for 1½ hours over low heat.

Peel potatoes and cut into large chunks. Add to casserole and cook, covered, for a further 20 minutes. Discard bouquet garni before serving.

Russian lamb burgers

Overall timing 30 minutes

Freezing Suitable: coat with flour and fry after thawing

To serve 2

1 oz	Fresh breadcrumbs	25 g
2 tbsp	Milk	2x15 ml
8 oz	Minced shoulder of lamb	225 g
1 oz	Gruyère cheese	25 g
1	Small egg	1
	Salt and pepper	
1 tbsp	Plain flour	15 ml
1 oz	Butter	25 g
8 oz	Can of tomatoes	226 g

Put breadcrumbs in a large bowl with the milk and soak for a few minutes. Add the lamb, grated cheese, egg and seasoning and mix well. Divide the mixture into four and shape into patties. Coat lightly with flour.

Melt butter in a frying pan and fry for 5 minutes on each side. Remove from pan with a spatula and place on a warmed serving dish. Keep hot.

Heat tomatoes in a saucepan. Drain and arrange on serving dish with the burgers. Serve a hot tomato sauce separately, if liked, and mashed potatoes topped with crisp fried breadcrumbs and bacon bits.

Shoulder of lamb with turnips

Overall timing 2 hours

Freezing Not suitable

To serve 6

3 lb	Boned shoulder of lamb	1.4 kg
	Salt and pepper	
1	Carrot	1
1	Onion	1
3 oz	Butter	75 g
	Bouquet garni	
¼ pint	Stock	150 ml
2 lb	Turnips	900 g
8 oz	Buttons onions	225 g

Preheat the oven to 350°F (180°C) Gas 4.

Season the lamb inside and out. Roll up and tie firmly with string into a neat shape. Peel and thinly slice carrot and onion.

Melt the butter in flameproof casserole, add onion and carrot and fry till golden. Add lamb and brown on all sides. Season and add bouquet garni and stock. Cover and cook in centre of oven for 1 hour.

Peel turnips and button onions. Place in a saucepan of cold salted water and bring to the boil. Drain and dry on kitchen paper. Arrange turnips and onions around the meat and adjust seasoning. Return to oven and cook for a further 45 minutes.

Remove bouquet garni and string. Transfer lamb to warmed serving plate and surround with turnips and onions.

Greek lamb stew with spinach

Overall timing 1½ hours

Freezing Not suitable

To serve 6

2 lb	Middle neck of lamb	900 g
1	Large onion	1
2 tbsp	Oil	2x15 ml
1 oz	Butter	25 g
1 lb	Ripe tomatoes	450 g
2 tbsp	Tomato purée	2x15 ml
	Dried oregano	
	Salt and pepper	
1 pint	Hot water or stock	560 ml
1¼ lb	Spinach	600 g

Cut the lamb into bite-size pieces. Peel and thinly slice the onion. Heat the oil and butter in a flameproof casserole, add the lamb and onion and fry over a moderate heat for about 10 minutes till browned, stirring occasionally.

Blanch, peel and chop the tomatoes. Add to the pan with the tomato purée, a pinch of oregano, seasoning and water or stock. Mix well and bring to the boil. Cover and simmer for 1¼ hours till the lamb is tender.

Wash spinach and shred finely. Add to the pan, stir, cover and cook for a further 10 minutes. Taste and adjust the seasoning. Pour into a warmed serving dish and serve.

Lamb with potatoes and onions

Overall timing 2½ hours

Freezing Not suitable

To serve 8

4½ lb	Leg of lamb	2 kg
4 oz	Butter	125 g
	Salt and pepper	
1 lb	Onions	450 g
2 lb	Potatoes	900 g
¾ pint	Stock	400 ml
	Sprigs of rosemary	
	Bouquet garni	

Preheat the oven to 350°F (180°C) Gas 4.

Place meat in roasting tin, spread with half the butter and season. Roast for 1¼ hours.

Peel and slice the onions. Peel and quarter potatoes. Melt remaining butter in frying pan, add onions and potatoes and fry till golden brown. Add stock, rosemary, bouquet garni and seasoning and cook for 5 minutes, stirring occasionally.

Arrange potato mixture around meat and roast for a further 45 minutes till meat is tender.

Remove bouquet garni. Place lamb on warmed serving dish and surround with potato mixture. Serve with green vegetables.

Stuffed breast of lamb

Overall timing 2½ hours

Freezing Not suitable

To serve 8

1 or 2	Boned breasts of lamb	1 or 2
2 lb	Potatoes	900 g
1½ lb	Small carrots	700 g
4	Turnips	4
2	Stalks of celery	2
4	Leeks	4
1	Onion	1
4	Cloves	4
2 oz	Butter	50 g
1 pint	Stock	560 ml
	Bouquet garni	
Stuffing		
3	Lambs' kidneys	3
8 oz	Streaky bacon	225 g
8 oz	Sausagemeat	225 g
½ teasp	Ground allspice	2.5 ml
3 tbsp	Chopped parsley	3x15 ml
1 teasp	Dried marjoram	5 ml
1	Egg	1
	Salt and pepper	

Preheat the oven to 325°F (170°C) Gas 3.

Prepare and finely chop kidneys. Derind and chop bacon. Mix all stuffing ingredients.

Cut a deep pocket in lamb and fill with stuffing. Sew up opening. If using two breasts, place together with skin side out and sew around sides.

Peel potatoes and carrots. Peel and halve turnips. Chop celery and leeks. Peel onion and spike with cloves. Melt butter in flameproof casserole, add meat and brown all over. Remove. Add vegetables and fry for 2 minutes. Return meat and add stock, bouquet garni and salt. Cover and cook in oven for 2 hours.

Slice meat. Arrange vegetables around meat, discarding onion. Boil stock till reduced by half. Strain over vegetables.

Lamb with vegetables

Overall timing 2 hours

Freezing Not suitable

To serve 6

1½ lb	Best end of neck of lamb	700 g
2 pints	Water	1.1 litres
1 lb	Small swedes	450 g
8 oz	Carrots	225 g
2	Large leeks	2
	Salt and pepper	
1 lb	Waxy potatoes	450 g
1 tbsp	Chopped parsley	15 ml
2 tbsp	Plain flour	2x15 ml

Wipe and trim the lamb, removing the skin. Put into a large saucepan with the water and bring slowly to the boil.

Meanwhile, peel the swedes thickly and cut into quarters. Scrape and thickly slice the carrots. Wash and trim the leeks; slice the white parts and reserve the green.

Add the prepared vegetables to the pan with salt and pepper and bring back to the boil. Cover and simmer for 1 hour.

Peel the potatoes and cut into quarters. Add to the pan and simmer for 20 minutes.

Shred the green part of the leeks and add to the pan with the parsley. Simmer for 5 minutes.

Remove the meat from the pan and keep hot. Blend the flour to a smooth paste with 5 tbsp (5x15 ml) water. Add to the cooking liquor and bring to the boil, stirring constantly. Simmer for 3 minutes. Taste and adjust the seasoning, then pour into a warmed serving dish. Arrange the meat on top and serve.

Lamb cutlets with garlic and anchovy

Overall timing 40 minutes

Freezing Not suitable

To serve 4

2 lb	Best end of neck lamb cutlets	900 g
2	Garlic cloves	2
5 tbsp	Oil	5x15 ml
	Salt and pepper	
	Sprigs of rosemary	
2	Anchovy fillets	2
3 tbsp	White wine vinegar	3x15 ml

Trim cutlets of all fat. Peel and crush one garlic clove. Heat the oil in a large frying pan. Add the garlic and cutlets. Fry quickly on both sides till golden, then season, reduce heat and cook for a further 10–15 minutes.

Put a few pieces of fresh rosemary, the remaining garlic clove, peeled, and the anchovies in a mortar. Pound with a pestle, gradually mixing in the vinegar. Add garlic mixture to pan and cook till the liquid reduces by half.

Arrange cutlets on warmed serving dish and spoon cooking juices over. Garnish with remaining rosemary sprigs.

Lamb fricassee

Overall timing 1¼ hours

Freezing Not suitable

To serve 4

1½ lb	Boned shoulder of lamb	700 g
1	Onion	1
1	Stalk of celery	1
2 oz	Butter	50 g
1 tbsp	Plain flour	15 ml
¼ pint	Milk	150 ml
¼ pint	Stock	150 ml
1	Carrot	1
2	Sprigs of parsley	2
2	Sprigs of basil	2
2	Sprigs of sage	2
	Salt and pepper	
2	Egg yolks	2
1 tbsp	Lemon juice	15 ml

Cut the lamb into neat pieces. Peel and chop the onion. Trim and chop the celery. Melt half the butter in a flameproof casserole. Add onion and celery and fry over low heat for 5 minutes without browning.

Stir in the flour and fry until golden. Gradually add milk and stock, stirring constantly. Bring to the boil, then remove from heat.

Scrape and chop carrot. Tie in a piece of muslin with parsley, basil and sage. Add to casserole with remaining butter, the lamb and seasoning. Stir well. Cover and cook gently for 1 hour, stirring occasionally. Remove muslin bag.

Beat the egg yolks in a bowl and blend with the lemon juice. Stir gently into the fricassee until blended; do not boil. Taste and adjust seasoning, then serve with creamed potatoes and minted peas.

Paprika lamb stew

Overall timing 2 hours

Freezing Suitable

To serve 6

2	Green peppers	2
2	Onions	2
1	Garlic clove	1
2 oz	Bacon rashers	50 g
2 tbsp	Oil	2x15 ml
2 lb	Boned shoulder of lamb	900 g
14 oz	Can of tomatoes	397 g
2 tbsp	Tomato purée	2x15 ml
1 teasp	Paprika	5 ml
1 teasp	Sugar	5 ml
1 pint	Stock	560 ml
	Salt and pepper	
$\frac{1}{4}$ pint	Carton of soured cream	150 ml

Deseed the peppers and cut into strips. Peel and finely chop the onions. Peel and crush the garlic. Derind and dice the bacon. Heat the oil in a flameproof casserole, add the onions, garlic and bacon and fry over a high heat till golden.

Cut the meat into cubes and add to casserole. Brown on all sides. Stir in peppers, tomatoes and their juice, tomato purée, paprika, sugar, stock and seasoning. Cover and cook gently for 1$\frac{1}{2}$ hours till meat is tender.

Taste and adjust seasoning and serve with boiled potatoes and soured cream for everyone to spoon on top of the stew.

Piquant kidneys

Overall timing 30 minutes

Freezing Not suitable

To serve 2

8 oz	Lamb's kidneys	225 g
2	Streaky bacon rashers	2
1	Onion	1
8 oz	Long macaroni	225 g
	Salt and pepper	
1 oz	Butter	25 g
1½ teasp	Plain flour	7.5 ml
½ pint	Beef stock	300 ml
1½ teasp	Tomato purée	7.5 ml
¼ teasp	Dried sage	1.25 ml

Prepare and thinly slice kidneys. Derind and dice bacon. Peel and chop onion. Cook macaroni in boiling salted water for 15 minutes till tender.

Meanwhile, melt butter in frying pan and fry kidneys for 3 minutes, stirring from time to time. Remove from pan.

Add bacon and onion to pan and fry gently till golden. Sprinkle flour over and cook, stirring, for 2 minutes. Add stock, tomato purée, sage and seasoning. Bring to the boil, stirring, then return kidneys to pan, reduce heat and simmer for 15 minutes.

Drain macaroni and arrange in warmed serving dish. Spoon kidneys and sauce over and serve hot with crisp lettuce and cucumber salad.

Kidneys in their jackets

Overall timing 45 minutes

Freezing Not suitable

To serve 4

8	Lamb kidneys in their suet	8
4	Slices of bread	4
	Salt and pepper	
1	Tomato	1
	Sprigs of parsley	

Preheat the oven to 400°F (200°C) Gas 6.

Place kidneys in their suet in a roasting tin. Bake for about 35 minutes till the fat is crisp and golden.

Pour a little of the melted fat from the roasting tin into a frying pan and fry the bread till golden on both sides. Arrange slices in warmed individual dishes.

Cut a deep cross in the top of the kidneys and open out like petals. Season inside and place on top of fried bread. Wash tomatoes and cut into wedges. Arrange with parsley sprigs on top of kidneys. Serve with sauté or mashed potatoes.

Kidney brochettes

Overall timing 25 minutes

Freezing Not suitable

To serve 4

4 oz	Unsalted butter	125 g
2 tbsp	Chopped parsley	2x15 ml
1 tbsp	Lemon juice	15 ml
1 lb	Lambs' kidneys	450 g
3	Tomatoes	3
1 teasp	Dried rosemary	5 ml
2 tbsp	Oil	2x15 ml
	Salt and pepper	

Mash the butter with the parsley and lemon juice until well combined. Form into a roll, wrap in greaseproof paper and chill until firm.

Preheat the grill.

Prepare kidneys and cut in half. Cut tomatoes into thin wedges. Thread kidneys and tomato wedges alternately on skewers. Sprinkle with rosemary and brush with oil.

Grill for 10–15 minutes, turning once. Season and garnish with pats of parsley butter. Serve immediately with matchstick chips and sprigs of watercress.

Swiss liver kebabs

Overall timing 35 minutes

Freezing Not suitable

To serve 4

1 lb	Calf's or lamb's liver	450 g
	Salt and pepper	
10	Sage leaves	10
10	Streaky bacon rashers	10
2 oz	Butter	50 g

Preheat the grill.

Cut the liver into 20 bite-size lengths. Season. Wash and dry sage leaves. Derind and stretch the bacon rashers, then cut in half. Wrap bacon rashers round liver pieces, including a sage leaf in alternate rolls. Thread on to four oiled skewers.

Melt the butter in the bottom of the grill pan. Balance the skewers across the pan and brush butter over. Grill for 10–15 minutes till cooked and crisp, turning frequently and brushing with butter. Serve immediately with boiled new potatoes.

Liver and bacon

Overall timing 20 minutes

Freezing Not suitable

To serve 4

4	Slices of lamb's or calf's liver	4
	Salt and pepper	
2 tbsp	Plain flour	2x15 ml
2 oz	Butter	50 g
8	Bacon rashers	8
1 tbsp	Chopped parsley	15 ml
1 tbsp	Lemon juice	15 ml

Trim and wipe the liver. Dust with seasoned flour.

Melt half the butter in a large frying pan, add the bacon rashers and fry till crisp and golden. Remove from pan and keep hot.

Melt the remaining butter in pan, add the liver and fry over a moderate heat for 3–4 minutes on each side.

Arrange liver on serving plate and put bacon on top. Add the parsley and lemon juice to the pan and bring to the boil. Season and spoon over liver. Serve immediately with watercress, matchstick chips and grilled whole tomatoes.

Liver and onions

Overall timing 20 minutes

Freezing Not suitable

To serve 6

1½ lb	Onions	700 g
6	Slices of calf's or lamb's liver	6
	Salt and pepper	
3 tbsp	Plain flour	3x15 ml
3 oz	Butter	75 g
2 tbsp	Chopped parsley (optional)	2x15 ml

Peel and slice onions. Trim and wipe liver. Season the flour and use to coat the liver.

Melt the butter in a large frying pan. Add the onions and fry till golden. Add liver slices and fry for 3–4 minutes on each side. Stir in parsley, if using.

Transfer to a warmed serving dish and top with fried onions. Spoon pan juices over. Serve with boiled potatoes and parsleyed baby carrots.

Liver and bacon kebabs

Overall timing 25 minutes

Freezing Not suitable

To serve 4

12 oz	Piece of lamb's liver	350 g
6 oz	Piece of streaky bacon	175 g
4 oz	Button mushrooms	125 g
2 oz	Melted butter	50 g
2 oz	Fine breadcrumbs	50 g
½ teasp	Paprika	2.5 ml
	Salt	
	Lemon slices	

Wipe and trim the liver and cut into 1 inch (2.5 cm) cubes. Derind the bacon; cut it into thick rashers, then into squares. Wipe and trim the mushrooms.

Preheat the grill. Line the grill pan with foil.

Thread the bacon, liver and mushrooms on to four skewers. Brush with melted butter. Mix the breadcrumbs, paprika and salt together on a plate. Turn the kebabs in the crumbs till evenly coated. Arrange on the grill pan and grill for about 15 minutes, turning the kebabs frequently and brushing them with the fat that runs from the bacon.

Arrange the kebabs on a warmed serving dish and serve immediately with lemon slices for squeezing, and saffron rice.

Brains Milan-style

Overall timing 15 minutes plus soaking and cooling

Freezing Not suitable

To serve 4

4	Lambs' brains	4
2 teasp	Vinegar	2x5 ml
	Salt and pepper	
	Bouquet garni	
4 tbsp	Plain flour	4x15 ml
1	Egg	1
4 tbsp	Fresh breadcrumbs	4x15 ml
2 oz	Butter	50 g
	Sage leaves	
	Lemon wedges	

Put the brains in a bowl of cold water with 1 teasp (5 ml) of the vinegar. Soak for 15 minutes.

Drain the brains. Holding them under running water, carefully pull away membranes and blood vessels. Put the brains into a saucepan and cover with cold water. Add the remaining vinegar, salt and bouquet garni. Bring to the boil, then remove from the heat. Leave to cool in the liquid.

Drain the brains and dry on kitchen paper. Break into small pieces and coat with the flour. Beat the egg. Dip the brains into the egg, then coat with the breadcrumbs.

Melt the butter in a frying pan till foaming. Add the brains and cook for 5 minutes till brown on all sides. Garnish with sage leaves and serve with lemon wedges.

Braised stuffed hearts

Overall timing 2 hours

Freezing Not suitable

To serve 6–8

1	Onion	1
2 oz	Butter	50 g
4 oz	Long-grain rice	125 g
¾ pint	Stock	400 ml
2	Calves' hearts *or*	2
4	Lambs' hearts	4
1	Lemon	1
2 tbsp	Chopped parsley	2x15 ml
1 tbsp	Chopped fresh sage	15 ml
1	Egg	1
	Salt and pepper	
8 oz	Streaky bacon rashers	225 g
2 tbsp	Dry sherry	2x15 ml

Preheat the oven to 350°F (180°C) Gas 4.

Peel and chop onion. Melt half the butter in a pan and fry onion till golden. Add rice and ½ pint (300 ml) of the stock. Bring to the boil, cover and simmer for 20 minutes till tender. Remove from the heat.

Prepare hearts, using kitchen scissors to cut through pockets inside. Wash well and dry with kitchen paper. Grate rind and squeeze juice from lemon. Add both to pan with parsley, sage, egg and seasoning. Mix well and spoon into hearts.

Derind bacon rashers and stretch with the back of a knife. Wrap around the hearts, tying them on with fine string.

Melt remaining butter in flameproof casserole and brown hearts all over. Pour over remaining stock, add sherry, cover and cook in the oven for 1 hour.

Remove string and slice hearts. Arrange on serving dish, garnish with sage and serve.

Hearts casseroled with potatoes and onions

Overall timing 1¾ hours

Freezing Not suitable

To serve 4

2	Calves' hearts or	2
4	Lambs' hearts	4
4 oz	Butter	125 g
1 pint	Beef stock	560 ml
	Bouquet garni	
6 oz	Streaky bacon	175 g
8 oz	Button onions	225 g
2 lb	Potatoes	900 g
2 tbsp	Oil	2x15 ml
	Salt and pepper	
2 tbsp	Redcurrant jelly	2x15 ml
1 tbsp	Chopped parsley	15 ml

Prepare hearts. Melt 2 oz (50 g) butter in saucepan, add hearts and brown on all sides. Pour in stock, add bouquet garni, cover and simmer for 1½ hours until tender.

Meanwhile, derind bacon and cut into strips. Peel onions. Peel and chop potatoes. Cook onions in boiling salted water for 5 minutes, then add potatoes and cook for a further 5 minutes. Drain well.

Melt remaining butter with oil in frying pan. Add bacon and fry till golden. Add potatoes, onions and seasoning and cook till golden brown, turning occasionally.

Remove hearts from pan and place on warmed serving dish. Keep hot. Reduce liquid in pan to about ¼ pint (150 ml), then stir in redcurrant jelly. Pour over vegetables in frying pan and cook for 2 minutes. Arrange vegetables around hearts. Spoon over cooking juices and serve sprinkled with parsley.

Sweetbread kebabs

Overall timing 35 minutes plus marination

Freezing Not suitable

To serve 4

1 lb	Prepared lambs' sweetbreads	450 g
4	Thick streaky bacon rashers	4
6 tbsp	Oil	6x15 ml
1 tbsp	Lemon juice	15 ml
	Salt and pepper	
$\frac{1}{2}$	Lemon	$\frac{1}{2}$
	Sprigs of parsley	

Cut the sweetbreads in half. Derind the bacon and cut into 1 inch (2.5 cm) pieces. Thread the sweetbreads and bacon alternately on to four greased skewers.

Mix the oil, lemon juice and seasoning in a shallow dish. Add the kebabs, turning them to coat with the marinade. Leave in a cool place for 1 hour.

Preheat the grill. Place each kebab on a piece of foil, shaping the foil into a dish so it will hold the marinade, and pour the marinade over. Arrange the kebabs on the grill pan and grill for 15–20 minutes, turning frequently in the marinade, till the sweetbreads are tender.

Arrange the kebabs on a warmed serving dish and pour the marinade over. Garnish with the lemon and parsley and serve immediately with crusty bread.

Honey-glazed bacon

Overall timing 1½ hours plus overnight soaking

Freezing Not suitable

To serve 6–8

4 lb	Collar bacon	1.8 kg
	Whole cloves	
2 tbsp	Clear honey	2x15 ml
3 tbsp	Soft brown sugar	3x15 ml
2	Granny Smith apples	2
2 oz	Butter	50 g

Put bacon into a large saucepan. Cover with cold water and leave to soak overnight.

The next day, drain the bacon. Return it to the same pan and cover with fresh water. Bring to the boil. Remove any scum. Reduce heat, cover and simmer gently for 1 hour.

Preheat the oven to 350°F (180°C) Gas 4.

Remove bacon from pan, allow to cool slightly then cut off the rind. Score fat in a lattice pattern and put a clove in the centre of each "diamond". Put in a roasting tin.

Gently heat honey and sugar in a small saucepan until melted. Brush over the surface of the bacon. Cook in the oven for 20 minutes, basting from time to time. Take care not to let the glaze burn.

Five minutes before the joint is cooked, peel, core and slice apples into ¼ inch (6 mm) thick rings. Melt butter in a frying pan and fry the apple rings on both sides until lightly golden and tender.

Serve bacon joint on a dish surrounded by apple rings.

Ham roasted in stout

Overall timing 2½ hours plus cooling

Freezing Suitable: slice meat and cover with sauce; reheat from frozen in moderate oven

To serve 6

3 lb	Lightly salted ham or bacon (collar, slipper, or gammon)	1.4 kg
2	Onions	2
½ pint	Stout	300 ml
1 oz	Butter	25 g
1 oz	Plain flour	25 g
¼ teasp	Crushed caraway seed	1.25 ml
	Pepper	

Preheat the oven to 400°F (200°C) Gas 4.

If using bacon joint, remove rind. Place ham or bacon in an ovenproof dish. Peel onions and slice into rings. Cover ham with onion rings. Pour stout over. Roast for 2 hours, turning meat once during cooking.

Remove meat from dish and place on warmed serving dish. Keep hot. Sieve cooking liquor, cool quickly and skim fat from surface. Place liquor in measuring jug and make up to ½ pint (300 ml) with water if necessary.

Melt butter in saucepan. Stir in flour and allow to brown lightly. Gradually add cooking liquor and simmer, stirring, till thickened. Season with crushed caraway seed and black pepper. Cook for 5 minutes, then pour over the roast and serve.

Bacon and cabbage casserole

Overall timing 1¼ hours

Freezing Not suitable

To serve 4

1	Medium-size white cabbage	1
2	Onions	2
1 oz	Lard	25 g
8 oz	Back bacon	225 g
1 lb	Minced beef	450 g
1 teasp	Caraway seeds	5 ml
¼ pint	Beef stock	150 ml
	Salt and pepper	
2 oz	Butter	50 g
8 oz	Streaky bacon rashers	225 g

Preheat the oven to 375°F (190°C) Gas 5.

Discard any marked outer leaves of the cabbage. Save two or three good ones. Cut the remaining cabbage in half. Remove the core, then shred the cabbage. Put with reserved leaves into a saucepan of cold water. Bring to the boil and drain. Set aside.

Peel and chop the onions. Melt the lard in a large saucepan, add the onions and cook gently for 3–4 minutes. Derind and chop back bacon. Add to the saucepan. Cook for 2–3 minutes. Add the minced beef and cook, stirring, until brown. Add the caraway seeds, stock and seasoning. Simmer for 10 minutes.

Melt the butter in a small saucepan. Put half of the shredded cabbage in the bottom of an ovenproof dish and pour the melted butter over. Spread the mince mixture evenly over the cabbage. Cover with remaining shredded cabbage and top with whole leaves. Arrange the streaky bacon rashers over the top of the cabbage. Bake for 45 minutes.

Frankfurters with apple purée

Overall timing 20 minutes

Freezing Suitable: add frankfurters when reheating

To serve 4

8	Dessert apples	8
½ pint	Sweet white wine or cider	300 ml
	Salt and pepper	
4 oz	Butter	100 g
8	Frankfurters	8

Peel, core and chop apples. Place in a saucepan with the wine or cider. Cover and cook over a low heat till the apples are soft, then beat until pulpy with a wooden spoon. Season to taste.

Melt butter in a frying pan, add the frankfurters, cover and cook gently over low heat till heated through.

Put apple purée on a warmed serving dish, place the frankfurters on top and serve immediately with crusty bread or jacket potatoes.

Bacon with lentils

Overall timing 2½ hours plus 3 hours soaking

Freezing Not suitable

To serve 6

2¼ lb	Middle cut bacon hock	1 kg
1	Carrot	1
2	Onions	2
1	Garlic clove	1
	Bouquet garni	
8	Peppercorns	8
1 lb	Continental lentils	450 g
	Salt and pepper	

Put bacon joint in a large saucepan and cover with cold water. Soak for 3 hours, changing the water several times.

Drain the bacon joint and cover with fresh water. Peel and slice the carrot; peel and quarter the onions; peel and halve the garlic. Add to the bacon with the bouquet garni and peppercorns. Bring to the boil, cover and simmer for 45 minutes.

Remove bouquet garni. Wash and pick over lentils. Add to bacon, cover and cook for a further hour till lentils are tender. Adjust seasoning, then arrange on warmed dish and serve with mustard.

Sausage surprise

Overall timing 35 minutes

Freezing Not suitable

To serve 4–6

2 lb	Potatoes	900 g
	Salt and pepper	
1 lb	Chipolatas	450 g
½ pint	Milk	300 ml
2 oz	Butter	50 g
6 oz	Cheese	175 g
½ teasp	Grated nutmeg	2.5 ml

Preheat the grill. Peel the potatoes and cut into quarters. Cook in boiling salted water for about 10 minutes till tender.

Meanwhile, grill the chipolatas for about 15 minutes, turning occasionally till well browned.

Drain the potatoes in a colander. Add the milk to the pan and bring just to the boil. Return the potatoes to the pan with the butter and mash till smooth.

Grate cheese and beat 4 oz (125 g) into potatoes with nutmeg and seasoning. Spread the mixture in a flameproof dish and push the chipolatas diagonally into the potato so that the tops are just showing.

Sprinkle the remaining cheese over and grill for about 5 minutes till golden.

Savoury mould

Overall timing 2½ hours plus setting

Freezing Not suitable

To serve 8–10

2 lb	Collar bacon	900 g
1	Onion	1
1	Clove	1
1	Stalk of celery	1
2	Garlic cloves	2
	Bouquet garni	
	Salt and pepper	
5 tbsp	Chopped parsley	5 x 15 ml
1 tbsp	White wine vinegar	15 ml
2 teasp	Powdered gelatine	2 x 5 ml
1 teasp	Dried tarragon	5 ml
1 teasp	Dried chervil	5 ml
2	Egg whites	2
	Cucumber peel	
1	Red pepper	1
1 oz	Stoned black olives	25 g

Put bacon in a pan, cover with water and bring to the boil. Drain. Peel onion and spike with clove. Chop celery. Peel garlic. Add vegetables to pan with 3½ pints (2 litres) water, the bouquet garni and seasoning. Bring to the boil and simmer for 1 hour.

Soak parsley in vinegar.

Lift bacon joint out of pan. Remove meat from bone and chop. Reduce cooking liquor to ½ pint (300 ml) by boiling fast. Strain cooking liquor and return to pan. Add gelatine and herbs. Lightly beat egg whites and add. Leave for 30 minutes, then bring nearly to the boil, whisking. Remove from heat and pour through a scalded jelly bag or several layers of muslin.

Spoon a little jelly into wet pudding basin. Chill till set.

Chop cucumber peel. Deseed and slice pepper. Arrange decoratively in basin with olives. Add a little more jelly and chill again till set. Arrange bacon pieces and parsley in layers in basin. Pour remaining jelly over, cover and chill overnight.

Sausage and vegetable stew

Overall timing 3¼ hours

Freezing Not suitable

To serve 6

1	White cabbage	1
3	Carrots	3
1	Leek	1
1	Bacon knuckle	1
1	Pig's knuckle	1
3½ pints	Water	2 litres
	Salt and pepper	
2	Large potatoes	2
8 oz	Sausages	225 g

Shred cabbage. Peel and chop carrots. Trim and slice leek. Put vegetables into a pan with the knuckles, water and seasoning. Bring to the boil, then cover and cook for 2½ hours.

Remove knuckles from pan and cut meat from bones. Peel potatoes and cut into large chunks. Cut sausages in half. Add meat, potatoes and sausages to pan and cook for a further 30 minutes. Taste and adjust seasoning before serving.

Sausages in cider sauce

Overall timing 50 minutes

Freezing Not suitable

To serve 4

1 lb	Boned pork chops	450 g
8	Pork chipolatas	8
1 oz	Lard	25 g
1	Large onion	1
1	Carrot	1
1	Stalk of celery	1
4	Large tomatoes	4
1	Garlic clove	1
¼ pint	Dry cider	150 ml
	Salt and pepper	
1 oz	Butter	25 g
12 oz	Long grain rice	350 g
1½ pints	Chicken stock	850 ml
3 tbsp	Grated Parmesan cheese	3 x 15 ml

Cut the pork chops into bite-size pieces. Twist each chipolata in half to make 16 small sausages. Melt the lard in a frying pan and fry the pork and sausages gently, turning frequently, for 10 minutes.

Meanwhile, peel and chop the onion and carrot. Trim and chop the celery. Quarter the tomatoes. Peel and crush the garlic. Add the vegetables to the frying pan with the cider and seasoning. Cover and simmer for 20 minutes.

Melt the butter in a saucepan, add the rice and fry, stirring, for 2 minutes. Add the stock and bring to the boil, stirring. Cover and simmer for about 15 minutes till rice is tender and liquid is absorbed.

Remove the rice from the heat and stir in the cheese. Taste and adjust the seasoning and fluff with a fork. Pile into a warmed serving dish and arrange sausages and pork on top. Spoon cider sauce over and serve immediately with a mixed salad.

Roast ginger chicken

Overall timing 1¼ hours

Freezing Not suitable

To serve 4

1	Cooking apple	1
1 inch	Piece of root ginger	2.5 cm
4 oz	Cooked long grain rice	125 g
5 oz	Carton of natural yogurt	141 g
3 oz	Softened butter	75 g
	Salt and pepper	
3 lb	Ovenready chicken	1.4 kg

Preheat the oven to 400°F (200°C) Gas 6.

Peel, core and grate apple. Grate or finely chop ginger and add to apple with rice, yogurt, 2 oz (50 g) of the butter and seasoning. Mix well together. Use to stuff chicken.

Place chicken on its side in a roasting tin and dot with remaining butter. Roast for 15 minutes, then turn chicken on to its other side and roast for 15 minutes. Turn chicken on to its back and continue roasting for a further 30 minutes or until tender. Baste frequently.

Remove chicken from roasting tin and place on warmed serving dish. Serve with gravy made from pan juices, green or mixed salad and sauté or creamed potatoes.

Alsatian chicken

Overall timing 1½ hours

Freezing Not suitable

To serve 4–6

8	Chicken legs and wings	8
1	Garlic clove	1
2 oz	Streaky bacon	50 g
4 tbsp	Oil	4x15 ml
2	Onions	2
8 fl oz	Dry white wine	225 ml
4 oz	Mushrooms	125 g
2	Bay leaves	2
2 tbsp	Chopped parsley	2x15 ml
2 tbsp	Chopped chives	2x15 ml
	Salt and pepper	
1 tbsp	Arrowroot	15 ml
¼ pint	Carton of single cream	150 ml
	Sprigs of fresh parsley	

Rub chicken all over with halved garlic clove. Derind and dice bacon. Fry in flameproof casserole till brown. Add oil and when hot brown chicken pieces on all sides.

Peel and finely chop onions. Add to casserole and brown. Pour in half of wine, cover and cook for 35 minutes.

Slice mushrooms and add to casserole with bay leaves, half the chopped parsley and chives and seasoning. Cover and cook for 10 minutes.

Discard bay leaves. Take out chicken pieces with a draining spoon and place on a warmed serving dish. Keep hot. If there's a lot of liquid in casserole, boil till reduced by half. Mix arrowroot with remaining wine and stir into pan juices. Cook, stirring, till sauce thickens, then gradually stir in cream. When hot (it must not boil) pour sauce over chicken. Garnish with remaining chopped parsley and chives and parsley sprigs.

Cheesy chicken rolls

Overall timing 45 minutes

Freezing Not suitable

To serve 6

6	Large chicken breasts	6
	Salt and pepper	
2 teasp	Made mustard	2x5 ml
6	Thin slices of Derby cheese	6
6	Thin streaky bacon rashers	6
	Plain flour	
2 oz	Butter	50 g
2 tbsp	Oil	2x15 ml
½ pint	Light ale	300 ml
12	Stoned green olives	12

Remove skin and bones from chicken breasts. Season underside of chicken breasts and spread with mustard, then place a slice of cheese on each. Roll up and wrap a rasher of bacon around. Tie rolls firmly with string and coat lightly in flour.

Heat butter and oil in flameproof casserole. Lightly brown chicken rolls all over. Add beer, taking care that it does not fill more than half the casserole. Add more seasoning if required. Cover and simmer for 10 minutes.

Meanwhile, scald olives in boiling water. Drain well and add to casserole. Cover and simmer for 10 minutes more. Carefully remove string from chicken rolls and serve with rice or potatoes.

Chicken with turnips

Overall timing 1 hour

Freezing Not suitable

To serve 6

8 oz	Button onions	225 g
6	Saffron strands	6
3 lb	Ovenready chicken	1.4 kg
1½ lb	Small turnips	700 g
8 oz	Courgettes	225 g
2 oz	Butter	50 g
2 tbsp	Oil	2x15 ml
½ pint	Chicken stock	300 ml
4	Bay leaves	4
	Salt and pepper	

Blanch and peel onions. Soak saffron in 2 tbsp (2x15 ml) warm water. Cut chicken into 12 portions. Peel and chop turnips. Slice courgettes.

Heat butter and oil in frying pan and brown chicken pieces all over. Remove from pan with a draining spoon. Add onions and turnips and fry for 3 minutes, then add courgettes and fry for a further 2 minutes till browned.

Return chicken to pan with saffron and soaking water, stock, bay leaves and seasoning. Cover and simmer for 20 minutes till chicken is tender.

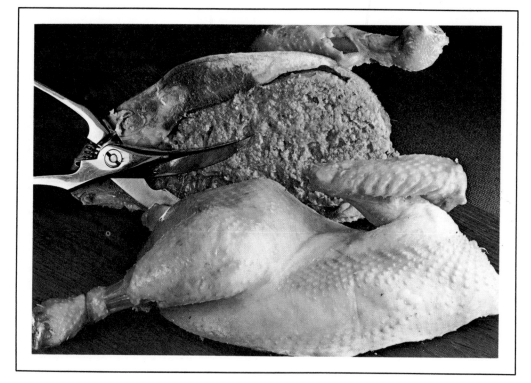

Lombardy chicken

Overall timing 2¼ hours

Freezing Not suitable

To serve 4

2 oz	Breadcrumbs	50 g
¼ pint	Milk	150 ml
4 oz	Cooked ham	125 g
3 lb	Chicken with giblets	1.4 kg
4 oz	Sausagemeat	125 g
2 tbsp	Chopped parsley	2x15 ml
1	Egg	1
2 oz	Grated Parmesan cheese	50 g
2 tbsp	Dry vermouth	2x15 ml
	Salt and pepper	
1	Stalk of celery	1
1	Carrot	1
1	Onion	1
2 teasp	Arrowroot	2x5 ml

Soak breadcrumbs in milk. Mince or finely chop ham, and liver and heart from giblets. Place in a bowl with the sausagemeat, parsley, egg, Parmesan, vermouth, salt and pepper. Squeeze liquid out of the breadcrumbs and add them to the mixture. Mix well together.

Wipe chicken and stuff with the mixture, leaving a little space for expansion. Close opening with a small skewer or by sewing with thick thread.

Half fill a large saucepan with lightly salted water and bring to the boil. Chop celery and carrot. Peel and quarter onion. Add them all to the pan and bring back to the boil.

Add the chicken and the rest of the giblets. Cover and simmer for 1¾ hours or until chicken is tender.

Lift chicken out of the stock and keep warm on serving dish. Dissolve the arrowroot in a little of the strained stock, then add a further ½ pint (300 ml) stock. Cook, stirring, until thick and clear.

Chicken à la king

Overall timing 35 minutes

Freezing Suitable

To serve 4

1 lb	Cooked boneless chicken	450 g
1	Onion	1
1	Large green pepper	1
2 oz	Butter	50 g
2 oz	Plain flour	50 g
2 tbsp	Cold milk	2x15 ml
½ pint	Warm milk	300 ml
	Salt and pepper	
	Grated nutmeg	
2 tbsp	Sherry	2x15 ml

Cut chicken into small pieces. Peel and finely chop onion. Deseed pepper and finely chop half of it.

Melt the butter in a saucepan and gently fry onion and pepper till onion is transparent.

Stir in the flour with a wooden spoon, then the cold milk. Remove from heat and gradually add the warm milk. Bring to the boil. Season with salt, pepper and a pinch of nutmeg. Reduce heat and simmer gently for 15 minutes.

Add chicken and sherry and cook for 5 minutes more. Stir frequently during this time to prevent mixture sticking.

Meanwhile, slice the remaining pepper and blanch in boiling water for 5 minutes.

Place chicken and sauce on a warmed serving plate and surround with the pepper slices. Serve with boiled rice or noodles.

Mustard chicken casserole

Overall timing 1 hour

Freezing Not suitable

To serve 4

3½ lb	Ovenready chicken	1.6 kg
1	Onion	1
4 tbsp	Oil	4x15 ml
	Salt and pepper	
1 lb	Potatoes	450 g
2 oz	Back bacon	50 g
1 tbsp	Vinegar	15 ml
2	Cloves	2
1	Bay leaf	1
¼ teasp	Grated nutmeg	1.25 ml
1 teasp	Powdered mustard	5 ml
¼ pint	Chicken stock	150 ml
8 oz	Can of tomatoes	227 g

Wipe the chicken and cut into 8 portions. Peel and finely slice the onion. Heat the oil in a flameproof casserole and fry the onion till transparent.

Add the chicken portions and fry for about 10 minutes, turning frequently. Season.

Meanwhile, peel and dice the potatoes. Add to the pan with the derinded bacon, vinegar, cloves, bay leaf, nutmeg and seasoning. Stir the mustard into the stock (made with cubes if necessary) and pour into pan with the canned tomatoes and juice. Mix well, pressing tomatoes to break them up, and bring to the boil. Reduce the heat and simmer for about 30 minutes till the chicken and potatoes are tender.

Adjust the seasoning and discard bay leaf before serving.

Chicken baked in salt

Overall timing 1¾ hours

Freezing Not suitable

To serve 4–6

3½ lb	Ovenready chicken	1.6 kg
1	Sprig of fresh tarragon	1
	Black pepper	
6 lb	Coarse sea-salt	2.6 kg

Preheat the oven to 450°F (230°C) Gas 8.

Wipe the chicken, put the tarragon inside and sprinkle inside and out with pepper. Truss with string.

Line a casserole with a large sheet of foil and spread with one-third of the salt. Place chicken breast-bone down on salt. Cover completely with remaining salt. Fold the foil over the top of the chicken and join together at top, sealing well. Bake, covered, near the top of the oven for 1½ hours.

Take the chicken out of the oven, unwrap and remove the crust of salt. Brush off any salt that clings, then carve the chicken in the usual way.

Pastry-wrapped stuffed chicken

Overall timing 2¼ hours

Freezing Not suitable

To serve 4

3 lb	Ovenready chicken	1.4 kg
	Salt	
1 oz	Butter	25 g
12 oz	Shortcrust pastry	350 g
1	Egg	1
Stuffing		
8 oz	Mushrooms	225 g
1 oz	Butter	25 g
2 tbsp	Sherry	2x15 ml
	Salt and pepper	
6 oz	Chicken livers	175 g
1	Small onion	1
2 oz	Dried breadcrumbs	50 g

First make stuffing. Slice mushrooms. Melt butter in a pan and fry mushrooms for 3 minutes. Add sherry and cook for 3 minutes. Season with salt and pepper.

Finely chop chicken livers. Peel and finely chop onion. Add both to pan with breadcrumbs and mix well. Heat gently for 5 minutes.

Season chicken inside and out with salt. Stuff with liver mixture and close the opening. Melt butter in a roasting tin and brown chicken on all sides for 20 minutes.

Preheat the oven to 400°F (200°C) Gas 6.

Roll out dough on a lightly floured surface till about ¼ inch (6 mm) thick and large enough to wrap round chicken. Remove chicken from roasting tin. Drain and allow to cool slightly, then place, breast side down, on dough. Moisten edges and wrap dough round chicken. Press edges together well.

Place chicken on greased baking tray with seam underneath. Use dough trimmings to decorate top. Brush with beaten egg and bake for 1½–1¾ hours. If pastry shows signs of overbrowning, cover with foil.

Chicken in soured cream

Overall timing 1 hour

Freezing Not suitable

To serve 4

3 lb	Chicken portions	1.4 kg
2 tbsp	Plain flour	2x15 ml
4 oz	Button mushrooms	125 g
1	Onion	1
2 oz	Butter	50 g
2 tbsp	Oil	2x15 ml
	Salt and pepper	
2 tbsp	Brandy	2x15 ml
¼ pint	Carton of soured cream	150 ml

Wash chicken portions and dry on kitchen paper. Coat lightly with the flour. Wipe and slice mushrooms. Peel and slice onion.

Heat butter and oil in a frying pan and fry onion till golden. Add floured chicken portions and brown on all sides. Season with salt and pepper. Cover and cook for 40 minutes.

Pour brandy over the chicken and heat for a few minutes, then set alight. When the flames have died down, add the sliced mushrooms and cook over a gentle heat for 5 minutes.

Add soured cream to pan. Heat through, stirring, for 2 minutes. Do not allow to boil. Serve at once with noodles and a mixed salad.

Poached chicken

Overall timing 2 hours

Freezing Not suitable

To serve 4

8	Chicken legs and wings	8
12 oz	Carrots	350 g
8 oz	Button onions	225 g
2	Stalks of celery	2
	Salt	
1 lb	Potatoes	450 g

Put chicken joints in a large saucepan and cover with cold water. Peel and chop carrots; peel onions; chop celery. Add a few pieces of carrot, four onions, all the celery and salt to chicken. Bring slowly to the boil, then reduce the heat until just simmering, cover and cook for about 1½ hours.

Meanwhile, cook remaining carrots and onions in boiling salted water for 5 minutes. Peel and chop potatoes and add to pan. Simmer for a further 20 minutes. Drain and keep hot.

Drain chicken (keep the cooking liquor and vegetables for soup) and serve on a warmed plate with the separately cooked carrots, onions and potatoes.

Chicken Kiev

Overall timing 1½ hours

Freezing Suitable: egg, crumb and fry after thawing

To serve 4

4 oz	Softened butter	125 g
2 tbsp	Lemon juice	2x15 ml
1	Garlic clove	1
1 tbsp	Chopped parsley	15 ml
	Salt and pepper	
4	Boneless chicken breasts	4
	Oil for frying	
3 tbsp	Plain flour	3x15 ml
1	Egg	1
3 tbsp	Fresh white breadcrumbs	3x15 ml

Work together the butter and lemon juice until smooth. Peel and crush the garlic and add to the butter with the parsley and seasoning. Mix well. Shape into a cylinder, wrap in foil and place in freezer for 1 hour to firm.

Place the chicken breasts between two sheets of dampened greaseproof paper on a flat surface and beat flat with a heavy knife or wooden mallet until thin.

Heat the oil in a deep-fryer to 350°F (170°C).

Place a piece of butter on each chicken breast. Roll chicken round butter and secure with a cocktail stick. Coat each piece of chicken all over with the flour, then dip in the beaten egg to cover and finally in the breadcrumbs, pressing them on well. Fry for 12–15 minutes until golden brown. Drain on kitchen paper, remove cocktail sticks and serve immediately with lemon wedges and a green salad.

Soufflé-topped chicken

Overall timing 1¼ hours

Freezing Not suitable

To serve 4–6

2 tbsp	Oil	2x15 ml
3 lb	Chicken portions	1.4 kg
	Salt and pepper	
1 lb	Can of sweetcorn kernels	450 g
2 tbsp	Fresh breadcrumbs	2x15 ml
Sauce		
3 oz	Butter	75 g
2 oz	Plain flour	50 g
¼ pint	Milk	150 ml
2	Eggs	2
¼ pint	Carton of single cream	150 ml
	Salt and pepper	
	Grated nutmeg	

Preheat the oven to 400°F (200°C) Gas 6.

Heat oil in flameproof casserole. Add chicken and cook for about 10 minutes until pieces are browned on all sides. Season with salt and pepper.

Drain corn and add to the casserole with 4 tbsp (4x15 ml) of the liquid.

To make the sauce, melt 2 oz (50 g) of the butter in a saucepan, sprinkle with the flour and cook till browned, stirring all the time. Gradually add milk and cook, stirring, for 5 minutes. Remove from heat.

Separate eggs. Mix cream, egg yolks, salt, pepper and a pinch of nutmeg in a bowl. Stir into the sauce and heat through but do not boil. Remove from heat and set aside.

Beat egg whites in a bowl until they hold stiff peaks. Fold into sauce with a metal spoon and pour over corn and chicken mixture. Sprinkle with breadcrumbs, dot with remaining butter and bake in the centre of the oven for 45 minutes. Serve with broccoli garnished with chopped hard-boiled eggs.

Crisp lemon chicken

Overall timing 30 minutes plus marination

Freezing Not suitable

To serve 4

8	Chicken portions	8
3 tbsp	Lemon juice	3x15 ml
2 tbsp	Oil	2x15 ml
2 oz	Plain flour	50 g
	Salt and pepper	
½ teasp	Paprika	2.5 ml
	Lemon wedges	

Wash and dry chicken portions. Mix together lemon juice and oil and rub into the chicken. Cover and leave to marinate for 2–3 hours.

Preheat the grill. Mix together the flour, seasoning and paprika.

Arrange chicken portions skin-side down on grill rack. Sift half the seasoned flour over the chicken and grill for 7–10 minutes.

Turn chicken portions over. Sprinkle with remaining sifted flour and grill for a further 7–10 minutes until crisp and golden, and juices run clear when a skewer is inserted. Arrange on a warmed serving dish and garnish with lemon wedges. Serve with a bean, cucumber and tomato salad.

Chicken Maryland

Overall timing 1¾ hours

Freezing Not suitable

To serve 8

8	Boned chicken breasts	8
	Salt	
	Cayenne pepper	
2 oz	Plain flour	50 g
2	Eggs	2
4 oz	Fresh breadcrumbs	125 g
	Oil for frying	
4	Bananas	4
12	Bacon rashers	12
Corn fritters		
4 oz	Plain flour	125 g
1	Whole egg	1
¼ pint	Milk	150 ml
11½ oz	Sweetcorn kernels	325 g
1	Egg white	1

To make the fritter batter, sift flour and pinch of salt into a bowl and make a well in the centre. Add the whole egg and gradually beat in the milk. Drain corn and add. Leave batter to stand.

Cut each chicken breast in half. Season with salt and cayenne pepper. Dip into the flour, then into beaten eggs, then into breadcrumbs.

Heat the oil in a deep-fryer until hot enough to brown a cube of bread in 30 seconds. Fry the chicken pieces a few at a time for about 10–15 minutes, depending on thickness. Remove from pan, drain on kitchen paper and keep hot. Skim surface of oil.

Peel bananas and cut into three, then halve each piece lengthways. Derind and stretch bacon rashers and cut in half. Wrap a piece of bacon round each piece of banana and secure with a wooden cocktail stick. Fry in hot oil, then drain and keep hot.

Whisk egg white till stiff and fold into fritter batter. Drop in spoonfuls into hot oil and fry till puffed and golden brown. Drain. Arrange fritters, chicken and bacon-wrapped bananas on plate and serve.

Tunisian chicken

Overall timing 2¼ hours

Freezing Not suitable

To serve 4

3 lb	Ovenready chicken with giblets	1.4 kg
	Salt and pepper	
5 oz	Sweetcorn kernels	150 g
3	Carrots	3
3	Medium potatoes	3
4	Tomatoes	4
4 oz	Cheddar cheese	125 g
1	Egg	1
2 tbsp	Breadcrumbs	2x15 ml
1	Hard-boiled egg	1
1	Stalk of celery	1
1	Sprig of parsley	1
2 oz	Butter	50 g
4 tbsp	Oil	4x15 ml

Season chicken inside and out. Chop heart, liver and gizzard. Drain sweetcorn. Peel carrots and potatoes. Blanch, peel and quarter tomatoes.

Dice the cheese and mix with the sweetcorn, giblets, egg and breadcrumbs. Mash the hard-boiled egg with a fork and add to the mixture with seasoning. Mix well. Stuff the chicken with the mixture, then close opening.

Put carrots, potatoes and tomatoes into a flameproof casserole with celery and parsley. Cover with 2½ pints (1.5 litres) water and bring to the boil. Lower heat and add chicken with half the butter. Cover and simmer for 1½ hours.

Remove chicken and drain on kitchen paper. Strain cooking liquor and return to casserole. Purée vegetables and add to casserole. Heat soup through.

Heat remaining butter and oil in a frying pan. Put in whole chicken and brown evenly, turning it over with two spoons. Bring chicken and soup to table in separate dishes.

Chicken pineapple salad

Overall timing 30 minutes plus chilling

Freezing Not suitable

To serve 4–6

4 oz	Long grain rice	125 g
	Salt and pepper	
4 oz	Frozen sweetcorn kernels	125 g
1	Celery heart	1
1	Cold roast chicken	1
8 oz	Can of pineapple rings	227 g
4	Small firm tomatoes	4
2 oz	Black olives	50 g
3 tbsp	Salad oil	3 x 15 ml
1 tbsp	Lemon juice	15 ml
1 tbsp	Chopped chives	15 ml
1	Round lettuce	1
1	Hard-boiled egg	1

Cook the rice in boiling salted water till tender, adding the sweetcorn for the last 5 minutes of cooking. Drain and rinse under cold water, then drain thoroughly.

Trim celery heart and cut into 2 inch (5 cm) lengths. Put into a large bowl with the celery leaves. Cut the chicken into bite-size pieces, discarding the skin and bones. Add to the bowl.

Drain the pineapple; chop three of the rings. Quarter the tomatoes and add to the bowl with the chopped pineapple, olives, rice and sweetcorn.

Mix together the oil, lemon juice, chives and seasoning. Pour over the salad and toss lightly. Chill for 30 minutes.

Wash and dry the lettuce and use to line a salad bowl. Pile the salad into the centre and garnish with the remaining pineapple rings and the hard-boiled egg quartered lengthways. Serve with crusty bread.

Chicken croquettes

Overall timing 30 minutes

Freezing Suitable: reheat in 375°F (190°C) Gas 5 oven for 20 minutes

To serve 4–6

12 oz	Cooked boneless chicken	350 g
3 oz	Butter	75 g
3½ oz	Plain flour	90 g
½ pint	Milk	300 ml
	Salt and pepper	
	Grated nutmeg	
2	Egg yolks	2
1 tbsp	Grated cheese	15 ml
1 tbsp	Chopped parsley	15 ml
	Oil for frying	
1	Egg	1
4 oz	Dried breadcrumbs	125 g
	Sprigs of parsley	
	Lemon wedges	

Finely chop or mince chicken.

To make sauce, melt the butter in a saucepan over a low heat and stir in 2 tbsp (2x15 ml) of the flour. When the mixture begins to froth, add the cold milk, salt, pepper and a pinch of grated nutmeg. Whisk until the sauce thickens.

Remove from heat and stir in egg yolks and cheese. Turn into a bowl and mix in chicken and chopped parsley. Cool.

Heat oil for frying to 340°F (170°C) or till bread cube browns in 1 minute.

Using your hands, shape chicken mixture into small cylindrical croquettes. Roll them in the remaining flour, then in the lightly beaten egg to coat them completely and finally in the breadcrumbs, pressing them on well with a palette knife or spatula.

Fry the croquettes, four or five at a time, in the hot oil until golden brown. Drain on kitchen paper and serve hot, garnished with parsley and lemon.

Welsh chicken and mace pie

Overall timing 1 hour

Freezing Not suitable

To serve 6

1½ lb	Cooked chicken	700 g
4 oz	Cooked tongue	125 g
1	Onion	1
4	Leeks	4
3	Stalks of celery	3
2 oz	Butter	50 g
1 teasp	Ground mace	5 ml
1 tbsp	Chopped parsley	15 ml
½ pint	Chicken stock	300 ml
	Salt and pepper	
12 oz	Shortcrust pastry	350 g
1	Egg	1

Preheat oven to 400°F (200°C) Gas 6.

Chop chicken into medium-size pieces. Cut the tongue into strips. Peel and thinly slice onion. Trim leeks, then cut into thin slices. Trim and finely chop the celery. Melt butter.

Put chicken, tongue and prepared vegetables in a bowl with mace, parsley and butter and mix well. Place in a large pie dish and add stock and seasoning.

Roll out dough and place on dish. Press edge to dish to seal. Lightly beat the egg and brush over the dough. Bake for 40 minutes, or until the pastry is golden. Serve immediately with mashed potatoes.

Chicken pieces with nutty sauce

Overall timing 1 hour plus marination

Freezing Not suitable

To serve 4

5	Onions	5
1	Garlic clove	1
2 oz	Walnuts	50 g
	Salt	
3 tbsp	Lemon juice	3x15 ml
4	Boned chicken breasts	4
2 tbsp	Groundnut oil	2x15 ml
	Pinch of chilli powder	
2 oz	Roasted peanuts	50 g
2 teasp	Soy sauce	2x5 ml
½ pint	Water	300 ml

Peel and finely chop two onions. Peel and crush garlic. Place both in a mortar or blender with walnuts and salt. Crush or blend to a paste, gradually adding 2 tbsp (2x15 ml) lemon juice to give a creamy mixture. Cut chicken into bite-size pieces. Place in a shallow dish and pour walnut mixture over. Leave to marinate for 1 hour, turning occasionally.

Meanwhile, peel and finely chop two onions. Heat half oil in a frying pan and fry onions till crisp and golden. Remove from pan and drain. Preheat the grill.

Peel and finely chop remaining onion and purée in mortar or blender with chilli powder, salt and peanuts till smooth. Heat remaining oil in pan and fry peanut mixture for 3 minutes, stirring constantly. Stir in soy sauce, water and remaining lemon juice. Cook over low heat for 5 minutes.

Thread chicken pieces on to four oiled skewers. Grill for 10 minutes, turning frequently and brushing with walnut mixture. Add any remaining walnut mixture and fried onions to peanut sauce and heat through.

Poule-au-pot

Overall timing 4 hours

Freezing Not suitable

To serve 6

2 oz	Streaky bacon	50 g
4 oz	Pork sausagemeat	125 g
2 oz	Fresh breadcrumbs	50 g
2 tbsp	Chopped parsley	2 x 15 ml
	Salt and pepper	
2	Eggs	2
3½ lb	Boiling chicken	1.6 kg
4	Medium-size onions	4
4	Small turnips	4
6	Large carrots	6
2	Leeks	2
4	Stalks of celery	4
2 oz	Dripping	50 g
	Bouquet garni	
12 oz	Long grain rice	350 g

Derind bacon, reserving rinds, and chop finely. Mix sausagemeat, bacon, breadcrumbs, parsley and seasoning and bind with eggs. Spoon into chicken and truss.

Peel onions, turnips and carrots. Trim leeks and celery. Heat dripping in a large pan and brown chicken all over. Add one of the onions, turnips, leeks and celery stalks and two carrots and fry for 3 minutes. Pour off excess fat.

Add bouquet garni, bacon rinds, giblets and cold water to cover the chicken and bring to the boil. Skim off any scum. Cover and simmer for about 2¼ hours.

Discard vegetables, bacon rinds and bouquet garni. Add remaining vegetables and seasoning. Cover and simmer for a further 45 minutes. Remove from heat. Strain 2¼ pints (1.3 litres) of stock into another saucepan. Keep chicken hot.

Add rice to stock with salt and cover tightly. Bring to boil and simmer for 15–20 minutes till rice is tender.

Fluff rice and arrange on a serving dish. Place chicken on rice and discard trussing strings. Arrange vegetables around chicken and serve.

Chicken supreme

Overall timing 2 hours

Freezing Not suitable

To serve 4

2	Carrots	2
2	Onions	2
2	Leeks	2
1	Stalk of celery	1
	Salt	
2½ pints	Water or stock	1.5 litres
3 lb	Ovenready chicken	1.4 kg
½	Lemon	½
8 oz	Rice	225 g
Sauce		
2 oz	Butter	50 g
1 tbsp	Plain flour	15 ml
2	Egg yolks	2
2 tbsp	Single cream	2x15 ml
	Salt and pepper	

Peel carrots and onions. Chop leeks and celery. Bring salted water or stock to the boil in a flameproof casserole, add prepared vegetables and cook for 15 minutes.

Rub chicken with the lemon. Add to casserole, cover and simmer gently for 1 hour. (If you prefer, chicken joints can be used instead of a whole chicken – they need only to be cooked for 45 minutes.)

Measure out 1 pint (560 ml) stock from casserole and place in a saucepan. Continue cooking chicken for a further 15 minutes. Bring stock in saucepan to the boil, add rice and cook for 15 minutes.

Meanwhile, prepare sauce. Melt butter in a saucepan and stir in flour. Measure out another 1 pint (560 ml) stock from casserole and gradually stir into pan. Cook, stirring till thickened. Remove from heat and stir in egg yolks and then cream. Season.

Drain rice and place on warmed serving dish. Remove chicken from casserole, cut into portions and arrange on top of rice. Pour sauce over and serve.

Chicken with aubergine and tomatoes

Overall timing 50 minutes

Freezing Not suitable

To serve 4

1	Aubergine	1
	Salt and pepper	
1	Green pepper	1
2	Large onions	2
6 tbsp	Oil	6x15 ml
4	Chicken joints	4
¾ pint	Tomato juice	400 ml
12 oz	Ripe tomatoes	350 g

Slice the aubergine. Sprinkle with salt and leave for 15 minutes. Meanwhile, deseed and slice the pepper. Peel and slice the onions.

Heat the oil in a flameproof casserole, add the chicken and fry over a moderate heat, turning frequently, till browned all over. Remove from the pan and reserve.

Add the onions and pepper and fry for 5 minutes. Return the chicken to the casserole, add the tomato juice and seasoning and bring to the boil.

Rinse the aubergine and pat dry on kitchen paper. Add to the chicken, cover and simmer for 25 minutes.

Blanch, peel and quarter the tomatoes. Add to the chicken and cook for a further 5 minutes. Serve with plain boiled rice and a green salad.

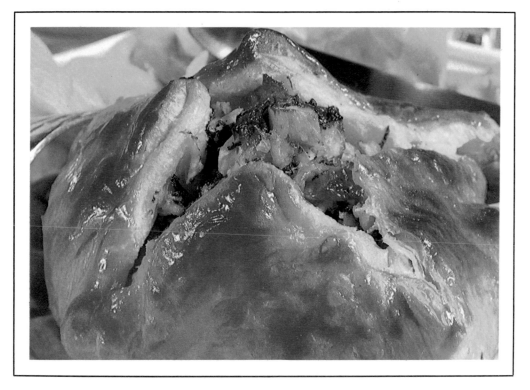

Chicken parcels

Overall timing 45 minutes

Freezing Suitable: bake from frozen, allowing 35–45 minutes

To serve 6

13 oz	Frozen puff pastry	375 g
1	Medium-size onion	1
1 oz	Butter	25 g
10 oz	Cooked boneless chicken	275 g
3 tbsp	Chopped parsley	3x15 ml
4 tbsp	Double cream	4x15 ml
	Salt and pepper	
3	Slices of cooked ham	3
1	Egg yolk	1
6	Lettuce leaves	6

Thaw pastry. Preheat oven to 400°F (200°C) Gas 6.

Peel and chop onion and fry in the butter till transparent.

Set aside six fairly large pieces of chicken and finely chop the rest. Put chopped chicken into a bowl with the parsley and fried onion. Lightly beat the cream, then stir into the chicken with seasoning.

Roll out the dough on a lightly floured surface. Cut out six 5 inch (12.5 cm) squares. Cut ham slices in half and place one piece in centre of each dough square. Top with a piece of chicken, then cover with chopped chicken mixture. Dampen dough edges with cold water. Fold corners to centre to cover the filling, pinching the edges together, but leaving a small hole in the top. Place parcels on a greased baking tray.

Beat the egg yolk with a pinch of salt and brush over parcels. Bake for 25 minutes or until well risen and golden brown. Serve the parcels on lettuce leaves.

Chicken in a basket

Overall timing 40 minutes

Freezing Not suitable

To serve 2

2x1 lb	Ovenready poussins	2x450 g
2 tbsp	Oil	2x15 ml
	Salt and pepper	
1 lb	Potatoes	450 g
	Oil for frying	
	Fresh parsley	
1	Small onion	1

Preheat the oven to 400°F (200°C) Gas 6.

Place the poussins in roasting tin. Brush with oil and season well. Roast for 30 minutes, or until juices from the legs run clear when pierced with a skewer.

Meanwhile, peel potatoes and cut into thin, matchstick chips. Heat oil in a deep-fryer to 340°F (170°C). Fry chips for 3–5 minutes till golden. Drain well.

Arrange napkins in two small baskets. Place chips in folds of cloth. Place poussins in baskets. Garnish with parsley sprigs and onion rings. Eat with your fingers or a knife and fork if preferred.

Variation

To make barbecue-style poussins, mix together 2 tbsp (2x15 ml) tomato purée, 1 tbsp (15 ml) Worcestershire sauce, 1 tbsp (15 ml) oil, 1 peeled and crushed garlic clove and seasoning. Spread over poussins, cover with foil and roast for 40 minutes. Serve as above.

Chicken with lentils

Overall timing 1¼ hours

Freezing Not suitable

To serve 6

12 oz	Continental lentils	350 g
1	Onion	1
1	Carrot	1
	Bouquet garni	
	Salt and pepper	
1 lb	Boned chicken	450 g
1 tbsp	Oil	15 ml
3 oz	Butter	75 g
1 tbsp	Chopped parsley	15 ml

Wash and pick over lentils. Place in a saucepan and add enough cold water just to cover. Peel and finely chop onion. Peel and halve carrot. Add to lentils with bouquet garni and seasoning. Bring to boil, cover and simmer for 35 minutes.

Meanwhile, cut chicken into neat pieces. Heat oil and half the butter in a frying pan, add chicken pieces and fry for 5 minutes, turning once. Add chicken to lentils, cover and simmer for a further 30 minutes.

Discard bouquet garni and carrot. Stir the remaining butter into lentils. Taste and adjust seasoning. Arrange chicken and lentils on a warmed serving dish and sprinkle with parsley. Serve immediately with a mixed salad.

Chicken with pineapple

Overall timing 45 minutes

Freezing Not suitable

To serve 2

1½ lb	Chicken joints	675 g
2 teasp	Potato flour or cornflour	2x5 ml
3 tbsp	Oil	3x15 ml
1 tbsp	Soy sauce	15 ml
1½ teasp	Dry sherry	7.5 ml
	Salt and pepper	
4 oz	Canned pineapple rings or chunks	125 g

Remove meat from chicken joints and cut it into chunky pieces.

Mix together potato flour or cornflour, half the oil, the soy sauce, sherry and seasoning in a bowl. Add the chicken pieces and coat well. Leave to marinate for 15 minutes.

Heat the rest of the oil in a heavy-based saucepan. Drain the chicken, saving the marinade, and add to the pan. Cook over a fairly high heat for 5 minutes, stirring constantly.

Drain the pineapple, reserving 4 tbsp (4x15 ml) of the syrup. Cut the rings into sections or halve the chunks. Add the reserved marinade from the chicken and the pineapple pieces to the pan and cook for a further 12 minutes, continually turning the chicken over.

When the chicken is golden brown, add the reserved pineapple syrup, adjust seasoning and cook for a further 5 minutes. Serve with saffron rice.

Chicken in foil

Overall timing 1 hour

Freezing Not suitable

To serve 2

2	Boned chicken or turkey breasts	2
	Salt and pepper	
1 tbsp	Plain flour	15 ml
2 oz	Butter	50 g
2	Sage leaves	2
1 tbsp	Brandy	15 ml
4 fl oz	Chicken stock	120 ml
4 oz	Chicken livers	125 g
2 oz	Mushrooms	50 g
1 oz	Cooked ham	25 g

Coat chicken or turkey breasts with seasoned flour. Melt half butter in a frying pan and fry chicken or turkey breasts on each side till golden. Add sage, brandy and stock and bring to boil. Cover and simmer for 15 minutes.

Preheat the oven to 400°F (200°C) Gas 6.

Finely chop chicken livers, mushrooms and ham. Melt remaining butter in another frying pan and stir-fry liver, mushrooms and ham for 5 minutes. Remove from heat.

Cut two large foil rectangles and put a chicken or turkey breast in centre of each. Spread liver mixture on top and spoon over pan juices. Wrap foil round to make secure parcels, then place in roasting tin. Bake for 20 minutes.

Stuffed turkey rolls

Overall timing 1¼ hours

Freezing Not suitable

To serve 2

1	Small onion	1
1	Garlic clove	1
2 oz	Butter	50 g
1	Large tomato	1
	Salt and pepper	
1 oz	Fresh breadcrumbs	25 g
1½ teasp	Chopped parsley	7.5 ml
½	Egg	½
2x6 oz	Turkey escalopes	2x175 g
2	Bacon rashers	2
5 tbsp	Dry white wine	5x15 ml
1 teasp	Lemon juice	5 ml

Peel and finely chop onion and garlic. Melt half butter in a saucepan and fry onion till golden.

Blanch, peel and chop tomato and add to pan with garlic and seasoning. Simmer till thick. Remove from heat; add crumbs, parsley and egg.

Season escalopes. Divide stuffing between them and roll up. Wrap a bacon rasher round each roll and secure with wooden cocktail sticks.

Melt remaining butter in frying pan and fry rolls till browned all over. Add wine and lemon juice, cover and simmer for 20 minutes.

Turkey fries

Overall timing 40 minutes plus marination

Freezing Not suitable

To serve 8

4 tbsp	Oil	4x15 ml
3 tbsp	Lemon juice	3x15 ml
	Salt	
8x4 oz	Slices of turkey breast	8x125 g
4 teasp	Dijon mustard	4x5 ml
2	Eggs	2
8 oz	Fresh breadcrumbs	225 g
2 oz	Butter	50 g
	Chopped parsley	
	Lemon wedges	

Mix 2 tbsp (2x15 ml) of the oil with the lemon juice and a pinch of salt in a shallow dish. Add the turkey, mix well and leave to marinate for 1 hour.

Drain the turkey and pat dry on kitchen paper. Spread thinly with the mustard. Beat the eggs lightly on a plate and use to coat turkey. Dip turkey slices into the breadcrumbs, pressing them on gently.

Melt the butter and remaining oil in a frying pan and gently fry the turkey for about 10 minutes on each side, till tender and golden.

Drain on kitchen paper and arrange on a warmed dish. Garnish with chopped parsley and lemon wedges and serve immediately with a tomato and onion salad dressed with vinaigrette.

Turkey with lemon sauce

Overall timing 30 minutes

Freezing Not suitable

To serve 6

6	Slices of turkey breast	6
	Salt and pepper	
2 tbsp	Plain flour	2x15 ml
2	Thick rashers of back bacon	2
3 oz	Butter	75 g
$\frac{1}{4}$ pint	Chicken stock	150 ml
2 tbsp	Lemon juice	2x15 ml
2 tbsp	Chopped parsley	2x15 ml
	Lemon slices	
	Sprigs of parsley	

Place each slice of turkey between two sheets of damp greaseproof paper and flatten with a rolling pin. Season the flour and use to coat the turkey. Derind bacon and cut into strips.

Melt the butter in a frying pan and cook the bacon for 5 minutes. Add turkey pieces and fry for 3–5 minutes on each side. Remove turkey and bacon from pan and arrange on a warmed serving plate. Keep hot.

Add any remaining seasoned flour to pan and stir well with a wooden spoon, scraping the sediment from the bottom of the pan. Gradually add the stock (made with a cube if necessary) and bring to the boil. Simmer gently for 5 minutes.

Remove pan from heat and stir in the lemon juice and chopped parsley. Taste and adjust seasoning. Pour over the turkey breasts and garnish with lemon slices and parsley sprigs. Serve immediately with a mixed salad.

Oven-fried rabbit

Overall timing 1¼ hours

Freezing Not suitable

To serve 4–6

2 lb	Young rabbit	900 g
	Salt and pepper	
3 tbsp	Plain flour	3x15 ml
½ teasp	Paprika	2.5 ml
2	Eggs	2
2 tbsp	Milk	2x15 ml
2 oz	Dried breadcrumbs	50 g
1 oz	Butter	25 g
4 tbsp	Oil	4x15 ml
4 tbsp	Thick mayonnaise	4x15 ml
2 tbsp	Horseradish sauce	2x15 ml
2 tbsp	Single cream	2x15 ml
1 teasp	Lemon juice	5 ml

Preheat the oven to 350°F (180°C) Gas 4.

Cut rabbit into small pieces, removing small bones. Season flour, add paprika and coat rabbit pieces.

Beat eggs with milk. Dip rabbit into egg mixture then into breadcrumbs.

Heat butter and oil in a frying pan and brown rabbit pieces on both sides. Place on baking tray and bake for about 40 minutes till tender.

Meanwhile, mix mayonnaise, horseradish sauce, cream, lemon juice and seasoning. Serve with rabbit.

Stuffed drumsticks

Overall timing 2 hours

Freezing Not suitable

To serve 4

2x1 lb	Turkey drumsticks	2x450 g
	Salt and pepper	
4 oz	Smoked back bacon	125 g
	Rosemary leaves	
2 oz	Butter	50 g
2 teasp	Plain flour	2x5 ml
¼ pint	Chicken stock	150 ml
4 tbsp	Dry vermouth	4x15 ml

Preheat the oven to 375°F (190°C) Gas 5.

Remove bone from drumsticks. Return drumsticks to their original shape, then season. Derind and chop bacon and stuff into cavities in the drumsticks. Close openings with skewers. Pierce the skin in several places and insert the rosemary leaves. Rub butter over drumsticks and place in a flameproof casserole. Cover and bake for about 1¼ hours.

Lift out the drumsticks and remove the skewers. Cut into thick slices, arrange on a serving dish and keep hot.

Add the flour to the casserole and stir over a low heat for 1 minute. Gradually add the stock and vermouth and bring to the boil, stirring. Simmer for 2 minutes then adjust the seasoning to taste.

Pour sauce over the turkey.

Rabbit carbonnade

Overall timing 2½ hours

Freezing Not suitable

To serve 4–6

2½ lb	Ovenready rabbit	1.1 kg
3 tbsp	Plain flour	3x15 ml
2	Carrots	2
1	Onion	1
4 oz	Streaky bacon rashers	125 g
2 oz	Butter	50 g
	Bouquet garni	
1	Garlic clove	1
	Salt and pepper	
1 pint	Pale ale	560 ml

Preheat the oven to 350°F (180°C) Gas 4.

Cut the rabbit into neat pieces. Toss in the flour till lightly coated.

Peel and thinly slice the carrots. Peel and chop the onion. Derind the bacon and cut into strips. Melt the butter in a flameproof casserole and fry the carrots, onion and bacon for 5 minutes. Add the rabbit pieces and fry till browned.

Add the bouquet garni, peeled and crushed garlic and seasoning. Pour the ale over, cover tightly and cook in the oven for 1¾–2 hours till the rabbit is tender. Serve with boiled potatoes.

Roast pigeons with mushrooms

Overall timing 50 minutes

Freezing Not suitable

To serve 2

4 oz	Small onions	125 g
2	Small ovenready pigeons	2
2	Sprigs of rosemary	2
4	Sage leaves	4
3 oz	Streaky bacon rashers	75 g
3 oz	Butter	75 g
4 oz	Mushrooms	125 g
5 tbsp	Dry white wine	5 x 15 ml
	Salt and pepper	

Preheat the oven to 450°F (230°C) Gas 8.

Blanch the onions in boiling water for 5 minutes, then peel. Wipe the pigeons and put a sprig of rosemary, two sage leaves and a rasher of bacon into each. Put into a roasting tin and spread half the butter over. Roast for about 15 minutes till browned.

Meanwhile, derind and chop the remaining bacon. Melt the remaining butter in a flameproof casserole and fry the onions and bacon till just golden. Thickly slice the mushrooms. Add to onions and bacon and fry for 2 minutes.

Remove the pigeons from the oven and reduce the temperature to 400°F (200°C) Gas 6. Put the pigeons into the casserole on top of the vegetables, pour the wine over and season.

Cover the casserole, place in the oven and cook for a further 15–20 minutes till the pigeons are tender. Adjust the seasoning before serving.

Pigeons with saffron

Overall timing 1 hour

Freezing Not suitable

To serve 6

3	Ovenready pigeons	3
	Salt and pepper	
1 tbsp	Plain flour	15 ml
1 tbsp	Oil	15 ml
2 oz	Butter	50 g
6	Saffron strands	6
3 tbsp	Lemon juice	3x15 ml
1	Small onion	1
2 tbsp	Chopped parsley	2x15 ml

Quarter the pigeons. Lightly coat with seasoned flour. Heat the oil and butter in a saucepan, add the pigeon pieces and fry for about 10 minutes till lightly browned on all sides.

Meanwhile, pound the saffron in a small bowl. Add 2 tbsp (2x15 ml) warm water and leave to soak for 10 minutes.

Add saffron, soaking liquid and lemon juice to the pan. Cover and cook over a low heat for 20 minutes till meat is tender. Remove pigeon pieces from the pan, place on a warmed serving dish and keep hot.

Peel and finely chop the onion. Add to the liquid in the pan with parsley and seasoning. Cook for 3 minutes, then spoon over the pigeon quarters and serve immediately with boiled rice.

Duck with oranges

Overall timing 2 hours

Freezing Not suitable

To serve 4

4 lb	Ovenready duck	1.8 kg
	Salt and pepper	
½ pint	Hot chicken stock	300 ml
2 teasp	Caster sugar	2x5 ml
2 tbsp	White wine vinegar	2x15 ml
4	Oranges	4

Preheat the oven to 400°F (200°C) Gas 6.

Prick duck all over with a fork. Season well and place on rack in roasting tin. Roast for 45 minutes till brown and crisp.

Remove all but 1 tbsp (15 ml) of the fat from the tin. Pour hot stock over duck. Cover and roast for a further 30 minutes till cooked.

Heat sugar gently in a pan until it caramelizes, then remove from heat and add vinegar. Remove duck and strain juices from roasting tin into sugar mixture. Replace duck in tin and keep warm.

Cut the rind from one orange into thin matchsticks. Squeeze the juice from two oranges and add to the pan with the rind. Cook gently for 5 minutes till the rind has softened.

Remove duck from oven and cut into portions. Arrange on warmed serving dish and spoon over a little of the orange sauce. Peel and segment remaining oranges and use to garnish duck. Serve with sautéed potatoes and peas, and with the rest of the sauce served in a sauce or gravy boat.

Duck with apples and cream

Overall timing 1 hour 20 minutes

Freezing Not suitable

To serve 4

3½ lb	Ovenready duck	1.6 kg
	Salt and pepper	
6	Granny Smith apples	6
1 oz	Butter	25 g
½ pint	Carton of single cream	284 ml

Preheat the oven to 400°F (200°C) Gas 6.

Sprinkle duck inside and out with salt and pepper. Prick all over with a fork and place on wire rack in roasting tin. Roast for 20 minutes, then reduce heat to 350°F (180°C) Gas 4.

Peel and core the apples. Cut two of them into quarters and leave the rest whole. Arrange around the duck, dot with butter and continue roasting for 1 hour or till tender.

Remove duck and apples from the tin. Place duck on serving plate. Keep hot. Pour off excess fat from pan juices, then stir in the cream. Replace apples in tin and baste thoroughly with the sauce. Cook for a further 5 minutes.

Arrange apples round duck. Spoon some sauce over. Serve rest separately.

Chicken liver brochettes

Overall timing 25 minutes

Freezing Not suitable

To serve 4

8 oz	Carton of chicken livers	225 g
2 oz	Piece of smoked streaky bacon	50 g
4 oz	Mushrooms	125 g
	Salt and pepper	
2 oz	Butter	50 g

Wash the chicken livers and dry on kitchen paper. Chop bacon into bite-size pieces. Wipe mushrooms.

Thread livers, bacon and mushrooms alternately on to skewers. Season with salt and pepper.

Melt the butter in a frying pan and cook brochettes for about 8 minutes, turning them from time to time. Alternatively, brush brochettes with oil and cook under a hot grill.

Serve hot with tomato sauce, rice and a mixed salad for lunch, or with crusty bread and butter for supper.

Chicken liver pancakes

Overall timing 45 minutes

Freezing Suitable: add cream and cheese and bake from frozen, covered, allowing 30–40 minutes

To serve 4

4 oz	**Chicken livers**	125 g
8 oz	**Button mushrooms**	225 g
1	**Small onion**	1
2 oz	**Butter**	50 g
	Salt and pepper	
6	**Slices of cooked ham**	6
3 tbsp	**Single cream**	3x15 ml
	Grated nutmeg	
2 oz	**Cheddar cheese**	50 g
Pancakes		
5 oz	**Plain flour**	150 g
¼ teasp	**Salt**	1.25 ml
2	**Eggs**	2
½ pint	**Beer**	300 ml
	Oil for frying	

Chop chicken livers. Chop mushrooms. Peel and finely chop onion. Melt butter in a saucepan and gently fry mushrooms and onion for 5 minutes. Add chopped livers and fry for 3–4 minutes. Season with salt and pepper.

To make pancakes, sift flour and salt into a bowl and make a well in the centre. Add eggs and beer and beat to a smooth batter. Heat a little oil in an 8 inch (20 cm) pancake or frying pan and make 12 pancakes.

Preheat oven to 400°F (200°C) Gas 6.

Cut slices of ham in half. Place one half on each pancake. Divide liver mixture between pancakes, then roll them up. Place side by side in greased baking dish. Pour cream over and sprinkle with nutmeg and grated cheese.

Bake for 15–20 minutes, or grill for 5 minutes. Serve hot.

Giblet fricassee

Overall timing 1½ hours

Freezing Not suitable

To serve 4

1¼ lb	Poultry giblets	600 g
1	Onion	1
3 tbsp	Oil	3x15 ml
¾ pint	Chicken stock	400 ml
1 teasp	Ground cumin	5 ml
	Salt and pepper	
1 tbsp	Plain flour	15 ml
2	Egg yolks	2
2 tbsp	Lemon juice	2x15 ml

Chop giblets. Peel and chop onion. Heat the oil in a saucepan and fry onion till transparent. Add giblets and brown on all sides. Pour in the stock and add cumin and seasoning. Bring to the boil, cover and simmer for about 1 hour or until giblets are tender.

Blend the flour with the egg yolks and mix in the lemon juice. Stir into fricassee and cook for a further 5 minutes, stirring. Serve with creamed potatoes and a mixed salad.

Savoury flans, pies and pizzas

Rich leek flan

Overall timing 1 hour

Freezing Suitable: reheat from frozen, covered, in 375°F (190°C) Gas 5 oven for 35 minutes

To serve 6–8

13 oz	Frozen puff pastry	375 g
2 lb	Leeks	900 g
2 oz	Butter	50 g
1 tbsp	Plain flour	15 ml
½ pint	Light stock	300 ml
	Salt and pepper	
1	Egg	1
1	Egg yolk	1
½ pint	Carton of single cream	284 ml

Thaw pastry. Preheat the oven to 425°F (220°C) Gas 7.

Trim leeks. Cut into 1 inch (2.5 cm) lengths. Blanch in boiling water for 5 minutes, then drain thoroughly.

Melt butter in a frying pan and fry the leeks for 5 minutes. Sprinkle with flour and cook until lightly browned. Gradually stir in the stock and bring to the boil. Season and cook gently for 10 minutes.

Meanwhile, roll out dough and use to line a 9 inch (23 cm) flan dish. Prick bottom several times with a fork.

Beat the whole egg, yolk and cream together in a bowl. Remove leeks from heat and add cream mixture. Pour into flan dish and spread evenly. Bake for 30 minutes till lightly set and golden. Serve hot.

Quiche lorraine

Overall timing 1½ hours

Freezing Suitable: reheat in hot oven

To serve 4–6

8 oz	Plain flour	225 g
	Salt and pepper	
5 oz	Butter	150 g
2 tbsp	Water	2x15 ml
2	Throughcut bacon rashers	2
3 oz	Cheddar cheese	75 g
2	Eggs	2
½ pint	Milk or single cream	300 ml

Sift the flour, salt and pepper into a bowl. Rub in 4 oz (125 g) of the butter till mixture resembles breadcrumbs. Gradually add the water and knead to a dough. Roll out and use to line a greased 8 inch (20 cm) pie plate or flan dish. Leave to stand for 30 minutes.

Preheat the oven to 400°F (200°C) Gas 6.

Derind and dice the bacon. Fry lightly in the remaining butter. Grate or thinly slice the cheese. Sprinkle bacon and cheese over the bottom of the flan case. Beat together the eggs, milk or cream and seasoning in a bowl. Pour mixture into flan. Do not overfill.

Bake for 15 minutes, then reduce heat to 325°F (170°C) Gas 3 and bake for further 25–30 minutes. Serve hot or cold with salad and potatoes.

Onion quiche

Overall timing 1½ hours

Freezing Suitable: reheat from frozen, covered, in 350°F (180°C) Gas 4 oven for 20 minutes

To serve 4

1 lb	Medium-size onions	450 g
2 oz	Lard	50 g
4 oz	Smoked streaky bacon	125 g
6 oz	Rich shortcrust pastry	175 g
3	Eggs	3
¼ pint	Milk	150 ml
¼ pint	Carton of single cream	150 ml
	Salt and pepper	

Preheat the oven to 400°F (200°C) Gas 6.

Peel and thinly slice the onions. Melt the lard in a frying pan and fry the onions over a moderate heat till pale golden.

Derind and dice the bacon and add to the pan. Fry for a further 4–5 minutes till the onions and bacon are golden brown.

Roll out the dough and use to line an 8½ inch (22 cm) flan dish. Prick the bottom and bake blind for 15 minutes.

Remove foil and baking beans and spread the onion and bacon mixture over the pastry base. Mix the eggs with the milk and cream and season to taste. Pour over the onions.

Bake for a further 25 minutes till lightly set and golden. Serve hot with mixed salads.

Bacon and corn flan

Overall timing 1 hour

Freezing Suitable: reheat in 425°F (220°C) Gas 7 oven for 10–15 minutes

To serve 6–8

4 oz	Streaky bacon rashers	125 g
8 oz	Shortcrust pastry	225 g
2	Eggs	2
¼ pint	Milk	150 ml
	Salt and pepper	
¼ teasp	Grated nutmeg	1.25 ml
	Cayenne pepper	
15 oz	Can of cream-style sweetcorn	425 g
4 oz	Strong Cheddar cheese	125 g

Preheat the oven to 450°F (230°C) Gas 8.

Derind and finely chop bacon. Put into a small ovenproof dish in the oven to draw off the fat.

Roll out the dough and use to line a 9 inch (23 cm) flan tin or pie plate.

Beat the eggs and milk together in a bowl and add salt, pepper, nutmeg and a pinch of cayenne pepper. Blend in the corn. Grate the cheese and mix three quarters of it into the egg and corn mixture.

Remove bacon from oven and brush a little of fat on the inside of the pastry case. Drain the bacon pieces and add half of them to the egg and corn mixture. Pour mixture into the pastry case. Sprinkle the rest of the cheese and remaining bacon on the top and bake in the centre of the oven for 20 minutes. Reduce the temperature to 350°F (180°C) Gas 4 and bake for a further 25 minutes. Serve hot or cool.

Welsh parsley flan

Overall timing 1 hour

Freezing Suitable: reheat from frozen in 350°F (180°C) Gas 4 oven for 25 minutes

To serve 4–6

8 oz	Shortcrust pastry	225 g
4 oz	Streaky bacon	125 g
1 oz	Butter	25 g
3	Eggs	3
½ pint	Milk	300 ml
3 tbsp	Chopped parsley	3x15 ml
	Salt and pepper	

Preheat the oven to 400°F (200°C) Gas 6.

Roll out the dough and use to line a 9 inch (23 cm) flan tin. Prick the bottom with a fork and bake blind for 15 minutes.

Meanwhile, derind and chop the bacon. Melt the butter in a frying pan and fry the bacon till golden. Arrange the bacon in the flan case. Reduce oven temperature to 350°F (180°C) Gas 4.

Beat the eggs, milk and parsley together, season to taste and pour over the bacon. Bake for a further 20–25 minutes till set. Serve hot or cold.

Tomato flan

Overall timing 1 hour plus chilling

Freezing Suitable: reheat in 350°F (180°C)
Gas 4 oven for 25–30 minutes

To serve 6

9 oz	Plain flour	250 g
	Salt	
4 tbsp	Soured cream	4x15 ml
5 oz	Butter	150 g
Filling		
5	Tomatoes	5
6 oz	Cheese	175 g
8	Thin slices of French bread	8
¼ pint	Carton of double cream	150 ml
¼ pint	Carton of soured cream	141 g
4	Eggs	4
	Salt	
	Grated nutmeg	
½ teasp	Paprika	2.5 ml
1 oz	Butter	25 g

Sift flour and salt into bowl. Add soured
cream, dot with butter pieces and knead
lightly until smooth. Chill for 30 minutes.

Thinly slice tomatoes. Slice cheese and cut
crusts off bread.

Preheat oven to 400°F (200°C) Gas 6.

Roll out dough and use to line 12 inch
(30 cm) flan tin. Cover with layer of sliced
tomatoes, then cheese and bread.

Beat double cream with soured cream, eggs,
a pinch each of salt and nutmeg, and paprika.
Pour into flan tin and dot top with butter. Bake
for 30–40 minutes until firm and golden. Serve
hot.

Onion flan

Overall timing 2¼ hours

Freezing Suitable: reheat from frozen in 350°F (180°C) Gas 4 oven for 20 minutes

To serve 4–6

1 teasp	Dried yeast	5 ml
	Pinch of sugar	
4 fl oz	Lukewarm water	120 ml
8 oz	Plain flour	225 g
1 teasp	Salt	5 ml
1	Egg	1
Filling		
5 oz	Bacon rashers	150 g
6 oz	Onions	175 g
1 oz	Butter	25 g
5 oz	Cheddar cheese	150 g

Mix yeast and sugar with most of the water and leave in a warm place for 15 minutes till frothy.

Sift flour and salt into bowl, make a well in the centre and add yeast mixture, any remaining water and egg. Mix well to a dough, then turn on to floured surface and knead for 5 minutes until smooth and elastic. Place dough in a clean bowl, cover with a damp cloth and leave to rise in a warm place for 45 minutes–1 hour, until doubled in size.

Preheat oven to 400°F (200°C) Gas 6.

Roll out dough on a floured surface and use to line a greased 10 inch (25 cm) loose-bottomed flan tin. Prove for 15 minutes.

Derind and chop bacon. Peel onions and cut into rings. Melt butter in a pan and fry onions for 5 minutes till golden. Slice the cheese.

Cover flan base with onions and bacon and arrange cheese slices on top. Bake for 30–35 minutes. Remove from tin and serve hot.

Asparagus quiche

Overall timing 1¼ hours

Freezing Suitable: thaw and refresh in hot oven for 10 minutes

To serve 4

8 oz	Shortcrust pastry	225 g
2 tbsp	Butter	2x15 ml
4 tbsp	Plain flour	4x15 ml
¾ pint	Milk	400 ml
	Salt and pepper	
	Pinch of grated nutmeg	
2	Eggs	2
4 oz	Mature cheese	125 g
12 oz	Can of asparagus	340 g

Preheat the oven to 425°F (220°C) Gas 7.

Roll out the dough to ¼ inch (6 mm) thick and use to line greased 10 inch (25 cm) flan ring or dish. Prick with fork. Bake blind for 5 minutes.

Melt the butter in a small saucepan. Stir in flour. Gradually stir in ½ pint (300 ml) of the milk. Season with salt, pepper and nutmeg. Bring to the boil, stirring constantly. Cook for 2 minutes. Remove pan from heat. Separate the eggs and stir one yolk into sauce. Grate the cheese and add to the sauce.

Pour the sauce into the flan case. Return to the oven and bake for 15 minutes.

Remove quiche from oven. Reduce heat to 375°F (190°C) Gas 5. Drain asparagus, cut into small lengths and arrange evenly over surface. Mix together the rest of the milk, the remaining egg yolk and 2 egg whites and pour this over top. Bake for 30 minutes more.

Tomato marjoram pizza

Overall timing 1½ hours

Freezing Suitable: cook in 450°F (230°C) Gas 8 oven for 35 minutes

To serve 4

Topping		
1½ lb	Ripe tomatoes	700 g
1	Large onion	1
2	Garlic cloves	2
4 tbsp	Oil	4x15 ml
2 teasp	Dried marjoram	2x5 ml
1 teasp	Sugar	5 ml
	Salt and pepper	
Base		
10 oz	Packet of bread mix	283 g
4 oz	Cheddar cheese	125 g
¼ teasp	Powdered mustard	1.25 ml

Blanch, peel and roughly chop the tomatoes. Peel and finely chop the onion. Peel and crush the garlic. Heat 3 tbsp (3x15 ml) of the oil in a saucepan and fry the onion till transparent. Add the tomatoes, garlic, 1 teasp (5 ml) of the marjoram, the sugar and seasoning. Bring to the boil, stirring. Cover and simmer for 15 minutes.

Empty the bread mix into a large bowl. Grate the cheese. Stir into mix with powdered mustard. Add hot water (according to packet instructions) and mix to a soft, but not sticky dough. Knead for 5 minutes, then roll out on a floured surface to a round 10 inches (25 cm) in diameter. Place in a greased 10 inch (25 cm) pizza pan or flan tin. Pinch up the edges to make a slight lip.

Spread the tomato mixture over the pizza base and sprinkle with the remaining marjoram. Put pizza in a warm place to rise for about 30 minutes till base has almost doubled its size.

Preheat the oven to 425°F (220°C) Gas 7.

Sprinkle the remaining oil over the pizza and bake for 25 minutes.

Storecupboard pizza

Overall timing 1 hour 10 minutes

Freezing Suitable: reheat from frozen in 400°F (200°C) Gas 6 oven for 40 minutes

To serve 4–6

14 oz	Can of tomatoes	396 g
2	Garlic cloves	2
1	Small onion	1
½ teasp	Dried basil	2.5 ml
	Salt and pepper	
4 oz	Can of sardines	125 g
6 oz	Cheddar cheese	175 g
1	Can of anchovy fillets	1
12	Small black olives	12
2 tbsp	Grated Parmesan cheese	2x15 ml
Base		
8 oz	Self-raising flour	225 g
	Pinch of salt	
3 tbsp	Oil	3x15 ml

Preheat oven to 450°F (230°C) Gas 8.

Mix together mashed tomatoes and juice, crushed garlic, chopped onion, herbs, seasoning and drained and chopped sardines. Leave for 15 minutes.

Meanwhile, for the base, sift flour and salt into a bowl. Stir in oil and sufficient water to mix to a soft dough. Roll out dough to a large round and place on a greased baking tray. Pinch up edge to make a ridge. Brush with oil.

Spread tomato mixture over base. Cover with grated or sliced Cheddar and arrange anchovy fillets in a lattice shape on top. Garnish with olives and sprinkle with Parmesan.

Bake for 15 minutes. Reduce heat to 375°F (190°C) Gas 5 and bake for a further 20–25 minutes.

Olive and caper pizza

Overall timing 1¾ hours

Freezing Not suitable

To serve 2

6 oz	Potatoes	175 g
	Salt and pepper	
8 oz	Self-raising flour	225 g
2 oz	Butter	50 g
12 oz	Tomatoes	350 g
4	Anchovy fillets	4
1 tbsp	Capers	15 ml
4 oz	Black olives	125 g
4 tbsp	Milk	4x15 ml
2 teasp	Dried oregano	2x5 ml
1 tbsp	Olive oil	15 ml

Preheat the oven to 425°F (220°C) Gas 7.

Peel potatoes and cut into small chunks. Cook in boiling salted water till tender.

Meanwhile, sift the flour into a bowl and rub in the butter till the mixture resembles fine breadcrumbs. Blanch, peel and chop tomatoes. Chop anchovy fillets. Drain capers. Stone olives.

Drain potatoes and mash well. Stir into rubbed-in mixture. Add milk and mix to form a soft dough. Knead lightly till smooth. Roll out dough and use to line a greased 9 inch (23 cm) pizza pan or flan tin.

Arrange tomatoes, anchovies, capers and olives on top. Sprinkle with salt, pepper and oregano. Sprinkle olive oil over and bake for about 55 minutes till well risen and golden. Cut into wedges to serve.

Spring vegetable pie

Overall timing 2 hours

Freezing Not suitable

To serve 6

1 lb	Spring greens	450 g
2	Small globe artichokes	2
1½ lb	Fresh peas	700 g
	Salt and pepper	
1	Large onion	1
3 oz	Butter	75 g
8 oz	Shortcrust pastry	225 g
4	Eggs	4
4 tbsp	Grated Parmesan cheese	4x15 ml
1 tbsp	Chopped parsley	15 ml

Pick over the spring greens, discarding any damaged parts, and chop coarsely. Remove stems and tough outer leaves from artichokes and cut artichokes into quarters, discarding the hairy chokes. Shell peas. Bring a pan of lightly salted water to the boil, add the artichokes and peas and simmer for 10 minutes.

Peel and chop onion. Melt butter in large saucepan, add onion and fry till golden.

Drain artichokes and peas and add to the onion with the spring greens and seasoning. Mix well, cover tightly and simmer for 10 minutes, shaking the pan occasionally. Cool.

Preheat oven to 400°F (200°C) Gas 6.

Roll out two-thirds of dough and use to line an 8 inch (20cm) springform tin. Spread vegetables in tin. Beat three of the eggs lightly with cheese and parsley, then pour over vegetables. Roll out remaining dough and cover filling. Beat remaining egg and brush over pie. Place tin on a baking tray and bake for 30 minutes.

Remove sides of tin. Brush sides of pie with egg and bake for a further 10–15 minutes till golden.

Sicilian fish pie

Overall timing 2 hours

Freezing Not suitable

To serve 8

12 oz	Rich shortcrust pastry	350 g
2 tbsp	Caster sugar	2x15 ml
$\frac{1}{2}$ teasp	Grated lemon rind	2.5 ml
12 oz	White fish steaks	350 g
1	Large stalk of celery	1
3 oz	Stoned green olives	75 g
1	Large onion	1
3 tbsp	Olive oil	3x15 ml
1 tbsp	Drained capers	15 ml
2 tbsp	Tomato purée	2x15 ml
	Salt and pepper	
3	Courgettes	3
1	Egg	1
3 tbsp	Plain flour	3x15 ml
	Oil for deep frying	
1	Egg yolk	1

Make pastry, adding sugar and lemon rind with 3 egg yolks. Cube fish; chop celery; slice olives. Peel and thinly slice onion. Heat oil in a saucepan, add onion and fry till golden. Add celery, olives, capers, tomato purée, fish, $\frac{1}{4}$ pint (150 ml) water and seasoning. Simmer for 15 minutes.

Preheat oven to 350°F (180°C) Gas 4.

Cut courgettes into thin fingers. Beat egg; season flour. Dip courgettes into egg, then into flour. Deep fry till golden. Drain.

Divide dough into thirds. Roll out one and use to line a greased and floured 8 inch (20 cm) springform tin. Roll out remaining dough to two 8 inch (20 cm) rounds.

Layer fish mixture, courgettes and dough rounds in tin. Brush with beaten egg yolk and bake for 50 minutes. Remove from tin and serve hot.

Pork and apple pie

Overall timing 1½ hours

Freezing Not suitable

To serve 6

Pastry		
10 oz	Plain flour	275 g
2 teasp	Salt	2x5 ml
¼ teasp	Powdered mustard	1.25 ml
5 oz	Lard	150 g
Filling		
4 oz	Streaky bacon rashers	125 g
2	Medium-size onions	2
1½ lb	Lean minced pork	700 g
¼ teasp	Dried sage	1.25 ml
¼ pint	Chicken stock	150 ml
	Salt and pepper	
3	Dessert apples	3
4 tbsp	Demerara sugar	4x15 ml
¼ teasp	Grated nutmeg	1.25 ml

Preheat the oven to 400°F (200°C) Gas 6.

Sift the flour, salt and mustard into a bowl and rub in the lard. Add enough cold water to mix to a soft but not sticky dough and knead till smooth. Roll out two-thirds of the dough and use to line an 8½ inch (22 cm) round pie dish.

Derind and dice the bacon. Peel and finely chop the onions. Mix the pork with the bacon, onions, sage, stock and plenty of seasoning.

Peel, quarter, core and slice the apples. Put into a bowl with the sugar and nutmeg and toss gently till mixed.

Spread one-third of the pork in the pie dish and arrange half the apple mixture on top. Repeat the layers, finishing with the pork mixture.

Roll out the remaining dough to a round and use to cover the pie. Crimp the edges to seal. Place the pie on a baking tray. Bake just above the centre of the oven for 1 hour, covering the top of the pie lightly with foil after the first 30 minutes.

Ham, veal and pork pie

Overall timing 2½ hours plus overnight marination and chilling

Freezing Suitable

To serve 6–8

12 oz	Pie veal	350 g
2	Bay leaves	2
1 tbsp	Brandy	15 ml
	Salt and pepper	
8 oz	Cooked ham	225 g
12 oz	Belly of pork	350 g
4 oz	Streaky bacon	125 g
1 lb	Plain flour	450 g
5 oz	Butter	150 g
6 fl oz	Water	175 ml
2	Egg yolks	2

Cut veal into thin strips and place in a bowl with bay leaves, brandy and a pinch of salt.

Leave to marinate overnight. Cut ham into thin strips, add to veal and leave to marinate for another 2 hours.

Preheat the oven to 375°F (190°C) Gas 5.

Pass pork and bacon through a mincer twice. Mix with a little of the marinade and seasoning.

Sift flour and 1 teasp (5 ml) salt into a large bowl and make a well in the centre. Melt butter in water and bring to the boil. Pour quickly into the flour and mix well. Add one egg yolk and knead to a smooth dough.

Working quickly, roll out two-thirds of dough and use to line a greased 2 lb (900 g) loaf tin. Spread half the pork mixture on bottom, cover with ham and veal mixture and spread remaining pork mixture on top. Roll out remaining dough to fit pie. Seal edges. Put strips from leftover dough on sides of rectangle, moistening first to secure.

Lightly beat remaining egg yolk with a pinch of salt and brush over dough. Bake for 1 hour, then reduce heat to 170°F (325°C) Gas 3, cover with foil to prevent over-browning and bake for another hour.

Australian-style lamb pie

Overall timing 1¼ hours

Freezing Suitable: cover with pastry after thawing, then bake

To serve 4

1½ lb	Boned shoulder of lamb	700 g
	Salt and pepper	
2 tbsp	Plain flour	2x15 ml
1	Onion	1
8 oz	Carrots	225 g
4 oz	Mushrooms	125 g
1 oz	Butter	25 g
2 tbsp	Oil	2x15 ml
¾ pint	Stock	400 ml
2 tbsp	Chopped parsley	2x15 ml
6 oz	Shortcrust pastry	175 g
1	Egg	1

Wipe meat and cut into thin slices. Coat in seasoned flour. Peel and chop onion. Scrape and grate carrots. Wipe and slice mushrooms.

Heat butter and oil in frying pan and brown meat on all sides. Add onion, carrots and mushrooms and cook for 5 minutes. Stir in stock (made from cubes if necessary) and add seasoning. Cover and simmer gently for 10 minutes.

Preheat oven to 400°F (200°C) Gas 6.

Transfer meat mixture to pie dish and sprinkle with parsley. Roll out pastry and cover pie dish. Brush surface with lightly beaten egg and bake for 40–45 minutes until golden brown. Serve hot with jacket potatoes and minted peas.

Suet and bacon tart

Overall timing 45 minutes plus resting

Freezing Not suitable

To serve 8

8 oz	Streaky bacon rashers	225 g
4 oz	Cracklings from rendered suet	125 g
12 oz	Self-raising flour	350 g
2 oz	Chopped suet	50 g
2	Eggs	2
1 tbsp	Tomato purée	15 ml
¼ teasp	Chilli sauce	1.25 ml
	Salt and pepper	

Derind the bacon, then grill till crisp. Allow to cool, then break into pieces and mix with the suet cracklings.

Grease an 8 inch (20 cm) loose-bottomed cake tin.

Sift flour into bowl and add half the crackling mixture, the suet, eggs, tomato purée, chilli sauce, salt and pepper. Mix to a soft but not sticky dough. Knead lightly, then press into cake tin. Leave to rest for 20 minutes.

Preheat oven to 400°F (200°C) Gas 6.

Sprinkle rest of crackling mixture over dough and press in lightly. Bake for about 30 minutes till well risen and golden.

Cottage pie

Overall timing 1¼ hours

Freezing: Suitable: reheat in 425°F (220°C) Gas 7 oven for 1 hour

To serve 6

2 lb	Floury potatoes	900 g
	Salt and pepper	
2	Large onions	2
1 oz	Beef dripping	25 g
2 lb	Minced beef	900 g
2 tbsp	Plain flour	2x15 ml
½ pint	Strong beef stock	300 ml
14 oz	Can of tomatoes	397 g
8 oz	Frozen vegetables	225 g
¼ pint	Milk	150 ml
2 oz	Butter	50 g

Peel and quarter the potatoes; cook in boiling salted water till tender.

Preheat the oven to 375°F (190°C) Gas 5.

Peel and thinly slice onions. Heat dripping in a flameproof casserole and fry onions till transparent. Add beef and fry till browned.

Sprinkle in the flour and cook, stirring for 1 minute. Gradually add stock and bring to the boil, stirring. Add tomatoes and juice, seasoning and frozen vegetables and simmer for 5 minutes.

Drain potatoes. Add milk and butter and mash well. Spread potato over beef mixture. Bake for 30 minutes.

Savoury strudel

Overall timing 1½ hours

Freezing Suitable: bake from frozen, allowing extra 10–15 minutes

To serve 4–6

13 oz	Frozen puff pastry	370 g
1	Onion	1
2	Tomatoes	2
1	Green pepper	1
3 tbsp	Oil	3x15 ml
1 lb	Minced beef	450 g
3 tbsp	Tomato ketchup	3x15 ml
½ teasp	Worcestershire sauce	2.5 ml
	Salt and pepper	
4 oz	Mature Cheddar cheese	125 g
1	Egg yolk	1

Thaw pastry. Preheat oven to 425°F (220°C) Gas 7. Grease baking tray.

Peel and finely chop onion and tomatoes. Deseed and finely chop pepper. Heat oil in a frying pan. Cook onion till golden, then add beef and pepper. Cook for 5 minutes, then add tomatoes. Cook for 5 more minutes. Cool, then stir in tomato ketchup, Worcestershire sauce and seasoning.

Roll out dough thinly to a rectangle about 12x8 inches (30x45 cm). Spread beef mixture over dough, leaving border clear. Grate cheese over beef mixture, then fold borders on short sides over filling. Roll up from a long side and seal join.

Place strudel on baking tray. Decorate with trimmings, then brush with beaten egg yolk. Bake for 20 minutes. Reduce heat to 350°F (180°C) Gas 4 and cook for a further 20 minutes. Cut into slices to serve.

Cottage spinach roll

Overall timing 1¾ hours

Freezing Not suitable

To serve 4–6

8 oz	Plain flour	225 g
	Salt and pepper	
2	Eggs	2
2 lb	Spinach	900 g
3 oz	Butter	75 g
8 oz	Cottage cheese	225 g
¼ teasp	Grated nutmeg	1.25 ml
6 tbsp	Grated Parmesan cheese	6x15 ml

Sift the flour and ½ teasp (2.5 ml) salt into a bowl. Beat the eggs lightly in a bowl, pour half into the flour and mix with a palette knife. Add enough of the remaining egg to make a stiff dough. Knead till smooth, then chill for 30 minutes.

Meanwhile, wash and pick over the spinach. Put into a saucepan with only the water that clings to it. Cover and cook gently for 5 minutes. Drain thoroughly, then shred.

Melt 1 oz (25 g) of the butter in a frying pan, add the spinach and cook for 5 minutes, stirring occasionally. Pour into a bowl and add the cottage cheese, nutmeg, half the Parmesan and seasoning. Mix well. Leave to cool.

Roll out the dough on a floured surface to a rectangle about 15x12 inches (38x30 cm). With a long side nearest you, spread the filling over the dough, leaving a 1 inch (2.5 cm) border. Fold the bottom border over the filling and roll up. Pinch the ends together to seal.

Wrap the roll in a double thickness of muslin, tying the ends with string. Place in a large pan of boiling salted water, cover and simmer for 25 minutes.

Drain and unwrap the roll and place on a warmed serving dish. Melt the remaining butter. Cut the roll into thick slices, pour the butter over and sprinkle with the remaining Parmesan. Serve immediately.

Brazilian meat pasties

Overall timing 50 minutes

Freezing Suitable: omit hard-boiled eggs and bake from frozen in 425°F (220°C) Gas 7 oven for 30 minutes

To serve 4

13 oz	Frozen puff pastry	375 g
1	Onion	1
4 oz	Belly pork rashers	125 g
1 oz	Butter	25 g
8 oz	Minced beef	225 g
3 tbsp	Seedless raisins	3x15 ml
	Pinch of ground cloves	
	Salt and pepper	
$\frac{1}{4}$ teasp	Paprika	1.25 ml
2	Hard-boiled eggs	2
8	Stoned green olives	8
1	Egg	1

Thaw the pastry. Roll out to a rectangle 8x16 inches (20x40 cm). Cut into eight 4 inch (10 cm) squares.

Preheat oven to 400°F (200°C) Gas 6.

Peel and finely chop the onion. Derind and mince the belly pork rashers. Melt the butter in a frying pan and fry the onion and pork till golden. Add the minced beef and fry briskly, stirring frequently, till brown.

Remove from heat and add the raisins, cloves, salt, pepper and paprika. Mix well. Shell and coarsely chop the hard-boiled eggs. Chop the olives, add to the pan with the eggs and mix well.

Place one eighth of the meat mixture on half of each dough square. Brush the edges with a little of the beaten egg and fold dough over. Crimp edges to seal.

Arrange on a dampened baking tray and brush tops with beaten egg. Bake for about 25 minutes till well risen and golden.

Raised chicken and ham pie

Overall timing 2¾ hours plus cooling

Freezing Suitable

To serve 6

12 oz	Hot water crust pastry	350 g
1½ lb	Boneless chicken	700 g
	Salt and pepper	
1 teasp	Grated lemon rind	5 ml
¼ teasp	Dried sage	1.25 ml
4 oz	Sliced cooked ham	125 g
1 teasp	Powdered gelatine	5 ml
6 tbsp	Chicken stock	6x15 ml
1	Egg	1

Roll out two-thirds of dough and use to line greased 6 inch (15 cm) loose-bottomed cake tin. Keep remaining dough for lid warm.

Preheat oven to 375°F (190°C) Gas 5.

Finely dice chicken, keeping breast and dark meat separate. Season both well and add lemon rind and sage. Dice ham. Cover dough bottom with half breast meat, then with half dark meat. Spread all ham on top, then repeat layering of dark and breast meats.

Moisten dough edges and place lid in position. Press down firmly to seal. Make a hole in centre and decorate top. Glaze with lightly beaten egg.

Bake for 1 hour, then reduce oven temperature to 350°F (180°C) Gas 4 and bake for a further 1–1¼ hours. Remove pie from oven, cool for 30 minutes then remove from tin and leave until cold.

Meanwhile, soften gelatine in cold stock in a small pan for 5 minutes. Then heat gently till gelatine dissolves; do not boil. Leave to cool.

When the jelly mixture begins to set, put a funnel or cone of foil or greaseproof paper into the centre hole in the pie. Pour in jelly and chill in refrigerator till set. Serve cold with salad.

Sausage in brioche

Overall timing 2½ hours plus rising

Freezing Not suitable

To serve 6–8

1 lb	Piece of fresh continental sausage	450 g
	Bouquet garni	
1	Onion	1
8 oz	Strong flour	225 g
¼ teasp	Salt	1.25 ml
1½ teasp	Dried yeast	7.5 ml
2 tbsp	Lukewarm water	2x15 ml
1 tbsp	Caster sugar	15 ml
2	Eggs	2
2 oz	Butter	50 g
1	Egg yolk	1

Put sausage into a saucepan with bouquet garni and peeled onion and cover with cold water. Bring to the boil and simmer very gently for 1¾ hours.

Meanwhile, sift flour and salt into a bowl. Sprinkle yeast on to the water, add a pinch of the sugar and mix well. Leave in a warm place till frothy, then add to flour with remaining sugar. Add eggs and melted butter to flour and mix to a soft dough. Knead till glossy, wrap in oiled polythene and leave in a warm place to rise.

Drain sausage, discarding flavourings, and allow to cool slightly. Remove the skin.

Preheat the oven to 425°F (220°C) Gas 7.

Roll out dough to a rectangle large enough to enclose the sausage. Place sausage in centre and fold dough round it, pinching edges to seal. Place, join down, on a baking tray. Leave to prove for 15 minutes.

Brush with beaten egg yolk and bake for about 25 minutes till crisp and golden. Serve hot, cut into thick slices.

Leek pie

Overall timing 1 hour

Freezing Suitable: reheat in 350°F (180°C) Gas 4 oven for 30 minutes

To serve 4

1½ lb	Leeks	700 g
2	Onions	2
2 oz	Butter	50 g
	Salt and pepper	
8 oz	Streaky bacon rashers	225 g
12 oz	Shortcrust pastry	350 g
1 tbsp	Cornflour	15 ml
¼ pint	Carton of single cream	150 ml
1	Egg	1

Preheat the oven to 400°F (200°C) Gas 6.

Wash, trim and slice leeks. Peel and slice onions. Melt butter in a frying pan and fry onions till golden. Add sliced leeks, salt and pepper and cook gently for 5 minutes.

Meanwhile, derind and lightly fry bacon rashers in another pan.

Roll out two-thirds of the dough and use to line a shallow pie dish. Cover with leek mixture and arrange bacon rashers on top. Mix cornflour with the cream and pour over.

Roll out remaining dough and cover filling. Seal and crimp edges, using any trimmings to decorate top. Glaze with beaten egg. Bake for 45 minutes until golden brown.

Ham pie

Overall timing 1 hour

Freezing Not suitable

To serve 4

8 oz	Shortcrust pastry	225 g
1 lb	Can of ham	453 g
1	Egg	1

Preheat the oven to 425°F (220°C) Gas 7.

Roll out the dough to ¼ inch (6 mm) thickness. Place ham in centre. Dampen the dough edges and fold around the ham. Seal well. Place in ovenproof dish and decorate with trimmings, if liked.

Lightly beat the egg and brush all over the dough. Bake for 40 minutes till golden.

Ham and vegetable bake

Overall timing 1 hour 10 minutes

Freezing Suitable: top with egg after reheating in 350°F (180°C) Gas 4 oven for 1¼ hours

To serve 4

8 oz	Frozen spinach	225 g
1 lb	Celeriac	450 g
2 lb	Potatoes	900 g
	Salt and pepper	
2½ oz	Butter	65 g
3 tbsp	Single cream	3x15 ml
3 fl oz	Hot milk	90 ml
1	Small stalk of celery	1
8 oz	Sliced ham	225 g
4 oz	Cheddar cheese	125 g
2	Eggs	2

Place spinach in a sieve to thaw. Peel celeriac and potatoes and cut into small chunks. Put prepared vegetable chunks into a saucepan of cold salted water and bring to the boil. Cook for 20 minutes till tender. Drain well and mash or purée with 2 oz (50 g) of the butter, the cream and enough milk to give a creamy purée. Season to taste.

Preheat oven to 400°F (200°C) Gas 6.

Wash and top and tail celery. Blanch in boiling water for 5 minutes. Drain well and cut into pieces.

Grease ovenproof dish with remaining butter. Spread the well-drained spinach over, arrange the chopped celery on top and cover with ham slices. Grate the cheese. Sprinkle over half the cheese and cover with the celeriac and potato purée. Bake on centre shelf of oven for 15 minutes.

In a bowl, lightly beat the eggs with salt and pepper. Pour over the purée, top with remaining cheese and return to oven. Bake for another 15 minutes till golden. Serve immediately.

Club sandwiches

Overall timing 30 minutes

Freezing Not suitable

To serve 4

12	Slices of bread	12
	Mayonnaise	
4	Slices of cooked chicken or turkey	4
4	Lettuce leaves	4
4–8	Back bacon rashers	4–8
5	Tomatoes	5

Preheat the grill.

Grill the bacon until crisp. Toast four slices of bread on both sides, but toast the remaining slices of bread on one side only. Slice the tomatoes.

To assemble the sandwiches, spread the untoasted sides of bread with mayonnaise. Place four pieces, toasted side down, on a board and top with the chicken or turkey slices. Cover with the completely toasted bread. Add the lettuce, bacon, tomato slices (reserving some for the garnish) and remaining bread, mayonnaise side down. Press lightly together, then halve the sandwiches diagonally. Garnish with the reserved tomato slices.

Country-style liver pâté

Overall timing 3 hours plus maturing

Freezing Suitable

To serve 12

1½ lb	Pig's liver	700 g
1 lb	Back bacon	450 g
8 oz	Lard	225 g
1	Egg	1
1 tbsp	Plain flour	15 ml
	Salt and pepper	
½ teasp	Ground allspice	2.5 ml
1	Pig's caul (optional)	1

Preheat the oven to 350°F (180°C) Gas 4.

Chop the liver. Derind and dice bacon. Put liver and bacon through a fine mincer. Melt the lard in a saucepan and gradually beat into minced liver and bacon in bowl. Beat egg and add with flour, seasoning and allspice. Mix well.

Line greased ovenproof dish with caul, if using, leaving edges hanging over sides. Add liver mixture and smooth top. Wrap caul edges over. Cover dish with lid or foil and place in a roasting tin containing 1 inch (2.5 cm) water. Bake for 1¾ hours.

Allow to cool, then leave in the refrigerator for 2–3 days to mature. Serve with crusty bread.

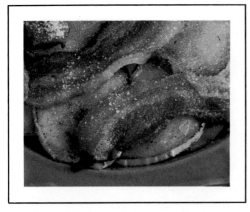

Bacon and apple rings

Overall timing 40 minutes

Freezing Not suitable

To serve 4

8 oz	Thin streaky bacon rashers	225 g
1 oz	Butter	25 g
2	Yellow Golden Delicious apples	2
2 tbsp	Caster sugar	2x15 ml

Derind the bacon. Melt the butter in a frying pan, add the bacon and fry till crisp. Drain on kitchen paper, place on a warmed serving plate and keep hot.

Wash, dry and core apples, but don't peel them. Cut into thin rings and cook in the frying pan till tender, turning them over with a spatula. Drain on kitchen paper, then arrange on the serving plate with the bacon.

Sprinkle with sugar and serve immediately with hot toast and butter.

Spanish kebabs

Overall timing 25 minutes plus marination

Freezing Not suitable

To serve 4

1 lb	Thick white fish fillets	450 g
2 tbsp	Oil	2x15 ml
2 tbsp	Lemon juice	2x15 ml
	Salt and pepper	
8 oz	Garlic sausage	225 g
8	Smoked streaky bacon rashers	8
16	Bay leaves	16
3 oz	Butter	75 g

Cut the fish into 16 neat cubes and put into a bowl with the oil, half the lemon juice and salt and pepper. Marinate for 1 hour, turning occasionally.

Preheat the grill and line the pan with foil. Cut the sausage into $\frac{1}{2}$ inch (12.5 mm) slices. Derind and stretch the bacon rashers and cut each in half. Thread the fish cubes, sausage, bay leaves and folded bacon on to greased skewers.

Place on the grill pan and brush the marinade over. Grill for about 10 minutes, turning and basting frequently, till the fish is tender.

Melt the butter in a saucepan and add the remaining lemon juice and seasoning. Serve this sauce with the kebabs.

Black pudding with apples

Overall timing 25 minutes

Freezing Not suitable

To serve 2

8 oz	Black pudding	225 g
2 oz	Butter	50 g
1	Onion	1
2	Dessert apples	2
	Fresh parsley	

Thickly slice the black pudding. Melt the butter in a frying pan and add the black pudding. Cook till crispy – if you cook them gently the slices will stay intact, instead of breaking away from the skin. Lift out with draining spoon and keep hot.

Peel onion and slice into rings. Fry gently in the butter till brown and just tender.

Core and slice the apples. Add to pan and cook for 5 minutes, turning slices over halfway. Add the pudding and cook the mixture for 2 minutes more.

Place black pudding, onion and apples on two warmed plates. Garnish with parsley sprigs and serve hot.

Crusty mushroom bread

Overall timing 1 hour

Freezing Suitable: cook after thawing

To serve 6–8

1	Round loaf of bread	1
4 oz	Butter	125 g
1 lb	Mushrooms	450 g
	Salt and pepper	
3 tbsp	Lemon juice	3x15 ml
½ pint	White sauce	300 ml
2	Eggs	2

Preheat the oven to 350°F (180°C) Gas 4.

Slice the top off the bread and scoop out most of the crumbs, leaving a ½ inch (12.5 mm) thick shell. Spread the inside with half the butter, place on a baking tray and bake for 10 minutes.

Meanwhile, finely chop the mushrooms. Melt the remaining butter in a saucepan and fry the mushrooms for 5 minutes, stirring frequently. Add salt, pepper and lemon juice. Stir the mushrooms into the white sauce.

Separate the eggs and beat the egg yolks, one at a time, into the sauce. Return to the heat and heat through gently. Whisk the egg whites till stiff but not dry. Gently fold into the mushroom mixture.

Pour the mixture into the bread shell and sprinkle the top with a few of the scooped out breadcrumbs, grated. Bake for 30 minutes till well risen and crisp. Serve hot.

Broccoli toasts

Overall timing 40 minutes

Freezing Not suitable

To serve 4

1 lb	Calabrese broccoli	450 g
½ pint	Beef stock	300 ml
8	Slices of bread	8
½ pint	Thick white sauce	300 ml
	Salt and pepper	
	Grated nutmeg	
½ teasp	Mixed herbs	2.5 ml
2	Hard-boiled eggs	2
1	Tomato	1
	Sprigs of parsley	
½	Red pepper	½

Trim broccoli and chop into large pieces. Bring stock to boil, add broccoli and cook for 7–10 minutes.

Toast bread and place on baking tray. Drain broccoli well, then divide it between toast.

Preheat oven to 375°F (190°C) Gas 5.

Heat sauce, then add seasoning, pinch of nutmeg and herbs. Finely chop one of the hard-boiled eggs and add to the sauce. Pour sauce over broccoli. Bake for 15 minutes.

Serve hot, garnished with remaining egg, sliced tomato, parsley and strips of pepper.

Pirozski

Overall timing 1 hour

Freezing Suitable: refresh in 350°F (180°C) Gas 4 oven for 10 minutes

To serve 6

7½ oz	Frozen puff pastry	212 g
8 oz	Liver pâté	225 g
1	Egg	1

Thaw pastry. Preheat the oven to 400°F (200°C) Gas 6.

Roll out dough very thinly on a floured surface and cut into 3 inch (7.5 cm) squares. Cut in half diagonally to make triangles. Put about 1 teasp (5 ml) liver pâté on half of the triangles. Moisten dough edges and cover with remaining triangles. Press edges together to seal.

Arrange triangles on greased baking tray and brush with beaten egg. Bake for 10–15 minutes till well risen and golden. Serve hot.

Provençal sandwiches

Overall timing 15 minutes

Freezing Not suitable

To serve 4

4	Crusty rolls	4
1	Garlic clove	1
4	Large lettuce leaves	4
2	Large tomatoes	2
2	Hard-boiled eggs	2
	Pickled vegetables or gherkins	
	Black olives	
	Cooked green beans	
	Anchovy fillets	
	Green or red pepper	
	Olive oil	
	Vinegar	

Halve the rolls and the garlic clove. Rub the cut surfaces of the rolls with the garlic. Place the lettuce leaves on the bottom halves of the rolls.

Slice the tomatoes. Shell and slice the eggs. Place the tomatoes and eggs on the lettuce, then add pickled vegetables or gherkins, olives, beans, anchovies and pepper strips, according to taste. Sprinkle with oil and vinegar, then place the tops of the rolls on the filling. Press gently together and serve.

Hot frankfurter salad

Overall timing 45 minutes

Freezing Not suitable

To serve 4

1 lb	Waxy potatoes	450 g
	Salt and pepper	
4	Frankfurters	4
2	Onions	2
4	Anchovy fillets	4
2 oz	Chopped gherkins	50 g
2 tbsp	Oil	2x15 ml
2 tbsp	White wine vinegar	2x15 ml

Peel and slice potatoes, then cook in boiling salted water for about 7 minutes till tender.

Heat frankfurters in boiling water for 5 minutes, then drain and slice. Peel and slice onions into rings. Finely chop anchovies and gherkins. Drain potatoes and mix with frankfurters and onions.

Beat together oil and vinegar, season and pour over the warm salad. Mix well and leave for 10 minutes. Add anchovies and gherkins and serve.

Tuna rolls

Overall timing 15 minutes

Freezing Not suitable

To serve 4

4	Long rolls	4
	Butter	
	Mayonnaise	
1x7 oz	Can of tuna fish	1x200 g
	Chopped parsley	
2	Hard-boiled eggs	2
	Radish roses	

Halve the rolls, not cutting all the way through, and butter the cut surfaces. Spread a thick layer of mayonnaise over the bottom cut surface.

Drain the tuna and flake it. Divide between the rolls and sprinkle with parsley. Arrange the sandwiches on a serving plate.

Shell and slice the eggs and use to garnish the sandwiches with radish roses.

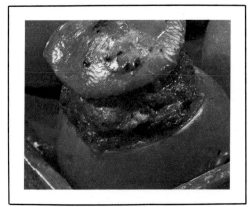

Beefy tomatoes

Overall timing 45 minutes

Freezing Not suitable

To serve 6

6	Large tomatoes	6
1	Large onion	1
8 oz	Corned beef	225 g
8 oz	Sausagemeat	225 g
2 tbsp	Chopped parsley	2x15 ml
1	Egg	1
¼ teasp	Ground allspice	1.25 ml
	Salt and pepper	
	Oil	

Preheat the oven to 425°F (220°C) Gas 7.

Cut tops off tomatoes and reserve. Scoop out most of the flesh and place it in a bowl. Peel and finely chop onion. Add to bowl with the corned beef, sausagemeat and chopped parsley. Mash well. Beat in the egg, allspice and seasoning and mix well.

Stuff tomatoes with beef mixture and put the reserved "lids" on top. Place on a baking tray and sprinkle with oil. Bake for 20 minutes. Serve with crusty bread.

Nutty beefburgers

Overall timing 45 minutes

Freezing Not suitable

To serve 4

4 oz	Hazelnuts	125 g
1 oz	Butter	25 g
1	Large onion	1
1 lb	Lean minced beef	450 g
2 tbsp	Capers	2x15 ml
	Grated rind of 1 lemon	
¼ teasp	Paprika	1.25 ml
½ teasp	Powdered mustard	2.5 ml
	Salt and pepper	
4	Egg yolks	4

Preheat the oven to 375°F (190°C) Gas 5.

Chop nuts. Melt butter in a frying pan and cook nuts till golden. Peel onion. Cut four equal rings and reserve. Finely chop remainder and mix with nuts, beef, half the capers, the lemon rind, paprika, mustard and seasoning.

Divide mixture into four portions. Shape into balls, place on a baking tray and flatten slightly making a well in centre of each. Bake for 25 minutes.

Place each burger on a lettuce leaf on serving plate. Press an onion ring into each well, then carefully place a raw egg yolk in each ring and garnish with remaining capers. If liked, bake for a further 10 minutes to cook egg yolk.

Ham and potato cake

Overall timing 1¼ hours

Freezing Not suitable

To serve 4

1½ lb	Medium-size potatoes	700 g
	Salt and pepper	
8 oz	Sliced cooked ham	225 g
8 oz	Cheese	225 g
3 oz	Butter	75 g
3 tbsp	Fresh breadcrumbs	3x15 ml
¼ pint	Milk	150 ml

Cook potatoes in boiling salted water for 20 minutes.

Meanwhile, chop the ham and grate cheese. Grease a 7 inch (18 cm) springform tin with a little of the butter and sprinkle breadcrumbs over the bottom and sides, shaking off any excess. Preheat oven to 350°F (180°C) Gas 4.

Drain and peel the potatoes, then cut into ¼ inch (6 mm) thick slices. Arrange a few of the slices, slightly overlapping, in the bottom of the tin. Melt the remaining butter and brush a little over the potatoes. Scatter some of the ham, then some of the cheese over and season. Continue layering, reserving a little of the butter, and finishing with a layer of potato topped with cheese. Pour the milk over and brush with remaining butter.

Bake for about 30 minutes till potatoes are tender and cheese has melted. Turn cake out of tin to serve.

Roast veal salad

Overall timing 20 minutes

Freezing Not suitable

To serve 2

½	Round lettuce	½
¼	Cucumber	¼
2	Large firm tomatoes	2
4	Radishes	4
2	Hard-boiled eggs	2
6 oz	Cold roast veal	175 g
2 tbsp	Oil	2x15 ml
2 teasp	White wine vinegar	2x5 ml
½ teasp	Powdered mustard	2.5 ml
	Salt and pepper	
	Sprigs of parsley	

Wash and dry lettuce. Use outside leaves to line a serving dish. Shred rest and put in bowl. Cut cucumber into matchsticks and add to shredded lettuce.

Cut tomatoes into wedges. Slice radishes. Add half of each to lettuce and cucumber.

Shell and halve hard-boiled eggs. Cut veal into neat cubes.

Put oil, vinegar, mustard and seasoning into a screw-top jar, cover and shake to mix. Add to shredded lettuce mixture and toss lightly. Place in lettuce-lined dish. Arrange eggs, veal and remaining tomatoes and radishes on top. Garnish with parsley.

Frankfurter kebabs

Overall timing 20 minutes

Freezing Suitable: cook from frozen

To serve 2

4	Frankfurters	4
12	Button onions	12
3 tbsp	Oil	3x15 ml
2 teasp	Coarse-grain mustard	2x5 ml

Preheat the grill.

Cut each frankfurter into three pieces. Blanch onions in boiling water for 5 minutes, then drain and peel. Thread onions and frankfurters alternately on to greased skewers.

Mix oil and mustard together. Brush over kebabs and grill for about 10 minutes, turning and brushing with mustard mixture frequently. Serve with mashed potatoes and pour any cooking juices over.

Welsh sausages

Overall timing 25 minutes

Freezing Suitable: reheat in 350°F (180°C) Gas 4 oven for 20–25 minutes

Makes 18–20

1	Small onion	1
5 oz	Hard cheese	150 g
9 oz	Fresh white breadcrumbs	250 g
1 tbsp	Chopped parsley or fresh fines herbes	15 ml
1 teasp	Powdered mustard	5 ml
	Salt and pepper	
2	Eggs	2
	Flour for coating	
2 oz	Dried breadcrumbs	50 g
	Oil for frying	

Peel and finely chop onion. Grate cheese. Place in bowl with fresh breadcrumbs, herbs, mustard and generous seasoning. Add 1 whole egg and 1 yolk and mix into ingredients with wooden spoon till well combined. Form mixture into small sausage shapes.

Lightly coat shapes in flour, then in lightly beaten egg white, then coat in dried breadcrumbs.

Heat ½ inch (12.5 mm) oil in a frying pan and when hot cook a few sausages at a time till crisp and golden all over. Drain on kitchen paper and serve hot or cold.

Peasant omelette

Overall timing 25 minutes

Freezing Not suitable

To serve 4

2	Waxy potatoes	2
1	Carrot	1
	Salt and pepper	
3 oz	Smoked streaky bacon rashers	75 g
3 oz	Butter	75 g
6	Eggs	6
1 tbsp	Chopped chives	15 ml
4	Thin slices of cheese	4

Peel and dice the potatoes; scrape and dice the carrot. Put into a pan, cover with cold salted water and bring to the boil. Simmer for 4 minutes, then drain.

Derind bacon and cut into strips. Preheat the grill.

Melt the butter in a frying pan and fry the bacon till transparent. Add the potatoes and carrots and fry over a moderate heat for 5 minutes, stirring frequently, till golden and tender.

Lightly beat the eggs in a bowl with salt, pepper and chives. Pour over the bacon and vegetables and cook till lightly set. Top with the slices of cheese and grill till melted. Serve immediately, cut into wedges.

Pilau rice

Overall timing 45 minutes plus soaking

Freezing Not suitable

To serve 4–6

1 lb	Patna rice	450 g
1	Large onion	1
1	Garlic clove	1
6	Whole allspice	6
8	Cardamom pods	8
4 oz	Butter or ghee	125 g
2 inch	Cinnamon stick	5 cm
8	Cloves	8
1 teasp	Ground turmeric	5 ml
	Salt	
2 oz	Flaked almonds	50 g
4 oz	Sultanas	125 g

Soak rice in cold water for 1 hour, then drain thoroughly.

Peel and finely chop the onion. Peel and crush garlic. Lightly crush allspice and cardamom pods. Melt 3 oz (75 g) of the fat in a saucepan. Add onion, garlic and spices and fry till onion is transparent but not browned.

Add rice and cook over a low heat, stirring, for 3–4 minutes. Add salt to taste and enough boiling water to come 1 inch (2.5 cm) above the rice. Cover pan tightly and simmer over a very low heat for about 20 minutes till water is absorbed and rice is tender.

Melt remaining fat in frying pan and fry almonds and sultanas for 3–5 minutes. Mix lightly into rice and serve immediately.

Curried cockles with rice

Overall timing 30 minutes

Freezing Not suitable

To serve 2

4 oz	Long grain rice	125 g
	Salt	
1 lb	Cockles	450 g
Curry sauce		
1	Small onion	1
1	Garlic clove	1
1 oz	Butter	25 g
1 tbsp	Curry powder	15 ml
	Ground cinnamon	
	Ground ginger	
	Sugar	
4 tbsp	Boiling water	4x15 ml
	Salt and pepper	

Cook the rice in boiling salted water till tender.

Meanwhile, scrub the cockles well under cold running water. Place them in a saucepan of salted water. Bring to the boil, cover and cook gently till the shells open. Discard any that do not open. Remove cockles from their shells and set aside. Strain the cooking liquor through a muslin-lined sieve into bowl.

Peel and finely chop onion and garlic. Melt butter in a frying pan and fry the onion and garlic till transparent. Add the curry powder and cook for a further 2 minutes. Add a large pinch each of cinnamon, ginger and sugar and the boiling water. Add 5 tbsp (5x15 ml) of the cooking liquor from the cockles. Taste, and season if necessary.

Stir the cockles into the sauce and heat through quickly. Put the drained rice on a warmed serving dish and pour the cockles and sauce over. Serve hot.

Prawn pilaf

Overall timing 1 hour

Freezing Not suitable

To serve 4

2	Large onions	2
2	Fresh green chillies	2
2	Garlic cloves	2
8 oz	Streaky bacon rashers	225 g
1 tbsp	Oil	15 ml
8 oz	Long-grain rice	225 g
14 oz	Can of tomatoes	397 g
	Salt	
¾ pint	Chicken stock	400 ml
1 lb	Shelled prawns	450 g
2 tbsp	Chopped parsley	2x15 ml
2 tbsp	Grated Parmesan cheese	2x15 ml

Peel and slice onions. Deseed and slice chillies. Peel and crush garlic. Derind and chop bacon.

Heat the oil in a flameproof casserole. Add bacon and fry until well browned. Add the onions, chillies and garlic to the casserole. Cook until onions are soft and transparent but not brown, stirring occasionally.

Add the rice and stir for 2–3 minutes until grains are coated with oil. Add the tomatoes with their juice, salt and chicken stock. Bring rapidly to the boil, then reduce heat, cover and simmer for 15 minutes on a very low heat.

Stir and add the prawns. Cover and cook for a further 5 minutes.

Turn mixture into warmed serving dish. Sprinkle with parsley and cheese and serve immediately.

Fish paella

Overall timing 45 minutes

Freezing Not suitable

To serve 6

1	Large onion	1
2	Garlic cloves	2
4 tbsp	Oil	4x15 ml
1 lb	Long grain rice	450 g
14 oz	Can of tomatoes	397 g
4	Saffron strands	4
3½ pints	Chicken stock or water	2 litres
	Salt and pepper	
1½ lb	White fish fillets	700 g
1	Red pepper	1
14 oz	Can of artichoke hearts	397 g
14 oz	Can of broad beans	397 g
8 oz	Frozen peas	225 g

Peel and chop the onion. Peel and crush the garlic. Heat the oil in a flameproof casserole, add the onion and fry till transparent. Add the rice and garlic and fry, stirring, for 2 minutes.

Add the tomatoes and juice, the saffron, stock or water and seasoning and bring to the boil. Reduce the heat and simmer for 10 minutes.

Meanwhile, cut the fish into chunks. Halve and deseed the pepper and cut into 1 inch (2.5 cm) pieces. Drain the artichoke hearts and cut in half lengthways. Drain the beans.

Add all these ingredients to the pan with the peas and mix lightly. Cover and cook for a further 10 minutes till the rice is tender and the liquid is absorbed. Fluff the mixture with a fork. Taste and adjust seasoning. Serve immediately.

Lentil risotto

Overall timing 1 hour

Freezing Not suitable

To serve 6

8 oz	Continental lentils	225 g
1	Onion	1
4 oz	Butter	125 g
	Salt and pepper	
12 oz	Long grain rice	350 g
2 pints	Stock	1.1 litres
2 oz	Grated Parmesan cheese	50 g

Wash and pick over lentils. Peel and finely chop the onion. Melt the butter in a large saucepan, add the onion and cook till transparent. Add the lentils and enough water to cover. Season and bring to the boil. Reduce heat, cover and simmer for 1 hour.

Add the rice and stock. Bring back to the boil, reduce heat, cover and simmer for a further 15–18 minutes or until rice is just tender.

Stir in the Parmesan, and taste and adjust seasoning. Serve hot.

Arabian pilaf

Overall timing 30 minutes

Freezing Not suitable

To serve 4

1 oz	Butter	25 g
2 oz	Capelli d'angelo (angels' hair pasta)	50 g
1¼ pints	Chicken stock	700 ml
8 oz	Long grain rice	225 g
2 tbsp	Grated Parmesan cheese	2x15 ml
	Salt and pepper	

Melt the butter in a saucepan. Break up the pasta, add to the pan and fry, stirring, over a moderate heat till golden. Remove from pan and reserve.

Add the stock to the pan and bring to the boil. Stir in the rice, bring back to the boil and simmer gently for 15 minutes till the rice is just tender.

Stir in the fried pasta and cook for 2–3 minutes till pasta and rice are tender and all the liquid has been absorbed. Stir in Parmesan and seasoning with a fork. Transfer to a warmed serving dish and serve immediately.

Cannelloni with tuna fish

Overall timing 1½ hours

Freezing Suitable: reheat in 350°F (180°C) Gas 4 oven for 1 hour

To serve 4

12	Sheets of lasagne	12
	Salt and pepper	
2	Onions	2
2	Garlic cloves	2
2 oz	Capers	50 g
7 oz	Can of tuna fish	198 g
2 oz	Fresh breadcrumbs	50 g
1 tbsp	Lemon juice	15 ml
1	Egg	1
2 tbsp	Chopped parsley	2x15 ml
14 oz	Can of tomatoes	397 g
2 tbsp	Grated Parmesan cheese	2x15 ml

Place lasagne in saucepan of boiling, salted water and cook for 10–15 minutes or until tender. Drain in a colander, rinse with boiling water and spread out on a damp tea-towel to cool for a few minutes.

Peel and chop onions. Peel and crush garlic. Drain capers. Drain tuna fish oil into a frying pan, heat, add onions and fry until golden. Add garlic, tuna fish and capers and cook over low heat for 5 minutes, stirring. Remove from heat.

Preheat oven to 400°F (200°C) Gas 6. Grease ovenproof dish.

Add breadcrumbs (reserving 2 tbsp/2x15 ml) to fish mixture with lemon juice, egg, parsley and seasoning. Mix well. Place some of the fish mixture in centre of each lasagne sheet and roll around filling. Arrange rolls, joins down, in ovenproof dish.

Press tomatoes in their juice through a sieve, season and spread over cannelloni. Sprinkle with reserved breadcrumbs and then with Parmesan. Cook in centre of the oven for 30 minutes.

Aubergine and pasta casserole

Overall timing 1 hour

Freezing Not suitable

To serve 4–6

1	Large aubergine	1
	Salt and pepper	
1	Onion	1
1	Garlic clove	1
3 oz	Butter	75 g
1 lb	Tomatoes	450 g
2 teasp	Chopped fresh basil	2x5 ml
3 fl oz	Oil	90 ml
12 oz	Rigatoni	350 g
3 oz	Mozzarella cheese	75 g

Preheat oven to 400°F (200°C) Gas 6.

Cut aubergine into thin slices lengthways. Arrange slices on a plate, sprinkle with salt and leave for 30 minutes.

Meanwhile, peel and chop onion. Peel and crush garlic. Melt 2 oz (50 g) of the butter in a saucepan, add onion and garlic and fry till transparent.

Blanch, peel and finely chop tomatoes. Add to onion with seasoning. Simmer gently for 15 minutes. Remove from heat and stir in basil.

Rinse aubergine slices under running cold water and pat dry with kitchen paper. Heat oil in frying pan, add slices and cook for 4–5 minutes each side. Drain on kitchen paper.

Cook rigatoni in boiling salted water till tender. Drain and mix with tomato sauce. Season to taste. Put half the rigatoni mixture into greased ovenproof dish and arrange aubergine slices on top. Add remaining rigatoni mixture. Thinly slice cheese and arrange on top. Dot with remaining butter· and bake for 15 minutes. Serve hot.

Seafood spaghetti

Overall timing 20 minutes

Freezing Not suitable

To serve 4

12 oz	Spaghetti	350 g
	Salt and pepper	
1	Garlic clove	1
3 tbsp	Oil	3 x 15 ml
8 oz	Large shelled prawns	225 g
10 oz	Can of baby clams or mussels	280 g
8 oz	Can of tomatoes	227 g
1 tbsp	Chopped parsley	15 ml

Cook spaghetti in boiling salted water till tender.

Meanwhile, peel and crush garlic. Heat oil in a large saucepan, add garlic and fry for 1 minute. Add prawns and fry, stirring, for 2–3 minutes.

Drain clams or mussels and add to pan with tomatoes and their juice and seasoning. Cook for about 3 minutes, stirring to break up tomatoes.

Drain spaghetti thoroughly. Add to seafood sauce with parsley and toss lightly over a low heat till well coated. Serve immediately.

Spaghetti with goat's cheese

Overall timing 35 minutes

Freezing Not suitable

To serve 2

1	Garlic clove	1
2	Anchovy fillets	2
2 tbsp	Olive oil	2x15 ml
1 tbsp	Chopped parsley	15 ml
	Salt and pepper	
8 oz	Spaghetti	225 g
4 oz	Firm goat's cheese	125 g
1 oz	Butter	25 g

Peel and crush the garlic into a bowl. Add the anchovy fillets and pound to a paste with a wooden spoon. Beat in the oil, parsley and seasoning. Leave to stand for 15 minutes.

Meanwhile, cook the spaghetti in boiling salted water till tender. Derind the cheese and cut into small cubes.

Drain the spaghetti in a colander. Melt the butter in the spaghetti pan and add the cheese. Cook, stirring, over a low heat for 2 minutes.

Return spaghetti to the pan and toss lightly till coated with butter. Arrange in a warmed serving dish, pour the anchovy dressing over and toss lightly before serving with crusty bread.

Crisp-topped macaroni with tuna

Overall timing 35 minutes

Freezing Not suitable

To serve 4

1	Onion	1
3 oz	Butter	75 g
¼ pint	Chicken stock	150 ml
	Salt and pepper	
1	Medium cauliflower	1
8 oz	Short-cut macaroni	225 g
6	Anchovy fillets	6
1 oz	Fresh breadcrumbs	25 g
7 oz	Can of tuna	198 g
4 tbsp	Grated Parmesan cheese	4x15 ml

Peel and chop the onion. Melt 1 oz (25 g) of the butter in a large saucepan and fry the onion till golden. Add the chicken stock and seasoning. Bring to the boil and simmer for 5 minutes.

Divide cauliflower into florets and cook in boiling salted water for 4 minutes. Remove with a draining spoon and reserve. Add macaroni to boiling water and cook till tender.

Meanwhile, melt remaining butter in a frying pan and fry cauliflower till golden. Roughly chop anchovies and add to pan with breadcrumbs. Fry till crisp. Remove from heat.

Preheat the grill.

Drain the macaroni and add to the stock mixture. Drain and flake tuna and stir carefully into the macaroni with half the Parmesan. Taste and adjust seasoning and heat through gently.

Pour the macaroni mixture into a flameproof dish and scatter cauliflower and breadcrumb mixture over it. Sprinkle with remaining cheese, then grill for 5 minutes till golden.

Lasagne alla bolognese

Overall timing 2 hours

Freezing Suitable: reheat in 350°F (180°C) Gas 4 oven for 1 hour

To serve 6

1	Onion	1
1	Carrot	1
1	Stalk of celery	1
4 oz	Streaky bacon	125 g
4 oz	Chuck steak	125 g
4 oz	Belly of pork	125 g
3 oz	Butter	75 g
1 tbsp	Tomato purée	15 ml
¼ pint	Hot stock	150 ml
3 tbsp	Dry white wine	3x15 ml
¼ pint	Milk	150 ml
1 lb	Fresh spinach	450 g
	Salt and pepper	
12 oz	Green lasagne	350 g
1 pint	White sauce	560 ml
3 oz	Grated Parmesan cheese	75 g

Peel and chop onion and carrot. Chop celery. Derind and chop bacon. Mince meats. Melt 1 oz (25 g) of butter in a saucepan, add bacon and meats and brown. Add vegetables, tomato purée, stock, wine and milk. Simmer gently for 45 minutes, stirring occasionally.

Meanwhile, wash spinach and remove coarse stalks. Place in a saucepan with 1 oz (25 g) of the butter and seasoning. Cook gently for 5–10 minutes. Chop finely and add to meat mixture.

Preheat oven to 375°F (190°C) Gas 5.

Cook lasagne in boiling, salted water till tender. Drain on damp tea-towel.

Cover bottom of greased ovenproof dish with a quarter of the lasagne. Spread half the meat mixture on top, then another quarter of the lasagne, half the white sauce and Parmesan. Repeat layers, finishing with white sauce and Parmesan. Dot with remaining butter. Bake for 20 minutes.

Spaghetti alla carbonara

Overall timing 20 minutes

Freezing Not suitable

To serve 4

12 oz	Spaghetti	350 g
	Salt and pepper	
2	Eggs	2
2 tbsp	Top of the milk	2x15 ml
4 oz	Streaky bacon rashers	125 g
1 tbsp	Oil	15 ml
2 oz	Grated Parmesan cheese	50 g

Cook the spaghetti in boiling salted water till tender.

Meanwhile, beat eggs, milk and pepper in a bowl. Derind and dice the bacon. Heat the oil in large frying pan, add the bacon and fry till crisp.

Drain the spaghetti and add to the bacon. Pour in the egg mixture, stirring, and toss over a gentle heat till the eggs just begin to set. Serve immediately, sprinkled with grated Parmesan.

Spaghetti with chicken sauce

Overall timing 1 hour

Freezing Suitable: cook spaghetti and almonds after reheating sauce

To serve 4

2	Thick rashers of streaky bacon	2
12 oz	Boned chicken breasts	350 g
2 oz	Butter	50 g
2 tbsp	Oil	2x15 ml
1 lb	Ripe tomatoes	450 g
1	Garlic clove	1
2 tbsp	Tomato purée	2x15 ml
½ teasp	Sugar	2.5 ml
	Salt and pepper	
¼ pint	Dry white wine	150 ml
12 oz	Spaghetti	350 g
1 oz	Chopped almonds	25 g

Derind and dice the bacon. Wipe and trim the chicken, discarding skin. Cut the meat into strips. Heat half the butter and the oil in a flameproof casserole, add the bacon and chicken and fry for 5 minutes till browned all over.

Blanch, peel and chop the tomatoes. Add to the pan with the peeled and crushed garlic, tomato purée, sugar and salt and pepper. Add the wine and bring to the boil, stirring. Reduce the heat, cover the pan tightly and simmer for 20 minutes.

Meanwhile, cook the spaghetti in boiling salted water till just tender. Drain in a colander.

Melt remaining butter in the saucepan, add the almonds and fry over a high heat till golden. Return the spaghetti to the pan with half the tomato chicken sauce, toss lightly and adjust seasoning to taste. Place in a warmed serving dish.

Season remaining sauce, pour into a warmed sauceboat and serve separately.

Turkey noodle bake

Overall timing 1½ hours

Freezing Not suitable

To serve 4

4 oz	Button mushrooms	125 g
8 oz	Noodles	225 g
	Salt and pepper	
3 tbsp	Plain flour	3x15 ml
1	Chicken stock cube	1
¼ teasp	Paprika	1.25 ml
5 tbsp	Single cream	5x15 ml
8 oz	Cooked turkey meat	225 g
2 oz	Cheddar cheese	50 g
1 oz	Fresh breadcrumbs	25 g
½ oz	Butter	15 g

Wipe and slice the mushrooms. Cook the noodles in boiling salted water for about 5 minutes till tender. Drain the noodles thoroughly, reserving 1 pint (560ml) of the cooking water.

Blend the flour in a small bowl with a little of the measured cooking water. Put rest of water into a saucepan, stir in blended flour, crumbled stock cube, salt, pepper and paprika. Bring to the boil, stirring. Reduce the heat and add the mushrooms. Simmer for 10 minutes.

Preheat the oven to 350°F (180°C) Gas 4. Grease an 8 inch (20cm) soufflé dish.

Remove pan from heat and stir in cream.

Spread half the drained noodles over the bottom of the soufflé dish. Dice the turkey and arrange half over the noodles. Cover with half the sauce. Repeat the layers, finishing with sauce. Grate cheese and scatter over top. Sprinkle with breadcrumbs and dot with butter. Bake for 30 minutes.

Corsican spaghetti

Overall timing 1 hour

Freezing Suitable (sauce only): add olives after reheating

To serve 2

1	Onion	1
2 oz	Butter	50 g
8 oz	Ripe tomatoes	225 g
1	Garlic clove	1
8 oz	Minced beef	225 g
½	Small dried chilli	½
	Salt and pepper	
8 oz	Spaghetti	225 g
6	Stoned green olives	6
1 oz	Cheese	25 g

Peel and finely chop onion. Melt half the butter in a saucepan and fry the onion till lightly browned.

Blanch, peel and chop the tomatoes. Peel and crush the garlic and add to onions with the minced beef, tomatoes, the dried chilli and salt. Simmer for 45 minutes.

Cook the spaghetti in boiling salted water till tender. Drain thoroughly in a colander, then add remaining butter and leave to melt.

Remove chilli from sauce. Slice the green olives and add to the sauce. Taste and adjust seasoning.

Pile spaghetti in a warmed serving dish and pour meat sauce over. Serve the grated cheese separately.

Cheesy macaroni

Overall timing 30 minutes

Freezing Not suitable

To serve 4

8 oz	Long macaroni	225 g
	Salt and pepper	
2	Eggs	2
4 oz	Cooked ham	125 g
6 oz	Cheddar cheese	175 g
3 oz	Butter	75 g
	Cayenne pepper	

Preheat the oven to 425°F (220°C) Gas 7. Grease an 8 inch (20 cm) soufflé dish.

Place macaroni in saucepan of boiling salted water and cook till tender.

Meanwhile, lightly beat the eggs. Coarsely chop the ham. Grate the cheese. Drain macaroni and place in soufflé dish. Add 2 oz (50 g) of the butter, 5 oz (150 g) of the cheese, the eggs and ham to the dish. Add a pinch of cayenne and season to taste. Mix well. Sprinkle with remaining cheese and dot with the rest of the butter.

Bake on top shelf of oven for 10 minutes or till golden and lightly set. Serve immediately with a tomato salad.

Cheesy noodles with ham

Overall timing 1 hour

Freezing Not suitable

To serve 4

8 oz	Tagliatelle	225 g
	Salt and pepper	
4 oz	Cheese	125 g
3	Eggs	3
¾ pint	White sauce	400 ml
4 oz	Sliced cooked ham	125 g

Preheat the oven to 400°F (200°C) Gas 6.

Cook the noodles in boiling salted water for about 10 minutes till tender.

Grate cheese. Separate eggs. Stir yolks, 3 oz (75 g) of the cheese and seasoning into sauce.

Cut ham into strips and stir into the sauce. Drain noodles thoroughly and fold into sauce. Season to taste. Whisk the egg whites in a bowl till stiff but not dry and fold into the mixture with metal spoon.

Pour the mixture into a greased ovenproof dish. Sprinkle remaining grated cheese over and bake for about 30 minutes till set and golden. Serve immediately with whole green beans mixed with flaked almonds and butter.

Spinach and veal ravioli

Overall timing 1 hour 35 minutes

Freezing Suitable: cook after thawing

To serve 2

2 oz	Spinach	50 g
6 oz	Veal	175 g
1 oz	Lean cooked ham	25 g
1 oz	Butter	25 g
2 tbsp	Fresh breadcrumbs	2x15 ml
1 tbsp	Milk	15 ml
1	Egg	1
2 oz	Grated Parmesan cheese	50 g
$\frac{1}{4}$ teasp	Dried marjoram	1.25 ml
	Pinch of grated nutmeg	
	Salt and pepper	
12 oz	Ravioli cases	350 g
$\frac{1}{4}$ pint	Tomato sauce	150 ml

Wash spinach and chop roughly. Blanch in boiling water for 5 minutes. Drain.

Chop the veal and ham into small pieces. Melt butter in frying pan and fry veal and ham till brown. Drain and cool. Soak breadcrumbs in milk till milk is absorbed.

Put meats and spinach through a mincer, then mix to a paste. Add egg, soaked breadcrumbs, 2 tbsp (2x15 ml) of the Parmesan, the marjoram, nutmeg and seasoning. Mix together well.

Use mixture to stuff ready-made ravioli cases, which can easily be obtained from delicatessens and supermarkets, then close them up. Cook ravioli in boiling, salted water for about 10 minutes. Drain, place in warmed serving dishes and cover with hot tomato sauce. Sprinkle the ravioli with remaining Parmesan. Serve with a crisp green salad.

Spaghetti omelette

Overall timing 30 minutes

Freezing Not suitable

To serve 4–6

12 oz	Spaghetti	350 g
	Salt and pepper	
1 oz	Cheddar cheese	25 g
1	Garlic clove	1
1 oz	Grated Parmesan cheese	25 g
4	Eggs	4
1 tbsp	Chopped parsley	15 ml
6	Basil leaves	6
2 oz	Butter	50 g

Cook the spaghetti in boiling salted water till tender.

Meanwhile, grate the Cheddar cheese. Peel and crush the garlic. Mix together the garlic, cheeses, eggs, parsley, chopped basil and seasoning.

Drain the spaghetti and put into a large bowl. Pour the egg and cheese mixture over and mix well. Melt 1 oz (25 g) butter in frying pan. Add spaghetti mixture and press down well with the back of a spoon to form a cake. Fry over a low heat for about 5 minutes, pressing down to keep the cake flat.

Run a knife round the edge of the omelette to loosen it, then turn it out on to a board. Add remaining butter to the pan and, when melted, slide the omelette back into the pan. Fry for 3–5 minutes till firmly set. Place on a warmed serving dish and serve immediately, cut into wedges.

Lasagne col pesto

Overall timing 1 hour

Freezing Suitable: reheat, covered with foil, in 350°F (180°C) Gas 4 oven for 1 hour

To serve 4

12 oz	Lasagne	350 g
	Salt	
4 tbsp	Grated Parmesan cheese	4x15 ml
2 oz	Butter	50 g
Pesto		
2	Garlic cloves	2
4 tbsp	Chopped fresh basil	4x15 ml
4 tbsp	Olive oil	4x15 ml
1 oz	Grated Parmesan cheese	25 g
	Pinch of salt	

Cook the lasagne in boiling salted water for 15–20 minutes till tender. Drain thoroughly and spread out on a damp cloth to cool.

Preheat oven to 350°F (180°C) Gas 4.

To make the pesto, peel and chop garlic and put in mortar with basil. Pound with pestle, gradually adding oil, Parmesan and salt.

Spread one-third of the lasagne over the bottom of a greased ovenproof dish. Spread with one-third of the pesto and sprinkle over 1 tbsp (15 ml) Parmesan. Repeat layers twice, adding extra Parmesan to the top. Dot with butter and bake for 20 minutes till heated through.

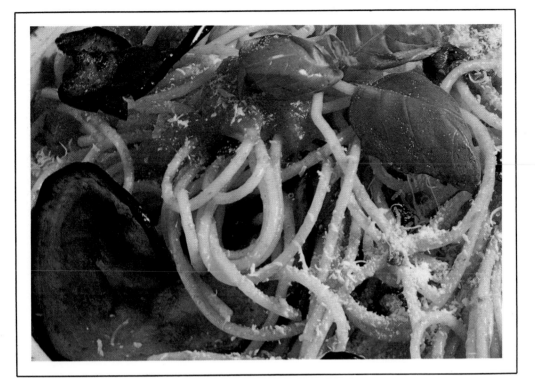

Spaghetti with aubergines

Overall timing 45 minutes plus draining

Freezing Not suitable

To serve 4

1	Large aubergine	1
	Salt and pepper	
1 lb	Ripe tomatoes	450 g
1	Garlic clove	1
	Oil	
2 teasp	Chopped fresh basil	2x5 ml
12 oz	Spaghetti	350 g
2 oz	Grated Parmesan cheese	50 g
	Sprig of basil	

Wash and thinly slice the aubergine. Put into a colander and sprinkle with salt. Leave to drain for 1 hour.

Blanch, peel and chop the tomatoes. Peel and crush garlic. Heat 3 tbsp (3x15 ml) oil in a saucepan, add garlic and fry for 1 minute. Add tomatoes, basil and seasoning, stir well and cook over a low heat for 15 minutes.

Cook spaghetti in boiling salted water till tender.

Meanwhile, rinse aubergine slices under running water and gently squeeze dry. Heat $\frac{1}{2}$ inch (12.5 mm) oil in a frying pan and fry aubergine slices, a few at a time, till crisp on both sides. Drain on kitchen paper and keep hot.

Drain spaghetti thoroughly. Put into a warmed serving dish and pour tomato sauce over. Add aubergine slices, sprinkle with cheese, garnish with sprig of basil and serve.

Macaroni niçoise

Overall timing 30 minutes

Freezing Not suitable

To serve 4

3	Anchovy fillets	3
12 oz	Tomatoes	350 g
1	Garlic clove	1
12 oz	Rigatoni	350 g
	Salt	
2 oz	Butter	50 g
2 oz	Grated Parmesan cheese	50 g
1 tbsp	Chopped fresh basil	15 ml

Chop the anchovies. Blanch, peel and cut tomatoes into thin slices. Place in a serving bowl with the anchovies and peeled and crushed garlic.

Cook the rigatoni in a large saucepan of boiling salted water till just tender. When cooked, drain in colander.

Melt butter in the saucepan and when frothy, add rigatoni and toss well. Add to the tomatoes and garlic, toss, then sprinkle with Parmesan and basil and serve immediately.

Spaghetti with bacon sauce

Overall timing 45 minutes

Freezing Not suitable

To serve 4

12 oz	Piece of smoked streaky bacon	350 g
1 tbsp	Oil	15 ml
1	Small red pepper	1
14 oz	Can of tomatoes	397 g
	Salt and pepper	
12 oz	Spaghetti	350 g
6 tbsp	Grated Parmesan cheese	6x15 ml

Remove the rind and any bones from the bacon. Cut into $\frac{1}{4}$ inch (6 mm) thick slices, then cut across into strips. Heat the oil in a saucepan, add the bacon and fry till golden all over.

Deseed and finely chop the pepper. Add to the pan and fry for 1 minute. Press the tomatoes and juice through a sieve into the pan and bring to the boil, stirring. Add seasoning, cover and simmer for 15 minutes.

Meanwhile, cook the spaghetti in boiling salted water till tender. Drain thoroughly and return to the pan. Add the sauce and all but 1 tbsp (15 ml) of the cheese. Toss lightly over a low heat for 2 minutes. Adjust the seasoning to taste.

Place spaghetti in a warmed serving dish and sprinkle with the remaining cheese. Serve immediately with fresh crusty bread.

Boer-style noodle supper

Overall timing 20 minutes

Freezing Not suitable

To serve 2

1 pint	Milk	560 ml
	Blade of mace	
6 oz	Noodles	175 g
1 oz	Butter	25 g
2	Eggs	2
¼ teasp	Ground cinnamon	1.25 ml
	Salt and pepper	

Put the milk in a saucepan with the mace and bring to the boil. Add the noodles and cook for about 5 minutes till tender. Drain, reserving the milk. Divide noodles between individual soup bowls and add half butter to each. Keep hot.

Separate the eggs. Beat the egg yolks in a bowl with the cinnamon and seasoning. Gradually strain the reserved milk on to the yolks, stirring constantly. Return to the pan.

Whisk the egg whites till stiff and fold into the yolk mixture. Cook over a low heat for 2–5 minutes without stirring till mixture begins to thicken. Do not allow to boil.

Pour egg mixture over the noodles and serve immediately with bread and a mixed salad.

Spaghetti with piquant sauce

Overall timing 50 minutes

Freezing Not suitable

To serve 4

1	Can of anchovy fillets	1
4 tbsp	Milk	4x15 ml
1 lb	Ripe tomatoes	450 g
1	Garlic clove	1
1	Dried red chilli	1
3 fl oz	Olive oil	90 ml
1 tbsp	Tomato purée	15 ml
2 tbsp	Capers	2x15 ml
12 oz	Spaghetti	350 g
	Salt and pepper	
4 oz	Stoned black olives	125 g

Drain the anchovies and put into a small bowl with the milk. Soak for 10 minutes. Blanch, peel and chop the tomatoes. Peel and crush the garlic; deseed and finely chop the chilli.

Heat the oil in a saucepan, add the garlic and cook for 2 minutes. Drain the anchovies, discarding the milk. Chop and add to the pan with the chilli. Fry for 3 minutes, pressing the anchovies with the back of a wooden spoon to break them up.

Add the tomatoes, tomato purée and capers. Bring to the boil, then cover and simmer for 15 minutes.

Meanwhile, cook the spaghetti in boiling salted water till tender. Drain thoroughly. Return to the pan and add the tomato and anchovy sauce and the black olives. Stir over a low heat for 3 minutes. Adjust seasoning to taste and serve hot.

Mushroom ravioli

Overall timing 45 minutes

Freezing Suitable: cook from frozen

To serve 4

12 oz	Strong flour	350 g
	Salt and pepper	
3	Eggs	3
1 lb	Mushrooms	450 g
1	Onion	1
2 oz	Butter	50 g

Sift flour and 1 teasp (5 ml) salt into a bowl. Add eggs and mix to a smooth, glossy dough.

Chop the mushrooms. Peel and finely chop onion. Melt half the butter in a frying pan and fry the onion for 5 minutes till transparent. Add mushrooms and seasoning and stir-fry over a high heat for about 5 minutes to evaporate any liquid. Reduce heat and cook gently for a further 5 minutes. Remove from heat and leave to cool.

Roll out the dough on a lightly floured surface and cut into 3 inch (7.5 cm) squares with a pastry wheel. Divide the mushroom mixture between the squares, then fold them over, pressing the edges together well to seal.

Put plenty of lightly salted water in a large saucepan and bring to the boil. Add the ravioli and cook for 10–15 minutes, then drain and place in a warmed serving dish. Melt the remaining butter, pour over the ravioli and toss well.

Neapolitan cannelloni

Overall timing 1½ hours

Freezing Suitable: reheat from frozen in 350°F (180°C) Gas 4 oven for 1 hour

To serve 4

12	Sheets of lasagne	12
8 oz	Mozzarella cheese	225 g
2 oz	Cooked ham	50 g
8 oz	Cream cheese	225 g
2	Eggs	2
	Salt and pepper	
1½ oz	Grated Parmesan cheese	40 g
Tomato sauce		
1	Onion	1
1	Garlic clove	1
1 tbsp	Oil	15 ml
14 oz	Can of tomatoes	397 g
1 tbsp	Chopped fresh basil	15 ml

Cook lasagne in boiling salted water for 10–15 minutes till tender. Drain and spread on a damp cloth to cool.

Thinly slice the Mozzarella. Dice ham. Place in a bowl with the cream cheese, eggs and seasoning. Mix well.

For the sauce, peel and finely chop onion. Peel and crush garlic. Heat oil in a saucepan, add onion and garlic and fry until golden. Add tomatoes in their juice, basil, salt and pepper. Cook for 10 minutes, stirring occasionally.

Preheat oven to 425°F (220°C) Gas 7.

Divide cheese mixture between lasagne sheets. Roll lasagne around filling and arrange, joins down, in greased ovenproof dish. Pour over the tomato sauce. Sprinkle half the Parmesan on top and bake for 15 minutes or until golden. Sprinkle with the rest of the Parmesan and serve immediately.

Spaghetti with sardine dressing

Overall timing 20 minutes

Freezing Not suitable

To serve 4

12 oz	Spaghetti	350 g
	Salt and pepper	
11½ oz	Can of sardines	326 g
2	Garlic cloves	2
3 oz	Butter	75 g

Cook the spaghetti in boiling salted water till tender.

Drain the sardines and put into a mortar. Peel and crush garlic and add to sardines. Pound to a paste with a pestle. Add the butter and mix well. Season to taste.

Drain the spaghetti and return to the pan. Add the sardine paste and toss lightly over a low heat till the spaghetti is coated. Place in a warmed serving dish and serve immediately with wedges of lemon.

Spaghetti with tomato sauce

Overall timing 30 minutes

Freezing Not suitable

To serve 4

1	Onion	1
2 lb	Cherry or plum tomatoes	900 g
	Bouquet garni	
	Pinch of sugar	
	Cayenne pepper or Tabasco sauce	
	Salt and pepper	
1 tbsp	Chopped fresh basil or parsley	15 ml
12 oz	Spaghetti	350 g

Peel and chop the onion. Halve the tomatoes. Put the onion and tomatoes in a saucepan with the bouquet garni and simmer gently until mushy.

Discard the bouquet garni, then rub the tomato sauce through a sieve, or purée in a blender. Return to the pan and add the sugar, a little cayenne or Tabasco sauce and seasoning. Stir in the herbs and reheat gently.

Meanwhile, cook the spaghetti in boiling salted water till just tender. Drain well and turn into a warmed serving dish. Pile the tomato sauce on top and serve.

Neapolitan rigatoni

Overall timing 50 minutes

Freezing Not suitable

To serve 2

2	Streaky bacon rashers	2
1	Onion	1
1	Garlic clove	1
1 oz	Lard	25 g
6 oz	Minced beef	175 g
5 tbsp	Beef stock	5x15 ml
5 tbsp	Red wine	5x15 ml
1 tbsp	Tomato purée	15 ml
1 teasp	Chopped fresh basil	5 ml
	Salt and pepper	
8 oz	Rigatoni	225 g

Derind and finely chop bacon. Peel and chop onion. Peel and crush garlic. Melt the lard in a saucepan, add bacon, onion and garlic and fry for 10 minutes till golden.

Add the minced beef and fry, stirring, till brown. Gradually stir in the stock, wine, tomato purée, basil and seasoning. Cover and simmer for 30 minutes.

Meanwhile, cook rigatoni in boiling salted water till tender. Drain thoroughly and pile on to a warmed serving dish. Keep hot.

Taste the sauce and adjust seasoning. Purée in a blender or press through a sieve, then reheat and spoon over rigatoni. Serve immediately with a mixed salad and grated Parmesan cheese.

Macaroni with mushrooms

Overall timing 30 minutes

Freezing Not suitable

To serve 4

4 oz	Button mushrooms	125 g
4 oz	Butter	125 g
8 fl oz	Carton of single cream	227 ml
12 oz	Short-cut macaroni	350 g
	Salt and pepper	
4 oz	Cooked ham	125 g
2 oz	Grated Parmesan cheese	50 g
½ pint	White sauce	300 ml

Finely chop the mushrooms. Place in a small saucepan with 2 oz (50 g) of the butter and cook gently for 5 minutes. Remove from heat and stir in cream.

Cook macaroni in boiling salted water till tender. Drain.

Cut the ham into pieces and add to the macaroni with 1 oz (25 g) of cheese, 1 oz (25 g) of butter and seasoning. Place macaroni in a flameproof dish with mushroom mixture and stir well. Cook gently for 10 minutes.

Preheat grill.

Pour white sauce over macaroni, sprinkle with remaining cheese and dot with remaining butter. Grill for 5 minutes.

Noodle tortilla

Overall timing 45 minutes

Freezing Not suitable

To serve 4

12 oz	Noodles	350 g
	Salt	
3 oz	Butter	75 g
4 oz	Cottage cheese	125 g
3	Eggs	3
¼ teasp	Ground allspice	1.25 ml
2 tbsp	Chopped parsley	2x15 ml

Cook the noodles in boiling salted water for about 5 minutes till tender. Drain thoroughly and put into a warm bowl. Stir in 2 oz (50 g) of the butter and the sieved cottage cheese. Lightly beat the eggs and stir into the noodles with salt, allspice and chopped parsley.

Preheat the grill. Melt the remaining butter in a frying pan. Add the noodle mixture and smooth the top. Cook over a moderate heat for 5 minutes till lightly set. Put the pan under the grill to brown the top.

Turn omelette on to a warmed serving plate and serve immediately.

Pasta with lamb and tomato sauce

Overall timing 1¼ hours

Freezing Not suitable

To serve 2

2	Bacon rashers	2
8 oz	Tomatoes	225 g
1	Onion	1
1	Garlic clove	1
2 tbsp	Oil	2x15 ml
6 oz	Minced lamb	175 g
¼ pint	Red wine	150 ml
	Salt and pepper	
8 oz	Pasta shapes	225 g

Derind and chop bacon. Blanch, peel and chop tomatoes. Peel and chop onion and garlic. Heat the oil in a saucepan, add the bacon and fry for 5 minutes. Add onion and garlic and fry gently till transparent. Add the minced lamb and fry for about 15 minutes till browned.

Stir in the red wine, tomatoes and seasoning. Cover and simmer for 40 minutes.

Meanwhile, cook pasta in boiling salted water till tender. Drain and place in warmed serving dish.

Spoon meat sauce over pasta and serve hot with a green salad.

Spaghetti with tuna

Overall timing 30 minutes

Freezing Not suitable

To serve 4

1	Onion	1
2	Garlic cloves	2
7 oz	Can of tuna	198 g
1 tbsp	Olive oil	15 ml
12 oz	Spaghetti	350 g
	Salt and pepper	
4	Anchovy fillets	4
2 tbsp	Tomato purée	2x15 ml
½ teasp	Sugar	2.5 ml
6 tbsp	Water	6x15 ml
1 tbsp	Chopped parsley	15 ml
2 teasp	Chopped fresh basil	2x5 ml

Peel and finely chop the onion; peel and crush the garlic. Drain the oil from the tuna into a saucepan. Add the olive oil and heat. Add the onion and garlic and fry till just golden.

Put the spaghetti into a saucepan of boiling salted water and cook gently till just tender.

Meanwhile, chop the anchovies and add to the onion with the tomato puree, sugar and water. Bring to the boil.

Flake the tuna fish and add to the pan with seasoning. Cover and simmer for 5 minutes.

Drain the spaghetti and add to the pan with the herbs. Toss lightly over a low heat for 2–3 minutes. Adjust seasoning to taste and serve immediately.

Striped vermicelli

Overall timing 45 minutes

Freezing Not suitable

To serve 4

1	Can of anchovies	1
6 tbsp	Milk	6x15 ml
1	Large onion	1
1	Garlic clove	1
2 tbsp	Oil	2x15 ml
14 oz	Can of tomatoes	397 g
	Salt and pepper	
	Chilli powder	
1 tbsp	Chopped parsley	15 ml
12 oz	Vermicelli	350 g
$\frac{1}{4}$ pint	Carton of double cream	150 ml

Drain the anchovies and soak in the milk for 10 minutes.

Meanwhile, peel and finely chop the onion; peel and crush the garlic. Heat the oil in a small saucepan, add onion and garlic and fry till transparent. Add tomatoes and juice, salt, a pinch of chilli powder and parsley. Simmer for 20 minutes, stirring frequently.

Drain the anchovies and add to the tomato mixture. Purée in a blender or rub through a sieve. Season and reheat gently.

Cook the vermicelli in boiling salted water for 3 minutes till tender. Drain thoroughly and arrange on a warmed flat serving dish. Smooth the top and keep hot.

Warm the cream, then spread it in a wide band across the centre of the vermicelli. Spread the tomato sauce in a wide band on either side of the cream. Serve with hot garlic bread.

Tagliatelli with ham

Overall timing 25 minutes

Freezing Not suitable

To serve 4

12 oz	Tagliatelli	350 g
	Salt and pepper	
1	Large onion	1
2 oz	Butter	50 g
2 tbsp	Oil	2x15 ml
1	Garlic clove	1
4 oz	Lean cooked ham	125 g
2 teasp	Dried marjoram	2x5 ml
14 oz	Can of tomatoes	397 g
6 tbsp	Grated Parmesan cheese	6x15 ml

Cook the tagliatelli in boiling salted water till tender.

Meanwhile, peel and finely chop the onion. Heat the butter and oil in a large saucepan and fry the onion till transparent. Peel and crush the garlic and add to the pan. Chop the ham very finely and add to the pan with the marjoram and tomatoes with their juice. Season and cook for 10 minutes, stirring to break up the tomatoes.

Drain the tagliatelli and place in a warmed bowl. Add the sauce and Parmesan and toss well, adding seasoning to taste. Serve immediately with a watercress, cucumber and lettuce salad.

Spinach ravioli

Overall timing 1¼ hours

Freezing Suitable: cook ravioli from frozen, then add to tomato sauce

To serve 4–6

12 oz	Strong flour	350 g
	Salt and pepper	
3	Eggs	3
2	Bacon rashers	2
1	Large onion	1
1 ·	Garlic clove	1
1 tbsp	Oil	15 ml
4 oz	Minced veal	125 g
4 oz	Sausagemeat	125 g
¼ teasp	Grated nutmeg	1.25 ml
6 tbsp	Dry white wine	6x15 ml
1 lb	Spinach	450 g
14 oz	Can of tomatoes	397 g
2 oz	Butter	50 g

Sift flour and 1 teasp (5 ml) salt into a bowl. Add eggs and mix to smooth, glossy dough.

Derind and dice bacon. Peel and finely chop onion; peel and crush garlic. Heat oil in a saucepan, add bacon, onion and garlic and fry for 5 minutes. Add the veal, sausagemeat and nutmeg and fry for 5 minutes. Stir in wine and seasoning and bring to the boil. Cover and simmer for 15 minutes.

Shred spinach and add to meat. Cover and simmer for a further 5 minutes.

Roll out dough to a large rectangle. Cut out rounds. Dot spoonfuls of spinach mixture on rounds. Fold in half and pinch edges to seal. Roll each half-moon round your forefinger and pinch ends together.

Cook ravioli in boiling salted water till tender. Drain. Press tomatoes through a sieve. Melt butter in pan, stir in tomatoes and seasoning and heat. Return ravioli to pan and toss lightly till coated.

Spaghetti with lamb sauce

Overall timing 1¾ hours

Freezing Not suitable

To serve 4

1½ lb	Boned shoulder of lamb	700 g
	Salt and pepper	
3 tbsp	Plain flour	3x15 ml
1	Large onion	1
3 tbsp	Olive oil	3x15 ml
2 teasp	Paprika	2x5 ml
¾ pint	Chicken stock	400 ml
2 tbsp	Tomato purée	2x15 ml
12 oz	Spaghetti	350 g

Cut the lamb into bite-size pieces. Season the flour and toss the meat in it till evenly coated. Peel and thinly slice the onion. Heat the oil in a saucepan, add the onion and fry till transparent. Add the meat and fry till browned all over. Sprinkle in any remaining flour and the paprika and cook for 1 minute, stirring.

Gradually add the stock and bring to the boil, stirring constantly. Add the tomato purée and seasoning, cover and simmer gently for about 1 hour till tender.

Break the spaghetti into 4 inch (10 cm) lengths. Add 1 pint (560 ml) water to the lamb and bring to the boil. Add the spaghetti and simmer till tender, stirring frequently.

Taste and adjust seasoning. Divide between warmed individual serving dishes, arranging the meat on top. Serve immediately.

Crusty noodle shapes

Overall timing 55 minutes

Freezing Not suitable

To serve 4

12 oz	Egg noodles	350 g
	Salt	
1 oz	Cheese	25 g
¾ pint	White sauce	400 ml
¼ teasp	Grated nutmeg	1.25 ml
2	Eggs	2
1 oz	Dried breadcrumbs	25 g
6 tbsp	Oil	6x15 ml
4 oz	Sliced cooked ham	125 g
4 oz	Mozzarella cheese	125 g
	Sprigs of parsley	
	Lemon	

Cook the noodles in boiling salted water for about 5 minutes till tender. Drain the noodles thoroughly and put into a bowl.

Grate the cheese and mix into the white sauce with nutmeg. Pour the sauce over the noodles and mix well. Press into a roasting tin to 1 inch (2.5 cm) thickness and leave to cool.

Preheat the oven to 450°F (230°C) Gas 8.

Beat the eggs in a bowl with salt. Spread the breadcrumbs on a sheet of greaseproof paper.

Cut the noodle mixture into diamond shapes or rounds with a biscuit cutter. Dip the shapes into the egg, then the breadcrumbs, pressing the crumbs on to the shapes to make them stick. Heat the oil in a frying pan and fry the shapes until golden on both sides. Drain on kitchen paper. Using a sharp knife, slice each one through the centre.

Halve each slice of ham and put a piece on the bottom half of each shape; top with a thin slice of Mozzarella. Replace the top half of each shape and arrange on a baking tray. Bake for about 10 minutes. Serve hot, garnished with parsley sprigs and lemon.

Ratatouille

Overall timing 1½ hours

Freezing Suitable

To serve 8

2	Large aubergines	2
1 lb	Courgettes	450 g
	Salt and pepper	
3	Large onions	3
2–3	Garlic cloves	2–3
2	Green peppers	2
1 lb	Ripe tomatoes	450 g
5 tbsp	Olive oil	5x15 ml
1 teasp	Sugar	5 ml

Cut the aubergines into 1 inch (2.5 cm) chunks. Cut courgettes into quarters lengthways, then into 1 inch (2.5 cm) lengths. Put the vegetables into a colander, sprinkle with salt and leave to drain for 30 minutes.

Meanwhile, peel and slice the onions. Peel and crush the garlic. Deseed and thinly slice the peppers. Blanch, peel and halve the tomatoes.

Heat the oil in a flameproof casserole, add the onions and garlic and fry gently till transparent. Dry the aubergines and courgettes on kitchen paper and add to the pan with the peppers, tomatoes, sugar and plenty of pepper. Cook for about 45 minutes till the vegetables are tender but not mushy. Adjust the seasoning and serve hot, or cool and chill before serving.

Aubergine cheese bake

Overall timing 2¼ hours

Freezing Suitable: bake from frozen in 350°F (180°C) Gas 4 oven for 45 minutes

To serve 4

1¼ lb	Aubergines	600 g
	Salt and pepper	
2 tbsp	Plain flour	2x15 ml
	Oil	
1	Small onion	1
14 oz	Can of tomatoes	397 g
½ teasp	Dried basil	2.5 ml
8 oz	Mozzarella cheese	225 g
3 oz	Grated Parmesan cheese	75 g

Remove stalks from aubergines and cut lengthways into ½ inch (12.5 mm) thick slices. Sprinkle with salt. Leave for 1 hour, then rinse and pat dry. Coat with flour.

Preheat the oven to 350°F (180°C) Gas 4.

Heat oil in a large frying pan and fry aubergine slices on both sides till golden. Drain on kitchen paper and keep warm.

Peel and finely chop onion. Fry till transparent, adding more oil to pan if necessary. Mash tomatoes and juice and add to pan with seasoning. Cook for 10 minutes. Stir in basil and simmer for a further 5 minutes.

Place a layer of aubergines in oiled oven-proof dish. Cover with slices of Mozzarella and spoon on a little tomato sauce. Sprinkle with Parmesan and a pinch of salt. Repeat layering, ending with Parmesan. Sprinkle a little oil over surface and bake for 15 minutes or until top begins to brown.

Aubergine boxes

Overall timing 1½ hours

Freezing Not suitable

To serve 4

1 lb	Aubergines	450 g
	Salt and pepper	
3	Anchovy fillets	3
2 oz	Mozzarella cheese	50 g
1 teasp	Dried basil	2x5 ml
2 teasp	Capers	2x5 ml
1	Large onion	1
2	Garlic cloves	2
2 tbsp	Oil	2x15 ml
14 oz	Can of tomatoes	397 g
1 tbsp	Worcestershire sauce	15 ml
4–5	Fresh tomatoes (optional)	4–5

Cook aubergines in boiling salted water for 5 minutes. Drain and leave to cool, then cut off stalks and make a lengthways cut through the aubergines leaving the halves still attached at one side. Ease open and remove most of the flesh with a teaspoon. Finely chop or mash the flesh and put into a bowl.

Drain and chop anchovies. Dice Mozzarella. Mix together aubergine flesh, anchovies, basil, Mozzarella, capers and seasoning. Stuff the hollowed-out aubergine shells with mixture.

Preheat the oven to 350°F (180°C) Gas 4.

Peel and chop onion. Peel and crush garlic. Heat oil in flameproof casserole and fry onion till brown. Stir in garlic, tomatoes, Worcestershire sauce and seasoning. Simmer gently for about 10 minutes or until the sauce has become quite "mushy".

Arrange the stuffed aubergines on top of sauce and bake for 45 minutes. You can add 4–5 fresh tomatoes about 15 minutes before the end of the cooking time – they add attractive colour as well as taste.

Cabbage parcels

Overall timing 1¼ hours

Freezing Not suitable

To serve 4

1	White cabbage	1
3 oz	Long grain rice	75 g
1	Small onion	1
6 tbsp	Oil	6x15 ml
8 oz	Minced beef	225 g
	Salt and pepper	
¼ teasp	Grated nutmeg	1.25 ml
1 teasp	Dried oregano	5 ml
8 fl oz	Stock	220 ml
1 oz	Butter	25 g
1 tbsp	Plain flour	15 ml
1	Egg	1
2	Egg yolks	2
6 tbsp	Lemon juice	6x15 ml
¾ pint	White sauce	400 ml

Remove core from cabbage and cook in boiling water for 5 minutes. Drain and cool, then peel away 16–20 leaves. Add rice to same pan of boiling water and cook till tender. Drain.

Peel and chop onion. Heat 4 tbsp (4x15 ml) oil in a frying pan and cook onion till transparent. Add mince, salt, pepper, nutmeg and oregano. Cook for 5–8 minutes. Cool, then mix in rice.

Place a little stuffing on each cabbage leaf. Fold in sides and roll into tight parcels. Heat rest of oil in flameproof casserole. Pack cabbage rolls tightly in casserole and pour in stock. Cut leftover cabbage heart in two and place on top. Cover and simmer gently for 40 minutes.

Transfer cabbage rolls to warmed serving dish. Pour cooking liquor into a measuring jug and make up to 8 fl oz (220 ml) with water if necessary.

Melt butter in saucepan, then stir in flour and cooking liquor and simmer until thickened. Beat egg and egg yolks with lemon juice till foamy. Add to pan off heat. Return to a gentle heat. Don't allow sauce to boil. Stir in white sauce and heat. Pour sauce over rolls

Braised lettuce

Overall timing 40 minutes

Freezing Not suitable

To serve 4

4	Small round lettuces	4
	Salt and pepper	
2	Onions	2
2	Carrots	2
4 oz	Streaky bacon rashers	125 g
1 oz	Butter	25 g
½ pint	Chicken stock	300 ml

Trim lettuces. Blanch in boiling salted water for 2 minutes, then drain thoroughly.

Peel and slice onions and carrots. Derind and thinly slice bacon. Melt butter in saucepan, add onions, carrots and bacon and fry gently for 10 minutes, stirring occasionally.

Pour in stock and add blanched lettuces and seasoning. Cover and simmer for 20 minutes.

Transfer bacon and vegetables to warmed serving dish and keep hot. Boil cooking liquor rapidly to reduce by half. Taste and adjust seasoning. Pour over lettuce and serve immediately with roast meats.

Casseroled lettuce rolls

Overall timing 1 hour

Freezing Not suitable

To serve 4

8 oz	Streaky bacon	225 g
10	Large lettuce leaves	10
2	Onions	2
2	Carrots	2
	Salt and pepper	
¼ pint	Stock	150 ml
2 tbsp	Lemon juice	2x15 ml
Stuffing		
1	Onion	1
2 tbsp	Oil	2x15 ml
8 oz	Chicken livers	225 g
2 oz	Long grain rice	50 g
½ pint	Chicken stock	300 ml
	Bouquet garni	
	Salt and pepper	

To make the stuffing, peel and chop onion. Heat oil in pan and fry onion till golden. Chop chicken livers. Add to pan and brown on all sides.

Add rice, stock, bouquet garni and seasoning. Bring to the boil. Cover and simmer for 15 minutes, shaking pan frequently.

Meanwhile, derind and halve bacon rashers, then use them to line bottom and sides of an ovenproof dish. Wash and dry lettuce leaves. Peel and slice onions into rings. Peel and thinly slice carrots. Blanch lettuce, onions and carrots in boiling salted water for 3 minutes. Drain thoroughly.

Preheat the oven to 350°F (180°C) Gas 4.

Spread out lettuce leaves. Taste stuffing and adjust seasoning. Divide between lettuce leaves. Fold in sides of leaves, then roll up tightly round stuffing. Arrange, join side down, in ovenproof dish. Add blanched onions and carrots. Mix stock, lemon juice and seasoning. Pour over lettuce. Cover tightly and bake for 25–30 minutes.

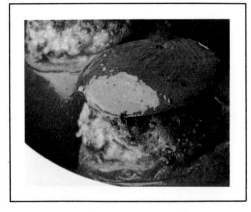

Sausagemeat tomatoes

Overall timing 45 minutes

Freezing Not suitable

To serve 4

8	Tomatoes	8
1	Large onion	1
4 tbsp	Oil	4x15 ml
12 oz	Pork sausagemeat	350 g
2 oz	Fresh breadcrumbs	50 g
1 tbsp	Chopped parsley	15 ml
	Salt and pepper	
1	Egg	1

Preheat the oven to 350°F (180°C) Gas 4.

Cut lids off the tomatoes and scoop out the flesh. Discard the seeds and chop the flesh. Peel and chop onion. Heat half the oil in a frying pan and fry onion till transparent. Add sausagemeat and fry until browned.

Remove from heat and stir in tomato flesh, breadcrumbs, parsley and seasoning. Bind with egg. Press mixture into tomato shells and replace lids.

Arrange tomatoes in ovenproof dish and brush with remaining oil. Bake for 30 minutes. Serve hot.

Lamb-stuffed onions

Overall timing 1¼ hours

Freezing Not suitable

To serve 6

6	Large onions	6
	Salt and pepper	
2 tbsp	Oil	2x15 ml
1½ teasp	Mixed spice	7.5 ml
1 lb	Minced lamb	450 g
1 oz	Fresh breadcrumbs	25 g
4 oz	Cottage cheese	125 g
1 oz	Butter	25 g
2 tbsp	Plain flour	2x15 ml
3 tbsp	Tomato purée	3x15 ml
½ pint	Light stock	300 ml

Peel onions and cook in boiling salted water for 15 minutes. Drain and cool. Remove slice from bottom of each onion. Cut slice from top and scoop out centres, leaving a ½ inch (12.5mm) shell. Put shells in flameproof casserole. Chop onion centres.

Heat oil and fry chopped onion with spice for 3 minutes. Add lamb and fry for 5 minutes. Stir in breadcrumbs, cheese and seasoning. Press into onion shells.

Melt butter, add flour and stir in tomato purée, stock and seasoning. Bring to the boil and pour over onions. Cover and simmer for 45 minutes till onions are tender.

Tomatoes stuffed with vegetables

Overall timing 30 minutes

Freezing Not suitable

To serve 4

3	Large waxy potatoes	3
3	Large carrots	3
4 oz	Green beans	125 g
2	Stalks of celery	2
	Salt and pepper	
4 oz	Frozen peas	125 g
6 tbsp	Mayonnaise	6x15 ml
	Lemon juice	
4	Large tomatoes	4
	Basil leaves	

Peel the potatoes. Scrape the carrots. Top and tail the beans. Wash and trim the celery. Dice all the vegetables. Cook in boiling salted water for 5 minutes. Add the peas and cook for a further 5 minutes or until tender. Drain well and cool.

Add the mayonnaise to the vegetables with a few drops of lemon juice and seasoning and mix well.

Halve the tomatoes and scoop out the seeds and centres. Fill with the vegetable mixture and arrange on a serving plate. Serve garnished with basil leaves.

Chicory bake

Overall timing 45 minutes

Freezing Not suitable

To serve 2

2	Heads of chicory	2
	Salt and pepper	
½ teasp	Sugar	2.5 ml
1 oz	Butter	25 g
½ teasp	Lemon juice	2.5 ml
2	Slices of Gruyère cheese	2
2	Tomatoes	2
	Lettuce leaves	

Place chicory in saucepan of boiling water. Add pinch of salt, sugar, a knob of butter and lemon juice. Cook for 30 minutes.

Preheat the oven to 425°F (220°C) Gas 7.

Drain chicory. Wrap each head in slice of cheese. Place seam-side down in greased ovenproof dish and surround with halved tomatoes. Season well, dot with the rest of the butter and bake for 15 minutes. Garnish with lettuce leaves and serve hot.

Corn prawn salad

Overall timing 15 minutes plus 1 hour chilling

Freezing Not suitable

To serve 2

11½ oz	Can of sweetcorn kernels	326 g
3	Tomatoes	3
8 oz	Shelled prawns	225 g
Dressing		
1	Onion	1
2 tbsp	Herb vinegar	2x15 ml
3 tbsp	Oil	3x15 ml
	Salt and pepper	
1 tbsp	Chopped fresh sage	15 ml
1 tbsp	Chopped parsley	15 ml
1 tbsp	Chopped chives	15 ml

Drain sweetcorn. Blanch and peel tomatoes and cut into strips. Put sweetcorn, tomatoes and prawns in a serving dish.

To make the dressing, peel and finely chop onion. Mix together vinegar, oil and seasoning, then add the onion, sage, parsley and chives.

Pour dressing over salad, mix in well, cover and chill for 1 hour before serving.

Chicory rolls in cheese sauce

Overall timing 1¼ hours

Freezing Suitable: bake from frozen in cold oven set to 350°F (180°C) Gas 4 for 1 hour; increase to 450°F (230°C) Gas 8 for extra 10 minutes

To serve 4–6

4 oz	Butter	125 g
8	Large heads of chicory	8
2 tbsp	Lemon juice	2x15 ml
1 teasp	Sugar	5 ml
	Salt and pepper	
1 oz	Plain flour	25 g
½ pint	Milk	300 ml
	Grated nutmeg	
2	Egg yolks	2
2 oz	Grated Parmesan cheese	50 g
8	Thin slices of cooked ham	8

Melt half butter in a saucepan and add chicory, lemon juice, sugar and seasoning. Cover and cook gently for about 30 minutes, turning the chicory occasionally.

Meanwhile, make the sauce. Melt 1 oz (25 g) of remaining butter in another saucepan and stir in the flour. Remove from heat and gradually add milk. Return to heat and bring to the boil, stirring until thickened. Remove from heat and stir in a pinch of nutmeg, egg yolks, cheese and seasoning.

Preheat the grill.

Lift out chicory with draining spoon. Reserve cooking liquor. Wrap each chicory head in a slice of ham and arrange in a greased ovenproof dish. Add reserved liquor to sauce, beat well, then pour over chicory. Dot with the rest of the butter and grill for 5–10 minutes till golden on top. Serve immediately.

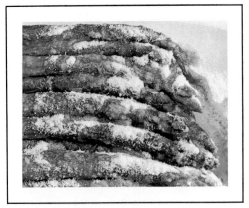

Asparagus milanese

Overall timing 30 minutes

Freezing Not suitable

To serve 4

1 lb	Asparagus	450 g
	Salt	
2 oz	Grated Parmesan cheese	50 g
2 oz	Butter	50 g

Cook asparagus in boiling salted water for 15–20 minutes till tender. Drain carefully on a tea-towel or kitchen paper, then place on a warmed serving dish and cool slightly. Sprinkle Parmesan over the asparagus tips.

Melt the butter in a small saucepan over a low heat. When golden brown, pour over the Parmesan. Serve immediately.

Alsace salad

Overall timing 15 minutes

Freezing Not suitable

To serve 6

2	Dessert apples	2
3	Boiled potatoes	3
1	Small cooked beetroot	1
2	Frankfurters	2
1	Onion	1
1	Hard-boiled egg	1
2 teasp	Chopped parsley	2x5 ml
	Sprigs of parsley	
8	Walnuts	8
3 tbsp	Olive oil	3x15 ml
1 tbsp	Wine vinegar	15 ml
1 teasp	Powdered mustard	5 ml
	Salt and pepper	

Peel, core and chop apples. Peel and dice potatoes and beetroot. Slice frankfurters. Peel onion and cut into rings. Shell egg and cut into 6 wedges.

Arrange prepared ingredients in rows in a serving dish and sprinkle with parsley. Garnish with parsley sprigs and walnuts.

To make dressing, mix oil with vinegar, mustard and seasoning. Pour dressing over salad and serve immediately.

Chive and mushroom pancakes

Overall timing 1¼ hours

Freezing Suitable: bake filled pancakes with sauce in 350°F (180°C) Gas 4 oven for 20 minutes

To serve 4–6

1 lb	Button mushrooms	450 g
1 oz	Butter	25 g
½ pint	Milk	300 ml
	Salt and pepper	
¼ teasp	Grated nutmeg	1.25 ml
1½ tbsp	Lemon juice	22.5 ml
½ pint	White sauce	300 ml
Pancakes		
5 oz	Plain flour	150 g
¼ teasp	Salt	1.25 ml
2	Eggs	2
2 tbsp	Chopped chives	2x15 ml
	Oil for frying	

Finely chop mushrooms. Melt butter in a saucepan and fry mushrooms for 3 minutes. Add milk, seasoning, nutmeg and lemon juice. Bring to the boil and simmer for 10 minutes. Strain, reserving the milk for the pancakes.

Make the pancakes as left, using the reserved milk instead of beer and adding the chives to the batter. Fry 12 pancakes.

Preheat the oven to 350°F (180°C) Gas 4.

Divide the mushroom filling between the pancakes and roll them to enclose the filling. Arrange in a greased ovenproof dish and pour the white sauce over. Bake for about 20 minutes. Serve immediately, garnished with extra fluted mushrooms, if liked.

Cottage baked potatoes

Overall timing 2 hours

Freezing Not suitable

To serve 6

6x8 oz	Potatoes	6x225 g
3 oz	Melted butter	75 g
	Salt and pepper	
3 oz	Cottage or cream cheese	75 g
5 tbsp	Milk	5x15 ml
2 teasp	Paprika	2x5 ml

Preheat the oven to 400°F (200°C) Gas 6.

Scrub and dry the potatoes and push a metal skewer lengthways through each one. Brush potatoes with a little melted butter and place on a baking tray. Bake for 1–1¼ hours till tender.

Take the potatoes out of the oven, remove skewers and cut a cross in the top of each. Lift the centre of each cross and scoop out some of the flesh. Put the flesh into a bowl and mash with a fork. Add half the remaining melted butter and mix thoroughly. Season well.

Mix the cheese, milk and rest of the butter in a bowl and beat till creamy. Spoon into the potatoes and cover with the mashed potato mixture. Sprinkle with paprika and salt.

Replace the potatoes on the baking tray and bake for about 15 minutes till the topping is golden. Arrange on a serving dish and serve immediately.

Carrots in batter

Overall timing 1 hour

Freezing Not suitable

To serve 4

1 lb	Carrots	450 g
1 oz	Butter	25 g
½ pint	Water	300 ml
¼ teasp	Salt	1.25 ml
	Oil for frying	
	Flour for coating	
Batter		
4 oz	Plain flour	125 g
6 tbsp	Milk	6x15 ml
2	Eggs	2
¼ teasp	Salt	1.25 ml
	Sprigs of parsley	

Scrape carrots and halve crossways. Melt butter in water in a saucepan. When boiling, add carrots and salt, cover and cook for 20 minutes.

To make the batter, sift flour into a large bowl and mix in the milk, eggs and salt until well combined and smooth.

Heat oil in deep fryer to 360°F (180°C).

Drain carrots and dry well on kitchen paper. Dip carrot pieces first in flour, then coat in batter. Use a skewer to lower carrots (four or five at a time) into the oil. Cook for 3 minutes till golden. Remove with a draining spoon, drain on kitchen paper and serve hot, garnished with parsley.

Country-style peas

Overall timing 45 minutes

Freezing Not suitable

To serve 6

4 oz	Button onions	125 g
2 lb	Fresh peas	900 g
3	Carrots	3
8 oz	New potatoes	225 g
1	Round lettuce	1
1	Thick streaky bacon rasher	1
2 oz	Butter	50 g
	Sprig of thyme	
	Sprig of tarragon	
	Bay leaf	
	Salt and pepper	

Blanch and peel onions. Shell peas; scrape and dice carrots. Scrub potatoes. Tear lettuce into pieces. Derind bacon and cut into strips.

Melt butter in a flameproof casserole and fry bacon and onions till bacon fat begins to run. Add remaining vegetables, herbs tied together, seasoning and ¼ pint (150 ml) water. Cover and simmer for 25 minutes till vegetables are tender. Remove herbs before serving.

Cheese and potato bake

Overall timing 1¼ hours

Freezing Not suitable

To serve 6

2 lb	New potatoes	900 g
3	Onions	3
2 tbsp	Oil	2x15 ml
1	Red pepper	1
8 oz	Sliced cooked ham	225 g
14 oz	Can of tomatoes	397 g
5	Small gherkins	5
12 oz	Red Leicester cheese	350 g
¼ pint	Soured cream	150 ml
2	Egg yolks	2
	Salt and pepper	
¼ teasp	Grated nutmeg	1.25 ml
2 oz	Butter	50 g

Preheat the oven to 400°F (200°C) Gas 6.

Scrub potatoes. Cook in boiling water for 30 minutes.

Peel and thinly slice onions. Fry in oil for 5 minutes. Deseed and slice red pepper, add to onion and fry for 5 minutes. Shred ham; add to pan with tomatoes, sliced gherkins and seasoning.

Drain potatoes and cool. Slice thickly. Slice cheese. Layer potatoes, cheese and tomato mixture in greased ovenproof dish. Mix soured cream, egg yolks, seasoning and nutmeg and pour over top. Dot with butter. Bake for 20 minutes.

Swiss style potatoes

Overall timing 1 hour

Freezing Not suitable

To serve 4

2 lb	Potatoes	900 g
3 tbsp	Caraway seeds	3x15 ml
1 tbsp	Sea-salt	15 ml
2 oz	Butter	50 g
8 oz	Curd cheese	225 g
4 fl oz	Milk	120 ml
1	Onion	1
2 tbsp	Chopped parsley	2x15 ml
2 tbsp	Chopped mustard and cress	2x15 ml
	Salt and pepper	
Garnish		
	Parsley sprigs	
	Mustard and cress	

Preheat the oven to 350°F (180°C) Gas 4.

Halve potatoes. Mix caraway seeds and sea-salt together in a bowl. Dip the cut sides of potatoes into mixture. Place potatoes in greased ovenproof dish with the caraway seeds facing up.

Melt the butter and pour a little over each potato half. Bake for 45 minutes.

Mix cheese with milk in a bowl. Peel and finely chop onion and add to bowl with parsley, mustard and cress and seasoning.

Divide cheese mixture between warmed serving plates and place the potatoes on top. Garnish with parsley and cress.

Tomatoes stuffed with buckling

Overall timing 40 minutes plus setting

Freezing Not suitable

To serve 2

1	Buckling	1
1½ tbsp	Thick mayonnaise	22.5 ml
2 teasp	Lemon juice	2x5 ml
	Salt	
1	Hard-boiled egg	1
1 teasp	Chopped parsley	5 ml
1 teasp	Chopped chives	5 ml
4 tbsp	Water	4x15 ml
	Pinch of sugar	
½ teasp	Vinegar	2.5 ml
2	Large tomatoes	2
2	Slices of Pumpernickel bread	2
	Butter	
	Lettuce leaves	
	Parsley	

Skin and bone the buckling. Chop flesh finely and place in a bowl. Add mayonnaise, lemon juice and salt. Shell and dice the hard-boiled egg and add with herbs to buckling mixture. Mix well.

Put water, sugar, pinch of salt and vinegar into a saucepan and heat till warm. Leave to cool, then add to buckling mixture.

Cut tops off tomatoes and remove the inside (this can be mixed into buckling mixture, if you like). Fill tomatoes with the buckling mixture and replace tops. Chill for 30 minutes.

Just before serving, put each tomato on to a slice of buttered Pumpernickel which should be slightly bigger than the base of the tomato. Serve on a bed of lettuce and garnish with parsley.

Courgettes with mozzarella

Overall timing 30 minutes plus chilling

Freezing Suitable: reheat from frozen in 350°F (180°C) Gas 4 oven for 45 minutes

To serve 2

1	Onion	1
1	Garlic clove	1
1 oz	Butter	25 g
3 tbsp	Oil	3x15 ml
8 oz	Can of tomatoes	226 g
¼ teasp	Dried basil	1.25 ml
4	Courgettes	4
2 tbsp	Plain flour	2x15 ml
	Salt and pepper	
4 oz	Mozzarella cheese	125 g

Peel and finely chop onion. Peel and crush garlic. Heat butter and 1 tbsp (15 ml) oil in a frying pan and fry onion and garlic till transparent.

Drain tomatoes. Add to pan with basil and cook over a low heat for 20 minutes. Purée mixture in a blender or push through a sieve.

Trim and slice courgettes. Coat slices with flour. Heat remaining oil in another frying pan and fry courgettes till lightly golden and tender. Drain on kitchen paper and season with salt and pepper.

Thinly slice Mozzarella. Layer courgettes, Mozzarella and tomato sauce in serving dish. Chill for 2–3 hours. Serve with hot garlic bread or toast and butter curls.

Deep-fried chicory

Overall timing 40 minutes

Freezing Not suitable

To serve 4

4	Heads of chicory	4
	Salt and pepper	
2 tbsp	Lemon juice	2x15 ml
	Oil for deep frying	
1	Egg	1
1 tbsp	Milk (optional)	15 ml
2 oz	Dried breadcrumbs	50 g

Blanch chicory in boiling salted water, with the lemon juice, for 10 minutes. Drain and leave on a wire rack until cool enough to handle, then pat dry with kitchen paper.

Heat oil in deep-fryer to 350°F (180°C).

Lightly beat egg in a large bowl with a pinch each of salt and pepper. If chicory heads are very large, add milk to the egg mixture to ensure there is sufficient coating mixture. Dip the chicory heads in the egg, then coat completely in the breadcrumbs.

Deep-fry coated chicory, two at a time, in the hot oil for 2–3 minutes or until golden brown. Drain on kitchen paper and keep warm while frying remaining chicory heads. Serve with any hot or cold meat and accompanied by sea-salt and butter to be added as you would with jacket potatoes – make a cross cut, add a knob of butter and freshly-ground sea-salt.

Deep-fried courgettes

Overall timing 2¼ hours

Freezing Not suitable

To serve 4

1¼ lb	Courgettes	600 g
	Salt	
3 tbsp	Plain flour	3x15 ml
	Oil for frying	

Trim courgettes and cut into thin strips. Sprinkle with salt and leave for 1½ hours.

Dry courgettes well on kitchen paper and coat in flour. Shake in a sieve to remove excess flour.

Heat oil in a deep-fryer.

Fry courgettes till lightly golden, then drain well on kitchen paper. Serve hot with tartare sauce.

Variations

Season the flour with a little paprika or ground coriander before coating courgettes.

Braised fennel

Overall timing 1 hour

Freezing Suitable

To serve 6

5	Bulbs of fennel	5
	Salt and pepper	
4 oz	Streaky bacon	125 g
1	Onion	1
2 oz	Butter	50 g
½ pint	Chicken stock	300 ml
	Bouquet garni	
	Sprigs of parsley	

Trim fennel. Cut each bulb in half and blanch in boiling salted water for 10 minutes. Drain.

Derind and finely chop bacon. Peel and chop onion. Melt butter in flameproof casserole and fry bacon for 5 minutes.

Arrange onion and fennel pieces on top of bacon. Cover with stock and add bouquet garni and seasoning. Cover and simmer for about 45 minutes till tender.

Remove bouquet garni. If liked, sprinkle fennel with grated Parmesan cheese. Garnish with parsley and serve with chicken or a bacon joint.

Tunisian stuffed courgettes

Overall timing 1¼ hours

Freezing Suitable: bake from frozen, covered, in 350°F (180°C) Gas 4 oven for about 45 minutes

To serve 4

1 lb	Courgettes	450 g
1	Onion	1
8 oz	Minced lamb	225 g
1 tbsp	Chopped parsley	15 ml
2	Eggs	2
	Cayenne	
	Salt and pepper	
4 tbsp	Plain flour	4x15 ml
4 tbsp	Oil	4x15 ml
8 oz	Can of tomatoes	227 g
	Parsley	

Trim courgettes. Using a long thin knife or melon-baller, scoop out centre of each whole courgette, working from both ends if necessary and trying to keep the sides an even thickness. Reserve cut-out flesh.

Peel and finely chop onion and mix with chopped courgette flesh, minced lamb, parsley, 1 egg, a pinch of cayenne and seasoning.

Fill courgettes with prepared mixture. Roll any leftover mixture into little meat balls. Beat remaining egg in a bowl and dip stuffed courgettes and meat balls in it. Coat lightly with flour.

Heat oil in a large frying pan. Add courgettes and meat balls and cook for about 20 minutes, turning to brown all sides. Remove from pan and drain on kitchen paper.

Sieve tomatoes and their juice. Add to pan juices with seasoning and cook over a moderate heat for about 15 minutes.

Return courgettes and meat balls to pan and cook for a further 15 minutes. Serve hot, sprinkled with chopped parsley.

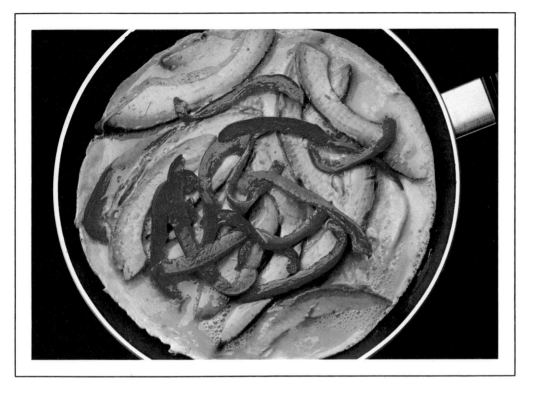

Avocado and pepper omelette

Overall timing 15 minutes

Freezing Not suitable

To serve 4

1	Red pepper	1
3 oz	Butter	75 g
2	Ripe avocados	2
1 tbsp	Lemon juice	15 ml
8	Eggs	8
1 tbsp	Water	15 ml
	Salt and pepper	

Deseed pepper and cut into long strips. Melt 1 oz (25 g) of the butter in an omelette or frying pan and fry pepper till just tender. Remove from pan and set aside.

Cut avocados in half lengthways and lift out stones. Peel, then cut avocado flesh into thick strips. Sprinkle with lemon juice to prevent discoloration.

Lightly beat together eggs, water and seasoning in a jug. Divide remaining butter into four pieces. Melt one piece in omelette pan.

Pour one-quarter of egg mixture into pan and cook till omelette starts to set. Run a spatula round the edge to loosen it and tilt the pan to let the uncooked egg run underneath. Continue to cook till the omelette is just soft and creamy.

Spread one-quarter of the pepper and avocado strips on top. Cook for 1 further minute, then fold over the omelette and slide it on to a warm serving plate. Serve immediately or keep it warm while you cook three more omelettes in the same way.

Avocado soufflé

Overall timing 45 minutes

Freezing Not suitable

To serve 2

1 oz	Butter	25 g
1 oz	Plain flour	25 g
¼ pint	Milk	150 ml
2	Ripe avocados	2
1 teasp	Lemon juice	5 ml
	Pinch of grated nutmeg	
	Salt and pepper	
	Pinch of ground cinnamon *or*	
1 teasp	Grated lemon rind (optional)	5 ml
3	Eggs	3

Preheat the oven to 400°F (200°C) Gas 6.

Melt the butter in a saucepan, stir in the flour and cook for 1 minute. Gradually stir in the milk. Bring to the boil, stirring till thickened. Remove from the heat.

Cut the avocados in half lengthways and lift out the stones. Cut out four very thin slices, sprinkle with lemon juice and reserve for the garnish. Remove remaining flesh with a teaspoon, place it in a bowl and mash well. Add to the sauce and beat vigorously until well blended. Add nutmeg, seasoning and cinnamon or lemon rind, if used.

Separate the eggs. Add the yolks one by one to the saucepan, beating well after each addition. Whisk egg whites with a pinch of salt till very stiff, then gently fold into the sauce.

Pour mixture into a greased 2 pint (1.1 litre) soufflé dish. Place on a baking tray and bake for about 30 minutes till well risen. Garnish with reserved avocado slices and serve immediately.

Endive ring

Overall timing 1 hour

Freezing Not suitable

To serve 4

2 lb	Curly endive	900 g
	Salt and pepper	
2 oz	Butter	50 g
2 oz	Plain flour	50 g
¾ pint	Milk	400 ml
	Grated nutmeg	
3	Eggs	3

Trim the endive and blanch in boiling salted water for 5 minutes. Plunge pan into cold water to cool quickly, then drain endive well and chop.

Preheat the oven to 325°F (170°C) Gas 3.

Melt butter in a saucepan, stir in flour and cook for 1 minute. Gradually stir in the milk. Bring to the boil, stirring, and simmer till thickened. Season with salt, pepper and nutmeg.

Remove pan from heat and stir in endive. Allow to cool slightly, then beat eggs into mixture. Turn into greased ring mould. Place mould in roasting tin with 1 inch (2.5 cm) water. Bake for 30 minutes. Invert on to a warmed serving dish and serve hot.

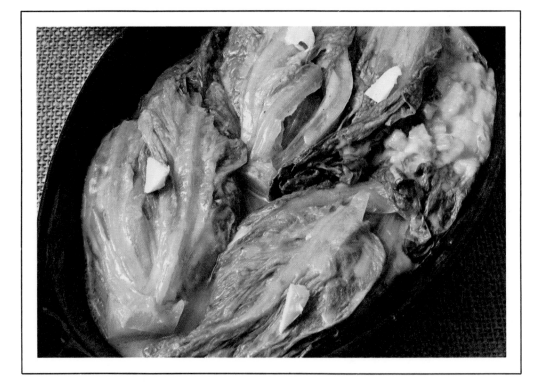

French stuffed lettuce

Overall timing 40 minutes

Freezing Not suitable

To serve 4

4	Round lettuces	4
1 pint	Chicken stock	560 ml
2 oz	Butter	50 g
1 oz	Plain flour	25 g
½ pint	Milk	300 ml
	Salt	
	Grated nutmeg	
4 oz	Cooked ham	125 g
3 oz	Mozzarella cheese	75 g
2	Egg yolks	2

Preheat the oven to 350°F (180°C) Gas 4.

Trim lettuces, discarding outer leaves if necessary. Bring stock to the boil in a large saucepan. Add lettuces, cover and cook for 5 minutes. Drain thoroughly, reserving cooking liquor. Allow lettuces to cool.

Melt 1 oz (25 g) of the butter in another saucepan. Add flour and cook, stirring, for 2 minutes. Gradually stir in milk. Bring to the boil, stirring, and cook for 3 minutes. Season with salt and a pinch of grated nutmeg.

Dice ham and Mozzarella and stir into sauce with egg yolks. Cook over a low heat for 2 minutes. Remove from heat and taste and adjust seasoning.

Cut cooled lettuces in half lengthways. Arrange four lettuce halves in a greased ovenproof dish, cut sides uppermost. Spoon sauce into each half and top with remaining lettuce halves. Add ¼ pint (150 ml) of the reserved cooking liquor and dot with remaining butter.

Cover with foil and bake for 15 minutes. Serve hot with French bread.

Baked sweet potatoes

Overall timing 1 hour

Freezing Not suitable

To serve 4

4x8 oz	Sweet potatoes	4x225 g
	Salt and pepper	
2 oz	Butter	50 g

Preheat the oven to 400°F (200°C) Gas 6,

Wash the sweet potatoes gently to avoid breaking the skins. Arrange on a greased baking tray and bake in the centre of the oven for about 45 minutes till tender when pierced with a skewer.

Arrange the sweet potatoes on a warmed serving dish and cut open along the top. Sprinkle a little salt and pepper into each and top with a knob of butter. Serve immediately.

Cauliflower ring

Overall timing 1¼ hours

Freezing Not suitable

To serve 4–6

1	Large cauliflower	1
	Salt and pepper	
4 oz	Butter	125 g
2 oz	Plain flour	50 g
¾ pint	Milk	400 ml
¼ teasp	Grated nutmeg	1.25 ml
4 oz	Gruyère or Cheddar cheese	125 g
3	Eggs	3
1 tbsp	Dried breadcrumbs	15 ml
	Sprigs of parsley	

Preheat oven to 375°F (190°C) Gas 5.

Trim cauliflower and divide into florets. Cook for 7–10 minutes in boiling salted water. Drain, chop and put in bowl.

To make sauce, melt 2 oz (50 g) of the butter in a pan, stir in flour and cook for 1 minute.

Gradually stir in milk. Bring to the boil, stirring, and cook for 1 minute. Add seasoning and nutmeg. Grate cheese and stir 3 oz (75 g) into sauce.

Remove pan from heat. Pour about two-thirds of the sauce into a bowl and set aside. Stir eggs into sauce left in pan. Mix sauce thoroughly into cauliflower.

Grease a 9½ inch (24 cm) ring mould with half remaining butter. Sprinkle breadcrumbs on bottom. Fill with cauliflower mixture, pressing down well, and bake for 30–35 minutes.

Remove from oven and immerse mould up to rim in cold water. Turn up oven to 450°F (230°C) Gas 8. Run a knife blade around the sides of the mould, then carefully turn out on to ovenproof dish (if any of the mixture sticks to mould, quickly smooth it back into position with a knife and a little of remaining sauce).

Spread reserved sauce over cauliflower ring and sprinkle with remaining cheese. Melt remaining 1 oz (25 g) butter and pour over. Return to oven and bake for about 15 minutes until golden brown. Serve hot.

Cauliflower bake

Overall timing 1½ hours

Freezing Not suitable

To serve 4

1	Cauliflower	1
	Salt and pepper	
	Grated nutmeg	
1	Soft bread roll	1
1 pint	Milk	560 ml
1	Onion	1
4	Tomatoes	4
8 oz	Minced beef	225 g
5	Eggs	5
½ teasp	Paprika	2.5 ml
2 oz	Butter	50 g

Remove any leaves and trim cauliflower stalk. Put whole cauliflower into a pan containing 1½ inches (4 cm) of boiling, salted water. Add a pinch of grated nutmeg, cover and cook for 10 minutes.

Crumble the bread roll into a little of the milk in a large bowl. Peel and chop the onion. Chop three of the tomatoes. Add the mince, onion, chopped tomatoes and 1 egg to the bowl. Season with salt and pepper and mix well.

Preheat oven to 400°F (200°C) Gas 6.

Drain cauliflower; place in greased oven-proof dish. Spoon meat mixture round. Mix remaining eggs with the rest of the milk. Season with salt, pepper, a pinch of nutmeg and paprika. Pour over cauliflower and meat.

Cut the butter into pieces and put on top. Cut remaining tomato into quarters and place round cauliflower. Bake in oven for 1 hour.

Broccoli vinaigrette

Overall timing 20 minutes plus 20 minutes marination

Freezing Not suitable

To serve 6

1 lb	Broccoli	450 g
	Salt and pepper	
10 tbsp	Oil	10x15 ml
1 teasp	Powdered mustard	5 ml
4 tbsp	White wine vinegar	4x15 ml
1 teasp	Brown sugar	5 ml
1	Onion	1
2 tbsp	Chopped chives	2x15 ml
2 tbsp	Chopped parsley	2x15 ml
1 tbsp	Chopped fresh tarragon	15 ml
5	Small gherkins	5
2	Hard-boiled eggs	2
2	Tomatoes	2
5	Radishes	5

Trim broccoli leaves and coarse stems, then cook in boiling salted water for about 10 minutes. Drain well, then chop and divide pieces between six serving dishes or place in salad bowl.

Beat together oil, mustard, vinegar, sugar and seasoning. Peel and finely chop the onion and add to dressing with herbs. Finely chop gherkins and eggs and stir into dressing.

Blanch, peel and finely chop tomatoes. Chop radishes and stir both into dressing. Pour over broccoli and mix well. Leave for 20 minutes until completely cold. Serve with buttered toast.

Celery in yogurt sauce

Overall timing 45 minutes

Freezing Not suitable

To serve 4–6

2 lb	Green celery	900 g
	Salt and pepper	
1	Onion	1
1 oz	Bacon fat or pork dripping	25 g
2 oz	Butter	50 g
1 pint	Chicken stock	560 ml
Sauce		
$\frac{1}{2}$ oz	Butter	15 g
$\frac{1}{2}$ oz	Plain flour	15 g
$\frac{1}{4}$ pint	Soured cream	150 ml
$\frac{1}{4}$ pint	Plain yogurt	150 ml
	Grated nutmeg	
	Salt and pepper	

Trim celery and cut into short lengths. Blanch in boiling salted water for 5 minutes, then drain well.

Peel and chop onion. Heat bacon fat or dripping and butter in large frying pan and fry onion till transparent. Add the celery and sprinkle with pepper. Add the stock, cover and cook over a low heat for 20–30 minutes.

Remove from heat and drain liquid into a measuring jug. There should be $\frac{1}{2}$ pint (300 ml) – make up to this amount with a little extra stock if necessary. Keep celery warm in a serving dish.

To make sauce, melt butter in a saucepan. Stir in flour and cook for 1 minute. Gradually stir in reserved stock. Bring to the boil stirring. Add soured cream, yogurt, a pinch of nutmeg and seasoning. Stir till smooth and creamy. Pour sauce over celery and serve hot.

Turkish potato fritters

Overall timing 50 minutes plus proving

Freezing Not suitable

To serve 4–6

8 oz	Floury potatoes	225 g
	Salt	
1 teasp	Bicarbonate of soda	5 ml
	Grated rind of $\frac{1}{2}$ lemon	
10 oz	Packet of white bread mix	283 g
	Oil for deep frying	
Syrup		
14 oz	Sugar	400 g
2 tbsp	Lemon juice	2x15 ml
1 tbsp	Rose-water or liqueur	15 ml

Peel and quarter potatoes. Cook in boiling salted water for 20 minutes till tender. Drain and mash. Beat in soda and lemon rind.

Put bread mix into a bowl and mix in mashed potatoes. Gradually add sufficient warm water to make a thick, smooth dough. Turn on to a floured board and knead till little bubbles appear on the surface. Place in a bowl, cover with oiled polythene and leave to rise in a warm place for about 1 hour till doubled in size.

Meanwhile, to make the syrup, place sugar in a saucepan with $\frac{3}{4}$ pint (400 ml) water, lemon juice and rose-water or liqueur and heat till sugar dissolves. Bring to the boil and boil gently for 15 minutes till syrupy. Remove from heat and keep warm.

Heat oil in a deep-fryer to 360°F (180°C).

Break off lumps of dough with a spoon and lower into oil on a draining spoon. Fry for 3–5 minutes, turning once, till golden all over. Remove and drain on kitchen paper. Keep hot while you fry the rest. Put in a deep dish and pour warm syrup over.

Stuffed tomatoes au gratin

Overall timing 50 minutes

Freezing Not suitable

To serve 4

4	Large tomatoes	4
1½ lb	Fresh peas	700 g
1	Onion	1
2 tbsp	Oil	2x15 ml
	Salt and pepper	
2 oz	Butter	50 g
3 tbsp	Plain flour	3x15 ml
½ pint	Milk	300 ml
4 oz	Cheese	125 g
1 tbsp	Fresh breadcrumbs	15 ml

Preheat the oven to 400°F (200°C) Gas 6.

Halve the tomatoes and scoop out the flesh. Discard the seeds and chop the flesh. Shell the peas. Peel and finely chop the onion.

Heat the oil in a frying pan and fry the onion till transparent. Add the peas, cover and cook for 5 minutes. Stir in the chopped tomato flesh, season and continue cooking, covered, for 10 minutes.

Meanwhile, melt the butter in a saucepan. Stir in the flour and cook for 1 minute. Gradually stir in the milk and bring to the boil, stirring until thickened.

Grate the cheese. Mix three-quarters into the sauce with the pea mixture. Use to fill the tomato halves and arrange in an ovenproof dish. Mix the remaining cheese with the breadcrumbs and sprinkle over the tomatoes. Bake for 20 minutes and serve hot.

Vegetable croquettes

Overall timing 1¼ hours plus chilling

Freezing Suitable: deep fry after thawing

To serve 4

1½ lb	Floury potatoes	700 g
1	Large parsnip	1
	Salt and pepper	
2	Large leeks	2
1	Stalk of celery	1
2	Large carrots	2
2 oz	Butter	50 g
2 tbsp	Chopped parsley	2x15 ml
¼ teasp	Grated nutmeg	1.25 ml
2	Eggs	2
	Oil for deep frying	
4 tbsp	Plain flour	4x15 ml
	Sprigs of parsley	

Peel and chop the potatoes and parsnip. Cook in boiling salted water for 15–20 minutes till tender.

Meanwhile, trim and finely shred leeks and celery. Peel and grate carrots. Melt butter in a frying pan, add leeks and celery and fry till golden.

Drain potatoes and parsnip, return to pan and shake over a low heat to dry throughly. Remove from heat and mash to a smooth purée. Stir in fried vegetables and any pan juices. Add carrots, parsley, nutmeg and seasoning. Beat in eggs. Spread the mixture on a plate, cool, then chill for 2–3 hours till firm.

Heat oil in a deep-fryer to 340°F (170°C). Shape vegetable mixture into 20 balls with floured hands. Fry, a few at a time, for 5–6 minutes, till crisp and golden. Drain on kitchen paper. Serve hot, garnished with parsley.

Endive soufflé

Overall timing 50 minutes

Freezing Not suitable

To serve 4

4 oz	Butter	125 g
2 tbsp	Finely chopped onion	2x15 ml
2 tbsp	Finely chopped bacon	2x15 ml
4 tbsp	Diced cooked potato	4x15 ml
2 tbsp	Plain flour	2x15 ml
½ pint	Milk	300 ml
6	Eggs	6
	Salt and pepper	
6 tbsp	Chopped endive	6x15 ml

Preheat the oven to 375°F (190°C) Gas 5.

Melt 2 oz (50 g) of the butter in a frying pan. Add onion and bacon and fry till onion is transparent. Drain mixture in a sieve. Add the diced potato and set aside.

Melt the remaining butter in the frying pan, stir in the flour and cook for 1 minute. Gradually stir in the milk and bring to the boil, stirring. Simmer for 3 minutes, then remove from heat and cool slightly.

Separate the eggs. Beat yolks into the sauce, then fold in the potato and bacon mixture and seasoning. Whisk the egg whites in a bowl till stiff. Stir 1 tbsp (15 ml) of the whites into the sauce to lighten it. Stir in the endive, then carefully fold in the remaining egg whites.

Turn the mixture into a greased 6 inch (15 cm) soufflé dish and bake for 25–30 minutes till the soufflé is well risen and golden in colour. Serve immediately.

Cauliflower polonaise

Overall timing 35 minutes

Freezing Not suitable

To serve 4

1	Small cauliflower	1
	Salt	
4	Hard-boiled eggs	4
4 oz	Butter	125 g
2 tbsp	Dried breadcrumbs	2x15 ml
1 teasp	Paprika	5 ml

Trim cauliflower and cook whole in boiling salted water for about 20 minutes till just tender.

Meanwhile, shell and finely chop eggs.

Drain cauliflower. Place in a warmed serving dish and sprinkle with the eggs. Keep warm.

Melt butter in frying pan. Add breadcrumbs and paprika and stir-fry until crisp. Sprinkle over cauliflower and serve.

Cauliflower fritters

Overall timing 25 minutes

Freezing Not suitable

To serve 4

1	Large cauliflower	1
	Salt	
1	Egg	1
1	Egg white	1
2 oz	Plain flour	50 g
4 oz	Dried breadcrumbs	125 g
	Oil for frying	
	Grated Parmesan cheese	
	Chopped parsley	

Trim cauliflower and divide into 25–30 florets. Cook in boiling salted water for 7–10 minutes or till just tender. Drain and allow to cool.

In a bowl, beat together egg, egg white and a pinch of salt till frothy. Dip each floret into flour, then into egg mixture, then roll in breadcrumbs till well coated.

Heat oil to 320°F (160°C). Deep fry cauliflower till golden brown and crisp. Remove cauliflower from pan with a draining spoon and drain on kitchen paper. Serve hot, sprinkled with salt and a little grated Parmesan and chopped parsley mixed together.

Brussels sprouts with chestnuts

Overall timing 1 hour

Freezing Not suitable

To serve 4–6

12 oz	Chestnuts	350 g
¾ pint	Hot beef stock	400 ml
1½ lb	Brussels sprouts	700 g
	Salt	
	Grated nutmeg	
2 oz	Butter	50 g

Make a cut in each chestnut with a sharp knife, then place them in a saucepan. Cover with cold water, bring to the boil and cook for 10 minutes.

Drain chestnuts and peel off both outer and inner skins. Add to the stock and simmer gently for about 20 minutes till tender.

Meanwhile, trim the sprouts and cut a cross in the base of each one. Cook in boiling salted water for 10–12 minutes till tender. Drain and season with nutmeg.

Melt the butter in a pan, then add the drained chestnuts and sprouts. Gently shake the pan to coat the vegetables with butter. Turn into a warmed serving dish and serve.

Potato and onion bake

Overall timing 1 hour

Freezing Not suitable

To serve 4

1½ lb	Potatoes	700 g
12 oz	Onions	350 g
3 oz	Butter	75 g
	Salt and pepper	

Preheat the oven to 400°F (200°C) Gas 6.

Peel the potatoes and slice very thinly (use a mandolin for best results). Put into a bowl of cold water to prevent discoloration. Peel and thinly slice the onions.

Drain the potatoes and dry with kitchen paper. Butter an ovenproof dish and cover the bottom with a layer of potato. Dot with butter, season and cover with a layer of onion. Dot with butter, season and repeat the layers till all the ingredients have been used, finishing with potato. Dot the top with the remaining butter.

Bake for about 40 minutes till the potatoes are tender and golden. Serve immediately.

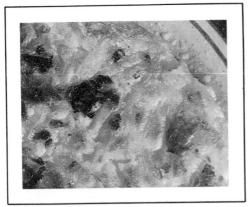

Potato cake

Overall timing 50 minutes

Freezing Not suitable

To serve 4

2 lb	Potatoes	900 g
6 oz	Cheese	175 g
3	Eggs	3
½ pint	Milk	300 ml
	Salt and pepper	

Preheat the oven to 375°F (190°C) Gas 5.

Peel potatoes and grate into bowl. Grate cheese and add to potatoes. Beat in eggs, milk and seasoning. Pour into an ovenproof dish and bake for 40 minutes till top is golden. Serve hot.

Potato omelette

Overall timing 30 minutes

Freezing Not suitable

To serve 4

4 x 6 oz	Waxy potatoes	4 x 175 g
	Salt and pepper	
8 oz	Butter	225 g
2	Sage leaves	2
12	Eggs	12

Peel and dice the potatoes. Cook in boiling salted water for 4 minutes. Drain and pat dry.

Melt 2 oz (50 g) of the butter in a frying pan, add the potatoes and sage and fry over a moderate heat for 5–10 minutes till the potatoes are tender and golden. Discard sage leaves, remove potatoes and keep hot.

Lightly beat three of the eggs in a bowl with salt and pepper. Heat omelette pan and add one-quarter of the remaining butter. Pour eggs into pan and cook omelette. When almost set, put one-quarter of the potatoes along the centre and fold the sides in to cover them. Turn on to a warm plate with the join down and keep hot while you cook the remaining three omelettes.

Just before serving, cut along the tops of the omelettes to expose the filling. Serve immediately with a mixed salad.

Vegetable moussaka

Overall timing 2 hours

Freezing Not suitable

To serve 4–6

2	Large onions	2
1	Garlic clove	1
1	Large aubergine	1
	Salt and pepper	
2 oz	Butter	50 g
4 oz	Continental lentils	125 g
2 tbsp	Tomato purée	2x15 ml
1 pint	Light stock	560 ml
4	Small globe artichokes	4
1 tbsp	Lemon juice	15 ml
	Bouquet garni	
4 tbsp	Oil	4x15 ml
	Sprigs of parsley	

Peel and finely chop onions; peel and crush garlic. Slice aubergine, sprinkle with salt and leave to drain for 15 minutes.

Melt the butter in a saucepan, add onion and garlic and fry till golden. Add lentils, tomato purée and stock and simmer for about 1 hour till a thick purée.

Meanwhile, remove stem and coarse outer leaves from artichokes. Bring a pan of water to the boil, add lemon juice, bouquet garni and artichokes and simmer for 20–30 minutes till tender.

Rinse aubergines and dry on kitchen paper. Heat oil in a frying pan, add aubergines and fry till crisp and golden.

Preheat oven to 350°F (180°C) Gas 4.

Drain artichokes thoroughly, cut in half and remove chokes. Arrange cut sides up in greased ovenproof dish. Pour half lentil mixture over artichokes, then cover with half fried aubergine slices. Repeat the layers of lentil and aubergine and press down lightly. Bake for 30 minutes. Turn out and serve hot, garnished with parsley.

Venetian green beans

Overall timing 1¼ hours

Freezing Suitable

To serve 4–6

1¼ lb	Runner or French beans	600 g
1 lb	Fresh tomatoes *or*	450 g
14 oz	Can of tomatoes	397 g
1	Medium onion	1
1	Garlic clove	1
2 oz	Butter *or*	50 g
2 tbsp	Oil	2x15 ml
	Bouquet garni	
¼ teasp	Dried oregano or marjoram	1.25 ml
	Salt and pepper	

Top and tail beans and remove strings, if necessary. If using fresh tomatoes, blanch, peel and chop them; drain and chop canned tomatoes. Peel and chop the onion. Peel and crush garlic.

Heat the butter or oil in a saucepan and fry the onion till browned. Add beans, tomatoes, garlic, bouquet garni, oregano or marjoram and seasoning. Cover and simmer over a very low heat for 1 hour. If necessary add a little boiling water during cooking to prevent sticking. Serve hot.

Potato gnocchi

Overall timing 1½ hours plus chilling

Freezing Not suitable

To serve 6

2 lb	Floury potatoes	900 g
	Salt and pepper	
8 oz	Plain flour	225 g
1 teasp	Baking powder	5 ml
2	Eggs	2
6 oz	Slices of cheese	175 g
2 oz	Butter	50 g
3 tbsp	Grated Parmesan cheese	3x15 ml

Scrub the potatoes and cook in boiling salted water for about 30 minutes till tender. Drain, peel and press through a sieve into a large bowl.

Sift the flour and baking powder together, add to the potatoes and mix in with a wooden spoon. Beat in the eggs and seasoning. Spread out on a plate and chill for 2–3 hours till firm.

Preheat oven to 425°F (220°C) Gas 7.

Bring a large pan of salted water to the boil, then reduce heat till simmering. Put teaspoonfuls of the potato mixture into the water and cook for about 4 minutes or till they rise to the surface. Remove with a draining spoon and keep hot while you cook the rest.

Layer cooked dumplings in an ovenproof dish with slices of cheese and butter and sprinkle Parmesan on top. Brown in the oven for 5–10 minutes.

Fried ham and spinach

Overall timing 30 minutes

Freezing Not suitable

To serve 4

2 lb	Spinach	900 g
	Salt and pepper	
6 oz	Slice of cooked ham	175 g
1	Garlic clove	1
3 tbsp	Oil	3x15 ml
2	Hard-boiled eggs	2
2 tbsp	Pine nuts (optional)	2x15 ml

Wash and pick over the spinach, discarding any withered leaves or coarse stalks. Drain thoroughly and blanch in lightly salted boiling water for 1 minute. Remove from heat, rinse under cold water and drain thoroughly. Chop coarsely.

Dice the ham and peel the garlic. Heat the oil in a large frying pan, add ham and garlic and fry for 2–3 minutes. Stir in the spinach, add plenty of pepper and fry gently for 5 minutes, stirring occasionally.

Meanwhile, shell and finely chop the eggs. Add to the pan with the pine nuts, if used, and cook for 2 minutes.

Discard garlic clove. Adjust seasoning to taste and arrange on a warmed serving dish. Serve immediately with thick slices of crusty bread.

Carrot soufflé

Overall timing 1 hour

Freezing Not suitable

To serve 4

1 lb	Carrots	450 g
2 oz	Butter	50 g
	Salt and pepper	
Sauce base		
2 oz	Butter	50 g
2 oz	Plain flour	50 g
1 pint	Milk	560 ml
	Salt and pepper	
3	Eggs	3

Peel and thinly slice the carrots, then cook in boiling water for 15 minutes. Drain and plunge into cold water to cool carrots quickly.

Melt butter in another pan, add drained carrots and cook for 5 minutes. Season with salt and pepper.

Preheat oven to 375°F (190°C) Gas 5.

For the sauce base, melt butter in a saucepan and stir in flour. Gradually add milk and bring to the boil, stirring until thickened. Season with salt and pepper and cool.

Separate the eggs. Mix the egg yolks and carrots into the sauce. Whisk the whites in a bowl until very stiff, then carefully fold into the carrot mixture. Pour into a greased 3 pint (1.7 litre) soufflé dish. Bake for about 30 minutes until the soufflé is golden and well risen. Serve immediately.

Bubble and squeak

Overall timing 15 minutes

Freezing Not suitable

To serve 4-6

1 lb	Mashed potatoes	450 g
1 lb	Cooked shredded cabbage	450 g
	Salt and pepper	
1 lb	Leftover cooked meat	450 g
2 oz	Butter	50 g

Beat together mashed potatoes and cabbage with a wooden spoon, adding plenty of seasoning. Dice meat.

Melt the butter in a heavy frying pan and add the potato and cabbage mixture, spreading it over the bottom of the pan. Mix in meat. Fry, turning the mixture occasionally, until crisp and golden brown. Serve immediately.

Boxty on the griddle

Overall timing 40 minutes

Freezing Suitable: reheat from frozen in 400°F (200°C) Gas 6 oven for 10 minutes

To serve 4

8 oz	Waxy potatoes	225 g
4 oz	Cooked mashed potatoes	125 g
4 oz	Plain flour	125 g
½ teasp	Bicarbonate of soda	2.5 ml
¾ pint	Milk	400 ml
	Salt and pepper	
	Oil for frying	

Peel the potatoes and grate into a large bowl. Add the mashed potatoes, sifted flour and bicarbonate of soda and mix together well. Make a well in the centre and gradually stir in enough milk to make a stiff batter. Season well.

Heat a lightly oiled griddle or heavy-based frying pan. Drop the batter in large spoonfuls on to the griddle or pan and cook over a moderate heat for 4 minutes on each side till crisp and golden.

Serve hot with fried black pudding, bacon and eggs.

Potato pancakes

Overall timing 45 minutes

Freezing Not suitable

To serve 4

1¼ lb	Waxy potatoes	600 g
2	Eggs	2
1 tbsp	Plain flour	15 ml
	Salt and pepper	
4 tbsp	Oil	4x15 ml

Peel the potatoes and grate coarsely into a bowl of cold water. Drain and squeeze dry in a cloth, then put into a dry bowl. Add the eggs, flour and seasoning and mix well.

Heat a little of the oil in a frying pan and add one-quarter of the potato mixture. Flatten into a pancake with the back of a fish slice and fry over a moderate heat for about 5 minutes till the edges are golden. Turn carefully and brown the other side. Remove from the pan and keep hot while rest of mixture is cooked.

Serve hot with roast or grilled meats and a green vegetable.

Rumanian vegetable casserole

Overall timing 1¼ hours

Freezing Not suitable

To serve 6–8

2	Waxy potatoes	2
2	Turnips	2
2	Medium-size onions	2
2	Garlic cloves	2
2	Carrots	2
1	Medium-size aubergine	1
2	Courgettes	2
2	Small leeks	2
4 oz	French beans	125 g
3	Large tomatoes	3
1 oz	Butter	25 g
2 tbsp	Oil	2x15 ml
4 oz	Shelled fresh peas	125 g
2 tbsp	Tomato purée	2x15 ml
	Bouquet garni	
	Salt and pepper	

Peel the potatoes, turnips, onions, garlic and carrots. Cut the potatoes, turnips, carrots, aubergine and courgettes into ¾ inch (2 cm) chunks. Cut the leeks and beans into 1 inch (2.5 cm) lengths. Quarter the tomatoes; slice the onions.

Heat the butter and oil in a flameproof casserole and fry the onions, leeks and garlic till golden. Add the remaining vegetables, tomato purée, bouquet garni and 1 pint (560 ml) water and mix well. Season and bring to the boil. Simmer gently for about 45 minutes till the vegetables are tender.

Bashed neeps

Overall timing 35 minutes

Freezing Not suitable

To serve 4–6

2 lb	Swedes	900 g
	Salt and pepper	
3 oz	Butter	75 g

Peel the swedes thickly, wash and cut into 1 inch (2.5 cm) chunks. Put into a saucepan of lightly salted cold water and bring to the boil. Reduce the heat, cover and simmer for 15–20 minutes till tender.

Drain thoroughly, then mash well till smooth with two-thirds of the butter. Season to taste.

Arrange in a warmed serving dish, top with the remaining butter and grind a little pepper over. Serve immediately.

Variations
"Clapshot" is a traditional mixed swede and potato dish from the Orkney Islands, off the north coast of Scotland. Cook equal quantities of swedes and floury potatoes in separate pans till tender. Drain well, then mash together with butter and seasoning and 1 small finely chopped onion or 2 tbsp (2x15 ml) chopped chives. Any leftovers can be fried in butter.

To turn Clapshot into a tasty lunch or supper dish, spread the mashed swede, potato and onion mixture in a shallow oven-proof dish. Make 4 hollows with the back of a spoon and break an egg into each one. Season and dot with butter, then bake in the centre of the oven, preheated to 425°F (220°C) Gas 7, for 8–10 minutes till the eggs are lightly set. Serve immediately with rashers of crispy fried bacon.

German broad beans

Overall timing 45 minutes

Freezing Suitable

To serve 4

2 lb	Unshelled broad beans	900 g
	Salt and pepper	
1	Chicken stock cube	1
2 oz	Streaky bacon	50 g
2	Onions	2
3 tbsp	Plain flour	3x15 ml
	Pinch of grated nutmeg	
½ pint	Carton of single cream	284 ml
1 tbsp	Chopped parsley	15 ml

Shell beans. Place in boiling, salted water and cook for 20 minutes or until tender. Drain cooking liquid into measuring jug and top up to ½ pint (300 ml) with water. Crumble in stock cube. Set beans and liquid in jug aside for the moment.

Derind and dice bacon; peel and chop onions. Put bacon and onions into a saucepan and fry gently for about 10 minutes. Remove pan from heat and stir in the flour. Gradually stir in the stock from the jug. Return pan to heat and cook gently for about 5 minutes, stirring constantly until sauce thickens. Remove from heat and season to taste with salt, pepper and nutmeg.

Stir in beans and cream and heat gently for a further 5 minutes, stirring. Transfer to warmed serving dish, garnish with parsley and serve.

Italian cauliflower omelette

Overall timing 20 minutes

Freezing Not suitable

To serve 2

12 oz	Cauliflower	350 g
	Salt and pepper	
1	Onion	1
2 oz	Butter	50 g
6	Eggs	6
2 tbsp	Grated Parmesan cheese	2x15 ml
$\frac{1}{2}$ teasp	Grated nutmeg	2.5 ml

Preheat the grill.

Cut cauliflower into tiny florets and cook in boiling salted water for 3–5 minutes till just tender.

Meanwhile, peel and finely chop onion. Melt butter in a frying pan and fry onion till golden. Add the drained cauliflower and seasoning and cook for 2 minutes, spreading evenly in the pan.

Beat the eggs in a bowl with the Parmesan and nutmeg. Pour evenly over the cauliflower and cook over a moderate heat till the omelette is nearly set.

Put the frying pan under the grill and cook till the top of the omelette is golden. Slide omelette on to a warmed serving plate and cut in two to serve.

Stuffed baked potatoes

Overall timing 1½ hours

Freezing Not suitable

To serve 8

8x8 oz	Waxy potatoes	8x225 g
1	Large onion	1
3 oz	Butter	75 g
8 oz	Cooked ham	225 g
6 tbsp	Dry white wine or cider	6x15 ml
2 oz	Fresh breadcrumbs	50 g
2 tbsp	Chopped parsley	2x15 ml
	Salt and pepper	
¼ pint	Chicken stock	150 ml

Preheat the oven to 400°F (200°C) Gas 6.

Peel the potatoes. Cut a slice from one end of each so they stand upright. Cut a slice from the other end of each and hollow out the centres with a sharp knife, leaving a thick shell. Finely chop the scooped out pieces and slices cut from the tops of the potatoes.

Peel and finely chop the onion. Melt 1 oz (25 g) of the butter in a saucepan and fry the onion till transparent. Dice the ham and add to the pan with the wine or cider, chopped potatoes and breadcrumbs. Cover and cook for 5 minutes, then stir in the parsley and seasoning.

Spoon the mixture into the potatoes, pressing it down firmly. Stand potatoes upright in a greased ovenproof dish. Melt remaining butter with the stock and pour into the dish.

Bake for 50 minutes to 1 hour, basting frequently, till the potatoes are tender. Serve hot with a green salad.

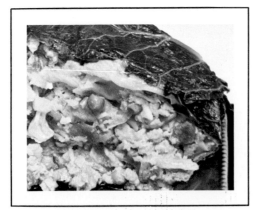

Stuffed cabbage

Overall timing 2 hours 10 minutes

Freezing Not suitable

To serve 6

8 oz	Streaky bacon	225 g
2	Onions	2
2 tbsp	Oil	2x15 ml
1	Green cabbage	1
2	Tomatoes	2
1	Garlic clove	1
1¾ lb	Sausagemeat	750 g
4 oz	Rice	125 g
4 oz	Frozen peas	125 g
	Salt and pepper	
1¾ pints	Hot beef stock	1 litre

Derind and chop bacon. Peel and finely chop onions. Heat oil in frying pan. Add bacon and cook till crisp. Add onions and cook gently for 10 minutes.

Remove all large outer leaves of cabbage. On a large piece of muslin make two layers of leaves in a circular shape. Finely chop remaining cabbage.

Finely chop tomatoes. Peel and crush garlic. Add tomatoes and garlic to chopped cabbage with sausagemeat, rice, peas, bacon and onion and seasoning. Mix well and form into a ball. Place in centre of cabbage leaves, then remake cabbage shape so leaves cover stuffing. Lift corners of muslin and tie at top. Place cabbage in stock, cover and simmer for 1½ hours.

Breton beans

Overall timing 1½ hours

Freezing Suitable

To serve 4–6

8 oz	Dried butter beans	225 g
2	Onions	2
2	Cloves	2
1	Carrot	1
1	Garlic clove	1
¼ teasp	Dried mixed herbs	1.25 ml
2	Bay leaves	2
	Salt and pepper	
1 lb	Tomatoes	450 g
2 oz	Butter	50 g

Place beans in a saucepan, cover with water and simmer for 15 minutes.

Peel one onion and spike with cloves; peel and slice carrot. Peel and crush garlic. Drain beans and return to pan. Add onion, carrot, garlic and herbs. Cover with water and bring to the boil. Cover and cook for 50 minutes; add salt and cook for another 20.

Meanwhile, peel and chop remaining onions. Blanch, peel and quarter tomatoes. Melt butter in a saucepan and add onions, tomatoes and seasoning. Simmer for 20 minutes.

Drain beans and mix into tomato sauce.

Italian fried vegetables

Overall timing 1 hour

Freezing Not suitable

To serve 6

1	Large aubergine	1
	Salt and pepper	
8 oz	Courgettes	225 g
$\frac{1}{2}$	Cauliflower	$\frac{1}{2}$
8 oz	Large flat mushrooms	225 g
2	Large dessert apples	2
4	Eggs	4
6 oz	Fine breadcrumbs	175 g
3 oz	Plain flour	75 g
	Oil for deep frying	
	Sprigs of parsley	

Cut aubergine into $\frac{1}{4}$ inch (6 mm) thick slices. Sprinkle with salt and leave for 15 minutes.

Meanwhile, halve courgettes lengthways, then cut into 2 inch (5 cm) lengths. Divide cauliflower into florets. Blanch in boiling salted water for 3 minutes, then drain and rinse under cold water.

Quarter mushrooms. Peel and core apples and cut into thick rings. Rinse aubergines and pat dry with kitchen paper.

Beat eggs in shallow dish and spread breadcrumbs on a board. Coat vegetables in seasoned flour, then dip into egg and bread-crumbs.

Heat oil in a deep-fryer to 340°F (170°C). Fry aubergine slices for about 4 minutes, turning occasionally, till crisp and golden. Drain on kitchen paper and keep hot.

Fry courgettes and cauliflower florets for 5–6 minutes, and mushrooms and apples for 3–4 minutes. Drain on kitchen paper and keep hot.

Arrange all the fried vegetables on a warmed serving dish and garnish with parsley. Serve immediately with Tartare sauce and a green salad.

Stuffed cucumbers

Overall timing 1 hour

Freezing Suitable

To serve 6

3	Large cucumbers	3
2 oz	Cooked ham	50 g
4 oz	Minced beef	125 g
2 tbsp	Fresh breadcrumbs	2x15 ml
1 tbsp	Chopped parsley	15 ml
3 tbsp	Milk	3x15 ml
1	Egg	1
	Salt and pepper	
Sauce		
1	Onion	1
1	Leek	1
2 oz	Butter	50 g
1 oz	Plain flour	25 g
½ pint	Stock	300 ml
1 tbsp	Chopped parsley	15 ml
	Paprika	
	Salt	
1 tbsp	Vinegar	15 ml
4 fl oz	Top of milk	120 ml

Peel cucumbers. Halve them lengthways and scoop out seeds. Finely chop ham and mix with beef, breadcrumbs, parsley, milk, egg and seasoning. Stuff cucumbers with mixture.

To make sauce, peel and finely chop onion. Trim and finely chop leek. Melt butter in a saucepan and fry onion and leek till golden. Sprinkle flour into pan and cook for 1 minute, stirring. Gradually stir in stock, then add parsley, a pinch each of paprika and salt and the vinegar. Bring to the boil, stirring.

Arrange cucumbers on top of sauce and surround with any leftover stuffing. Cover and cook gently for 30 minutes. Turn cucumbers over halfway through cooking time.

Stir milk into sauce and heat through uncovered for 2 minutes.

Stuffed celeriac

Overall timing 1½ hours

Freezing Not suitable

To serve 4

4	Bulbs of celeriac	4
	Salt and pepper	
1 tbsp	Lemon juice	15 ml
2 oz	Streaky bacon	50 g
1	Large onion	1
8 oz	Minced beef	225 g
1 oz	Fresh breadcrumbs	25 g
1 oz	Grated Parmesan cheese	25 g

Cook celeriac in boiling salted water with lemon juice for 20 minutes. Drain and allow to cool slightly, then cut off tops and reserve. Scoop out insides and reserve.

Preheat the oven to 400°F (200°C) Gas 6.

Derind and dice bacon, then cook for 3 minutes in frying pan. Peel and finely chop onion, cutting a few large pieces for the garnish. Fry onions till golden. Remove large pieces and set aside.

Add mince to pan and cook for 5 minutes. Chop inside of two celeriac bulbs and add to pan with breadcrumbs, Parmesan and seasoning.

Fill celeriac with meat mixture. Replace tops, then place in greased ovenproof dish. Bake for 40 minutes, basting with pan juices halfway through. Serve garnished with reserved onion pieces.

Spanish stuffed peppers

Overall timing 1 hour

Freezing Suitable: bake for 1 hour

To serve 4

1 lb	Tomatoes	450 g
1	Onion	1
1	Garlic clove	1
¼ pint	Olive oil	150 ml
1 tbsp	Caster sugar	15 ml
	Pinch of cayenne	
½ teasp	Dried oregano	2.5 ml
	Salt and pepper	
8	Firm green peppers	8
14 oz	Smoked bacon	400 g
4 oz	Fresh breadcrumbs	125 g

Blanch, peel and chop tomatoes. Peel and chop onion. Peel and crush garlic. Heat 2 tbsp (2x15 ml) oil in saucepan, add tomatoes, onion, garlic, sugar, cayenne, oregano and seasoning. Simmer till reduced by half.

Cut off stalk end of each pepper, then deseed. Blanch in boiling salted water for 5 minutes, then drain.

Preheat the oven to 400°F (200°C) Gas 6.

To make stuffing, derind and mince bacon. Mix with crumbs and pepper to taste.

Pour 1 teasp (5 ml) oil into each pepper, then fill with stuffing. Pour remaining oil into ovenproof dish. Place peppers in dish with tomato sauce between them. Cover with foil and bake for 45 minutes.

Romanian peppers

Overall timing 1¼ hours

Freezing Not suitable

To serve 6

1 lb	Lean pork	450 g
2	Onions	2
2 oz	Butter	50 g
4 oz	Button mushrooms	125 g
8 oz	Tomatoes	225 g
½ pint	Water	300 ml
	Salt and pepper	
½ teasp	Paprika	2.5 ml
6	Green peppers	6
2 teasp	Cornflour	2x5 ml
4 tbsp	Top of milk	4x15 ml
	Tabasco sauce	

Dice the pork. Peel and finely chop onions. Melt butter in saucepan. Fry onions and pork for 10 minutes.

Slice mushrooms. Blanch, peel and chop tomatoes. Add mushrooms and tomatoes to the saucepan. Pour in water and cook for 40 minutes over a low heat. Season with salt, pepper and paprika.

Cut tops off peppers. Remove seeds. Place peppers and their tops in a saucepan of boiling water and cook for 5 minutes or until just soft. Lift out and drain. Keep warm.

Blend cornflour with top of milk. Stir into pork mixture, then bring just to the boil to thicken. Season with a few drops of Tabasco sauce. Mix well, then use mixture to fill peppers. Place tops on peppers to serve.

Leeks with mustard sauce

Overall timing 30 minutes

Freezing Not suitable

To serve 4–6

2 lb	Leeks	900 g
	Salt and pepper	
4 oz	Cheese	125 g
1	Small onion	1
1	Garlic clove	1
2 oz	Butter	50 g
2 tbsp	Plain flour	2x15 ml
$\frac{3}{4}$ pint	Milk	400 ml
1 tbsp	Made mustard	15 ml

Trim leeks. Cook in boiling salted water for 15–20 minutes till tender. Drain, saving $\frac{1}{4}$ pint (150 ml) cooking liquor. Arrange leeks in warmed serving dish. Keep hot.

Grate cheese. Peel and chop onion and garlic. Melt the butter in a saucepan and fry the onion and garlic till golden. Stir in the flour and cook for 1 minute. Gradually add reserved cooking liquor and milk. Bring to the boil, stirring, and cook for 3 minutes. Stir in mustard, cheese and seasoning and heat through gently without boiling. Pour over leeks and serve immediately.

Leek and cheese soufflé

Overall timing 1 hour

Freezing Not suitable

To serve 4

2 oz	Butter	50 g
2 oz	Plain flour	50 g
¼ pint	Warm milk	300 ml
2 oz	Red Leicester cheese	50 g
8 oz	Leeks	225 g
	Salt and pepper	
3	Large eggs	3

Melt the butter in a pan, stir in the flour and cook for 1 minute. Gradually add warm milk and bring to the boil, stirring. Simmer for 2 minutes. Remove from heat and leave to cool.

Grate the cheese. Trim and finely chop leeks. Blanch in boiling water for 5 minutes and drain thoroughly. Stir the grated cheese and leeks into sauce and season. Separate eggs. Beat the yolks into the sauce.

Whisk egg whites in a bowl till stiff but not dry. Stir 1 tbsp (15 ml) whisked whites into sauce to lighten it, then carefully fold in the rest. Turn mixture into greased 2 pint (1.1 litre) soufflé dish, place on baking tray and bake for 30–35 minutes till well risen and golden. Serve immediately.

Irish cabbage

Overall timing 40 minutes

Freezing Not suitable

To serve 4–6

14 oz	Potatoes	400 g
2	Small leeks	2
	Milk	
1 lb	Green cabbage	450 g
	Salt and pepper	
	Pinch of mace	
4 oz	Butter	125 g
	Sprigs of parsley	

Cook unpeeled potatoes in lightly salted water till just tender. Meanwhile, trim the leeks, then roughly chop both white and green parts. Just cover with milk and cook gently till soft.

Roughly chop cabbage and cook in boiling, lightly salted water for 7 minutes. Drain and cut into smaller pieces. Keep cabbage warm.

Drain potatoes; peel and put through a food mill or mash well. Mash in the leeks/milk mixture and season well with salt, pepper and mace. Place bowl over a pan of boiling water and gradually beat in the cabbage till light and fluffy.

Melt butter. Place vegetable mixture in warmed serving dish, make a well in the centre and pour in the hot butter. Garnish with parsley sprigs and serve immediately.

Stuffed mushrooms

Overall timing 1 hour

Freezing Suitable: reheat in 375°F (190°C) Gas 5 oven for 10 minutes

To serve 4

8	Cup mushrooms	8
2 oz	Fresh breadcrumbs	50 g
¼ pint	Warm milk	150 ml
1	Garlic clove	1
	Salt and pepper	
1	Egg	1
1	Egg yolk	1
4 oz	Grated Parmesan cheese	125 g
2 teasp	Chopped fresh marjoram	2 x 5 ml
8 teasp	Oil	8 x 5 ml
	Fresh parsley	

Preheat the oven to 350°F (180°C) Gas 4.

Carefully detach mushroom caps from stalks. Wipe caps and reserve. Chop stalks.

Soak breadcrumbs in warm milk, then squeeze out well, reserving milk. Peel garlic and place in mortar or blender with mushroom stalks, a little of the reserved milk and seasoning. Pound or blend till well combined. Put mixture into a bowl and add egg, egg yolk, grated Parmesan, marjoram and 2 teasp (2x5 ml) of oil. Mix well until creamy, then add salt.

Spread stuffing into hollow of each mushroom cap using a dampened knife. Arrange the stuffed mushrooms in an oiled baking dish. Sprinkle the top with the remaining oil and pepper and bake for about 30 minutes. Garnish with parsley and serve hot.

Sweet-sour beans

Overall timing 2½ hours plus 2 hours soaking

Freezing Not suitable

To serve 4

8 oz	Dried haricot beans	225 g
1 teasp	Salt	5 ml
1	Carrot	1
1	Onion	1
8	Green olives	8
Dressing		
6 tbsp	Oil	6x15 ml
2 tbsp	Wine vinegar	2x15 ml
1 teasp	Soft brown sugar	5 ml
½ teasp	Ground cinnamon	2.5 ml
	Salt and pepper	
1	Garlic clove	1
1 teasp	Dried savory	5 ml

Put the beans in a saucepan, cover with boiling water and leave to soak for 2 hours.

Add the salt, bring to the boil, cover and simmer for 2–2½ hours or till tender. Drain beans and cool.

Peel and slice carrot. Peel and chop onion. Place in bowl and add beans and olives.

To make dressing, mix all ingredients together. Pour over beans and toss.

Sweetcorn fritters

Overall timing 30 minutes

Freezing Not suitable

To serve 4

1 lb	Can of sweetcorn kernels	450 g
1	Egg	1
2 oz	Plain flour	50 g
	Salt	
1 tbsp	Oil	15 ml
	Grated rind of ½ lemon	
	Oil for deep frying	
	Grated Parmesan cheese	

Drain sweetcorn. Separate egg. Sift flour and pinch of salt into a mixing bowl. Make a well in centre, then put in egg yolk, oil and grated lemon rind. Stir until a smooth batter forms.

In another bowl, whisk egg white till stiff. Fold into batter with sweetcorn.

Heat oil in deep-fryer to 340°F (170°C).

Drop spoonfuls of batter into the hot oil – be careful because corn can burst – a few at a time, and fry for 5 minutes on each side or until golden. Remove with a fish slice and drain on kitchen paper. Keep warm while frying the rest.

Sprinkle grated Parmesan over and serve hot.

Lemon-braised leeks

Overall timing 1 hour

Freezing Not suitable

To serve 4

2 lb	Leeks	900 g
	Salt and pepper	
2	Carrots	2
1	Onion	1
3 oz	Butter	75 g
¼ pint	Stock	150 ml
2 tbsp	Plain flour	2x15 ml
½	Lemon	½

Preheat the oven to 350°F (180°C) Gas 4.

Trim leeks and blanch in boiling salted water for 5 minutes. Drain.

Peel and chop carrots. Peel and slice onion. Melt 1 oz (25 g) of the butter in a flameproof casserole and fry the carrots and onion till golden. Arrange leeks on top and add stock and seasoning.

Cream remaining butter with the flour to make a paste. Squeeze juice from lemon and work into the mixture with a fork. Spread over the leeks. Cover and cook in oven for 30–35 minutes. Serve with side dish of grated cheese and chunks of brown bread.

Cheesy vegetables

Overall timing 10 minutes

Freezing Not suitable

To serve 6

8 oz	Cream cheese	225 g
¼ pint	Carton of single cream	150 ml
2 lb	Hot cooked mixed vegetables (including beans, cauliflower, peas, carrots and mushrooms)	900 g
2 tbsp	Grated Parmesan cheese	2x15 ml
	Salt and pepper	

Beat the cream cheese and cream together in a bowl. Place the bowl over a pan of simmering water and heat through gently, stirring occasionally. Do not boil.

Arrange the vegetables in a warmed serving dish. Keep hot.

Beat the Parmesan into the cream cheese mixture and season to taste. Pour the hot sauce over the vegetables and serve immediately with roast or grilled meat, or as vegetarian lunch.

Greek pumpkin

Overall timing 1 hour

Freezing Not suitable

To serve 4–6

2 lb	Pumpkin	900 g
2	Medium onions	2
3 tbsp	Olive oil	3x15 ml
14 oz	Can of tomatoes	397 g
¼ teasp	Ground cumin	1.25 ml
2	Sprigs of flat-leafed parsley	2
	Salt and pepper	
½ pint	Water	300 ml

Scrape the seeds and fibrous centre out of the pumpkin. Cut into chunks, leaving the skin on. Peel the onions and cut through the root into eight wedges.

Heat the oil in a saucepan, add onions and fry till transparent. Add the tomatoes and juice, cumin and pumpkin. Chop the parsley and add with seasoning and the water. Bring to the boil, then cover and simmer for 25–35 minutes till the pumpkin is tender.

Adjust the seasoning and pour into a warmed serving dish. Serve hot with roast or grilled meat.

Lentils with bacon

Overall timing 1½ hours

Freezing Suitable

To serve 4

8 oz	Continental lentils	225 g
1	Large onion	1
8 oz	Smoked streaky bacon	225 g
3 tbsp	Oil	3x15 ml
1 teasp	Salt	5 ml
3 tbsp	Tomato purée	3x15 ml
1½ pints	Stock	850 ml

Wash and pick over the lentils. Peel and finely chop the onion. Derind and dice the bacon. Heat oil in a saucepan and fry onion and bacon till golden. Add the lentils and salt and cook for 10 minutes, stirring frequently.

Stir in the tomato purée and the stock and simmer for about 1 hour until the lentils are tender. Taste and adjust seasoning. Serve on slices of fried bread with a mixed salad.

Lentils with courgettes and potatoes

Overall timing 1½ hours

Freezing Not suitable

To serve 6

8 oz	Continental lentils	225 g
	Salt and pepper	
2	Bay leaves	2
1	Onion	1
2 tbsp	Oil	2x15 ml
12 oz	Courgettes	350 g
1	Garlic clove	1
2 tbsp	Lemon juice	2x15 ml
5	Fennel leaves	5
	Basil leaves	
	Sprig of rosemary	
1 teasp	Cumin seed	5 ml
8 oz	Potatoes	225 g
1 oz	Butter	25 g
	Chopped parsley	

Put lentils in a large saucepan. Add 2 pints (1.1 litres) water, seasoning and bay leaves. Bring to the boil and simmer for 5 minutes, then drain, reserving the liquid.

Peel and finely chop onion. Heat oil in a large saucepan and fry onion till transparent. Trim and thickly slice courgettes. Add to pan and stir-fry for 5 minutes. Peel and crush garlic and add to pan with lentils and lemon juice.

Finely chop fennel leaves and add to pan with a few basil leaves, a sprig of rosemary, the cumin and reserved lentil liquor. Simmer for 45 minutes.

Meanwhile, peel potatoes and cut into large chunks. Add to pan and simmer for a further 20 minutes or till the lentils are cooked.

Add the butter, and taste and adjust seasoning. Sprinkle with chopped parsley and serve hot with grated cheese or slices of boiled bacon.

Russian potatoes with cream

Overall timing 1¼ hours

Freezing Not suitable

To serve 4

1½ lb	Waxy potatoes	700 g
	Salt and pepper	
2 oz	Button mushrooms	50 g
1	Small onion	1
2 oz	Butter	50 g
¼ pint	Soured cream	150 ml
2 tbsp	Chopped parsley	2x15 ml

Cook the potatoes in boiling salted water for about 30 minutes till tender. Drain and peel the potatoes, then cut into ¼ inch (6mm) thick slices. Slice the mushrooms. Peel and thinly slice the onion.

Melt the butter in a frying pan and fry the onion till transparent. Add the mushrooms and fry for 2–3 minutes, stirring. Add the sliced potatoes and fry for 5 minutes, turning once.

Pour the cream over and season well. Turn potatoes gently till coated and continue cooking over a low heat for about 10 minutes till the potatoes have absorbed most of the cream.

Stir in the parsley, adjust the seasoning and serve hot.

Lettuce and ham supper

Overall timing 40 minutes

Freezing Not suitable

To serve 4

4	Round lettuces	4
1	Onion	1
1 oz	Butter	25 g
½ pint	Chicken stock	300 ml
	Salt and pepper	
4	Thick slices of cooked ham	4
1 teasp	Cornflour	5 ml
2 tbsp	Water	2x15 ml
¼ pint	Sherry	150 ml

Trim and wash lettuces. Drain well and cut in half lengthways. Peel and chop the onion.

Melt the butter in a saucepan and fry onions till golden. Add lettuces and fry for 3 minutes. Add stock, salt and pepper. Tightly cover pan and simmer gently for 15–20 minutes.

Cut ham slices in half and add to pan. Heat through gently for 3 minutes.

Carefully lift out the lettuce halves and ham, draining thoroughly. Arrange on a warmed serving dish and keep hot.

Blend cornflour with water, then stir into cooking liquor. Bring to the boil, stirring continuously. Remove from heat and stir in sherry. Taste and adjust seasoning. Pour over lettuce and ham and serve immediately with mashed potatoes and wholemeal bread.

Savoury pumpkin

Overall timing 1¼ hours plus 30 minutes standing

Freezing Not suitable

To serve 4–6

2 lb	Pumpkin	900 g
	Salt and pepper	
8 oz	Cheese	225 g
¼ teasp	Ground cumin	1.25 ml
3	Eggs	3
2 oz	Fresh breadcrumbs	50 g
2 tbsp	Chopped parsley	2x15 ml
1 oz	Butter	25 g

Scrape the seeds and fibrous centre out of the pumpkin. Remove the skin and grate the flesh into a bowl. Sprinkle with salt, mix well and leave to stand for 30 minutes.

Preheat the oven to 350°F (180°C) Gas 4.

Press the pumpkin with the back of a spoon to squeeze out as much liquid as possible. Grate the cheese and add to the pumpkin with cumin, eggs, breadcrumbs, parsley and seasoning and beat the mixture till smooth.

Pour into a greased ovenproof dish and smooth the top. Dot with butter and bake for about 45 minutes till set. Serve immediately with a tomato salad and fresh crusty bread and butter.

Macaroni with artichokes

Overall timing 35 minutes

Freezing Not suitable

To serve 2

2	Small globe artichokes	2
1 teasp	Lemon juice	5 ml
1	Garlic clove	1
2 tbsp	Olive oil	2x15 ml
1 tbsp	Chopped parsley	15 ml
8 oz	Penne macaroni	225 g
	Salt and pepper	

Cut off stems, tough outer leaves and pointed tops of artichokes and snip off the tips of outside leaves. Cut artichokes into quarters, remove chokes and place in bowl with lemon juice. Cover with water and leave to soak for 10 minutes.

Peel and crush garlic. Heat the oil in saucepan. Drain artichokes and add to pan with garlic. Cook gently over low heat for about 10 minutes till tender, turning them several times. Add parsley and cook for a further 5 minutes, stirring occasionally.

Meanwhile, cook macaroni in boiling salted water till tender. Drain thoroughly and add to artichokes. Mix well to coat pasta with oil and parsley, adding lots of seasoning, then turn into warmed serving dish. Serve hot with grated Parmesan cheese.

Lyonnaise beans

Overall timing 1 hour plus soaking

Freezing Not suitable

To serve 6

12 oz	Dried butter beans	350 g
	Salt and pepper	
2	Medium onions	2
2 oz	Butter	50 g
1 tbsp	Chopped parsley	15 ml

Soak beans in water to cover overnight. Drain.

Place beans in saucepan and add 1¾ pints (1 litre) fresh water. Cover and cook for about 1 hour till tender. Add a little salt towards the end of cooking time.

Peel and finely chop onions. Melt the butter in a saucepan and add the onions, parsley and seasoning. Cook gently till onions are transparent.

Drain beans well, then toss them in the onion and parsley mixture. Transfer to a warmed serving dish and serve.

Sicilian broad beans

Overall timing 1 hour 20 minutes plus optional cooking

Freezing Not suitable

To serve 4

12 oz	Fresh broad beans	350 g
12 oz	Fresh peas	350 g
1	Small onion	1
2 tbsp	Oil	2x15 ml
4 tbsp	Water or stock	4x15 ml
	Pinch of grated nutmeg	
	Salt and pepper	
4	Canned artichoke hearts	4
6	Leaves of fresh mint	6
½ teasp	Sugar	2.5 ml
2 teasp	Vinegar	2x5 ml

Shell beans and peas. Peel and chop onion. Heat oil in a saucepan and fry onion till transparent. Add beans, peas, water or stock, nutmeg and seasoning. Cover the pan and simmer gently for 30 minutes.

Drain artichokes and cut into eighths. Add to pan and continue cooking for 10 minutes. Stir in mint (some whole leaves, some chopped) and cook for 5 minutes more. Leave to cool slightly before serving.

If you wish to serve this dish cold, add sugar and vinegar with the mint. Stir well, then transfer to a serving dish and leave till cold. Chill for 15 minutes before serving.

Scalloped Chinese leaves

Overall timing 45 minutes

Freezing Not suitable

To serve 4

2 lb	Chinese leaves	900 g
1	Onion	1
1 pint	Milk	560 ml
	Salt and pepper	
1	Egg	1
2 tbsp	Chopped parsley	2x15 ml
1 oz	Butter	25 g
4 oz	Cheese	125 g

Preheat the oven to 375°F (190°C) Gas 5.

Trim stalk end of Chinese leaves. Remove any damaged outer leaves, then separate remaining leaves. Rinse and drain.

Peel and slice the onion and put into a large saucepan with the milk and a little salt. Bring just to boil, then add the Chinese leaves. Cover and simmer for 5 minutes.

Lift the Chinese leaves out of the milk with a draining spoon and arrange in a shallow ovenproof dish. Beat the egg in a bowl with the parsley and gradually add the milk, beating constantly. Add pepper and the butter and stir till melted. Pour over the Chinese leaves. Grate the cheese and sprinkle over the top. Bake for about 30 minutes till golden. Serve immediately with brown bread rolls.

Spicy stuffed peppers

Overall timing 1¼ hours

Freezing Not suitable

To serve 4

8	Green or red peppers	8
	Salt and pepper	
1	Onion	1
2 tbsp	Oil	2x15ml
1 lb	Minced beef	450g
1 pint	Beef stock	560ml
6 oz	Long grain rice	175g
1 teasp	Grated nutmeg	5ml
1 tbsp	Brown sugar	15ml
2 oz	Cheese	50g

Cut stalk ends off peppers and remove seeds and membrane. Blanch in boiling salted water for 5 minutes, then drain. Arrange in a greased ovenproof dish.

Peel and chop onion and pepper lids. Heat oil in a saucepan and fry onion and pepper lids till just golden. Add beef and brown well. Stir in stock and bring to the boil. Add rice, nutmeg, sugar and seasoning and simmer for 15–20 minutes till rice is tender and has absorbed the stock.

Remove from heat. Grate cheese and stir into stuffing. Use to fill the peppers. Cover the dish with foil and bake for 20 minutes. Remove foil and bake for a further 10 minutes till golden.

Stuffed baked turnips

Overall timing 1¼ hours

Freezing Not suitable

To serve 4

4x8oz	Turnips	4x225g
	Salt and pepper	
1	Onion	1
1 oz	Butter	25g
2 oz	Fresh breadcrumbs	50g
8 oz	Sliced cooked ham	225g
1	Egg yolk	1
¼ pint	Chicken stock	150ml
3 oz	Cheese	75g

Preheat the oven to 375°F (190°C) Gas 5.

Peel turnips. Cut off top third of each to make a lid. Scoop flesh out of base, leaving a thick shell, and chop flesh. Cook shells and lids in boiling salted water for 5 minutes, then drain.

Peel and chop onion. Melt butter in a saucepan, add onion and chopped turnip and fry till golden. Stir in breadcrumbs. Reserve four slices of ham, chop rest and add to stuffing with seasoning and egg yolk.

Press stuffing into turnips. Place a slice of ham on each and cover with lids. Put in ovenproof dish. Pour stock over, cover and bake for 20 minutes.

Grate cheese. Uncover turnips, sprinkle over cheese and bake for a further 10–15 minutes.

Marrow ratatouille

Overall timing 40 minutes

Freezing Suitable: add olives and Parmesan after reheating

To serve 2

1 lb	Marrow	450 g
	Salt and pepper	
1	Onion	1
1	Garlic clove	1
2	Tomatoes	2
1 oz	Butter	25 g
1 tbsp	Oil	15 ml
1 tbsp	Tomato purée	15 ml
5 tbsp	Stock	5x15 ml
1 teasp	Chopped fresh marjoram	5 ml
1 teasp	Chopped fresh basil	5 ml
½ teasp	Chopped fresh thyme	2.5 ml
6	Black olives	6
2 tbsp	Grated Parmesan cheese	2x15 ml

Peel the marrow, cut in half lengthways and scoop out seeds. Cut flesh into 2 inch (5 cm) slices. Blanch in boiling salted water for 5 minutes. Drain well.

Peel and slice the onion. Peel and crush the garlic. Blanch, peel and chop the tomatoes.

Heat butter and oil in a frying pan, add onion and garlic and cook for 5 minutes till transparent. Add marrow, tomatoes, tomato purée, stock, herbs and seasoning. Simmer for 10–15 minutes till the marrow is just tender.

Add the olives and sprinkle with grated Parmesan cheese. Serve hot with chunks of crusty fresh bread, or as an accompaniment to grilled meats.

Spinach dumplings

Overall timing 40 minutes plus setting

Freezing Suitable: cook from frozen for 12–15 minutes, then add melted butter and cheese.

To serve 6

2 lb	Spinach	900 g
$\frac{1}{2}$	Chicken stock cube	$\frac{1}{2}$
5 tbsp	Warm milk	5 x 15 ml
12 oz	Plain flour	350 g
3	Eggs	3
	Salt and pepper	
4 oz	Butter	125 g
8 oz	Fresh breadcrumbs	225 g
$\frac{1}{4}$ teasp	Grated nutmeg	1.25 ml
1 tbsp	Chopped parsley	15 ml
1 tbsp	Chopped chives	15 ml
4 oz	Emmenthal cheese	125 g

Wash spinach and put into a saucepan with only water that clings to it. Cover and cook for 5 minutes.

Dissolve stock cube in milk. Sift flour into a bowl, add eggs, milk and seasoning and mix to a soft dough.

Drain spinach thoroughly and chop finely. Melt half the butter in a frying pan, add breadcrumbs and fry till crisp and golden. Add to dough with nutmeg, parsley and chives. Add spinach and mix to a stiff dough.

Roll dough between floured hands into long sausage-shapes about $\frac{1}{2}$ inch (12.5 mm) in diameter. Leave to set.

Cut across dough into 1 inch (2.5 cm) lengths. Cook in boiling salted water for about 10 minutes till they float to the surface.

Lift out dumplings with a draining spoon, drain thoroughly and arrange in a warmed serving dish. Melt remaining butter, pour over dumplings and sprinkle with grated cheese. Toss lightly before serving with casseroles.

Spinach omelette

Overall timing 15 minutes

Freezing Not suitable

To serve 2

6 oz	Spinach	175 g
2 oz	Butter	50 g
	Salt and pepper	
6	Eggs	6
2 tbsp	Single cream	2x15 ml

Cut away blemishes and stalks from spinach. Wash, then shred coarsely. Melt 1½ oz (40 g) of the butter in a saucepan, add spinach and seasoning, cover and cook over a low heat for about 5 minutes till a purée.

Lightly beat the eggs in a bowl with seasoning. Melt the remaining butter in an omelette pan, add the egg mixture and cook gently till the omelette is lightly set.

Spread the spinach purée over half the omelette and spoon the cream over. Slide omelette out of the pan on to a warmed serving dish, tilting the pan so the omelette folds in half. Serve immediately with chips and a salad.

Marseilles marrow

Overall timing 45 minutes

Freezing Not suitable

To serve 6

1½ lb	Marrow	700 g
	Salt and pepper	
12 oz	Ripe tomatoes	350 g
2	Large onions	2
3 tbsp	Olive oil	3x15 ml
4 oz	Long grain rice	125 g
1 pint	Water	560 ml
1 tbsp	Chopped parsley	15 ml

Blanch marrow in boiling salted water for 10 minutes. Drain thoroughly. Cut in half lengthways, then cut across each half into 1 inch (2.5 cm) thick slices, removing the seeds.

Blanch, peel and halve the tomatoes. Peel and slice the onions. Heat the oil in a flameproof casserole and fry onions till pale golden.

Add the rice to the casserole and fry, stirring, for 2 minutes till the oil is absorbed. Add the water, tomatoes, marrow and seasoning. Bring to the boil, then cover and simmer gently for 15–20 minutes till rice is tender and most of the water has been absorbed.

Taste and adjust the seasoning, sprinkle with parsley and serve hot.

Sweet potato soufflé

Overall timing 1¼ hours

Freezing Not suitable

To serve 2

8 oz	Yam or sweet potatoes	225 g
¼ pint	Milk	150 ml
	Salt	
1 oz	Butter	25 g
1½ teasp	Plain flour	7.5 ml
2	Eggs	2
	Pinch of cayenne	
2 oz	Cheese	50 g

Preheat the oven to 375°F (190°C) Gas 5.

Peel the yam or sweet potato and cut into ½ inch (12.5 mm) cubes. Put into a saucepan with the milk and a little salt and bring to the boil. Cover and simmer for about 20 minutes till tender. Drain the yam or sweet potato, reserving the cooking liquor, then return it to the pan and mash over a low heat to make a dry, fluffy purée.

Melt the butter in a saucepan, add the flour and cook for 1 minute. Make the reserved cooking liquor up to ¼ pint (150 ml) with extra milk if necessary and gradually add to the roux. Bring to the boil, stirring constantly, and simmer for 2 minutes. Remove from the heat and allow to cool slightly.

Separate the eggs and beat the yolks into the sauce with the cayenne, grated cheese, a little salt and the yam or potato purée. Whisk the egg whites till stiff and fold into the sauce with a metal spoon.

Pour the mixture into a greased soufflé dish and bake for 30–35 minutes till well risen and golden. Serve immediately.

Mixed vegetables in milk

Overall timing 35 minutes

Freezing Not suitable

To serve 4

1	Large potato	1
1	Bulb of celeriac	1
2	Carrots	2
1	Turnip	1
1	Small cauliflower	1
8 oz	Green beans	225 g
¾ pint	Milk	400 ml
2 oz	Butter	50 g
	Salt and pepper	
2 tbsp	Plain flour	2x15 ml
4 tbsp	Single cream	4x15 ml

Peel and dice potato, celeriac, carrots and turnip. Divide cauliflower into small florets. Top and tail beans, remove strings and chop.

Heat milk with half the butter and salt. Add potato, celeriac, carrots and turnip and cook for 10 minutes. Add cauliflower and beans and cook for a further 5 minutes. Drain vegetables, reserving milk.

Melt remaining butter in pan, stir in flour and cook for 1 minute. Gradually stir in reserved milk and simmer till thickened. Add cooked vegetables and heat through. Remove from heat and stir in cream and seasoning to taste.

Peas bonne femme

Overall timing 45 minutes

Freezing Not suitable

To serve 4

2 lb	Fresh peas	900 g
6	Small onions	6
1	Round lettuce	1
1	Thick streaky bacon rasher	1
3 oz	Butter	75 g
1 tbsp	Chopped parsley	15 ml
½ teasp	Sugar	2.5 ml
¼ pint	Water	150 ml
	Salt and pepper	
1 teasp	Plain flour	5 ml

Shell peas. Blanch onions in boiling water for 5 minutes, then peel. Shred lettuce. Derind and chop bacon.

Melt 2 oz (50 g) butter in a saucepan and fry peas, onions, lettuce, parsley and bacon for 3 minutes, stirring. Add sugar, water and seasoning. Bring to the boil, cover and simmer for 15–20 minutes till peas and onions are tender.

Mix flour with remaining butter to a paste and add in small pieces to the vegetable mixture, stirring constantly. Cook for 3 minutes. Taste and adjust the seasoning and serve hot.

Stir-fried celery

Overall timing 15 minutes

Freezing Not suitable

To serve 4

1	Large bunch of celery	1
2 teasp	Salt	2x5 ml
3 tbsp	Oil	3x15 ml
2 tbsp	Soy sauce	2x15 ml
½ teasp	Sugar	2.5 ml

Cut off leaves from celery, then chop into 2 inch (5 cm) pieces. Sprinkle with salt.

Heat oil in frying pan. When oil is very hot, add the celery and stir-fry for 5 minutes. Add soy sauce and sugar, mix well and serve immediately.

Mushrooms in batter

Overall timing 30 minutes

Freezing Not suitable

To serve 2–4

12 oz	Large open mushrooms	350 g
4½ oz	Plain flour	140 g
1 teasp	Salt	5 ml
1	Egg	1
1 tbsp	Oil	15 ml
¼ pint	Milk or water	150 ml
2	Egg whites	2
	Oil for frying	
	Sprigs of parsley	

Trim the mushrooms, then toss in ½ oz (15 g) of the flour.

Sift the remaining flour and salt into a bowl and make a well in the centre. Add the egg and oil and begin to mix with a wooden spoon, drawing the flour into the liquid. Gradually stir in the milk or water to make a thick smooth batter. Whisk the egg whites in a bowl till stiff but not dry and fold gently into the batter.

Heat oil in a deep-fryer to 340°F (170°C).

Spear a mushroom on a long skewer and dip into the batter. Using a second skewer, carefully push the mushroom off the skewer into the oil. Fry the mushrooms, a few at a time, for 3–4 minutes till crisp and golden. Remove from the pan with a draining spoon and drain on kitchen paper. Pile on to a warmed serving plate and garnish with sprigs of parsley.

Mushroom casserole

Overall timing 2½ hours

Freezing Not suitable

To serve 4

2 lb	Flat mushrooms	900 g
1 oz	Butter	25 g
1	Onion	1
1	Garlic clove	1
8 oz	Cooked ham	225 g
8 oz	Lean pork	225 g
4 oz	Streaky bacon	125 g
4	Sprigs of parsley	4
2	Eggs	2
1 tbsp	Fresh breadcrumbs	15 ml
	Salt and pepper	
½ oz	Dripping	15 g
1 tbsp	Oil	15 ml
1 teasp	Wine or cider vinegar	5 ml

Preheat the oven to 325°F (170°C) Gas 3.

Separate mushroom stalks from the caps. Halve or quarter caps if large and reserve. Chop the stalks. Melt the butter in a saucepan, add the chopped mushroom stalks and fry over a high heat until all the liquid has evaporated. Remove pan from heat.

Peel and finely chop the onion and garlic. Mince the ham, pork, derinded bacon and parsley. Add all these ingredients to the saucepan with the eggs, breadcrumbs and generous seasoning. Mix well.

Heat the dripping and oil in flameproof casserole. When hot, remove from heat and put in a layer of the mince mixture (don't pack tightly), followed by a layer of mushroom caps. Repeat until all the ingredients have been used up. Cover and bake for about 2 hours. Sprinkle with vinegar just before serving with a mixed salad.

Sweet-sour red cabbage

Overall timing 1 hour 20 minutes

Freezing Suitable

To serve 4

2 lb	Red cabbage	about 1 kg
2 oz	Streaky bacon	50 g
1	Onion	1
1	Cooking apple	1
6	Whole allspice	6
½ teasp	Salt	2.5 ml
2 teasp	Honey	2 x 5 ml
3 fl oz	Red wine or wine vinegar	90 ml

Discard any damaged outer leaves from the cabbage. Quarter, cut away core and thick ribs and shred leaves.

Derind and chop bacon. Peel and chop onion. Cook bacon in flameproof casserole over a low heat until fat starts to run. Add onion and cook for 5 minutes, stirring.

Peel, core and chop apple and add to casserole with cabbage. Crush allspice and add to casserole with salt, honey and wine or vinegar. Mix well, then cover and simmer for 1 hour.

If there's too much liquid at the end of cooking time, remove the lid and continue simmering. Serve hot.

Neapolitan beans

Overall timing 1½ hours plus soaking

Freezing Not suitable

To serve 4

4 oz	Dried haricot beans	125 g
1	Stalk of celery	1
1	Carrot	1
1	Garlic clove	1
2 tbsp	Oil	2x15 ml
2 tbsp	Chopped parsley	2x15 ml
14 oz	Can of tomatoes	397 g
1 tbsp	Chopped fresh savory	15 ml
	Salt and pepper	
1 pint	Strong chicken stock	560 ml
8 oz	Short macaroni	225 g

Put beans in a large pan and cover with plenty of cold water. Bring to the boil and boil for 2 minutes. Remove from heat, cover and leave to soak for 2 hours.

Drain beans well, then cover with boiling water and cook for 1 hour.

Chop celery. Peel and chop carrot. Peel and crush garlic. Heat oil in a saucepan, add celery, carrot, garlic and parsley and fry for 5 minutes.

Sieve tomatoes and juice and add to vegetables with savory and seasoning. Drain beans and purée two-thirds of them in a vegetable mill or press through a sieve. Add bean purée, whole beans and stock to vegetables. Bring to the boil.

Add the macaroni and stir well. Cook for 15–20 minutes, stirring occasionally. Taste and adjust seasoning before serving.

Norwegian cauliflower

Overall timing 25 minutes

Freezing Not suitable

To serve 4

1	Cauliflower	1
	Salt and pepper	
1 oz	Butter	25 g
2 oz	Fresh white breadcrumbs	50 g
$\frac{1}{2}$ pint	Milk	300 ml
	Pinch of sugar	
4 oz	Shelled prawns	125 g
1 tbsp	Brandy (optional)	15 ml
3 tbsp	Single cream	3x15 ml
	Sprigs of parsley	

Remove any leaves from the cauliflower and trim the stalk. Put cauliflower into a saucepan containing $1\frac{1}{2}$ inches (4 cm) of boiling salted water, cover and cook for 20 minutes.

Meanwhile, melt the butter in another pan, add breadcrumbs and milk and cook for a few minutes, stirring. Add salt, pepper and sugar. Set aside a few shelled prawns for the garnish and add the rest to the pan. Cook for 5 minutes more, stirring.

Remove pan from heat and add brandy, if used, and cream. Return to a gentle heat for 1 minute.

Drain cauliflower, place on a warmed serving dish and pour over sauce. Garnish with reserved prawns and parsley.

Mushroom loaf

Overall timing 1 hour

Freezing Not suitable

To serve 4

1½ lb	Button mushrooms	700 g
1½ oz	Butter	40 g
½ pint	White sauce	300 ml
	Salt and pepper	
	Grated nutmeg	
3	Eggs	3

Preheat the oven to 350°F (180°C) Gas 4.

Trim the mushrooms. Reserve four for decoration and finely chop the rest. Melt 1 oz (25 g) butter in a saucepan and cook the chopped mushrooms for 5 minutes. Stir in the white sauce, then season with salt, pepper and a little grated nutmeg to taste.

Remove pan from heat and allow to cool slightly, then beat in the eggs one at a time. Pour the mixture into a greased 6 inch (15 cm) soufflé dish and bake for about 45 minutes till set.

Meanwhile, flute one of the reserved mushrooms and thinly slice the other three. Melt remaining butter in a saucepan and fry mushrooms till golden.

Turn out mushroom loaf and serve hot, garnished with fried mushrooms, on a bed of lettuce leaves.

Moravian mushrooms

Overall timing 30 minutes

Freezing Not suitable

To serve 6

1¼ lb	Button mushrooms	600 g
1 oz	Butter	25 g
½ teasp	Salt	2.5 ml
1 teasp	Cumin seeds	5 ml
1 tbsp	Finely chopped parsley	15 ml
1 tbsp	Plain flour	15 ml
1 teasp	Vinegar or lemon juice	5 ml
4 fl oz	Milk	120 ml
2 tbsp	Double cream	2x15 ml

Trim and slice the mushrooms.

Melt the butter in a saucepan and add the mushrooms, salt, cumin seeds and chopped parsley. Stir-fry over a high heat for 5 minutes, then stir in flour.

Gradually add vinegar or lemon juice and milk, stirring constantly. Lower the heat and simmer for 10 minutes, stirring frequently. Stir in cream and serve.

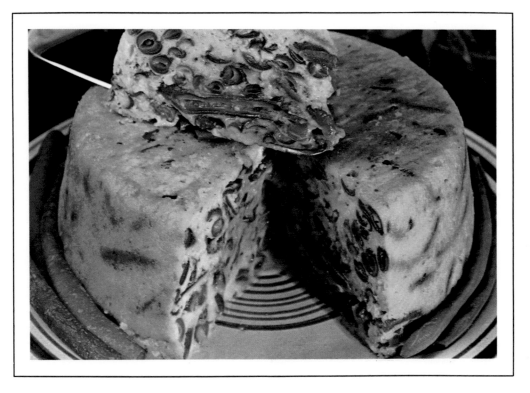

Bean cake

Overall timing 1¼–1½ hours

Freezing Suitable: reheat after thawing in 300°F (150°C) Gas 2 oven for 30 minutes

To serve 4

1 lb	Green beans	450 g
	Salt and pepper	
1	Celery stalk	1
3 oz	Butter	75 g
2 tbsp	Oil	2x15 ml
1 tbsp	Chopped onion	15 ml
1 tbsp	Chopped parsley	15 ml
1 oz	Plain flour	25 g
9 fl oz	Milk	250 ml
4 oz	Mature cheese	125 g
2 tbsp	Crisp breadcrumbs	2x15 ml
3	Eggs	3

Preheat the oven to 425°F (220°C) Gas 7.

String beans. Blanch for 5 minutes in boiling salted water. Drain.

Chop celery. Melt 2 oz (50 g) of the butter with the oil in a frying pan and brown the onion, celery and chopped parsley. Add beans, cover and cook very gently for 10 minutes.

Meanwhile, melt the remaining butter in a saucepan. Stir in flour and cook for 2 minutes, then gradually stir in milk. Simmer until thick. Grate cheese and add to sauce with seasoning.

Grease ovenproof dish and coat bottom and sides with breadcrumbs. Drain bean mixture and mix it into sauce until well combined, then mix in lightly beaten eggs. Spoon mixture into dish. Place dish in roasting tin of water and bake for 25 minutes. Reduce heat to 400°F (200°C) Gas 6 and bake for 10 more minutes.

Remove dish from oven, leave to stand for 5 minutes, then invert on to serving plate. Serve hot or cold.

Bean gratin

Overall timing 40 minutes

Freezing Not suitable

To serve 6

2 oz	Bread	50 g
	Milk	
1	Garlic clove	1
1 tbsp	Chopped parsley	15 ml
8 oz	Leftover cooked lamb or beef	225 g
	Salt and pepper	
2x14 oz	Cans of green beans *or*	2x397 g
1 lb	Frozen beans *or*	450 g
1¼ lb	Fresh cooked beans	600 g
1 oz	Butter	25 g
1 oz	Plain flour	25 g
¾ pint	Milk	400 ml
3 oz	Cheese	75 g
1	Egg	1

Preheat oven to 450°F (230°C) Gas 8.

Soak the bread in a little milk. Squeeze out, then put through a mincer with the peeled garlic, parsley and meat. Season with salt and pepper.

If using canned beans, drain them. Fill a well-greased gratin dish with alternate layers of beans and meat mixture, finishing with a bean layer.

Melt butter in a saucepan. Stir in flour and cook for 1 minute, then gradually add milk. Bring to the boil, stirring until thickened. Grate cheese and add to sauce. Cool slightly, then mix in beaten egg and seasoning.

Cover bean mixture in gratin dish with the sauce. Bake for about 10 minutes until the sauce is lightly browned.

Beans with egg sauce

Overall timing 25 minutes

Freezing Not suitable

To serve 6

1½ lb	French beans *or*	700 g
2x14 oz	Cans of whole or cut green beans	2x397 g
	Salt	
2 oz	Butter	50 g
4 tbsp	Fresh breadcrumbs	4x15 ml
1 oz	Margarine	25 g
1 oz	Plain flour	25 g
	Nutmeg	
1 teasp	Lemon juice	5 ml
¼ teasp	Dried mixed herbs	1.25 ml
3 tbsp	White wine or cider	3x15 ml
2	Hard-boiled eggs	2
1 teasp	Chopped chives	5 ml

If using fresh beans wash, top and tail them and remove strings. Break or cut into short lengths. Cook for 10–15 minutes in boiling, salted water until tender. Drain, saving 9 fl oz (250 ml) of the cooking liquor, and put beans into a warmed serving dish. Heat canned beans in their liquid and use this, made up to required amount with water, for sauce.

Melt the butter in a saucepan, add the breadcrumbs and lightly brown. Sprinkle over beans and keep warm.

To make the sauce, melt the margarine in the saucepan then stir in the flour. Remove pan from heat and blend in the reserved cooking liquor. Stir sauce over a medium heat until it comes to the boil and thickens, then add pinches of salt and nutmeg, lemon juice and mixed herbs.

Remove pan from heat and stir in wine or cider, chopped hard-boiled eggs and chives. Pour sauce over beans. Serve with lamb steaks and potato croquettes.

Boston baked beans

Overall timing 8 hours

Freezing Not suitable

To serve 6

1 lb	Dried haricot beans	450 g
2 tbsp	Black treacle	2x15 ml
2 oz	Brown sugar	50 g
2 teasp	French mustard	2x5 ml
½ teasp	White pepper	2.5 ml
1 lb	Piece of fat bacon with rind	450 g

Soak the beans for 2 hours.

Preheat oven to 350°F (180°C) Gas 4.

Drain the beans and cover them with fresh cold water. Bring to the boil and simmer for about 1½ hours. Drain and reserve ½ pint (300 ml) of the cooking liquor.

Add the treacle, sugar, mustard, pepper and reserved cooking liquor to the beans.

Derind bacon and score the skin in several places. Cut 2 or 3 slices from the bacon, and place these in the bottom of a heavy-based casserole. Pour in the bean mixture and top with the rest of the bacon and also the rind. Cover tightly and bake for 4½–5 hours or till the beans are tender and deep brown.

Use two forks, one in each hand, to shred the bacon rind and mix it in with the beans. Serve hot.

Baked stuffed onions

Overall timing 1½ hours

Freezing Not suitable

To serve 6

6	Large white onions	6
3 oz	Long grain rice	75 g
	Salt and pepper	
3 tbsp	Chopped parsley	3x15 ml
1 oz	Butter	25 g

Peel the onions, then blanch in boiling water for 10 minutes. Drain and cool.

Meanwhile, cook the rice in boiling salted water for 20 minutes or until tender. Drain if necessary, then mix with the parsley, butter and seasoning.

Cut a thin slice from the tops of the onions, then hollow out the centres with a spoon. Fill with the rice mixture.

Arrange the onions around a roasting joint for the last 30–45 minutes of the cooking time, till tender.

Celeriac with onions

Overall timing 50 minutes

Freezing Not suitable

To serve 4–6

1½ lb	Celeriac	700 g
	Salt and pepper	
1 tbsp	Lemon juice	15 ml
2	Medium onions	2
2 oz	Butter	50 g
1 oz	Pork dripping *or*	25 g
2 tbsp	Oil	2x15 ml
2 tbsp	Plain flour	2x15 ml
¾ pint	Chicken stock	400 ml

Peel celeriac and cut into ⅛ inch (3 mm) slices. Blanch in boiling salted water with the lemon juice for 5 minutes, then drain.

Peel and finely chop onions. Heat half the butter and all the dripping or oil in a large frying pan. Add onions and celeriac and cook till onions are transparent, turning the celeriac over once with tongs – take care not to break up the fragile slices.

Tilt the pan, sprinkle the flour over the fat and stir. Add the stock and seasoning. Move the pan to distribute the liquids evenly, then cover and cook over a very low heat for 30 minutes.

Transfer celeriac to a warmed serving dish. Strain the cooking juices, stir in remaining butter and seasoning to taste and pour over the celeriac.

Sunshine salad

Overall timing 15 minutes plus chilling

Freezing Not suitable

To serve 2

8 oz	Poached smoked haddock	225 g
1	Orange	1
1	Grapefruit	1
1	Green pepper	1
1	Onion	1
1 tbsp	Chopped parsley	15 ml
3 tbsp	Olive oil	3x15 ml
1 tbsp	Lemon juice	15 ml
	Salt and pepper	
2 oz	Black olives	50 g

Cut the haddock into small strips. Peel orange and grapefruit and slice or chop the flesh. Deseed and slice pepper. Peel onion and cut into thin rings.

Put prepared ingredients into salad bowl with the parsley. Add oil, lemon juice and seasoning. Toss salad well and chill. Garnish with stoned olives just before serving.

Sweet and sour corn salad

Overall timing 45 minutes including chilling

Freezing Not suitable

To serve 6

8 oz	Can of sweetcorn kernels	225 g
2 tbsp	Wine vinegar	2x15 ml
3 tbsp	Oil	3x15 ml
	Salt and pepper	
1 lb	Cold boiled potatoes	450 g
8 oz	Tomatoes	225 g
8 oz	Can of pineapple chunks	247 g
2	Bananas	2
5 tbsp	Lemon juice	5x15 ml
1	Small lettuce	1
Dressing		
1 tbsp	French mustard	15 ml
¼ pint	Soured cream or plain yogurt	150 ml
2 tbsp	Milk	2x15 ml
	Salt and pepper	
1 teasp	Paprika	5 ml

Drain sweetcorn and place in a bowl. Mix together vinegar, oil and seasoning and add to bowl. Mix well. Cover and chill.

Peel and dice potatoes. Slice tomatoes. Drain pineapple, reserving 2 tbsp (2x15 ml) of the juice. Peel and slice bananas. Put all these in a bowl and pour lemon juice over.

Mix together dressing ingredients with reserved pineapple juice. Add to potato mixture. Chill for 30 minutes.

Line serving dish with lettuce leaves and spoon potato mixture in a ring round the edge. Pile sweetcorn in the middle and serve.

Bacon and potato salad

Overall timing 55 minutes

Freezing Not suitable

To serve 6–8

2 lb	Medium-size waxy potatoes	900 g
	Salt and pepper	
8 oz	Streaky bacon rashers	225 g
1	Large onion	1
4 tbsp	White wine vinegar	4x15 ml
4 tbsp	Water	4x15 ml
1 teasp	Powdered mustard	5 ml
1 tbsp	Chopped chives	15 ml

Scrub the potatoes, cover with cold salted water and bring to the boil. Cook for about 30 minutes till tender.

Meanwhile, derind and dice the bacon and fry over a moderate heat till crisp and brown. Lift out of the pan with a draining spoon and put into a warmed serving dish. Cover with foil to keep hot.

Drain the potatoes and cut into ½ inch (12.5 mm) thick slices. Add to the bacon and cover again.

Peel and roughly chop the onion, add to the bacon fat in the pan and fry over a moderate heat till golden. Add the vinegar, water, salt, pepper and mustard and bring to the boil.

Pour over the potatoes and bacon, turning them carefully till coated. Sprinkle with chives and serve immediately with fresh crusty bread.

Swiss salad

Overall timing 35 minutes

Freezing Not suitable

To serve 4

12 oz	Boiled new potatoes	350 g
1	Dessert apple	1
2 tbsp	White wine vinegar	2x15 ml
1 teasp	Made mustard	5 ml
4 tbsp	Oil	4x15 ml
	Salt and pepper	
$\frac{1}{2}$	Round lettuce	$\frac{1}{2}$
6 oz	Gruyère cheese	175 g
4	Hard-boiled eggs	4
2 teasp	Chopped chives	2x5 ml
1 teasp	Paprika	5 ml

Peel and slice the potatoes into a bowl. Peel, core and slice the apple and toss in the vinegar. Add to the potatoes.

Mix the mustard, oil and seasoning together in a bowl and pour over the potatoes and apple. Toss lightly.

Wash and dry the lettuce leaves and use to line salad bowl. Arrange the potato mixture on the lettuce.

Cut the cheese into matchsticks. Scatter the cheese round the edge and in the centre of the salad. Shell and slice the eggs and arrange on the salad. Sprinkle with the chives and paprika and serve immediately with crusty or wholemeal bread or rolls and butter.

Tropical salad

Overall timing 25 minutes plus cooling

Freezing Not suitable

To serve 2

Salad		
3½ oz	Packet of frozen prawns	100 g
4 oz	Long grain rice	125 g
1	Leek	1
8 oz	Cooked chicken	225 g
1	Small onion	1
Dressing		
2 tbsp	Mango chutney	2x15 ml
2 tbsp	Oil	2x15 ml
2 tbsp	Lemon juice	2x15 ml
1 teasp	Vinegar	5 ml
½ teasp	Worcestershire sauce	2.5 ml
½ teasp	Curry powder	2.5 ml
	Salt and pepper	
Garnish		
	Lettuce leaves	
1	Banana	1

Thaw prawns. Put rice in a pan of boiling salted water and cook for 10 minutes.

Wash, trim and finely slice the leek. Add to the pan and cook for a further 5 minutes or until rice is cooked. Drain and leave to cool.

Slice cooked chicken into thin strips. Peel and finely slice the onion. Add both to the rice with the prawns and mix.

To make the dressing, finely chop the mango chutney and put into a bowl with the oil, lemon juice, vinegar, Worcestershire sauce, curry powder and salt and pepper. Mix well.

Arrange rice mixture on top of lettuce leaves in a serving dish. Garnish with slices of banana and pour dressing over.

Tuna salad

Overall timing 15 minutes

Freezing Not suitable

To serve 4

1	Bulb of fennel	1
	Salt and pepper	
4	Tomatoes	4
6½ oz	Can of tuna	184 g
3 tbsp	Oil	3x15 ml
1 tbsp	Wine vinegar	15 ml
	Chopped parsley	
1 oz	Black olives	25 g

Trim and slice the fennel. Blanch in boiling salted water for 5 minutes. Drain. Slice tomatoes. Drain tuna.

Place tuna in centre of serving dish and arrange fennel and tomato slices around it.

In a bowl, mix together oil, vinegar and seasoning. Pour dressing over salad and sprinkle with chopped parsley. Garnish with black olives and fennel leaves, if available.

Apple and salami salad

Overall timing 40 minutes

Freezing Not suitable

To serve 4

3	Small onions	3
3	Apples	3
8 oz	Salami	225 g
2	Large gherkins	2
1 tbsp	Vinegar	15 ml
1 tbsp	Lemon juice	15 ml
3 tbsp	Oil	3x15 ml
	Salt and pepper	
	Pinch of caster sugar	
$\frac{1}{4}$ teasp	Celery or mustard seeds	1.25 ml

Peel onions and cut into thin rings. Peel, core and chop apples. Dice salami and gherkins. Put them all in a salad bowl and mix well together.

Combine all remaining ingredients to make the dressing and pour over salad, mixing it in well. Leave for 20 minutes to blend the flavours before serving, with crusty bread and butter.

Spinach and avocado salad

Overall timing 20 minutes plus cooling

Freezing Not suitable

To serve 6

8 oz	Spinach	225 g
½	Lettuce	½
1	Avocado	1
1 tbsp	Oil	15 ml
1 tbsp	Lemon juice	15 ml
	Salt and pepper	
4 tbsp	Thick mayonnaise	4x15 ml
1	Hard-boiled egg	1

Trim spinach and wash thoroughly. Put into a pan with no extra water, cover and cook for 8–10 minutes till tender. Turn into a colander and press with wooden spoon to remove excess liquid. Leave to cool.

Wash, trim and dry lettuce. Reserve six medium-size leaves and finely shred the rest. Cut avocado in half and remove stone. Scoop out flesh and chop finely. Place in bowl with cooled spinach, shredded lettuce, oil and lemon juice. Mix together well and season to taste.

Arrange reserved lettuce leaves on serving plate and divide spinach mixture between them. Pipe or spoon mayonnaise on top. Cut hard-boiled egg into wedges and use to garnish.

Avocado and pine nut salad

Overall timing 15 minutes plus chilling

Freezing Not suitable

To serve 2

1	Large ripe avocado	1
1½ teasp	Lemon juice	7.5 ml
2	Gherkins	2
1 tbsp	Pine nuts	15 ml
1½ tbsp	Olive oil	22.5 ml
	Salt and pepper	
1	Garlic clove	1
4	Fresh mint leaves	4
2 tbsp	Plain yogurt	2x15 ml

Cut the avocado in half and remove the stone. Peel away the skin, dice the flesh and put into a bowl. Sprinkle with lemon juice and toss lightly till the avocado is coated.

Slice the gherkins thinly and add to the avocado with the pine nuts. Sprinkle with oil, season and toss.

Peel and crush the garlic into a small bowl. Wash the mint leaves and shred finely. Add to the garlic with the yogurt and mix well. Pour over the avocado and toss lightly. Chill for 1 hour.

Divide salad between two individual dishes and serve immediately with crusty rolls.

Asparagus and potato salad

Overall timing 25 minutes plus chilling

Freezing Not suitable

To serve 4

1 lb	New potatoes	450 g
	Salt and pepper	
1	Small onion	1
1 tbsp	Lemon juice	15 ml
¼ pint	Thick mayonnaise	150 ml
12 oz	Can of asparagus spears or tips	340 g
1	Hard-boiled egg	1
4	Anchovy fillets	4
2 teasp	Drained capers	2 x 5 ml

Scrape the potatoes and cut into even-sized chunks. Cook in boiling salted water for about 5 minutes till tender. Drain and place in a large bowl.

Peel the onion and chop finely. Stir gently into the potatoes with the lemon juice and plenty of seasoning. Add the mayonnaise and mix well.

Drain the asparagus (if using spears, cut into 2 inch/5 cm lengths), and fold gently into the salad. Arrange in a serving dish.

Shell the hard-boiled egg and cut into quarters lengthways. Arrange round the dish. Arrange anchovy fillets in a cross on the salad. Garnish with capers and chill for 30 minutes before serving with wholemeal or black bread.

Esau's salad

Overall timing 1 hour plus cooling

Freezing Not suitable

To serve 6

1 lb	Continental lentils	450 g
2 oz	Smoked bacon	50 g
4 tbsp	Oil	4x15 ml
2	Frankfurters	2
1 tbsp	Vinegar	15 ml
1 teasp	Made mustard	5 ml
	Salt and pepper	
1	Onion	1
1	Green pepper	1
2	Tomatoes	2
2	Hard-boiled eggs	2
1 tbsp	Chopped parsley or chives	15 ml

Put lentils in a saucepan and add enough water just to cover. Bring to the boil, cover and simmer for about 1 hour till tender. Drain and leave to cool.

Derind bacon and cut into strips. Heat 1 tbsp (15 ml) of the oil in a frying pan, add bacon and cook until golden. Remove from pan and allow to cool.

Put frankfurters in a pan, cover with water and bring to the boil. Drain and leave to cool.

Meanwhile, beat together the rest of the oil, the vinegar, mustard and seasoning in a serving dish.

Peel and slice onion. Deseed and slice pepper. Put cooled lentils, bacon, onion and pepper into the dish with the dressing and mix well.

Cut tomatoes into wedges. Shell eggs and cut into wedges. Slice frankfurters. Arrange on top of lentil salad and sprinkle with parsley or chives. Serve with black bread.

Fennel and tomato salad

Overall timing 30 minutes

Freezing Not suitable

To serve 4

1	Large bulb of fennel	1
	Salt and pepper	
1	Onion	1
4	Tomatoes	4
3 tbsp	Oil	3x15 ml
1 tbsp	Wine vinegar or lemon juice	15 ml

Trim fennel. Cut into thin slices and blanch in boiling salted water for 5 minutes. Drain.

Peel onion and cut into rings. Slice tomatoes. Arrange fennel, onion and tomatoes in layers in salad bowl.

In another bowl, mix together oil, vinegar or lemon juice and seasoning. Pour over salad. Chill for 15 minutes before serving.

Fish and potato salad

Overall timing 25 minutes

Freezing Not suitable

To serve 4

1	Onion	1
1	Carrot	1
1	Stalk of celery	1
2 pints	Cold water	1.1 litres
1	Slice of lemon	1
1 lb	Boneless white fish	450 g
1½ lb	Waxy potatoes	700 g
1 tbsp	Wine vinegar	15 ml
½ teasp	Powdered mustard	2.5 ml
4 tbsp	Oil	4x15 ml
2 tbsp	Chopped parsley	2x15 ml
	Salt and pepper	

Peel and halve the onion; scrape and halve the carrot. Wash, trim and halve the celery. Put into a saucepan with the water and slice of lemon and bring slowly to the boil.

Meanwhile, cut the fish into 2 inch (5 cm) pieces. Peel the potatoes and cut into ¼ inch (6 mm) thick slices. Add the fish and potatoes to the boiling court bouillon, and bring almost back to boiling point. Skim off any scum, reduce the heat, cover and poach for 8–10 minutes till the potatoes and fish are tender.

Drain the fish and potatoes carefully in a colander, discarding the other vegetables and lemon.

Put the wine vinegar, mustard and oil into a serving dish with the parsley and mix well. Add the fish and potatoes and toss lightly till coated. Taste and add seasoning if necessary. Serve while still warm with a crisp green salad.

Florida salad

Overall timing 20 minutes plus chilling

Freezing Not suitable

To serve 4

1	Fresh red chilli	1
3 tbsp	Olive oil	3x15 ml
2 teasp	Vinegar	2x5 ml
	Salt and pepper	
4	Slices of fresh pineapple *or*	4
8 oz	Can of pineapple slices in natural juice	227 g
1	Red pepper	1
1	Yellow or green pepper	1
3	Medium bananas	3
1	Large avocado	1

Deseed and finely chop the chilli. Put into a bowl with the oil, vinegar and seasoning and mix well with a fork.

Peel and chop the fresh pineapple, or drain and chop the canned pineapple, and add to the bowl. Deseed and chop the peppers and add to the bowl. Peel and slice the bananas. Halve the avocado, discard the stone, peel and cut into chunks. Add to the bowl with the bananas.

Toss the salad lightly and put into a serving dish. Chill for 30 minutes before serving with chicken or seafood.

Vegetable and herb salad

Overall timing 30 minutes

Freezing Not suitable

To serve 6

1 lb	Potatoes	450 g
	Salt and pepper	
8 oz	Cauliflower	225 g
4 oz	Green beans	125 g
4 oz	Frozen peas	125 g
4 tbsp	Oil	4x15 ml
2 tbsp	Vinegar	2x15 ml
2 tbsp	Chopped fresh mixed herbs	2x15 ml

Scrub the potatoes and cut into small chunks. Place in a saucepan, cover with water, add salt and bring to the boil. Boil gently for 2 minutes.

Divide cauliflower into florets. Add to the pan. Bring back to the boil. Cut beans into 1 inch (2.5 cm) lengths and add to pan with the peas. Simmer gently for 5 minutes or until the potatoes are tender.

Meanwhile, whisk together the oil, vinegar, herbs and seasoning.

Drain the vegetables well and place in salad bowl. While still hot, pour dressing over the vegetables and toss well. Allow to cool before serving.

Egg and parsley mayonnaise

Overall timing 15 minutes plus chilling

Freezing Not suitable

To serve 4

8	Hard-boiled eggs	8
2	Spring onions	2
3 tbsp	Chopped parsley	3x15 ml
¼ pint	Thick mayonnaise	150 ml
¼ pint	Carton of soured cream	150 ml
	Salt and pepper	

Shell and slice the hard-boiled eggs. Trim the spring onions and slice thinly. Arrange half the eggs in a shallow dish and sprinkle the spring onions and 2 tbsp (2x15 ml) of the parsley over.

Mix together the mayonnaise and soured cream and add seasoning to taste. Spoon three-quarters of the mayonnaise mixture over the eggs. Arrange the remaining egg slices decoratively on top and spoon the rest of the mayonnaise between them.

Chill for 1 hour before serving. Sprinkle with the reserved parsley and serve with slices of crusty brown bread.

Walnut cabbage salad

Overall timing 30 minutes plus maceration

Freezing Not suitable

To serve 4

½	Red cabbage	½
4 tbsp	Walnut or olive oil	4x15 ml
2 tbsp	Lemon juice	2x15 ml
2	Large oranges	2
1	Large dessert apple	1
1	Banana	1
2 oz	Walnut halves	50 g
1 oz	Seedless raisins	25 g

Shred the cabbage and toss with the oil and lemon juice. Leave to macerate in the refrigerator for 1 hour.

Peel the oranges and separate into segments. Peel, core and chop the apple. Peel and thickly slice the banana. Add the fruit to the cabbage with the walnuts and raisins. Toss together well, then serve.

Asparagus and ham salad

Overall timing 20 minutes plus chilling

Freezing Not suitable

To serve 4

12 oz	Can of asparagus spears	340 g
4 oz	Cooked ham	125 g
4	Pineapple rings	4
	Lettuce leaves	
8 tbsp	Mayonnaise	8x15 ml
½ teasp	Brandy (optional)	2.5 ml
2 tbsp	Lemon juice	2x15 ml
	Pinch of cayenne	
Garnish		
2	Tomatoes	2
2	Hard-boiled eggs	2
	Chopped parsley	

Drain and chop asparagus and place in a mixing bowl. Dice ham. Chop the pineapple rings. Add both to asparagus and mix together well.

Place lettuce in the bottom of individual glasses. Divide asparagus mixture evenly between them.

Mix mayonnaise with brandy, if using, lemon juice and cayenne. Divide dressing equally between glasses. Garnish with chopped tomato, sliced hard-boiled egg and chopped parsley. Chill for 10 minutes before serving.

Caesar salad

Overall timing 15 minutes plus chilling

Freezing Not suitable

To serve 4

6 tbsp	Oil	6x15 ml
2 tbsp	Vinegar	2x15 ml
2	Garlic cloves	2
	Salt and pepper	
½	Cos lettuce	½
4	Eggs	4
2	Slices of bread	2
2 oz	Roquefort or Parmesan cheese	50 g
4	Anchovy fillets	4

Beat together 4 tbsp (4x15 ml) of the oil, the vinegar, 1 peeled and crushed garlic clove and seasoning in a bowl. Cover and chill for 30 minutes.

Wash and dry lettuce. Tear leaves into pieces, put in a bowl and leave in the refrigerator to crisp.

Put eggs in a pan of cold water, bring to the boil and cook for 4–5 minutes. Drain and place in a bowl of cold water. Shell.

Rub bread slices all over with remaining halved garlic clove, then cut into 1 inch (2.5 cm) cubes. Fry in rest of oil till golden. Drain croûtons on kitchen paper.

Divide lettuce and croûtons between serving plates. Arrange eggs on top of lettuce, sprinkle over crumbled or grated cheese, then spoon dressing over. Garnish with rolled anchovy fillets and serve with crusty bread.

Carrot and cabbage slaw

Overall timing 15 minutes plus chilling

Freezing Not suitable

To serve 4

8 oz	Carrots	225 g
8 oz	White cabbage	225 g
4 tbsp	Wine vinegar	4x15 ml
5 tbsp	Oil	5x15 ml
½ teasp	Caraway seeds	2.5 ml
¼ teasp	Sugar	1.25 ml
	Salt and pepper	
2 oz	Streaky bacon	50 g
1	Large onion	1

Peel and grate carrots. Shred cabbage. In a salad bowl, mix together vinegar, 4 tbsp (4x15 ml) of the oil, caraway seeds, sugar and seasoning. Add carrots and cabbage and mix well. Cover the bowl and chill for 30 minutes.

Derind and chop the bacon. Heat remaining 1 tbsp (15ml) oil in frying pan and fry bacon for 3 minutes till crisp. Peel and finely chop onion, saving a few rings for garnish. Add chopped onion to pan and fry for a few minutes.

Remove salad from refrigerator. Put the hot bacon and onion mixture on top and garnish with onion rings. Serve with roasts or cold meat.

Cauliflower mayonnaise

Overall timing 30 minutes plus chilling

Freezing Not suitable

To serve 4

1	Large cauliflower	1
	Salt and pepper	
6 tbsp	Oil	6x15 ml
2 tbsp	Lemon juice	2x15 ml
3	Tomatoes	3
8	Lettuce leaves	8
¼ pint	Thick mayonnaise	150 ml

Divide cauliflower into large florets. Cook in boiling salted water for 5–10 minutes till just tender.

Meanwhile, put the oil, lemon juice and seasoning into a bowl and mix together with a fork.

Drain the cauliflower thoroughly and add to the dressing while still hot. Toss lightly, then chill for 1 hour.

Meanwhile, slice two of the tomatoes; cut the other in half in a zigzag pattern.

Arrange six lettuce leaves on a serving dish and pile the cauliflower on top. Shred the remaining lettuce and scatter over the cauliflower. Put a tomato half on top and arrange the tomato slices round the edge.

Pipe or spoon the mayonnaise into the tomato half and between the florets. Serve immediately with cold meats or smoked fish.

Chef's salad

Overall timing 20 minutes

Freezing Not suitable

To serve 4–6

1	Round lettuce	1
2	Heads of radicchio *or*	2
$\frac{1}{4}$	Red cabbage	$\frac{1}{4}$
4 oz	Cooked ham	125 g
3 oz	Gruyère or Emmenthal cheese	75 g
1	Small onion	1
2	Tomatoes	2
Dressing		
2 tbsp	Oil	2x15 ml
1 tbsp	Wine vinegar	15 ml
1 teasp	Dijon mustard or made English mustard	5 ml
	Salt and pepper	

Wash and dry lettuce. Line salad bowl with crisp whole leaves. Tear the rest into bite-size pieces and arrange on top.

Wash and dry radicchio and tear into pieces, or shred cabbage. Cut ham into $\frac{1}{2}$ inch (12.5 mm) dice. Slice cheese, then cut into small strips. Peel and slice onion and separate into individual rings. Cut tomatoes into wedges. Arrange all the prepared ingredients on top of the lettuce.

Mix together the dressing ingredients and pour over the salad. Toss thoroughly but gently. Garnish with garlic croûtons (see page 74), if liked.

Tunisian tuna salad

Overall timing 25 minutes plus chilling

Freezing Not suitable

To serve 6

2	Green peppers	2
1	Small onion	1
2x7 oz	Cans of tuna in oil	2x198 g
	Olive oil	
2 teasp	Red wine vinegar	2x5 ml
1 teasp	Lemon juice	5 ml
	Salt and pepper	
1	Garlic clove	1
4 oz	Gruyere or Cheddar cheese	125 g
4 oz	Stoned green olives	125 g
1 lb	Large firm tomatoes	450 g

Deseed the peppers and cut into thin strips. Peel the onion and slice thinly into rings.

Drain the oil from the tuna and put into a small bowl with enough olive oil to make it up to 4 tbsp (4x15 ml). Add the vinegar, lemon juice, seasoning and peeled and crushed garlic.

Flake the tuna; slice the cheese thickly, then cut into thin strips. Put into a large bowl with the onion, pepper and olives. Pour the dressing over and toss lightly till ingredients are evenly coated.

Wash and thinly slice the tomatoes and use to line the salad bowl. Arrange the tuna mixture on top, cover and chill for 30 minutes before serving.

Waldorf salad

Overall timing 15 minutes plus 1 hour refrigeration

Freezing Not suitable

To serve 4

4	Stalks of celery	4
8 oz	Dessert apples	225 g
1 tbsp	Lemon juice	15 ml
	Salt and pepper	
6 tbsp	Thick mayonnaise	6x15 ml
2 oz	Nuts	50 g

Chop celery. Peel, core and dice apples. Place in salad bowl with celery, lemon juice and a little salt. Chill for about 1 hour.

Remove from refrigerator and stir in mayonnaise, chopped nuts and seasoning to taste.

If serving this salad on a special occasion, divide mixture between hollowed-out apples that have been sprinkled with lemon juice. For a simpler, yet still effective presentation, serve on lettuce (shredded or leaves) in individual glass dishes and garnish with fine lemon slices.

Bean and herring salad

Overall timing 1½ hours

Freezing Not suitable

To serve 2

6 oz	Green beans	175 g
	Salt and pepper	
½ oz	Butter	15 g
2	Matjes herring fillets	2
2	Cooked potatoes	2
1	Onion	1
2 tbsp	Mayonnaise	2x15 ml
2 tbsp	Plain yogurt	2x15 ml
1 teasp	Lemon juice	5 ml
	Sugar	
	Chopped parsley	

Top and tail the beans and remove strings. Cut into short lengths. Put the beans into a saucepan of boiling salted water, add butter and cook for 10 minutes till just tender. Drain and leave to cool.

Slice the herrings and potatoes. Peel and finely chop the onion. Place in salad bowl and add herrings and potatoes. Lightly mix in beans.

Make the dressing by combining mayonnaise, yogurt, lemon juice and pepper and sugar to taste. Pour over the salad and chill for 1 hour. Serve garnished with chopped parsley.

Beetroot and apple salad

Overall timing 1 hour 40 minutes plus cooking

Freezing Not suitable

To serve 4–6

1¾ lb	Beetroot	750 g
	Salt	
4 tbsp	Oil	4x15 ml
2 tbsp	Wine vinegar or lemon juice	2x15 ml
1 teasp	Sugar	5 ml
8 oz	Dessert apples	225 g
1	Onion	1

Wash beetroot, then cut off tops. Take care not to pierce the skin when you are preparing beetroot or the colour will boil out, leaving them a rather washed out pink. Place prepared beetroot in saucepan and cover with water. Add a little salt, cover and simmer for 1¼ hours over a low heat. Leave to cool.

Drain beetroot, cut off root and pull off skin. Slice with a mandolin or fluted grater. Dry slices and put them in layers in a salad bowl.

Mix together oil, wine vinegar or lemon juice and sugar and pour over beetroot. Chill for 2 hours.

Peel, core and chop apples. Peel and finely chop onion. Mix into beetroot and serve before the beetroot has time to colour the apple and onion.

Buckling and potato salad

Overall timing 30 minutes

Freezing Not suitable

To serve 4–6

3	Buckling	3
8 oz	Cold boiled potatoes	225 g
8 oz	Red apples	225 g
2	Tomatoes	2
2	Hard-boiled eggs	2
	Sprig of dill or fennel	
Dressing		
4 tbsp	Olive oil	4x15 ml
3 tbsp	Lemon juice	3x15 ml
	Salt and pepper	

Slice buckling along backbone. Skin and fillet, then blanch in boiling water for 3 minutes. Break fish into large pieces and place in serving bowl.

Cut the potatoes into cubes and add to bowl. Core and dice apples. Add to fish and potatoes.

Mix the olive oil, lemon juice and seasoning together to make a dressing. Pour over the fish mixture. Toss carefully and leave for 15 minutes for the flavours to develop.

Wash tomatoes and cut into eighths. Shell and slice eggs and arrange with the tomatoes and herbs around the salad. Serve with hot, crusty bread.

Salade Béatrice

Overall timing 10 minutes plus chilling

Freezing Not suitable

To serve 4

1 lb	Cooked green beans	450 g
	Salt and pepper	
3 tbsp	Oil	3 x 15 ml
1 tbsp	White wine vinegar	15 ml
2	Tomatoes	2
1	Bunch of watercress	1
1	Hard-boiled egg yolk	1

Break or cut the beans into short lengths and put into a salad bowl. Season, add oil and vinegar and mix together well. Chill for 15 minutes.

Cut tomatoes into quarters and arrange around the edge of the salad bowl with the watercress.

Just before serving, garnish with sieved or finely chopped egg yolk. Toss salad at the table.

Salade niçoise

Overall timing 25 minutes

Freezing Not suitable

To serve 4

1 lb	Waxy potatoes	450 g
	Salt and pepper	
8 oz	Green beans	225 g
4 oz	Large black olives	125 g
2 tbsp	Drained capers	2x15 ml
1	Garlic clove	1
4 tbsp	Olive oil	4x15 ml
1 tbsp	Tarragon vinegar	15 ml
1 teasp	Lemon juice	5 ml
1 tbsp	Chopped parsley	15 ml
1	Large firm tomato	1
6	Anchovy fillets	6

Peel and dice the potatoes. Cook in boiling salted water for about 5 minutes till just tender. Top, tail and string the beans and cut into 1 inch (2.5 cm) lengths. Cook in another pan of boiling salted water for 5 minutes till tender.

Drain the vegetables and rinse under cold water. Drain thoroughly and put into a salad bowl. Add half the olives and the capers.

Peel and crush the garlic clove into a bowl. Add the oil, vinegar, lemon juice, parsley and pepper to taste and mix well, then pour over vegetables. Toss lightly till evenly coated.

Cut the tomato into thin wedges. Arrange on the salad with the remaining olives. Cut the anchovies into strips and arrange in a lattice on top of the salad. Serve immediately with French bread.

Raw mushroom salad

Overall timing 20 minutes plus chilling

Freezing Not suitable

To serve 4

12 oz	Button mushrooms	350 g
1 teasp	Lemon juice	5 ml
1 teasp	Made mustard	5 ml
2 tbsp	Single cream	2x15 ml
2 tbsp	Oil	2x15 ml
1½ teasp	White wine vinegar	7.5 ml
	Salt and pepper	
	Chopped parsley	

Thinly slice the mushrooms. Put into a salad bowl and sprinkle with the lemon juice.

Mix together the mustard, cream, oil, vinegar and seasoning. Pour this dressing over the mushrooms and toss carefully. Sprinkle chopped parsley on top. Chill for 30 minutes before serving.

Spanish salad

Overall timing 45 minutes plus 1 hour refrigeration

Freezing Not suitable

To serve 4

½	Cucumber	½
	Salt and pepper	
12 oz	Potatoes	350 g
12 oz	Can of asparagus spears	340 g
8 fl oz	Mayonnaise	220 ml
1 tbsp	French mustard	15 ml
½ teasp	Dried tarragon	2.5 ml
½	Red pepper	½

Peel and slice cucumber. Sprinkle with salt and chill for 1 hour.

Peel and dice potatoes, then cook in boiling salted water for 10 minutes. Drain and leave to cool.

Drain asparagus and dry spears on kitchen paper.

Mix together potatoes, mayonnaise, mustard, tarragon and seasoning and put into a shallow dish. Arrange asparagus on top like the spokes of a wheel. Drain cucumber slices and place one between each asparagus spear and one in the centre. Deseed and dice pepper and place on top of cucumber to add colour.

Sausage and potato salad

Overall timing 25 minutes

Freezing Not suitable

To serve 2

12 oz	Medium-size new potatoes	350 g
	Salt and pepper	
1 tbsp	Dry white wine	15 ml
4–6 oz	German spicy sausage	125–175 g
1½ teasp	Chopped parsley	7.5 ml
½ teasp	Made mustard	2.5 ml
2 tbsp	Oil	2x15 ml
1½ teasp	Vinegar	7.5 ml
	Sprigs of parsley	

Scrub the potatoes, put into a saucepan, cover with cold salted water and bring to the boil. Simmer for about 15 minutes till tender. Drain and peel, then slice thickly and put into a serving dish. Sprinkle with the white wine.

Remove outer covering from the sausage and slice thickly. Add to the potatoes with the chopped parsley.

Mix the mustard, oil, pepper and vinegar together and pour over the salad. Toss gently. Garnish with sprigs of parsley and serve warm or cold.

Rice salad with anchovy dressing

Overall timing 40 minutes plus chilling

Freezing Not suitable

To serve 4

8 oz	Long grain rice	225 g
	Salt and pepper	
1	Can of anchovy fillets	1
2	Large hard-boiled eggs	2
1 teasp	Powdered mustard	5 ml
5 tbsp	Olive oil	5x15 ml
1	Carrot	1
1	Small onion	1
1	Green chilli	1
1	Red pepper	1
1	Small bulb of fennel	1
2 oz	Stoned black olives	50 g
1 teasp	Chopped chives	5 ml

Cook rice in boiling salted water for 15 minutes till tender. Drain and rinse under cold water to cool.

Drain anchovies and reserve half for garnish. Put the rest into a mortar and pound to a paste with the pestle. Shell and finely chop eggs. Add to mortar with mustard and pound together, gradually adding oil a few drops at a time. Season.

Peel carrot and cut shallow grooves at intervals along its length. Slice thinly and place in large bowl with rice.

Peel and finely chop onion; thinly slice chilli: deseed and slice pepper. Add these to the rice. Thinly slice fennel; chop fennel tops and add to salad. Toss lightly. Chill salad and dressing for 30 minutes.

Put salad into a serving dish and arrange reserved anchovies on top with olives and chives. Serve with dressing.

Greek salad

Overall timing 40 minutes including chilling

Freezing Not suitable

To serve 2

2	Large tomatoes	2
¼	Cucumber	¼
1	Small onion	1
2 oz	Black olives	50 g
8	Anchovy fillets	8
4 oz	Fetta or Wensleydale cheese	125 g
Dressing		
3 tbsp	Olive oil	3 x 15 ml
1 tbsp	Lemon juice	15 ml
	Salt and pepper	
	Pinch of dried marjoram	

Quarter tomatoes. Slice cucumber. Peel onion and cut into rings. Stone olives (optional). Roll up anchovy fillets. Cut cheese into chunks. Place all these ingredients in a serving bowl or divide them between two serving dishes.

To make the dressing, mix the oil and lemon juice with pinch of salt, pepper to taste and marjoram. Pour over salad, mix well and chill for 30 minutes before serving.

Another good alternative to Fetta is white Stilton – the important thing is to use a crumbly white cheese with a slightly sour taste. As in the authentic Greek version, it will absorb all the flavour of the oil dressing.

Kipper salad

Overall timing 20 minutes

Freezing Not suitable

To serve 4

4	Kipper fillets	4
4	Cold boiled potatoes	4
1	Cooked beetroot	1
1 tbsp	Chopped onion	15 ml
8 tbsp	Mayonnaise	8x15 ml
	Sprigs of parsley	

Place kippers upright in a jug, fill with boiling water and leave for 5 minutes. Drain, pat dry with kitchen paper, then chop into pieces. Cube potatoes and beetroot.

Put kippers, potatoes, beetroot and onion in salad bowl. Mix well. Spoon mayonnaise over and garnish with parsley sprigs.

Israeli sweet-sour salad

Overall timing 20 minutes plus chilling

Freezing Not suitable

To serve 4

2 tbsp	Sultanas	2x15 ml
1 lb	Carrots	450 g
4	Oranges	4
2	Avocados	4
2 tbsp	Lemon juice	2x15 ml
3 tbsp	Oil	3x15 ml
1 tbsp	Wine or cider vinegar	15 ml
	Salt and pepper	
	Ground ginger	

Put the sultanas into a bowl, cover with warm water and leave to soak.

Peel carrots and grate into serving dish. Add the juice of two of the oranges and mix well. Peel remaining oranges and separate into segments.

Peel avocados and remove stones. Cut flesh into chunks and sprinkle with lemon juice.

Drain sultanas and add to serving dish with oranges and avocados.

In a small bowl, beat the oil and vinegar with a pinch each of salt, pepper and ground ginger. Pour over salad and toss. Chill for 15 minutes before serving.

Fruity celeriac salad

Overall timing 45 minutes

Freezing Not suitable

To serve 4

8 oz	Celeriac	225 g
2	Apples	2
1	Orange	1
2 tbsp	Lemon juice	2x15 ml
2 oz	Cooked tongue	50 g
Dressing		
3 tbsp	Single cream	3x15 ml
5 tbsp	Plain yogurt	5x15 ml
½ teasp	Strong made mustard	2.5 ml
	Pinch of sugar	
	Salt and pepper	

Peel celeriac. Peel and core apples. Peel orange and roughly chop flesh. Grate celeriac and apples into a bowl, add orange and sprinkle with lemon juice. Cut tongue into thin strips and add to salad.

To make the dressing, mix together the cream, yogurt, mustard, sugar and seasoning. Add to salad, toss well and chill for 30 minutes before serving.

Tangy avocado salad

Overall timing 15 minutes plus chilling

Freezing Not suitable

To serve 4–6

2	Avocados	2
2	Dill pickles	2
2 oz	Pine nuts	50 g
1	Small onion	1
2 tbsp	Oil	2x15 ml
1 tbsp	Lemon juice	15 ml
	Salt and pepper	
2	Garlic cloves	2
1 tbsp	Chopped fresh mint	15 ml
½ pint	Plain yogurt	300 ml

Halve avocados and remove stones. Scoop out flesh and dice. Grate or chop pickles. Roughly chop pine nuts. Peel and finely chop onion.

Put prepared ingredients into serving dish and stir in oil, lemon juice and seasoning.

Peel and crush garlic and put into a bowl with mint and yogurt. Beat lightly with a fork. Pour over salad and mix in well. Chill for 1 hour.

Russian salad

Overall timing 30 minutes

Freezing Not suitable

To serve 4

3	Medium potatoes	3
2	Carrots	2
4 oz	Green beans	125 g
2	Stalks of celery	2
	Salt and pepper	
4 oz	Frozen peas	125 g
2 tbsp	Capers	2x15 ml
	Juice of $\frac{1}{2}$ lemon	
8 fl oz	Carton of double cream	227 ml
2	Hard-boiled eggs	2

Peel and dice potatoes and carrots. Top and tail beans and remove strings. Cut beans into small pieces. Trim and finely dice celery.

Place potatoes in boiling salted water and cook for 5 minutes. Remove with draining spoon, place in colander and rinse under cold water. Add carrots to pan and cook for 5 minutes. Remove and rinse. Add beans, peas and celery to pan and cook for 4 minutes. Remove and rinse.

Drain cooled vegetables and place in bowl with capers. Add lemon juice and salt and pepper. Pour cream over and mix carefully. Pile salad on to a serving plate.

Shell and quarter eggs and arrange round the edge of the plate.

Tunisian mixed salad

Overall timing 25 minutes plus chilling

Freezing Not suitable

To serve 4

1½ lb	Cooked waxy potatoes	700 g
8 oz	Cooked carrots	225 g
3	Canned artichoke hearts	3
6 oz	Cooked peas	175 g
2 tbsp	Drained capers	2x15 ml
12	Stoned black olives	12
12	Stoned green olives	12
4 tbsp	Olive oil	4x15 ml
2 tbsp	Lemon juice	2x15 ml
1 tbsp	Chopped parsley	15 ml
¼ teasp	Ground coriander	1.25 ml
	Salt and pepper	

Dice the potatoes and carrots. Drain the artichokes and cut into quarters. Put all the vegetables into a serving dish with the capers and olives.

Whisk the oil and lemon juice together with the parsley, coriander and plenty of seasoning. Pour the dressing over the salad and toss lightly. Chill for 30 minutes before serving with crusty bread.

Goat's cheese salad

Overall timing 15 minutes plus 1 hour chilling

Freezing Not suitable

To serve 4

12 oz	Goat's cheese	350 g
	Salt and pepper	
4 tbsp	Olive oil	4x15 ml
2 tbsp	Wine vinegar	2x15 ml
4	Stalks of celery	4
2 oz	Walnuts	50 g
	Fennel seed (optional)	

Slice cheese and put into serving bowl. Grind black pepper over it. Beat 2 tbsp (2x15 ml) oil and 1 tbsp (15 ml) vinegar together and pour over cheese.

Chop celery. Add celery and nuts to bowl. Toss lightly.

Beat together the rest of the oil and vinegar and pour over. Sprinkle with salt and crushed fennel seed, if used, and chill for 1 hour. Serve with crusty French bread.

Gouda salad

Overall timing 15 minutes

Freezing Not suitable

To serve 4–6

Salad		
1	Webb's lettuce	1
2 oz	Corn salad or watercress	50 g
1	Head of white chicory	1
4	Tomatoes	4
1	Hard-boiled egg	1
1	Onion	1
2 oz	Black olives	50 g
4 oz	Gouda cheese	125 g
Dressing		
2 tbsp	Oil	2x15 ml
1 tbsp	Wine vinegar	15 ml
1 tbsp	Chopped fresh fines herbes *or*	15 ml
1 teasp	Dried fines herbes	5 ml
	Salt and pepper	

Trim and wash lettuce and corn salad or watercress. Dry thoroughly. Trim, wash and shred chicory. Arrange lettuce leaves in salad bowl, scatter the chicory over and arrange corn salad or watercress in the centre.

Wipe and slice tomatoes. Shell and quarter hard-boiled egg. Peel and finely slice onion. Arrange on top of lettuce with the olives.

Cut cheese into thin matchstick strips. Sprinkle over top of salad.

To make dressing, put the oil, vinegar, herbs, salt and pepper into a bowl and mix well together. Pour over salad just before serving and toss.

Mimosa salad

Overall timing 15 minutes

Freezing Not suitable

To serve 4

3 tbsp	Single cream	3x15 ml
1 tbsp	Lemon juice	15 ml
	Salt and pepper	
1	Lettuce	1
1	Orange	1
4 oz	Black and white grapes	125 g
1	Banana	1
1	Hard-boiled egg yolk	1

In a salad bowl, mix together the cream, lemon juice and seasoning.

Wash and dry lettuce leaves. Peel the orange and cut into thin slices. Wash grapes. Peel and slice banana. Place the lettuce, orange, grapes and banana in salad bowl on top of dressing. Toss just before serving and garnish with sieved egg yolk.

Normandy salad

Overall timing 10 minutes plus chilling

Freezing Not suitable

To serve 4

1	Round lettuce	1
2	Dessert apples	2
½	Lemon	½
3 tbsp	Single cream	3x15 ml
1 tbsp	Cider vinegar	15 ml
	Grated nutmeg	
	Salt and pepper	
2 oz	Walnut halves	50 g

Wash and dry lettuce. Peel and core apples. Cut into thin rings. Rub cut surface of the lemon half over both sides of the apple rings to prevent browning. Place lettuce leaves and apple in a salad bowl and chill for 15 minutes.

Mix together the cream, cider vinegar, a pinch of grated nutmeg and seasoning in a small bowl. Just before serving, pour dressing over salad and toss. Garnish with walnut halves.

Pepper salad

Overall timing 30 minutes including cooling

Freezing Not suitable

To serve 4

4	Large red and yellow peppers	4
8 tbsp	Olive oil	8x15 ml
1 oz	Parmesan or strong Cheddar cheese	25 g
1 tbsp	Dried breadcrumbs	15 ml
2 tbsp	Capers	2x15 ml
	Pinch of dried marjoram or mint	
	Sea-salt	
1 tbsp	Vinegar	15 ml

Preheat the grill.

Halve peppers and place, rounded side up, under grill. Cook for a few minutes till skins are charred, then peel. Cut in half again and deseed.

Heat oil in frying pan and fry peppers gently for 7 minutes on each side. Arrange peppers in serving dish, alternating colours to achieve a spoked effect.

Grate cheese. Sprinkle over peppers with breadcrumbs, capers, marjoram or mint and sea-salt. Leave to cool slightly, then pour vinegar over. Serve straight away or cool and serve chilled.

Prawn and chicory salad

Overall timing 30 minutes plus chilling

Freezing Not suitable

To serve 4

2	Small heads of chicory	2
3 tbsp	Lemon juice	3x15 ml
4	Tomatoes	4
1	Fresh green chilli	1
8 oz	Shelled prawns	225 g
1 tbsp	White wine vinegar	15 ml
	Salt and pepper	
4 oz	Cream cheese	125 g
3 tbsp	Plain yogurt	3x15 ml
1	Garlic clove	1
$\frac{1}{4}$ teasp	Powdered mustard	1.25 ml
2 tbsp	Oil	2x15 ml

Remove any wilted outside leaves from the chicory, cut off the bases and scoop out the cores. Cut across into $\frac{1}{2}$ inch (12.5 mm) thick slices. Put into a bowl, add 2 tbsp (2x15 ml) of the lemon juice and toss.

Blanch, peel and quarter the tomatoes. Deseed and thinly slice the chilli. Put into a salad bowl with the tomatoes, prawns, vinegar and seasoning. Add the chicory and toss together lightly.

Put the cheese and yogurt into a bowl and beat till smooth. Add the peeled and crushed garlic, mustard, oil and remaining lemon juice. Season to taste and trickle over the salad. Chill for 15 minutes.

Just before serving, toss salad lightly till ingredients are evenly coated.

Prawn and egg salad

Overall timing 35 minutes

Freezing Not suitable

To serve 4–6

1	Lemon	1
12 oz	Shelled prawns	350 g
¼ teasp	Tabasco sauce	1.25 ml
	Salt and pepper	
4–6	Hard-boiled eggs	4–6
¼ pint	Thick mayonnaise	150 ml
1 teasp	Tomato purée	5 ml
½ teasp	Anchovy essence	2.5 ml
	Lettuce leaves	
2 oz	Black olives	50 g
4 oz	Unshelled prawns	125 g

Cut lemon in half across the segments; reserve one half. Finely grate rind of the other and reserve. Squeeze juice into a bowl.

Add shelled prawns to lemon juice with Tabasco sauce and seasoning. Leave to marinate for 15 minutes.

Meanwhile, shell eggs and cut in half lengthways. Divide the mayonnaise between two bowls. Add tomato purée and anchovy essence to one and grated lemon rind to the other.

Put the yellow mayonnaise mixture into a piping bag fitted with a star nozzle and pipe on to half the eggs. Pipe the pink mixture on to the remaining eggs.

Line a serving dish with lettuce leaves. Arrange the marinated prawns in a circle in the centre. Place eggs around the edge, alternating the colours, and garnish with the black olives.

Cut remaining lemon half into a basket shape and place in centre of the dish. Hang the whole unshelled prawns on the lemon and serve immediately.

Chicory and anchovy salad

Overall timing 15 minutes

Freezing Not suitable

To serve 4

4	Heads of chicory	4
4	Anchovy fillets	4
2 tbsp	Lemon juice	2x15 ml
½ teasp	Salt	2.5 ml
2 tbsp	Chopped parsley	2x15 ml
2	Hard-boiled egg yolks	2
Dressing		
1 tbsp	Wine or cider vinegar	15 ml
1 teasp	French mustard	5 ml
	Salt and pepper	
3 tbsp	Oil	3x15 ml

Trim and chop chicory. Drain and chop anchovy fillets. Place both in salad bowl. Add lemon juice and salt.

To make the dressing, mix together vinegar, mustard and seasoning in a small bowl. Gradually beat in oil until the dressing thickens.

Pour dressing over salad and toss. Sprinkle with chopped parsley and sieved or crumbled egg yolks.

Cockle salad

Overall timing 1 hour 20 minutes

Freezing Not suitable

To serve 4

2 lb	Fresh cockles	900 g
	Coarse salt	
1	Small onion	1
¼ pint	Dry white wine	150 ml
1	Lettuce	1
1 tbsp	Strong made mustard	15 ml
3 tbsp	Oil	3x15 ml
1 tbsp	Vinegar	15 ml
1 tbsp	Chopped parsley or chives	15 ml
	Salt and pepper	

Scrub cockles well under running cold water. Add as much coarse salt to a bowl of water as will dissolve and place the cockles in the water so that they open and release any sand or grit.

Remove cockles from bowl, then rinse under cold running water and drain.

Peel and chop onion. Put into saucepan with wine and boil till wine begins to evaporate. Add cockles and cook, stirring, for about 3 minutes till the shells open. Discard any that do not open. Strain the juice and reserve.

Line salad bowl with lettuce leaves. Remove cockles from shells and pile them on the lettuce. Mix together the reserved strained juice, mustard, oil, vinegar, parsley or chives and seasoning. Pour over cockles just before serving.

Crispy lettuce and cheese salad

Overall timing 15 minutes plus chilling

Freezing Not suitable

To serve 4–6

1	Large bulb of fennel	1
	Salt and pepper	
1	Cos lettuce	1
1	Onion	1
4 tbsp	Oil	4x15 ml
1 tbsp	Lemon juice	15 ml
3 oz	Grated Parmesan cheese	75 g
1 tbsp	Chopped parsley	15 ml

Trim fennel. Cut into small pieces and blanch in boiling salted water for 2 minutes. Drain.

Wash and dry lettuce. Shred finely. Peel and thinly slice onion. Put into a salad bowl with blanched fennel and lettuce and mix well together. Chill for 15 minutes to crisp.

Meanwhile, beat the oil and lemon juice together in a small bowl. Add salt and lots of freshly-ground black pepper.

Add Parmesan and chopped parsley to salad bowl and pour dressing over. Toss and serve immediately.

This salad makes a good accompaniment to many Italian-style dishes incorporating pasta and tomato sauce.

Cucumber and cider salad

Overall timing 10 minutes plus 1 hour chilling

Freezing Not suitable

To serve 4

2	Cucumbers	2
¼ pint	Dry cider	150 ml
3 tbsp	Chopped parsley	3x15 ml
1 teasp	Sugar	5 ml
	Salt and pepper	

Peel cucumbers. Cut them in half lengthways and scoop out the seeds with a spoon. Thinly slice cucumbers and put into a bowl.

Mix together the cider, parsley, sugar and seasoning. Pour over the cucumber and chill for at least 1 hour. Toss gently before serving.

Cucumber and fruit salad

Overall timing 15 minutes

Freezing Not suitable

To serve 2

$\frac{1}{2}$	Cucumber	$\frac{1}{2}$
1	Orange	1
$\frac{1}{4}$	Honeydew melon	$\frac{1}{4}$
2 oz	Black grapes	50 g
	Sprigs of dill	
Dressing		
3 tbsp	Soured cream	3x15 ml
$1\frac{1}{2}$ teasp	Lemon juice	7.5 ml
1 tbsp	Caster sugar	15 ml
1 tbsp	Chopped fresh dill	15 ml
	Salt and pepper	

Thinly slice cucumber. Put into a bowl. Peel orange, remove pips and cut flesh into pieces. Peel melon, remove seeds and cut flesh into thin slices. Add orange and melon to cucumber with grapes. Chill for 20 minutes.

To make the dressing, beat soured cream, lemon juice, sugar, dill and seasoning in a bowl.

Divide salad between two serving glasses and spoon a little of the dressing over each. Garnish with dill sprigs and keep in refrigerator till ready to serve.

Pears in chocolate sauce

Overall timing 40 minutes plus chilling

Freezing Not suitable

To serve 6

6	Firm pears	6
¾ pint	Water	400 ml
1 tbsp	Lemon juice	15 ml
4 oz	Caster sugar	125 g
1	Vanilla pod	1
3½ oz	Plain dessert chocolate	100 g
½ oz	Butter	15 g
	Vanilla ice cream	
	Crystallized violets (optional)	

Peel the pears and remove the stalks. Put the water, lemon juice, sugar and vanilla pod into a saucepan and heat gently till the sugar dissolves. Bring the syrup to the boil, add the pears and simmer for about 15 minutes till just tender. Leave pears to cool in the syrup, then lift them out with a draining spoon and chill for several hours. Reserve the syrup.

Break the chocolate into small pieces and put into a heatproof bowl with the butter. Stand the bowl over a pan of simmering water and stir till melted. Remove from the heat and beat in 2 tbsp (2x15 ml) of the pear syrup.

Arrange the pears in a serving dish and place scoops of ice cream between them. Decorate with crystallized violets, if liked. Spoon the chocolate sauce over the pears and serve.

Spicy fruit purée

Overall timing 1½ hours plus overnight maceration and cooling

Freezing Suitable

To serve 2

8 oz	Mixed dried fruit (figs, apricots, peaches, pears, prunes)	225 g
1 pint	Water	560 ml
3 oz	Granulated sugar	75 g
1	Apple	1
1 teasp	Ground cinnamon	5 ml
1 tbsp	Cornflour	15 ml

Put the dried fruit in a large bowl with three-quarters of the water and the sugar and leave to soak overnight.

Stone the prunes. Transfer fruit to a saucepan, add remaining water and bring to the boil. Cook over a low heat for about 15 minutes.

Peel, core and slice the apple and add with cinnamon to the pan. Cook for a further 45 minutes.

Drain fruit and return liquid to the pan. Push fruit through a sieve or blend to a purée, then return to the pan.

Mix cornflour with 1 tbsp (15 ml) cold water in a bowl, then stir into fruit mixture. Bring to the boil and boil for 5 minutes, stirring, until thick. Remove from heat and allow to cool. Pour into two serving glasses and chill for 2 hours before serving.

Spicy pumpkin dessert

Overall timing 45 minutes plus chilling

Freezing Not suitable

To serve 6

14 oz	Can of pumpkin purée	398 ml
2 oz	Butter	50 g
½ pint	Milk	300 ml
5 tbsp	Sugar	5x15 ml
3	Eggs	3
½ teasp	Ground cinnamon	2.5 ml
¼ teasp	Ground ginger	1.25 ml
¼ teasp	Grated nutmeg	1.25 ml
	Salt	
¼ pint	Carton of whipping cream	150 ml
	Glacé cherries	
	Candied angelica	

Preheat the oven to 350°F (180°C) Gas 4.

Put the pumpkin purée into a bowl and beat in the melted butter, milk, sugar, eggs, spices and a pinch of salt. In a separate bowl, whip the cream till it forms soft peaks, and fold into the mixture.

Pour the mixture into a greased 2 pint (1.1. litre) brioche mould and bake for about 30 minutes. Remove from the oven and leave to cool completely, then chill for 3–4 hours till firm.

Turn out the dessert on to a serving dish and decorate with glacé cherries and angelica. Serve with pouring cream.

Singapore coconut pudding

Overall timing 45 minutes plus 30 minutes soaking

Freezing Not suitable

To serve 4

3 oz	Desiccated coconut	75 g
4 fl oz	Boiling water	120 ml
8 oz	Caster sugar	225 g
3	Eggs	3
	Pinch of salt	
4 tbsp	Grated fresh coconut	4x15 ml

Put desiccated coconut in a bowl and pour over boiling water. Soak for 30 minutes, then pour through muslin or a fine sieve into a jug. Squeeze out liquid from coconut. Discard coconut.

Preheat the oven to 350°F (180°C) Gas 4.

Beat the sugar, eggs and salt till thick and foamy. Gradually add reserved coconut liquid.

Turn the mixture into a lightly greased 1 pint (560 ml) mould or four ovenproof dishes and place in roasting tin half-filled with hot water. Bake for 30 minutes.

Allow to cool, then invert over a serving plate to turn out. Chill until ready to serve, sprinkled with grated fresh coconut.

Upside-down cheesecake

Overall timing 1¼ hours plus chilling

Freezing Suitable

To serve 8

8 oz	Nice biscuits	225 g
4 oz	Butter	125 g
3 tbsp	Light soft brown sugar	3x15 ml
1 teasp	Ground cinnamon	5 ml
Filling		
12	Petits suisses	12
4 tbsp	Single cream	4x15 ml
4 teasp	Plain flour	4x5 ml
3 oz	Caster sugar	75 g
1 teasp	Vanilla essence	5 ml
1	Lemon	1
4	Eggs	4

Preheat the oven to 350°F (180°C) Gas 4.

Crush biscuits. Put butter, sugar and cinnamon into a saucepan and heat gently till sugar dissolves. Remove from heat and stir in biscuit crumbs. Press all but 4 tbsp (4x15 ml) over bottom and sides of greased 9 inch (23 cm) loose-bottomed flan tin.

Beat cheese with cream, flour, sugar, vanilla essence, grated rind of the lemon and 1 tbsp (15 ml) of the juice. Separate eggs. Beat yolks into the cheese mixture. Whisk whites till stiff and fold into cheese mixture. Pour into crumb case and smooth the top. Sprinkle remaining crumbs on top and press down lightly.

Bake for 45 minutes till set. Switch off the oven, open the door slightly and leave cheesecake in oven till cold. Chill for 2–3 hours, then invert on to a serving dish.

Raspberries jubilee

Overall timing 10 minutes plus 2 hours maceration

Freezing Not suitable

To serve 6

12 oz	Fresh or frozen raspberries	350 g
2–4 oz	Caster sugar	50–125 g
3 tbsp	Lemon juice	3x15 ml
1½ pints	Vanilla ice cream	850 ml
3 tbsp	Kirsch or brandy	3x15 ml

Put raspberries, sugar (add according to taste) and lemon juice in a bowl and macerate for 2 hours in the refrigerator. Chill serving plate.

Transfer raspberries and soaking juices to a saucepan and heat through gently.

Remove ice cream from freezer and place on serving plate. Spoon raspberries and syrup over. Warm Kirsch or brandy in ladle. Set alight and pour over ice cream. Serve immediately.

Marbled ice cream with chocolate sauce

Overall timing 20 minutes

Freezing Not suitable

To serve 4–6

2 teasp	Cornflour	2x5 ml
½ pint	Cold milk	300ml
2 oz	Plain dessert chocolate or chocolate dots	50g
2 tbsp	Granulated sugar	2x15 ml
½ teasp	Vanilla essence	2.5 ml
	Chocolate and vanilla ice cream	
4–6	Sponge fingers	4–6

Blend the cornflour in a bowl with a little milk. Put rest of milk in saucepan with the broken up chocolate or chocolate dots. Heat slowly until the chocolate melts, then stir in cornflour. Cook, stirring constantly, until the sauce comes to the boil and thickens. Stir in sugar and vanilla essence and cook, stirring, for 3 minutes more.

Turn ice cream out on to chilled serving plate and press sponge fingers into the top. Pour some of the sauce over. Serve immediately with the remaining sauce.

Rum and almond pastry cake

Overall timing 2¼ hours

Freezing Suitable: refresh from frozen in 350°F (180°C) Gas 4 oven for 30 minutes

Serves 6–8

13 oz	Frozen puff pastry	375 g
3 oz	Butter	75 g
3 oz	Caster sugar	75 g
2	Eggs	2
4 oz	Ground almonds	125 g
2 tbsp	Rum	2x15 ml
1 tbsp	Icing sugar	15 ml

Thaw pastry. To make filling, cream butter with sugar till light and fluffy. Beat in one whole egg and one egg yolk, reserving white. Fold in the ground almonds and rum. Cover and chill for 40 minutes.

Roll out dough to ¼ inch (6 mm) thickness. Cut out two rounds, one 8 inch (20 cm) and the other 9 inch (23 cm). Place smaller one on a dampened baking tray. Place almond filling in a ball in centre of dough round, leaving at least a 2 inch (5 cm) border all round. Brush edges with water.

Place second dough round on top and press edges together to seal. Using a knife, trim, then knock up edges and crimp. Chill for 15 minutes.

Preheat the oven to 450°F (230°C) Gas 8.

Brush pie with reserved beaten egg white. Leave for 1 minute, then brush again. Using the tip of a sharp knife, score top of pie to make a swirl pattern. Bake for 20 minutes, then reduce temperature to 400°F (200°C) Gas 6 and bake for a further 25 minutes, or until well risen and golden brown.

Remove from oven and increase heat to 475°F (240°C) Gas 9. Sift icing sugar over pie and return to oven to bake for 4–5 minutes to glaze. Remove from baking tray with palette knife and place on serving plate.

Strawberries and cream

Overall timing 15 minutes plus chilling

Freezing Not suitable

To serve 4

1 lb	Strawberries	450 g
Crème Chantilly		
8 fl oz	Carton of double cream	227 ml
¼ teasp	Vanilla essence	1.25 ml
	Icing sugar	

Hull and wipe the strawberries. Divide between individual serving dishes and chill for 1 hour.

Whip the cream till stiff peaks form, then fold in the vanilla essence and sugar to taste. Pipe the cream on top of the strawberries and serve immediately.

Variation

Sprinkle the strawberries with fresh orange juice, or an orange liqueur such as Cointreau, before chilling.

Honey and lemon cheesecake

Overall timing 1¼ hours plus cooling

Freezing Suitable

To serve 12

6oz	Rich shortcrust pastry	175g
2	Eggs	2
1lb	Curd cheese	450g
6 tbsp	Thick honey	6x15ml
2	Lemons	2
4oz	Sultanas	125g

Preheat the oven to 400°F (200°C) Gas 6.

Roll out dough and use to line 8½ inch (22 cm) loose-bottomed flan tin, reserving any trimmings. Prick bottom. Bake blind for 10 minutes, then remove from oven and reduce temperature to 350°F (180°C) Gas 4.

Separate the eggs. Put the yolks into a bowl with the cheese, honey and the grated rind of one of the lemons. Squeeze juice from both lemons and add to the bowl with the sultanas. Mix well.

In another bowl, whisk the egg whites to soft peaks and fold into the cheese mixture with a metal spoon. Pour into flan case and smooth the surface.

Roll out dough trimmings and cut into thin strips with a pastry wheel. Arrange in a lattice pattern over the filling. Bake for 50–55 minutes till set. Cool in tin, then turn out and serve cold.

Strawberries melba

Overall timing 15 minutes plus maceration

Freezing Not suitable

To serve 4–6

1 lb	Strawberries	450 g
4 oz	Raspberries	125 g
4 tbsp	Caster sugar	4x15 ml
2 teasp	Lemon juice	2x5 ml
1 oz	Slivered almonds	25 g

Hull the strawberries and pile in a serving dish.

Sieve the raspberries, then stir in the sugar and lemon juice until the sugar has dissolved. Pour over the strawberries and toss gently to coat. Leave to macerate for 1 hour.

Scatter the almonds over the top and serve.

Peach sundae

Overall timing 40 minutes plus maceration

Freezing Not suitable

To serve 2

2	Large ripe peaches	2
1 tbsp	Maraschino or peach brandy	15 ml
1½ oz	Caster sugar	40 g
1 tbsp	Apricot jam	15 ml
	Peach or vanilla ice cream	

Peel, halve and stone one of the peaches. Roughly chop the flesh and put into a bowl with the Maraschino or peach brandy and sugar. Macerate in the refrigerator for 30 minutes.

In a saucepan, melt the apricot jam with 1 tbsp (15 ml) of macerating liquid. Peel, halve and stone remaining peach. Divide chopped fruit and juices between two serving dishes and top each with cubes of ice cream and a peach half. Spoon the warmed jam over and serve immediately.

Pineapple jelly cream

Overall timing 20 minutes plus chilling

Freezing Suitable

To serve 2

$\frac{1}{2}$	Pineapple jelly tablet	$\frac{1}{2}$
$\frac{1}{4}$ pint	Cold water	150 ml
7 oz	Canned crushed pineapple	200 g
6 tbsp	Whipping cream	6x15 ml
1	Egg white	1

Break up the jelly tablet and put into a small saucepan with half the water. Heat gently, stirring, till the jelly melts, then remove from heat.

Add the crushed pineapple and remaining water, mix well and pour into a large bowl. Chill till beginning to set.

Whip the cream till soft peaks form. Whisk the egg white till stiff but not dry. Fold the cream into the pineapple jelly mixture with a metal spoon, then carefully fold in the egg white.

Pour into two small dishes, smooth the top and chill till lightly set.

Clementines niçoise

Overall timing 15 minutes plus 2 hours maceration

Freezing Not suitable

To serve 8

8	Large clementines	8
1	Peach	1
4 oz	Cherries	125 g
8 oz	Can of pineapple rings	227 g
2 oz	Caster sugar	50 g
2 tbsp	Cointreau	2x15 ml
	Vanilla ice cream	

Slice the top off each clementine with a sharp knife and reserve. Scoop out the flesh with a teaspoon, taking care not to break the shell. Cover the empty shells and the tops and chill.

Cut the flesh into neat pieces, discarding the pips and pith. Peel the peach, cut in half and discard the stone. Cut into cubes. Stone the cherries, then chop flesh. Drain the pineapple and cut into pieces.

Put all the fruit into a bowl with the sugar and liqueur and leave to macerate for 2 hours.

Remove clementine shells and tops from the refrigerator. Divide the fruit and juices between the shells, add a scoop of ice cream and place the lids on top. Serve immediately in individual glass dishes.

Clementine rice mould

Overall timing 1¼ hours plus cooling

Freezing Not suitable

To serve 4–6

4 oz	Pudding rice	125 g
5	Clementines	5
¾ pint	Milk	400 ml
1 teasp	Vanilla essence	5 ml
	Salt	
4 oz	Caster sugar	125 g
1	Egg	1
1 oz	Butter	25 g
	Candied angelica	
Syrup		
¼ pint	Water	150 ml
3 oz	Sugar	75 g

Put the rice in a large saucepan of water, bring to the boil and boil for 5 minutes. Drain well.

Finely chop the peel and flesh of one clementine. Put into a saucepan with milk and bring almost to the boil. Remove from the heat, cover and leave to infuse for 10 minutes. Strain milk and return to pan. Add vanilla essence, a pinch of salt and rice. Cook gently, stirring occasionally, for 25–30 minutes till all milk has been absorbed. Add sugar and cook for a further 5 minutes.

Lightly beat egg. Remove cooked rice from heat and mix in egg and butter. Pour into a greased 2 pint (1.1 litre) soufflé dish. Cool, then chill for 2–3 hours.

To make syrup, put water and sugar into a saucepan and heat gently, stirring, till sugar has dissolved. Cut remaining clementines into wedges and add to syrup. Boil gently for 25 minutes till tender and syrup has caramelized.

Turn out rice mould onto serving plate. Arrange clementine wedges and angelica on top and around sides. Spoon over any remaining caramel, if liked, and serve with cream.

Coconut milk jelly

Overall timing 1 hour plus overnight chilling

Freezing Not suitable

To serve 6–8

1	Fresh coconut	1
	Milk	
	Pinch of salt	
7 oz	Caster sugar	200 g
½ teasp	Vanilla essence	2.5 ml
5 teasp	Powdered gelatine	5x5 ml

Use clean nail and hammer to pierce black "eyes" of coconut. Drain any milk inside into a measuring jug. Remove white flesh, but not inner rind, with grapefruit knife and grate.

Add sufficient milk to the coconut milk to make up to 1¾ pints (1 litre). Put milk in a saucepan with the salt, sugar and grated coconut and bring to the boil. Remove pan from heat, stir in vanilla essence and leave to cool.

Meanwhile, dissolve the gelatine in 3 tbsp (3x15 ml) cold water in a small bowl.

Stir gelatine into coconut mixture. Pour into a dampened 2 pint (1.1 litre) decorative jelly mould. Chill overnight.

To turn out, dip mould bottom into hot water for a few seconds, then invert jelly on to serving plate, tapping mould sharply so jelly slides out intact. Serve with coconut macaroons or biscuits.

Coffee water ice

Overall timing 2 hours

Freezing See method

To serve 6–8

9 oz	Granulated sugar	250 g
1 tbsp	Vanilla sugar	15 ml
1 pint	Water	560 ml
8 teasp	Instant coffee granules	8x5 ml
½ pint	Carton of whipping cream	300 ml
	Peppermint essence (optional)	

Put granulated and vanilla sugar and water in a saucepan. Stir until sugar has completely dissolved, then bring to the boil and boil for 5 minutes. Skim if necessary. Stir in the coffee granules and remove pan from heat. Allow mixture to cool completely.

Pour coffee mixture through a fine sieve or muslin-lined sieve into a freezer tray. Place in freezer or freezing compartment of refrigerator and leave for about 1 hour or until the mixture forms a granular mass. Do not stir.

In a bowl whip cream till just holding soft peaks, then add a few drops of peppermint essence, if using, to taste. Scrape out contents of freezer tray with a fork and divide ice between chilled serving glasses. Top each glass with peppermint-flavoured cream and serve with biscuits.

Rum and apricot pudding cake

Overall timing 55 minutes

Freezing Not suitable

To serve 6

1 pint	Milk	560 ml
½ teasp	Vanilla essence	2.5 ml
4	Eggs	4
4 tbsp	Caster sugar	4x15 ml
4 oz	Sponge cake	125 g
2 tbsp	Rum	2x15 ml
4 oz	Chopped glacé fruits	125 g
1 oz	Butter	25 g
8 oz	Apricot jam	225 g

Preheat the oven to 375°F (190°C) Gas 5.

Put the milk and vanilla essence into a saucepan and bring to the boil. Meanwhile, separate the eggs. Add the sugar to the yolks and beat together with a fork. Pour the hot milk over the yolks, stirring constantly.

Crumble the sponge cake into a bowl. Strain the custard over the cake and mix in half the rum, the glacé fruits and butter. Leave to cool.

Whisk the egg whites till stiff. Fold into the crumb mixture with a metal spoon. Pour the mixture into a greased and lined 2 pint (1.1 litre) soufflé dish and smooth the top. Bake for about 35–40 minutes till well risen and golden.

Put the apricot jam into a saucepan with remaining rum and heat gently till melted.

Serve the cake hot from the dish, with the apricot sauce separately in a sauceboat. Or, leave the cake to cool completely and turn out on to a serving dish. Pour the hot apricot sauce on top and serve immediately.

Sherry trifle

Overall timing 1½ hours including chilling time

Freezing Not suitable

To serve 6–8

1 pint	Milk	560 ml
3 tbsp	Custard powder	3x15 ml
2 tbsp	Sugar	2x15 ml
6 oz	Leftover sponge cake	175 g
2 tbsp	Raspberry jam	2x15 ml
1 lb 13 oz	Can of sliced peaches	822 g
6 tbsp	Sherry	6x15 ml
¼ pint	Carton of double or whipping cream	150 ml
1 oz	Toasted split almonds	25 g

Blend 6 tbsp (6x15 ml) of the milk with the custard powder and sugar. Bring remaining milk to the boil, then pour on to powder and stir well. Return to pan and bring back to the boil, stirring continuously until thickened. Put to one side to cool, covering surface with wet greaseproof to prevent a skin forming.

Cut sponge into small pieces and spread with jam. Arrange around the bottom and sides of serving dish.

Drain peaches. Mix 3 tbsp (3x15 ml) of syrup from can with the sherry and sprinkle over the sponge. Reserve a few peaches for decoration and arrange the rest on top of sponge.

Remove greaseproof paper and beat cooled custard well. Pour over fruit and chill for 1 hour.

Whip cream until stiff, then pipe on to trifle. Decorate with reserved peaches and sprinkle with toasted almonds.

Lemon sherbet

Overall timing 20 minutes plus freezing

Freezing See method

To serve 6

8 oz	Caster sugar	225 g
1 pint	Water	560 ml
$\frac{1}{4}$ pint	Fresh lemon juice	150 ml
1	Egg white	1

Put the sugar and water in a pan and heat slowly, stirring until sugar dissolves. Bring to the boil and simmer for 10 minutes without stirring – do not let the syrup colour. Remove from heat and leave to cool.

Add lemon juice to syrup, then strain into freezer tray and freeze until mushy.

Remove mixture from freezer, turn into a bowl and beat well to break down crystals. Whisk egg white till soft peaks form. Fold into frozen mixture. Return to freezer tray and freeze till firm.

Plum crumb pudding

Overall timing 1½ hours plus chilling

Freezing Not suitable

To serve 8

4 oz	Sponge cake	125 g
3	Eggs	3
2 oz	Caster sugar	50 g
1 pint	Milk	560 ml
1 oz	Butter	25 g
	Grated rind of 1 lemon	
½ teasp	Ground cinnamon	2.5 ml
1 lb	Red plums	450 g

Preheat oven to 350°F (180°C) Gas 4. Grease and base-line a 9 inch (23 cm) springform tin.

Crumble the cake into a bowl. Separate two of the eggs, putting the yolks and remaining whole egg into a bowl with the sugar. Put the milk and butter into a saucepan and bring almost to the boil.

Beat the yolks and sugar together and pour the milk on to them, stirring constantly. Strain over the cake crumbs. Add the lemon rind and cinnamon, mix well and leave to stand for 15 minutes.

Meanwhile, wash and halve the plums, discarding the stones. Dry thoroughly on kitchen paper.

Whisk the 2 egg whites in a large bowl till stiff but not dry and fold into the crumb mixture with a metal spoon. Pour the mixture into the tin.

Arrange the plums cut sides down on the mixture and bake in the centre of the oven for about 50 minutes till set.

Remove from the oven and leave to cool in the tin, then chill for 3–4 hours. Remove pudding from tin and place on a serving dish. Serve cut into slices, with pouring cream.

Loganberry jelly ring

Overall timing 25 minutes plus chilling

Freezing Suitable

To serve 6

14½ oz	Can of loganberries	411 g
1	Raspberry jelly tablet	1
¼ pint	Carton of whipping cream	150 ml
	Langue de chat biscuits	

Drain loganberries, reserving syrup, and press through a sieve. Make up jelly, using loganberry syrup as part of the required amount of liquid. Stir in sieved fruit and leave to cool and set slightly.

Whip cream and fold into berry mixture, then pour into dampened 1½ pint (850 ml) ring mould. Chill till firm (2–4 hours). Chill serving plate at the same time.

Dip the mould in hot water to loosen, turn out on to chilled serving plate and arrange biscuits in centre of ring just before serving.

Chocolate mousse

Overall timing 15 minutes plus 3 hours chilling

Freezing Not suitable

To serve 4

1	Orange	1
3½ oz	Plain chocolate	100 g
1 oz	Butter	25 g
4	Eggs	4
	Pinch of salt	

Grate the orange rind finely, being careful not to remove any pith. Break the chocolate into pieces and melt in the top half of a double saucepan, or in a heatproof bowl over gently boiling water. Immediately the chocolate has melted pour into a heavy-based pan and add the butter and orange rind.

Separate the eggs. Add the yolks to the chocolate, stirring vigorously with a wooden spoon to prevent the mixture from boiling. Remove from heat. Cool.

Add pinch of salt to egg whites and whisk till stiff peaks form. Fold one or two spoonfuls into the chocolate mixture, to make it more liquid, then gently fold in the rest of the whites with a spatula or metal spoon. Take care not to let the mixture become flat and heavy.

Pour into a serving bowl and chill for 3 hours before serving.

Blackcurrant sorbet

Overall timing 4½ hours including refrigeration

Freezing See method

To serve 8

2 lb	Blackcurrants	900 g
	Blackcurrant cordial or liqueur	
9 oz	Caster sugar	250 g
2	Egg whites	2

Reserve a handful of blackcurrants, and put the rest through a food mill or sieve to make a purée. Measure the purée – you should have about 1 pint (560 ml). Top up with blackcurrant cordial or liqueur and/or water if necessary.

Add the sugar to the purée and mix well to dissolve sugar. Pour into a freezer tray and freeze for about 2 hours till mushy.

Beat the egg whites till stiff. Turn blackcurrant mixture into a bowl, mash lightly with a fork, then fold in the whisked egg whites, stirring to distribute evenly through purée. Turn into lightly oiled or dampened 1½ pint (850 ml) shallow container or 1¾ pint (1 litre) mould. Freeze for 2 hours till firmly set.

Immerse mould in hot water up to the rim, then quickly turn sorbet out on to a serving dish. Decorate sorbet with remaining blackcurrants, and allow to soften at room temperature for 20 minutes before serving.

Glacé fruit bombe

Overall timing 15 minutes plus maceration and freezing

Freezing See method

To serve 6–8

4 oz	Chopped glacé fruit	125 g
4 tbsp	Apricot brandy or sweet sherry	4x15 ml
1¾ pints	Non-dairy vanilla ice cream	1 litre
8 oz	Apricot jam	225 g

Put a 2 lb (900 g) loaf tin in the freezer or freezing compartment of the refrigerator. Place fruit in a bowl, add apricot brandy or sherry and leave to macerate for 30 minutes.

Put ice cream into a bowl, add fruit and liqueur and quickly mix well with a wooden spoon.

Remove tin from freezer and coat bottom and sides with a thick layer of the ice cream mixture. Spoon jam into the centre of the tin, then cover with remaining ice cream. Smooth surface with a dampened knife.

Freeze for at least 2 hours. Turn out of tin and cut into slices to serve.

Coffee charlotte

Overall timing 50 minutes plus chilling

Freezing Suitable

To serve 8

2 tbsp	Brandy	2x15 ml
30	Sponge fingers	30
5 oz	Caster sugar	150 g
¼ pint	Strong black coffee	150 ml
2 teasp	Powdered gelatine	2x5 ml
4	Egg yolks	4
2 tbsp	Vanilla sugar	2x15 ml
½ pint	Carton of double cream	300 ml
15	Sugar coffee beans	15

Mix brandy with ¼ pint (150 ml) water in a shallow dish. Dip sponge fingers quickly in mixture to moisten them, then use to line sides of greased 10 inch (25 cm) springform tin. Place biscuits upright, sugared sides against tin, and trim ends to height of tin. Press lightly into place.

Put caster sugar and 3 tbsp (3x15 ml) water in heavy-based saucepan. Stir to dissolve sugar, then heat until golden brown. Stir in coffee and simmer for 2 minutes till caramel dissolves. Cool.

Dissolve gelatine in 2 tbsp (2x15 ml) cold water.

Put egg yolks and vanilla sugar in a bowl over a pan of hot water and whisk together till light and foamy. Stir coffee caramel into egg mixture and whisk till it starts to thicken. Stir in gelatine, then leave to cool until just on the point of setting.

Whip two-thirds of the cream until it holds soft peaks. Using a metal spoon, fold lightly into coffee mixture. Pour into centre of sponge finger-lined tin and chill till set.

Unclip tin and carefully transfer charlotte to a serving plate. Whip remaining cream until it holds stiff peaks. Pipe 15 rosettes round edge of charlotte. Place a coffee bean on top of each one. Pipe smaller rosettes round base.

Strawberry vacherin

Overall timing 2¼ hours plus cooling

Freezing Not suitable

To serve 8

6	Egg whites	6
12 oz	Caster sugar	350 g
1 lb	Strawberries	450 g
Crème Chantilly		
½ pint	Carton of double cream	284 ml
1 tbsp	Cold milk	15 ml
1	Ice cube	1
1 tbsp	Caster sugar	15 ml
¼ teasp	Vanilla essence	1.25 ml

Preheat the oven to 300°F (150°C) Gas 2.

Line two baking trays with non-stick paper. Draw a 10 inch (25 cm) square on one, and a 6 inch (15 cm) square on the other.

Whisk egg whites till stiff and dry. Sprinkle over 2 tbsp (2x15 ml) of the sugar and whisk in, then gradually whisk in remaining sugar to make a stiff, glossy meringue.

Using the marked squares as a guide, put large spoonfuls of meringue on to paper to make two squares with scalloped edges. Swirl into peaks. Place large square in centre of oven with small square below. Bake for about 1¼ hours till slightly browned and crisp. Cool.

Meanwhile, hull strawberries. To make the Crème Chantilly, whip cream with milk, ice cube, sugar and vanilla essence till it forms soft peaks. Chill till required.

Just before serving, carefully peel the paper from the meringue squares and place the large one on a flat board or serving dish. Spread or pipe two-thirds of the Crème Chantilly over and arrange two-thirds of the strawberries on top. Place the small meringue square on top and spread with the remaining crème. Decorate with remaining strawberries and serve immediately.

Champagne sorbet

Overall timing 20 minutes plus freezing

Freezing See method

To serve 6

8 oz	Caster sugar	225 g
1 pint	Water	560 ml
$\frac{1}{4}$ pint	Champagne or dry cider	150 ml
1 tbsp	Lemon juice	15 ml
2	Egg whites	2

Put the sugar and water in a pan and heat gently, stirring until sugar dissolves. Bring to the boil and simmer for 10 minutes without stirring. Do not let the mixture colour. Remove from the heat and cool.

Add the Champagne or cider and lemon juice to the syrup, then pour into a 2 pint (1.1 litre) freezer tray. Freeze till mushy.

Remove mixture from freezer, turn into a bowl and beat well to break down any ice crystals. Whisk the egg whites until stiff and fold into the mixture. Return to the freezer tray and freeze till firm.

Strawberry milk ring

Overall timing 30 minutes plus setting

Freezing Not suitable

To serve 6

1	Lemon	1
5 teasp	Powdered gelatine	5x5 ml
5 tbsp	Caster sugar	5x15 ml
1	Large can of evaporated milk	1
½ pint	Buttermilk	300 ml
	Pink food colouring	
1	Egg white	1
¼ pint	Carton of double cream	150 ml
1 lb	Fresh strawberries	450 g

Grate the rind from the lemon and reserve. Squeeze out the juice and place in a small bowl. Sprinkle the gelatine over and dissolve. Stir in the sugar. Allow to cool slightly.

Pour the well-chilled evaporated milk into a large bowl and whisk till very thick and foamy. Whisk in the buttermilk, gelatine mixture, reserved lemon rind and a few drops of food colouring. Pour into a dampened 2 pint (1.1 litre) ring mould and chill for 3–4 hours till set.

Dip the mould up to the rim in hot water for a few seconds and turn out on to a serving plate.

Whisk the egg white till stiff. Whip the cream till stiff and fold into the whisked egg white. Hull the strawberries and pile half in the centre of the ring. Pipe the cream mixture on top and around the base of the ring. Decorate with the remaining strawberries and serve immediately.

Crème caramel

Overall timing 45 minutes

Freezing Not suitable

To serve 6

1 pint	Milk	560 ml
$\frac{1}{2}$	Vanilla pod	$\frac{1}{2}$
1	Piece lemon rind	1
4	Eggs	4
4 oz	Caster sugar	125 g

Preheat the oven to 350°F (180°C) Gas 4.

Put the milk, vanilla pod and lemon rind in a saucepan and bring to the boil. Remove from heat and lift out the vanilla pod and lemon rind.

In a bowl, beat eggs with half sugar and gradually pour in the hot milk, stirring constantly.

Melt the remaining sugar in a saucepan over a moderate heat till golden brown. Divide between six small moulds and turn them so the caramel coats the bottoms and sides.

Strain the custard mixture into the moulds and place them in a roasting tin half-filled with hot water. Bake for 45 minutes till set. Allow to cool in moulds and chill before turning out.

Blackberry special

Overall timing 4 hours including chilling but not cooling

Freezing Not suitable

To serve 6–8

6 oz	Plain flour	150 g
2	Egg yolks	2
3 oz	Caster sugar	75 g
3 oz	Butter	75 g
¼ teasp	Salt	1.25 ml
Filling		
1 lb	Blackberries	450 g
2 oz	Chopped mixed peel	50 g
3	Egg whites	3
6 oz	Caster sugar	175 g
6 oz	Ground almonds	175 g
1 teasp	Grated lemon rind	5 ml
¼ teasp	Ground cinnamon	1.25 ml
2 oz	Flaked almonds	25 g

Sift flour into a mixing bowl. Add egg yolks, sugar, small flakes of butter and salt. Mix to a pliable dough. Chill for 2 hours.

Preheat the oven to 375°F (190°C) Gas 5.

Roll out dough and use to line 9 inch (23 cm) flan ring on a baking tray. Bake blind for 15 minutes.

Remove flan case from oven and reduce heat to 300°F (150°C) Gas 2. Remove foil and beans. Add blackberries to flan and sprinkle with peel.

Whisk egg whites until very stiff. Fold in sugar followed by ground almonds, lemon rind and cinnamon. Put 3 tbsp (3x15 ml) of the mixture in a piping bag fitted with a large rose nozzle. Spread the remainder over black-berries. Sprinkle edges of flan with flaked almonds and decorate the top with swirls of piped egg white mixture.

Bake for 1 hour 10 minutes. Remove from oven and cut flan into wedges before it cools. When cold, remove flan ring and serve.

Caramel cornmeal mould

Overall timing 1 hour

Freezing Not suitable

To serve 6–8

¾ pint	Milk	400 ml
	Pinch of salt	
4 oz	Sugar	125 g
1	Bay leaf	1
18	Sugar lumps	18
9 tbsp	Warm water	9x15 ml
1 tbsp	Lemon juice	15 ml
5	Eggs	5
3 oz	Fine maizemeal	75 g

Preheat the oven to 400°F (200°C) Gas 6.

Put the milk in a saucepan with the salt, sugar and bay leaf. Bring to the boil. Remove from the heat, cover and leave to infuse for 10 minutes.

Put the sugar lumps, water and lemon juice into a small saucepan and heat gently, stirring till sugar dissolves. Bring to the boil and boil without stirring till a deep golden caramel colour. Watch pan carefully to see that caramel does not burn. Pour into an 8 inch (20 cm) round deep cake tin, turning it so that the bottom and sides are coated with the caramel.

Separate the eggs. Put the egg yolks and maizemeal into a bowl and mix together with a wooden spoon. Remove bay leaf from the milk. Gradually pour the hot milk on to the egg yolks, stirring continuously. Whisk the egg whites till stiff and fold into the mixture.

Pour the mixture into the prepared tin and place in a roasting tin containing 1 inch (2.5 cm) hot water. Bake for 35–40 minutes. While still warm, run knife round edge of mould and invert on to serving plate. Serve warm or cold, with pouring cream.

Cider and grape ring

Overall timing 15 minutes plus setting

Freezing Not suitable

To serve 4-6

1 pint	Medium-sweet cider	600 ml
1 tbsp	Powdered gelatine	15 ml
1 tbsp	Lemon juice	15 ml
8 oz	White grapes	225 g
8 oz	Black grapes	225 g
2 tbsp	Caster sugar	2x15 ml

Put 6 tbsp (6x15 ml) of the cider in a heatproof bowl, sprinkle over the gelatine and leave until spongy – about 5 minutes.

Dissolve gelatine over a pan of hot water, then stir in the remaining cider and lemon juice. Remove bowl from the heat. Spoon enough of the cider jelly into a dampened 1½ pint (850 ml) ring mould just to cover it. Leave it to set in the refrigerator.

Reserve half of each kind of grape. Wash and cut remainder in half and remove pips. Arrange halves over the set jelly, then cover with more liquid jelly and leave to set. Continue layers, ending with jelly, then chill in refrigerator till set. Wash remaining grapes and remove most of moisture. Toss in caster sugar.

Dip the mould quickly in and out of hot water and invert over a serving plate so jelly slides out. Fill centre with sugared grapes. Serve with whipped cream and ginger biscuits.

Fruit salad with prunes

Overall timing 15 minutes plus maceration and chilling

Freezing Not suitable

To serve 6

8 oz	Plump prunes	225 g
¾ pint	Hot strong tea	400 ml
3	Oranges	3
1	Grapefruit	1
2	Bananas	2
1 tbsp	Lemon juice	15 ml
8 oz	Can of pineapple slices	227 g
2 tbsp	Brandy or sherry	2x15 ml

Put stoned prunes in a bowl and cover with strained tea. Soak for 30 minutes.

Cut the rind and pith away from the oranges and grapefruit with a serrated knife. Cut into slices across the segments, cutting large slices in halves or quarters. Place in glass serving bowl.

Peel and cut the bananas into thick slices and sprinkle with lemon juice to prevent discoloration. Add to bowl with drained prunes, lemon juice and pineapple slices with their syrup. Stir in the brandy or sherry and chill for at least 1 hour before serving.

Rum trifle

Overall timing 35 minutes plus chilling

Freezing Not suitable

To serve 4–6

2 tbsp	Cocoa powder	2x15 ml
4 oz	Caster sugar	125 g
1¼ pints	Milk	700 ml
4	Egg yolks	4
2 oz	Plain flour	50 g
4 tbsp	Rum	4x15 ml
4 tbsp	Water	4x15 ml
8	Trifle sponges	8

Mix the cocoa with 1 oz (25 g) of the sugar. Heat the milk in a saucepan and add ¼ pint (150 ml) of it to the cocoa mixture. Stir till well blended.

In another bowl, beat the egg yolks with remaining sugar and flour. Gradually add the remaining hot milk. Return to the saucepan and bring to the boil, stirring. Cook for 2 minutes till custard thickens. Pour half of the custard back into bowl and stir in cocoa mixture.

Line a glass bowl with greaseproof paper. Put rum and water on a plate. Split the sponges in half, then halve each half. Dip sponges in rum mixture just to moisten. Line bottom and sides of bowl with half the sponges.

Pour in the plain custard and cover with a layer of sponges. Pour the chocolate custard into the mould and cover with remaining sponges. Cover with foil or cling film and chill for at least 3 hours but preferably overnight.

Turn trifle out on to a plate, carefully remove greaseproof paper and decorate with whipped cream, if liked.

Cherry bread pudding

Overall timing 1 hour

Freezing Not suitable

To serve 4–6

7	Slices of bread	7
15 oz	Can of cherries	425 g
4	Eggs	4
4 oz	Caster sugar	125 g
¾ pint	Milk	400 ml
	Grated rind of ½ lemon	
1 tbsp	Icing sugar	15 ml

Preheat the oven to 350°F (180°C) Gas 4.

Cut the slices of bread into quarters diagonally. Arrange eight of the bread triangles over the bottom of an ovenproof dish.

Drain the cherries; halve and remove stones. Spread half the cherries over bread and cover with eight more triangles. Sprinkle over the remaining cherries and cover with the remaining bread, arranged in overlapping rows.

Beat the eggs with the sugar and add the milk. Sprinkle lemon rind over the bread and strain the egg mixture over. Sprinkle the surface with icing sugar and bake for 35 minutes. Serve hot.

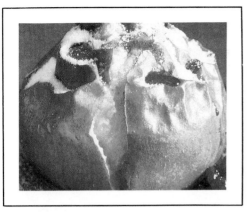

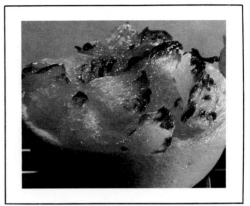

Baked apples

Overall timing 35 minutes

Freezing Not suitable

To serve 4

4	Large apples	4
8 tbsp	Jam	8x15 ml
1 oz	Butter	25 g
4 tbsp	Water	4x15 ml
4 tbsp	Caster sugar	4x15 ml

Preheat oven to 375°F (190°C) Gas 5.

Wash, dry and core apples. Place in a greased ovenproof dish and fill each apple with jam. Add small knob of butter to each.

Put water in bottom of dish, then bake for 25 minutes. Serve sprinkled with sugar.

Caramelized grapefruit

Overall timing 20 minutes

Freezing Not suitable

To serve 4

2	Grapefruit	2
1 teasp	Ground cinnamon	5 ml
4 tbsp	Caster sugar	4x15 ml

Preheat the grill.

Cut grapefruit in half. Remove flesh with grapefruit knife, separate segments and discard membranes. Put segments into a bowl. Mix cinnamon with half the sugar and sprinkle over fruit.

Fill grapefruit shells with segments and sprinkle with remaining sugar. Grill for a few minutes till golden brown. Serve hot.

Redcurrant pudding

Overall timing 1½ hours

Freezing Suitable: reheat from frozen in 350°F (180°C) Gas 4 oven for 1 hour

To serve 6–8

12 oz	Redcurrants	350 g
12	Slices of stale bread	12
2 oz	Butter	50 g
1 pint	Milk	560 ml
1	Vanilla pod	1
2	Eggs	2
6 tbsp	Caster sugar	6x15 ml

Wash and drain the redcurrants. Remove the stalks. Remove the crusts from the bread. Spread with butter and cut into triangles.

Sprinkle a few redcurrants over the bottom of a well-greased 3 pint (1.7 litre) ovenproof dish and arrange some of the bread on top. Cover with redcurrants, then a layer of bread. Repeat the layers.

Put the milk and vanilla pod into a saucepan and bring to the boil. Remove from the heat and lift out the vanilla pod. Whisk the eggs with 5 tbsp (5x15 ml) of the sugar till frothy, then pour in the hot milk, whisking continuously. Strain the custard over the redcurrants and bread. Leave to soak for 20 minutes.

Preheat the oven to 375°F (190°C) Gas 5.

Sprinkle the remaining sugar over the pudding and bake for about 40 minutes till golden. Serve immediately.

Russian pudding

Overall timing 30 minutes

Freezing Not suitable

To serve 4–6

1½ pints	Milk	850 ml
	Pinch of salt	
	Grated rind of ½ lemon	
4 oz	Granulated sugar	125 g
3 oz	Semolina or ground rice	75 g
1	Egg	1
1 lb	Can of cherries	453 g
2 tbsp	Redcurrant jelly	2x15 ml

In a saucepan, heat the milk, salt, lemon rind and 2 oz (50 g) of the sugar. Stir in the semolina or ground rice. Remove from the heat.

Separate the egg and add the beaten yolk to the saucepan.

In a bowl, beat the egg white till stiff and carefully fold into the semolina or ground rice mixture.

Drain cherries. Place cherries and 2 tbsp (2x15 ml) of the juice in a pan. Stir in the redcurrant jelly and cook for 5 minutes.

Preheat the grill. Grease a flameproof serving dish. Pour in half the semolina or rice mixture, then all the cherry mixture and finally the rest of the semolina or rice. Sprinkle with the remaining sugar and place under the grill. Cook till the sugar caramelizes and turns golden but not brown – it should take about 3 minutes. Serve immediately.

Spotted Dick

Overall timing 2¼ hours

Freezing Suitable: boil for a further 2 hours

To serve 8

5 oz	Self-raising flour	150 g
½ teasp	Salt	2.5 ml
5 oz	Fresh breadcrumbs	150 g
5 oz	Shredded suet	150 g
3 oz	Caster sugar	75 g
8 oz	Currants	225 g
¼ pint	Milk	150 ml

Mix together the flour, salt, breadcrumbs, suet, sugar and currants in a large bowl. Make a well in the centre. Gradually add enough milk to make a soft but not sticky dough, using a knife to mix the dry ingredients into the liquid.

Form the dough into a roll on a floured surface. Wrap in greased greaseproof paper with a pleat in the top to allow room for the dough to rise. Wrap the roll loosely in foil, allowing room for expansion, and seal the joins tightly to keep water out.

Place in a large pan of boiling water, cover and simmer for 2 hours.

Remove from the heat, unwrap carefully and roll the pudding off the paper on to a warmed serving plate. Serve hot in slices with pouring custard.

Apricot dumplings

Overall timing 1¼ hours including refrigeration

Freezing Not suitable

Makes 16

2 oz	Butter	50 g
8 oz	Cottage cheese	225 g
	Pinch of salt	
2	Eggs	2
5 oz	Plain flour	150 g
16	Small apricots	16
16	Sugar lumps	16
To finish		
6 oz	Butter	175 g
2 tbsp	Caster sugar	2x15 ml
8 tbsp	Dried breadcrumbs	8x15 ml
1 teasp	Ground cinnamon	5 ml
	Icing sugar	

Beat together butter, sieved cheese, salt, eggs and flour. Chill 30 minutes.

Make a small slit in each apricot. Remove stone and replace with a sugar lump.

Roll out dough on a floured board. Cut into 16x2 inch (5 cm) squares. Put an apricot on to each square and draw dough around to form a dumpling. Drop dumplings into simmering water, cover and cook for 10 minutes. Turn over halfway through cooking.

Melt butter in a saucepan. Stir in sugar, breadcrumbs and cinnamon. Drain dumplings and toss in butter mixture. Dredge with icing sugar and serve hot.

Blackcurrant pancake tower

Overall timing 45 minutes

Freezing Suitable: assemble tower and make sauce after reheating pancakes

To serve 4–6

1½ lb	Blackcurrants	700 g
5 oz	Caster sugar	150 g
Pancakes		
6	Eggs	6
	Pinch of salt	
4 tbsp	Milk	4x15 ml
4 oz	Plain flour	125 g
2 tbsp	Caster sugar	2x15 ml
6 tbsp	Oil	6x15 ml

Put blackcurrants into a bowl and sprinkle with sugar.

To make pancakes, separate eggs. Beat yolks with salt and milk, then gradually beat in flour.

In another bowl, whisk egg whites till frothy. Add sugar and whisk until stiff. Fold whites into yolk mixture.

Heat 1 tbsp (15 ml) of oil in 8 inch (20 cm) frying pan. Add one-sixth of the batter and cook till pancake is golden brown underneath. Turn and cook other side. Place on serving dish and top with some of the fruit. Cook five more pancakes in the same way, placing each one on the "tower" as it is cooked with a layer of fruit.

Serve hot with custard.

Almond apricot desserts

Overall timing 1¼ hours

Freezing Not suitable

To serve 6

1 oz	Butter	25 g
1 oz	Caster sugar	25 g
8 oz	Apricot jam	225 g
3 tbsp	Lemon juice	3x15 ml
3	Eggs	3
2 oz	Ground almonds	50 g

Preheat the oven to 300°F (150°C) Gas 2.

Melt the butter in a saucepan and use to grease six small ovenproof dishes. Coat the inside of each dish with sugar.

Put the apricot jam and lemon juice into a saucepan and heat gently, stirring. Put pan into water to cool mixture quickly.

Separate the eggs. Stir the yolks and almonds into the jam mixture. Beat the egg whites in a mixing bowl until very stiff. Gently fold into the jam mixture.

Fill each dish to the top with the mixture. Place on a baking tray and bake for about 45 minutes.

Serve in the dishes or turn desserts out on to serving plates. Serve hot with custard, whipped cream or ice cream.

Sultana and macaroon pudding

Overall timing 1 hour 20 minutes

Freezing Suitable: serve cold

To serve 6

1 pint	Milk	560 ml
4 oz	Fresh breadcrumbs	125 g
3 oz	Butter	75 g
3	Eggs	3
2 oz	Caster sugar	50 g
8 oz	Sultanas	225 g
8 oz	Macaroons	225 g
Rum cream		
4	Eggs	4
3 oz	Caster sugar	75 g
4 tbsp	Rum	4x15 ml
	Juice of ½ lemon	

Preheat the oven to 400°F (200°C) Gas 6.

Put the milk into a saucepan and bring to the boil. Add the breadcrumbs and cook gently – just simmering – for 10 minutes.

Meanwhile, cream butter in a bowl till softened. Separate the eggs. Whisk the yolks with the sugar till light and fluffy, then gradually beat into the butter. Add the milk and breadcrumbs and the sultanas and mix well. Whisk the egg whites till stiff and fold into the mixture.

Arrange the sultana mixture and the macaroons in layers in a greased 8 inch (20 cm) brioche or kugelhopf mould, beginning and ending with the sultana mixture. Bake for 1 hour.

To make the rum cream, mix the eggs, sugar, rum, lemon juice and 3 fl oz (90 ml) water in a bowl. Place the bowl over a pan of simmering water and cook, stirring constantly, till the mixture is thick enough to coat the back of the spoon. Strain into a warmed sauceboat or serving dish.

Turn the pudding on to a warmed serving plate and serve hot, cut into thick wedges, with the rum cream.

Grapefruit soufflés

Overall timing 45 minutes

Freezing Not suitable

To serve 6

6	Grapefruit	6
3 oz	Butter	75 g
2 oz	Plain flour	50 g
	Finely grated rind of 1 orange	
1–2 oz	Caster sugar	25–50 g
3	Eggs	3

Preheat the oven to 375°F (190°C) Gas 5.

Slice tops off grapefruit and squeeze juice out of flesh very gently – measure out ½ pint (300 ml). Remove flesh and membranes with grapefruit knife and discard. Retain shells.

Melt the butter in a saucepan, stir in the flour and cook for 2 minutes. Gradually stir in the grapefruit juice. Bring to the boil and cook, stirring, for 2 minutes or until the sauce thickens. Add orange rind and sugar and stir until sugar dissolves. Remove from heat and leave to cool slightly.

Separate the eggs and beat the yolks into the sauce. Whisk the egg whites in a bowl till stiff, then carefully fold into the sauce mixture.

Place empty grapefruit shells in a foil-lined bun tin and fill with the mixture. Bake for 15–20 minutes till well risen and golden. Serve immediately.

Sussex pond pudding

Overall timing 4 hours

Freezing Not suitable

To serve 6–8

8 oz	Self-raising flour	225 g
4 oz	Shredded suet	125 g
¼ pint	Milk	150 ml
4 oz	Butter	125 g
4 oz	Soft brown sugar	125 g
1	Large thin-skinned lemon	1

Mix the flour and suet in a large bowl. Add the milk a little at a time to give a soft, but not sticky, dough. Knead the dough lightly. Roll out three-quarters of the dough and use to line a well-greased 2½ pint (1.5 litre) pudding basin.

Cream the butter and sugar together until fluffy and spread half the mixture over the bottom and sides of the pastry.

Pierce the lemon all over with a fine skewer (to help the juices run out during cooking). Stand the lemon upright in centre of the basin, then add the remaining creamed mixture.

Roll out remaining dough and cover the filling, sealing pastry edges well. Cover the basin with a piece of greased greaseproof paper which has a large pleat to allow for expansion. Cover with pleated foil and tie with string, making a handle to aid removal from saucepan.

Place basin in saucepan containing 3 inches (7.5 cm) boiling water. Cover and leave to boil for 3½ hours, topping up with extra boiling water as it evaporates.

Lift basin from saucepan. Remove foil and paper and run a knife round the sides of the basin to release the pudding. Invert on to a warmed serving plate and serve hot with pouring custard or cream.

Tapioca and caramel mould

Overall timing 1¼ hours

Freezing Not suitable

To serve 6

4 oz	Seed pearl tapioca	125 g
1½ pints	Milk	850 ml
4 tbsp	Caster sugar	4x15 ml
	Grated rind of 1 lemon	
4 oz	Granulated sugar	125 g
1 oz	Butter	25 g
3	Eggs	3

Preheat the oven to 400°F (200°C) Gas 6.

Put the tapioca, milk, caster sugar and lemon rind into a saucepan and bring to the boil, stirring. Simmer for 15 minutes, stirring occasionally with a wooden spoon to prevent the mixture sticking to the pan.

Meanwhile, put the granulated sugar into a saucepan with 2 tbsp (2x15 ml) water and stir over a low heat till the sugar dissolves. Stop stirring and boil steadily till golden brown. Pour into a 7 inch (18 cm) round cake tin, turning so the bottom and sides are coated.

Remove the tapioca from the heat and beat in the butter. Separate the eggs, putting the whites into a large bowl. Beat the yolks into the tapioca, then leave to cool, stirring occasionally.

Whisk the egg whites till stiff but not dry and fold gently into the tapioca with a metal spoon. Pour the mixture into the caramel-lined tin and bake for about 35 minutes till well risen and golden.

Run a knife round the edge of the mould and turn out on to a serving dish. Serve hot or cold with pouring cream.

Viennese sweet semolina

Overall timing 50 minutes

Freezing Not suitable

To serve 4–6

2 oz	Sultanas	50 g
1 pint	Milk	560 ml
1½ oz	Butter	40 g
3 oz	Semolina	75 g
4 tbsp	Caster sugar	4x15 ml

Preheat the oven to 350°F (180°C) Gas 4.

Soak the sultanas in warm water. Put the milk into a saucepan with butter. Heat till warm, then pour in the semolina and bring to the boil, stirring constantly. Simmer for 5 minutes, then stir in all but 1 tbsp (15 ml) of the sugar.

Drain sultanas and mix into semolina. Turn into a greased ovenproof dish and smooth top. Bake for 30 minutes.

Remove dish from oven and increase heat to 400°F (200°C) Gas 6. Mix the semolina with a fork to break it up. Return dish to oven for 5 minutes till mixture is dry and crisp. Turn on to a warmed serving dish, sprinkle with the reserved sugar and serve hot.

Coconut and cherry surprise

Overall timing 1 hour

Freezing Suitable: reheat in 375°F (190°C) Gas 5 oven for 10 minutes

To serve 8–10

8 oz	Shortcrust pastry	225 g
2½ oz	Ground almonds	65 g
14 oz	Can of cherry pie filling	379 g
1 oz	Desiccated coconut	25 g
Filling		
3 oz	Butter	75 g
3 oz	Caster sugar	75 g
2	Eggs	2
¼ teasp	Almond essence	1.25 ml
2 tbsp	Milk	2x15 ml
2 oz	Self-raising flour	50 g
2 oz	Desiccated coconut	50 g
1½ oz	Ground almonds	40 g

Topping		
3 tbsp	Desiccated coconut	3x15 ml
1	Egg yolk	1
1 teasp	Milk	5 ml

Roll out dough and use to line greased 10 inch (25 cm) springform tin. Sprinkle ground almonds over. Spread pie filling to within 1 inch (2.5 cm) of edge, then cover with coconut.

Preheat the oven to 400°F (200°C) Gas 6.

Make filling by creaming butter with sugar till pale and fluffy. Add eggs, essence and 1 tbsp (15 ml) milk and beat well. Fold in flour, followed by remaining milk, coconut and almonds.

Place mixture in blobs over pie filling and smooth evenly so no fruit is visible. Sprinkle with coconut and bake for 30 minutes.

Mix egg yolk and milk together. Brush over tart and bake for a further 10 minutes. Serve hot.

Flamed fruit salad

Overall timing 30 minutes

Freezing Not suitable

To serve 4

	Selection of any firm fresh fruit: apple, banana, cherries, orange, clementine, pear, peach, strawberries and grapes		
1	Lemon	1	
1 oz	Butter	25 g	
3 tbsp	Caster sugar	3x15 ml	
2 oz	Flaked almonds	50 g	
3 tbsp	Rum	3x15 ml	

Prepare the fruit and chop it into pieces. Mix these together in a bowl. Grate lemon and squeeze out juice. Add juice to fruit.

Put the butter and caster sugar into a saucepan. Heat without stirring, until the sugar caramelizes and becomes light brown. This will take about 5 minutes. Add the grated lemon rind and almonds. Cook for about 5 minutes, stirring occasionally, until the caramel and nuts are golden brown.

Remove pan from the heat. Add juices from mixed fruits and stir until caramel becomes a smooth syrup. Add the fruit and heat through for about 5 minutes, turning the mixture over frequently to distribute the syrup. Remove from heat.

Warm rum in a metal ladle, then set it alight and pour over fruit. Serve immediately with whipped cream or ice cream.

Fruit brochettes

Overall timing 20 minutes

Freezing Not suitable

To serve 6

3	Bananas	3
2	Oranges	2
1	Lemon	1
8 oz	Can of pineapple chunks	227 g
2 tbsp	Rum	2x15 ml
4 oz	Caster sugar	125 g
1 oz	Butter	25 g
3	Thick slices of bread	3

Peel the fruit. Cut bananas into 1 inch (2.5 cm) pieces; divide oranges and lemon into segments; drain pineapple chunks. Place fruit in a bowl, pour rum over and sprinkle with 2 tbsp (2x15 ml) of the sugar.

Preheat grill.

Butter the bread on both sides, cut into small cubes and roll in sugar to coat. Thread fruit and bread cubes on to skewers.

Cook under the grill (or on a barbecue) for 10 minutes, turning brochettes over from time to time and sprinkling them with any remaining sugar. Serve immediately with whipped cream or vanilla ice cream.

Apricot pancakes

Overall timing 45 minutes

Freezing Suitable: fill pancakes after thawing and reheating

To serve 4

2	Eggs	2
¼ pint	Milk	150 ml
2 fl oz	Water	60 ml
3 oz	Plain flour	75 g
1 oz	Caster sugar	25 g
	Vanilla essence	
	Pinch of salt	
3½ oz	Butter or lard	100 g
8 tbsp	Apricot jam	8x15 ml
	Icing sugar	
1 oz	Ground hazelnuts	25 g

Put eggs, milk and water into a bowl. Add the flour, caster sugar, a few drops of vanilla essence and salt. Whisk or beat well together until creamy and smooth.

Melt a knob of butter or lard in a small frying pan. Pour in a little of the batter and spread in a thin layer over the pan, using a spatula. When underside is cooked, flip the pancake over to brown the other side.

As soon as each pancake is ready, spread with apricot jam and roll up. Put on to a dish and keep warm in the oven while you cook the other pancakes, adding more butter or lard to the pan as necessary.

Before serving, dredge with icing sugar and sprinkle with ground hazelnuts or chopped nuts of your choice.

Blackberry pancakes

Overall timing 30 minutes

Freezing Not suitable

To serve 2

1½ oz	Plain flour	40 g
2 teasp	Caster sugar	2x5 ml
	Pinch of salt	
1	Egg	1
3 fl oz	Milk	90 ml
	Oil for frying	
Topping		
4 oz	Canned blackberries	125 g
3 tbsp	Honey	3x15 ml
1½ tbsp	Brandy	22.5 ml
	Vanilla ice cream	
1 oz	Walnuts	25 g

Sift flour, sugar and salt into a bowl. Make a well in the centre and add egg and milk. Whisk till smooth. Pour into jug and leave to stand for 5 minutes.

Lightly oil an 8 inch (20 cm) pancake pan and heat. Make four thin pancakes. Fold into quarters, arrange on a warmed serving plate and keep hot.

Place drained blackberries in a sieve and rinse under running water. Turn on to kitchen paper to drain.

Gently heat honey with brandy in a saucepan. Remove from heat before it boils.

To assemble pancakes, put a cube of ice cream on top of each and scatter with blackberries. Pour over hot honey mixture and sprinkle with chopped walnuts. Serve immediately.

Baked bananas

Overall timing 15 minutes

Freezing Not suitable

To serve 4

4	Large ripe bananas	4
2 oz	Butter	50 g
2 teasp	Caster sugar	2x5 ml
2 tbsp	Water	2x15 ml
	Ground cinnamon	

Preheat oven to 425°F (220°C) Gas 7.

Peel the bananas three-quarters of the way down. Fold back the skin to give a petal effect. Place in a greased ovenproof dish and dot each banana with butter. Sprinkle with sugar, water and a little ground cinnamon.

Bake for 10 minutes. Serve immediately with custard or vanilla ice cream.

Baked noodle pudding

Overall timing 1 hour

Freezing Not suitable

To serve 4

½ pint	Milk	300 ml
1 pint	Water	560 ml
8 oz	Noodles	225 g
2 oz	Butter	50 g
2	Eggs	2
2	Large dessert apples	2
2 oz	Walnut pieces	50 g
3 oz	Caster sugar	75 g
2 teasp	Poppy seeds	2x5 ml

Preheat the oven to 325°F (170°C) Gas 3.

Put the milk and water into a saucepan and bring to the boil. Add the noodles, bring back to the boil and simmer till tender. Drain noodles and put into a large bowl. Stir in the melted butter and beaten eggs till lightly coated.

Spread one-third of the noodles over the bottom of a greased ovenproof dish. Core and thinly slice the apples. Arrange half the slices over the noodles with half the walnuts. Sprinkle with one-third of the sugar and poppy seeds.

Repeat the layers, finishing with a layer of noodles arranged in a lattice pattern. Sprinkle with the remaining sugar and poppy seeds.

Bake for about 35 minutes till the apples are tender. Remove from the oven and cool completely before serving.

Bananas flambé

Overall timing 15 minutes

Freezing Not suitable

To serve 4

¼ pint	Water	150 ml
3 oz	Caster sugar	75 g
8	Bananas	8
5 tbsp	Rum	5x15 ml
1	Small block of vanilla ice cream	1
2 oz	Flaked almonds	50 g

Put the water and sugar into a saucepan and cook until it starts to turn golden.

Peel the bananas. Leave whole or cut in half crossways. Add to the pan. Cook, uncovered, for 7 minutes, spooning syrup over occasionally. Remove from heat, stir in 4 tbsp (4x15 ml) of the rum and keep warm.

Place scoops of ice cream on a chilled serving dish. Cover with the bananas and spoon the syrup over.

Warm the remaining rum in a metal spoon or ladle. Set alight and pour over the bananas. Decorate with flaked almonds and serve immediately, while flaming.

Plum pudding

Overall timing 5½ hours plus maceration

Freezing Suitable: boil from frozen for about 2 hours

To serve 8–10

1 lb	Mixed sultanas, raisins and currants	450 g
12 oz	Prunes	350 g
5 oz	Chopped mixed peel	150 g
4 tbsp	Rum	4x15 ml
¼ pint	Light ale or lager	150 ml
3	Eggs	3
8 oz	Flaked almonds	225 g
1	Apple	1
2 teasp	Mixed spice	2x5 ml
2 teasp	Salt	2x5 ml
12 oz	Brown sugar	350 g
2	Oranges	2
2	Lemons	2
8 oz	Shredded suet	225 g
6 oz	Plain flour	175 g
5 oz	Fresh breadcrumbs	150 g

Put dried fruits and candied peel in a large bowl, add 3 tbsp (3x15 ml) rum and ale or lager and leave to macerate overnight.

Drain fruit, reserving liquid. Stone prunes, then add eggs, almonds, grated apple, mixed spice, salt, sugar and the juice and grated rind of oranges and lemons. Mix well.

Put suet in a bowl and work in flour and breadcrumbs. Mix in any liquid from macerated fruit and add a little more beer if mixture is too dry. Knead to a dough and mix in all remaining ingredients. Tip mixture on to a clean, floured tea-towel and tie the corners together. Suspend from a long wooden spoon in a large saucepan half filled with boiling water. Boil for 5 hours.

Drain pudding for 5 minutes before removing tea-towel. Warm remaining rum, set alight and pour over pudding. Serve hot with custard.

Fruity pancakes

Overall timing 1 hour

Freezing Not suitable

To serve 2

1½ oz	Plain flour	40 g
2 teasp	Caster sugar	2x5 ml
	Pinch of salt	
1	Egg	1
4 tbsp	Milk	4x15 ml
2 tbsp	Cider or white wine	2x15 ml
	Grated rind of ½ orange	
	Vanilla essence	
3	Sugar lumps	3
1	Orange	1
½ teasp	Ground cinnamon	2.5 ml
2	Dessert apples	2
	Oil for frying	

Sift flour, sugar and salt into a bowl. Make a well in the centre and add egg, milk, cider or wine, orange rind and a few drops of vanilla essence. Whisk till smooth. Pour batter into a jug.

Rub sugar lumps over surface of orange to absorb zest. Crush them and add cinnamon.

Peel orange, then chop flesh roughly. Place in a bowl. Peel, core and cube apples, then mix well with orange.

Preheat the grill.

Lightly oil an 8 inch (20 cm) pancake pan and heat. Pour in one-quarter of the batter and cook for 1–2 minutes till base bubbles and is firm. Spoon over one-quarter of the fruit and crushed sugar and cinnamon mixtures. Place under grill and cook for a few minutes till bubbling. Fold pancake and lift out on to a warmed serving dish. Cover and keep hot while you cook three other pancakes in the same way.

Serve whipped cream flavoured with orange juice separately, or serve with vanilla ice cream.

Honey-baked bananas

Overall timing 40 minutes

Freezing Not suitable

To serve 4

4	Bananas	4
4 tbsp	Lemon juice	4x15 ml
3 tbsp	Honey	3x15 ml
2 oz	Blanched almonds	50 g
3 tbsp	Fresh breadcrumbs	3x15 ml
2 oz	Butter	50 g
¼ pint	Soured cream	150 ml
3 tbsp	Orange juice	3x15 ml

Preheat the oven to 400°F (200°C) Gas 4.

Peel bananas. Arrange side by side in a greased ovenproof dish. Pour over lemon juice and honey. Mix the chopped almonds with the breadcrumbs and sprinkle over bananas. Cut butter into small pieces and scatter over bananas.

Bake for 30 minutes. Serve with soured cream mixed with orange juice.

Plum soufflé

Overall timing 1 hour

Freezing Not suitable

To serve 6

1½ lb	Ripe plums	700 g
2–4 oz	Sugar	50–125 g
6 tbsp	Water	6x15 ml
2½ oz	Butter	65 g
1 tbsp	Dried breadcrumbs	15 ml
2 oz	Plain flour	50 g
½ pint	Warm milk	300 ml
3	Large eggs	3
	Grated rind of 1 orange	

Preheat oven to 375°F (190°C) Gas 5.

Stone the plums and cut into quarters. Put into a saucepan with the sugar and water. Bring to the boil, cover and simmer for 10 minutes.

Grease a 3 pint (1.7 litre) soufflé dish with ½ oz (15 g) butter and coat with the breadcrumbs. Put two thirds of the plums in the dish with any juice.

Melt the remaining butter in a large saucepan, stir in the flour and cook for 1 minute. Gradually add the warm milk and bring to the boil, stirring constantly. Simmer for 2 minutes, then remove from the heat. Cool slightly.

Separate the eggs. Beat the yolks into the sauce with the orange rind and remaining plums. Whisk the egg whites till stiff but not dry. Stir one spoonful into sauce and fold in remainder. Pour mixture over the plums in the dish.

Stand dish in a roasting tin containing 1 inch (2.5 cm) hot water. Bake for 30–35 minutes till well risen and golden. Serve immediately.

Baked apricots

Overall timing 1 hour

Freezing Suitable: reheat from frozen in 400°F (200°C) Gas 6 oven for 15 minutes, then add syrup

To serve 6–8

12	Large apricots	12
½ pint	Milk	300 ml
2 tbsp	Custard powder	2x15 ml
1 tbsp	Caster sugar	15 ml
4 oz	Blanched almonds	125 g
5 oz	Macaroons	150 g
1½ oz	Candied orange peel	40 g
	Pinch of ground cinnamon	
6 tbsp	Redcurrant jelly	6x15 ml
4 tbsp	Water	4x15 ml

Preheat the oven to 400°F (200°C) Gas 6.

Halve apricots and remove stones. Arrange, cut sides up, in a greased ovenproof dish.

Prepare the custard according to packet instructions, using the milk, custard powder and sugar. Cool quickly by standing the pan in cold water. Stir the custard frequently to prevent a skin forming.

Chop almonds, macaroons and candied peel finely and stir into the custard with the cinnamon. Fill apricot halves with custard mixture. Bake for 30 minutes.

Meanwhile, mix together the redcurrant jelly and water in a small pan over a low heat. Spoon syrup carefully over the apricots and bake for a further 10 minutes.

Serve hot with whipped cream, or leave to cool, then chill and serve with ice cream or whipped cream.

Apple and marmalade charlotte

Overall timing 1 hour

Freezing Suitable: reheat in 400°F (200°C) Gas 6 oven for 10 minutes

To serve 8

2½ lb	Cooking apples	1.1 kg
4 tbsp	Water	4x15 ml
1 oz	Sugar	25 g
4 oz	Marmalade	125 g
1½ lb	Stale sliced bread	700 g
3 oz	Butter	75 g

Preheat oven to 400°F (200°C) Gas 6.

To make the filling, peel apples, core and slice into a large saucepan. Add water, cover and bring to the boil. Cook over medium heat for 12 minutes without removing the lid at all during cooking. Remove from heat and beat in sugar and marmalade with a wooden spoon.

Remove crusts and butter bread. Cut a third of slices into triangles, and the rest into wide fingers.

Grease a 3 pint (1.7 litre) charlotte mould and line the bottom with some of the bread triangles, buttered-side out. Overlap the slices as the bread tends to shrink during cooking. Line sides of mould with overlapping bread fingers, butter-side out.

Pour in apple mixture and top with remaining bread triangles, butter-side up. Cook on centre shelf of the oven for 30–40 minutes till golden brown.

Remove from oven. Leave to cool slightly in the mould. Run a knife around the edge and turn out on to a warmed serving plate. Serve hot with custard or cream.

Fruity rice pudding

Overall timing 1¼ hours

Freezing Suitable: reheat in 300°F (150°C) Gas 2 oven for 30 minutes

To serve 6–8

1¼ pints	Milk	700 ml
	Salt	
4	Strips of lemon rind	4
5 oz	Round grain rice	150 g
1½ lb	Apples	700 g
2	Bananas	2
1 oz	Butter	25 g
4 oz	Caster sugar	125 g
1 teasp	Ground cinnamon	5 ml
4 oz	Bottle of sweet cherries	125 g
2 oz	Shelled walnuts	50 g
3	Eggs	3

Preheat oven to 350°F (180°C) Gas 4.

Put the milk, pinch of salt and strips of lemon rind into a saucepan and bring to the boil. Add the rice. Cover and cook for 40 minutes on a low heat, stirring occasionally.

Meanwhile, peel and slice the apples and bananas. Melt the butter and 2 oz (50 g) of the sugar in a saucepan until golden brown. Add the apples and cook for 5 minutes, then add the bananas and cook for 2–3 minutes more. Sprinkle on the cinnamon, then stir in drained cherries and chopped walnuts.

Remove from heat, put mixture into a greased ovenproof dish and smooth over. Work quickly to prevent caramel setting.

Separate the eggs. Cream together the yolks and 1 oz (25 g) sugar in one bowl. In another, beat the whites and remaining sugar together until mixture is very stiff. Fold both mixtures into the cooked rice (take out the lemon peel first) then pour over the fruit. Bake for 30 minutes. Serve hot with cream.

Jam omelettes

Overall timing 10 minutes

Freezing Not suitable

To serve 2

3	Eggs	3
	Pinch of salt	
1 oz	Butter	25 g
3 tbsp	Jam	3x15 ml
1 tbsp	Caster sugar	15 ml

Beat eggs with salt in a bowl. Melt half butter in omelette pan. Add half the egg mixture and cook until set. Slip omelette out of pan on to plate, cooked side down.

Repeat with remaining egg mixture to make another omelette. Spoon jam into the middle of each omelette. Roll them up like pancakes and sprinkle with caster sugar.

To make the caramelized stripes, heat a skewer or toasting fork over a naked flame, then press lightly on top of the omelettes at intervals. Serve at once.

Nutty apple pudding

Overall timing 50 minutes

Freezing Not suitable

To serve 4–6

1½ lb	Cooking apples	700 g
¼ pint	Water	150 ml
2 oz	Flaked almonds	50 g
2 oz	Sultanas	50 g
7 oz	Wholemeal bread	200 g
4 oz	Demerara sugar	125 g
2 oz	Butter	50 g

Preheat the oven to 425°F (220°C) Gas 7.

Peel and core apples and slice into a saucepan. Add water, almonds and sultanas. Cover and cook over a gentle heat for 10 minutes. Remove from heat.

Crumble the bread into a bowl and mix in half the sugar. Grease an ovenproof dish with some of the butter and spread half the bread mixture over the bottom. Cover with apple mixture, then top with remaining bread. Sprinkle on rest of sugar and dot with remaining butter. Bake for about 20 minutes.

Peach meringue pudding

Overall timing 50 minutes

Freezing Not suitable

To serve 6

1 pint	Milk	560 ml
4 tbsp	Semolina	4x15 ml
2	Eggs	2
3 oz	Caster sugar	75 g
4	Ripe peaches	4
3 tbsp	Peach or raspberry jam	3x15 ml
1 oz	Toasted flaked almonds	25 g

Preheat the oven to 350°F (180°C) Gas 4.

Heat the milk in a saucepan and sprinkle in the semolina, stirring constantly. Bring to the boil and cook, stirring, for 3 minutes till thickened. Remove from the heat.

Separate the eggs. Beat the yolks into the semolina with 1 oz (25 g) of the sugar. Pour mixture into a 7 inch (18 cm) soufflé dish and smooth surface.

Peel and halve the peaches. Remove stones. Place a little jam in each peach half. Arrange in soufflé dish, some with the cut sides pressing against the sides of the dish and the rest jam-side down on the semolina.

Whisk the egg whites till stiff, then whisk in half the remaining sugar. Fold in the finely chopped almonds and the rest of the sugar. Pipe or spoon the meringue over the peaches.

Bake for 20 minutes till the meringue is lightly browned. Serve hot or leave to cool completely and chill before serving.

Pear brown betty

Overall timing 1 hour

Freezing Not suitable

To serve 6–8

2 lb	Ripe pears	900 g
8 oz	Stale breadcrumbs	225 g
4 oz	Caster sugar	125 g
2 oz	Butter	50 g

Preheat the oven to 375°F (190°C) Gas 5.

Peel and halve the pears. Remove the cores and cut flesh into ¼ inch (6 mm) slices.

Cover the bottom of a greased 8 inch (20 cm) springform tin with a quarter of the breadcrumbs. Arrange one-third of the pears on top and sprinkle with a little sugar. Repeat the layers till all the ingredients have been used.

Dot with the butter and bake for about 45 minutes till the pears are tender and the top is crisp and golden. Remove from the tin and serve hot or cold with pouring cream or custard.

Pear dumplings

Overall timing 1¼ hours plus chilling

Freezing Not suitable

To serve 4

12 oz	Plain flour	350 g
¼ teasp	Salt	1.25 ml
6 oz	Butter	175 g
	Grated rind of 1 orange	
2 tbsp	Caster sugar	2x15 ml
1	Egg yolk	1
Filling		
4	Ripe pears	4
2 oz	Butter	50 g
2 tbsp	Soft brown sugar	2x15 ml
½ teasp	Ground cinnamon	2.5 ml

Sift flour and salt into a bowl and rub in butter. Stir in the grated orange rind and caster sugar and add enough water to bind to a dough. Knead till smooth. Chill for 30 minutes.

Preheat the oven to 400°F (200°C) Gas 6. Roll out dough and cut into four 8 inch (20 cm) squares.

Peel and halve pears and remove cores. Cream butter with soft brown sugar and cinnamon till pale and fluffy. Use to fill centres of pears. Press halves together and place one on each dough square.

Brush edges of dough squares with water. Bring the four corners of each square together at top of pears, sealing edges well. Roll out dough trimmings and cut into leaves. Lightly beat egg yolk with 1 tbsp (15 ml) water and brush over dough. Dip leaves in egg and press in place on top.

Place on a greased baking tray and bake for about 30 minutes till crisp and golden. Serve hot with whipped cream or vanilla ice cream.

Pineapple fritters

Overall timing 25 minutes

Freezing Not suitable

To serve 6

15½ oz	Can of pineapple rings	439 g
4 oz	Plain flour	125 g
1½ teasp	Caster sugar	7.5 ml
1	Whole egg	1
1 tbsp	Oil	15 ml
4 fl oz	Milk or water	120 ml
2	Egg whites	2
	Oil for frying	
3 tbsp	Icing sugar	3x15 ml

Drain the pineapple rings and dry on kitchen paper.

Sift flour and sugar into bowl. Beat in egg, oil and liquid till smooth. Whisk egg whites till stiff and fold into batter.

Heat oil in a deep-fryer to 340°F (170°C). Spear the pineapple rings on a fork, dip into the batter and carefully lower into the oil. Fry three at a time for 2–3 minutes till crisp and golden. Remove from the pan, drain on kitchen paper and keep hot while remaining fritters are cooked.

Arrange on a warmed serving plate, sift the icing sugar over and serve immediately with whipped cream.

French toast

Overall timing 25 minutes

Freezing Not suitable

To serve 4–6

10	Thin slices of bread	10
½–¾ pint	Milk	300–400 ml
2–3	Eggs	2–3
2 oz	Butter	50 g
2 oz	Caster sugar	50 g
1 teasp	Ground cinnamon (optional)	5 ml

Place bread on a baking tray or Swiss roll tin and pour over the milk. The more stale the bread, the more milk you will need to make the bread spongy. Soak for 10 minutes.

Whisk the eggs in a shallow dish till creamy. Lightly press bread with a fork to remove excess milk.

Melt butter in frying pan (reserve some if you cannot cook all slices at once). Dip bread in egg to coat, add to pan and fry for 3–4 minutes on each side. Sprinkle with caster sugar and cinnamon, if used, and serve immediately, with jam or golden or maple syrup.

Apple strudel

Overall timing 1¾ hours

Freezing Not suitable

To serve 8

10 oz	Strong plain flour	275 g
1	Large egg	1
4 oz	Butter	125 g
	Pinch of salt	
2½ lb	Bramley apples	1.1 kg
3 oz	Caster sugar	75 g
2 teasp	Ground cinnamon	2x5 ml
4 oz	Seedless raisins	125 g
1 tbsp	Grated lemon rind	15 ml
4 oz	Ground almonds	125 g
2 oz	Fresh breadcrumbs	50 g

Sift flour on to a work surface. Add egg. Melt half butter in a pan, then add 3 tbsp (3x15 ml) water and salt. Add mixture to flour and mix to a soft, sticky dough. Knead till smooth.

Leave in a warm place for 20 minutes.

Meanwhile, peel and core apples, then slice half very thinly. Coarsely grate rest into a bowl and mix in sugar, cinnamon, raisins, lemon rind, almonds and half breadcrumbs.

Place a large patterned tea-towel on a flat surface and sprinkle it with flour. Roll out dough on top till it is same shape as towel. Slide your hands between dough and tea-towel. Lift and stretch dough till thin enough to see pattern of tea-towel through. The rectangle should eventually measure about 20x16 inches (50x40 cm).

Preheat the oven to 400°F (200°C) Gas 6.

Brush dough with half remaining melted butter. Sprinkle with remaining breadcrumbs, leaving a 1 inch (2.5 cm) border all round. Spread almond mixture evenly over dough. Arrange apple slices on top. Fold border over filling, then roll up. Place on greased baking tray, curving to fit.

Brush with remaining butter and bake for 10 minutes. Reduce heat to 375°F (190°C) Gas 5 and bake for a further 30 minutes. Sprinkle with icing sugar and serve warm.

Apple soufflé omelette

Overall timing 50 minutes

Freezing Not suitable

To serve 2

2	Eggs	2
2 tbsp	Caster sugar	2x15 ml
4 tbsp	Milk	4x15 ml
¼ teasp	Vanilla essence	1.25 ml
1 oz	Butter	25 g
	Icing sugar	
2 tbsp	Brandy	2x15 ml
Filling		
12 oz	Cooking apple	350 g
1 tbsp	Water	15 ml
½ oz	Butter	15 g
3 tbsp	Granulated sugar	3x15 ml
	Vanilla essence	

To make the filling, peel, core and roughly chop apple. Place in saucepan with water and butter, cover and cook for 15 minutes. Remove from heat and add sugar and few drops of vanilla essence. Mix well, then cool.

To make omelette, separate one egg. Put the yolk in a bowl with the whole egg and the caster sugar and beat till light and frothy. Stir in milk and vanilla essence.

In another bowl, beat the egg white till very stiff. Stir 1 tbsp (15 ml) into yolk mixture to lighten it, then carefully fold in the rest with a metal spoon.

Preheat the grill.

Melt the butter in an omelette pan. When it begins to turn a light brown, pour in the egg mixture. Cook over a low heat for 5–7 minutes. Place under the grill until the top has set. Spread over the filling and fold over in half. Slide onto a warmed serving dish. Dredge with icing sugar. Warm the brandy, pour over the omelette and set alight. Serve flaming.

Individual coconut soufflés

Overall timing 45 minutes

Freezing Not suitable

To serve 8

½ pint	Milk	300 ml
5 tbsp	Caster sugar	5x15 ml
2 tbsp	Plain flour	2x15 ml
2 oz	Butter	50 g
4	Eggs	4
4 oz	Desiccated coconut	125 g
1 tbsp	Icing sugar	15 ml

Whisk 4 tbsp (4x15 ml) of the milk with 3 tbsp (3x15 ml) of the caster sugar and the flour. Bring the remaining milk to the boil in a saucepan. Add 2 tbsp (2x15 ml) of the boiling milk to the sugar mixture and whisk in well, then add to the milk in the pan, whisking vigorously all the time. Simmer gently till thickened, then cover, remove from heat and leave to cool for 15 minutes.

Preheat the oven to 375°F (190°C) Gas 5. Grease eight ovenproof moulds or ramekins with the butter and sprinkle with 1 tbsp (15 ml) of the sugar.

Separate the eggs. Add the yolks to the sauce with the coconut, whisking all the time. In a large bowl, whisk the egg whites till they hold stiff peaks, gradually adding the remaining sugar. Fold into the egg yolk mixture.

Three-quarters fill the moulds or ramekins with the mixture and sprinkle with icing sugar. Place on baking tray and bake for 20 minutes. Serve hot.

Banana pudding with rum sauce

Overall timing 1¼ hours

Freezing Suitable: reheat in 350°F (180°C) Gas 4 oven

To serve 6

2 lb	Bananas	900 g
3½ oz	Caster sugar	100 g
2 oz	Softened butter	50 g
2 oz	Plain flour	50 g
	Grated nutmeg	
2	Eggs	2
2 tbsp	Icing sugar	2x15 ml
1 tbsp	Rum or rum flavouring	15 ml
¼ pint	Carton of single cream	150 ml

Preheat the oven to 350°F (180°C) Gas 4.

Reserve half a large or 1 medium-sized banana for decoration. Peel the rest. Mash them with a fork in a bowl with sugar, butter, flour and a pinch of nutmeg.

Separate the eggs. Add yolks to banana mixture and beat well with a wooden spoon until smooth and creamy. Beat the egg whites till very stiff, then gently fold into the banana mixture.

Lightly grease and flour a pudding basin. Fill with the banana mixture and bake for 1 hour.

Remove from oven. Leave to cool slightly then turn out on to a warmed serving plate. Sprinkle with icing sugar and decorate with the reserved banana, sliced. Mix rum or rum flavouring into single cream and serve separately.

Banana soufflés

Overall timing 25 minutes

Freezing Not suitable

To serve 2

4	Ripe bananas	4
1 oz	Butter	25 g
3 oz	Caster sugar	75 g
	Vanilla essence	
2 tbsp	Rum	2x15 ml
2	Large eggs	2
2 tbsp	Icing sugar	2x15 ml

Preheat the oven to 425°F (220°C) Gas 7.

Make two lengthways slits with a sharp knife near to the top of each banana, leaving the skin joined at the stalk end. Roll back skin. Remove banana pulp with a teaspoon and place in a bowl. Mash well to a purée.

Put the banana purée into a saucepan with the butter, caster sugar, a few drops of vanilla essence and the rum. Cook for about 3 minutes over a low heat, stirring constantly. Remove from heat.

Separate eggs. Stir yolks into the banana mixture. Place pan in cold water to cool mixture quickly. Beat egg whites till firm, then lightly fold into cold banana mixture with a metal spoon.

Fill banana skins with mixture. Place on a baking tray and bake for about 10 minutes. Sprinkle with icing sugar and serve immediately with pouring cream.

Blackberry and pear meringue

Overall timing 50 minutes

Freezing Not suitable

To serve 6–8

12 oz	Ripe blackberries	350 g
2 oz	Caster sugar	50 g
3 tbsp	Ground almonds	3x15 ml
4	Large ripe pears	4
3	Egg whites	3
7 oz	Icing sugar	200 g

Preheat the oven to 350°F (180°C) Gas 4.

Hull the berries and arrange over the bottom of a shallow ovenproof dish. Mix the caster sugar and 2 tbsp (2x15 ml) of the almonds together and sprinkle over the berries.

Peel and halve the pears lengthways. Remove the cores. Arrange cut sides down in a single layer on the berries. Bake on the centre shelf of the oven for 20 minutes.

Put the egg whites and sifted icing sugar into a large heatproof bowl over a pan of simmering water. Whisk till the meringue is stiff and glossy. Spoon or pipe the meringue over the pears and sprinkle with the reserved almonds.

Return to the oven and bake for a further 10 minutes till lightly browned. Serve immediately.

Baked apple toasts

Overall timing 40 minutes

Freezing Not suitable

To serve 4

3 oz	Butter	75 g
4	Thick slices of crusty bread	4
4	Dessert apples	4
6 tbsp	Demerara sugar	6x15 ml

Preheat the oven to 425°F (220°C) Gas 7.

Butter the bread thickly on one side and arrange on a baking tray, buttered side up.

Peel, core and thinly slice the apples. Arrange half the slices on the bread so they overlap slightly and cover the bread. Sprinkle with a little of the sugar and place remaining apples on top.

Sprinkle apples with remaining sugar and bake for about 25 minutes till the sugar melts and caramelizes. Serve hot.

Berry-stuffed apples

Overall timing 30 minutes

Freezing Suitable: reheat from frozen in 375°F (190°C) Gas 5 oven for 20 minutes

To serve 4

14½ oz	Can of loganberries	411 g
4	Large apples	4
2 oz	Butter	50 g
4 tbsp	Brown sugar	4x15 ml

Preheat the oven to 375°F (190°C) Gas 5.

Drain loganberries, reserving syrup. Core apples. Place in a greased ovenproof dish and fill centres with loganberries. Surround with remaining berries and reserved syrup. Place a knob of butter on each apple and sprinkle with 1 tbsp (15 ml) sugar.

Bake for 25 minutes, basting occasionally with the juices in the dish, till tender. Serve apples hot with pouring cream.

Cherry pudding with jam sauce

Overall timing 1¾ hours

Freezing Not suitable

To serve 4–6

4 oz	Butter	125 g
4 oz	Caster sugar	125 g
2	Eggs	2
6 oz	Self-raising flour	175 g
4 oz	Glacé cherries	125 g
3 tbsp	Milk	3x15 ml
½ teasp	Almond essence	2.5 ml
Sauce		
4 tbsp	Red jam	4x15 ml
¼ pint	Water	150 ml
1 teasp	Arrowroot	5 ml
1 tbsp	Lemon juice	15 ml

Cream butter with sugar till pale and fluffy. Gradually beat in the eggs one at a time. Fold in the sifted flour and cherries, adding milk and almond essence to give a soft dropping consistency. Place in greased basin and cover with greased foil.

Put basin into a pan and fill up to rim of basin with boiling water. Cover and steam for 1½ hours.

To make the sauce, melt the jam with the water in a small pan, then sieve. Blend arrowroot with lemon juice and stir into sauce. Bring to the boil, stirring.

Turn pudding out of mould and serve immediately with the hot jam sauce.

Irish lemon pudding

Overall timing 1 hour

Freezing Not suitable

To serve 4–6

4 oz	Butter	125 g
6 oz	Caster sugar	175 g
4	Eggs	4
1	Lemon	1
3 tbsp	Plain flour	3x15 ml
½ pint	Milk	300 ml
1 tbsp	Icing sugar	15 ml

Preheat the oven to 400°F (200°C) Gas 6.

Cream the butter and caster sugar in a bowl till light and fluffy. Separate the eggs and add the yolks to the creamed mixture. Beat well. Grate rind from lemon and squeeze out juice. Beat into the creamed mixture. Gradually stir in the flour, then the milk.

Beat egg whites till stiff, then carefully fold into mixture. Turn into a greased 7 inch (18 cm) soufflé dish and sift icing sugar over. Place dish in roasting tin containing 1 inch (2.5 cm) hot water. Bake for 40–50 minutes till the pudding has risen and the top is golden. Serve hot or cold.

Caribbean pancakes

Overall timing 40 minutes

Freezing Not suitable

To serve 6

2½ oz	Plain flour	65 g
	Pinch of salt	
¼ teasp	Ground ginger	1.25 ml
1	Egg	1
¼ pint	Milk	150 ml
2 oz	Butter	50 g
Filling		
15½ oz	Can of pineapple rings	439 g
15½ oz	Can of creamed rice	439 g
4 tbsp	Rum	4x15 ml
6	Glacé cherries	6

Sift the flour, salt and ginger into a bowl. Add the egg and milk and beat till smooth. Melt butter and add one-quarter to batter.

Brush a little butter over an 8 inch (20 cm) pan and heat. Pour one-sixth of the batter into the pan, tilting it so that the bottom is covered. Cook till pancake is golden brown underneath, then flip over and cook other side. Make five more pancakes in this way.

Preheat the oven to 375°F (190°C) Gas 5.

Drain the pineapple rings, and reserve three. Finely chop the rest and put into a bowl. Add creamed rice and mix well. Divide the mixture between the pancakes. Roll up the pancakes loosely and arrange in an ovenproof dish. Heat through in the oven for 10 minutes.

Meanwhile, cut the reserved pineapple rings in half. Warm the rum in a small saucepan. Remove pancakes from oven and decorate with the halved pineapple rings and cherries. Pour the warm rum over, set alight and serve flaming, with scoops of vanilla ice cream.

Walnut pear pie

Overall timing 1 hour plus chilling

Freezing Suitable: decorate with cream after thawing

To serve 6–8

6 oz	Plain flour	175 g
4 oz	Butter	125 g
2 oz	Caster sugar	50 g
2 oz	Walnuts	50 g
2 teasp	Ground cinnamon	2x5 ml
1	Egg	1
Filling		
4	Ripe dessert pears	4
1½ oz	Caster sugar	40 g
¼ pint	Whipping cream	150 ml

Sift flour into a large bowl and rub in butter. Stir in sugar, finely chopped walnuts and cinnamon. Add egg with enough water to bind to a firm dough. Chill for 1 hour.

Preheat the oven to 375°F (190°C) Gas 5.

Roll out two-thirds of dough and use to line an 8 inch (20 cm) fluted flan dish. Peel, core and quarter pears. Arrange over pastry in a circle, core-side downwards and with the stem ends pointing towards the centre but not joining up. Sprinkle with 1 oz (25 g) caster sugar.

Roll out remaining dough and place over pears. Trim edges and pinch together to seal. Using a 3 inch (7.5 cm) pastry cutter, cut a circle out of the centre of the pastry lid. Brush pastry with egg white (from egg shell) and dredge with remaining caster sugar. Bake for 15 minutes, then reduce oven temperature to 350°F (180°C) Gas 4 and bake for a further 25 minutes. Cool in tin.

Whip cream and spoon or pipe into centre of pie before serving.

Traditional apple pie

Overall timing 1 hour

Freezing Not suitable

To serve 4–6

8 oz	Plain flour	225 g
	Pinch of salt	
4 oz	Butter	125 g
1½ lb	Cooking apples	700 g
4 tbsp	Brown sugar	4x15 ml
½ teasp	Ground cinnamon	2.5 ml
¼ teasp	Grated nutmeg	1.25 ml
¼ teasp	Ground cloves	1.25 ml
2 oz	Sultanas	50 g
	Milk	
1 tbsp	Caster sugar	15 ml

Preheat oven to 400°F (200°C) Gas 6.

Sift flour and salt together into a bowl and rub in butter. Add enough water to mix to a firm dough.

Peel, core and slice apples into a bowl. Add brown sugar, spices and sultanas. Put mixture in buttered 2 pint (1.1 litre) pie dish. Sprinkle over 2 tbsp (2x15 ml) of water.

Roll out dough and cover pie. Decorate with dough trimmings. Brush with milk and sprinkle with caster sugar.

Bake for 20 minutes. Reduce heat to 350°F (180°C) Gas 4 and bake for a further 20 minutes.

West Indian peanut pie

Overall timing 1¼ hours

Freezing Not suitable

To serve 6–8

Pastry		
4 oz	Self-raising flour	125 g
½ teasp	Salt	2.5 ml
2 tbsp	Caster sugar	2x15 ml
2 oz	Softened butter	50 g
1	Egg yolk	1
2 tbsp	Milk	2x15 ml
Filling		
4 oz	Roasted unsalted peanuts	125 g
1	Egg	1
3 oz	Sugar	75 g
4 oz	Golden syrup	125 g
½ teasp	Vanilla essence	2.5 ml

Preheat the oven to 350°F (180°C) Gas 4.

To make pastry, sift flour, salt and sugar into a bowl. Rub in the butter. Add egg yolk and gradually mix in enough milk to bind to a soft dough. Roll out dough and use to line an 8 inch (20 cm) fluted flan ring.

To make filling, preheat the grill. Remove the shells from the peanuts. Place nuts on a baking tray and grill them for 2 minutes, shaking the tray so they brown lightly all over. Remove and allow to cool.

Whisk the egg and sugar in a bowl till light and frothy. Add syrup and continue to beat till thick. Stir in the peanuts and vanilla essence.

Pour the peanut mixture into the flan ring and bake for 30 minutes. Cover with foil and bake for a further 5–10 minutes. Lift off the foil, leave the pie till almost cool, then remove from tin.

Apple and mincemeat tart

Overall timing 1 hour

Freezing Suitable: reheat in 350°F (180°C) Gas 4 oven for 40 minutes

To serve 6

8 oz	Shortcrust pastry	225 g
14½ oz	Jar of mincemeat	411 g
1 lb	Bramley apples	450 g
3 oz	Caster sugar	75 g
½ teasp	Ground allspice	2.5 ml
2 oz	Butter	50 g
1 tbsp	Plain flour	15 ml

Preheat the oven to 425°F (220°C) Gas 7. Roll out the dough and line a 9½ inch (24 cm) fluted loose-bottomed flan tin. Spread mincemeat evenly over pastry.

Peel, core and finely slice the apples. Mix with 2 oz (50 g) of sugar and the allspice. Arrange in circles on mincemeat.

In a bowl, cut and fold the butter with remaining 1 oz (25 g) sugar and flour until the mixture resembles fine breadcrumbs. Sprinkle evenly over the apples. Place flan on a baking tray.

Bake in oven for 15 minutes, then reduce to 375°F (190°C) Gas 5 and bake for a further 30 minutes. Remove from oven and allow to cool.

Lift tart from flan tin and place on serving plate. Spoon any topping from baking tray on to tart. Serve warm or cold, with whipped cream or vanilla ice cream.

Blackcurrant boats

Overall timing 1 hour 20 minutes

Freezing Not suitable

Makes 8

3 oz	Plain flour	75 g
1½ oz	Caster sugar	40 g
1	Egg	1
	Vanilla essence	
1½ oz	Butter	40 g
Filling		
11 oz	Can of blackcurrants	300 g
2 oz	Caster sugar	50 g
1 oz	Flaked almonds	25 g
¼ pint	Carton of double cream	150 ml
1 tbsp	Icing sugar	15 ml

Preheat the oven to 425°F (220°C) Gas 7.

Sift flour into a bowl, make a well in the centre and add sugar, egg and a few drops of vanilla essence. Add the butter, cut into pieces, and knead to a dough. Chill for 30 minutes.

Roll out dough to ¼ inch (6 mm) thick and use to line eight barquette tins. Prick and bake blind for 15–20 minutes till cooked and golden brown. Cool.

Drain blackcurrants and place in bowl. Sprinkle over the caster sugar and leave for 1 hour.

Preheat the grill. Spread flaked almonds on grill pan and toast. Whip cream till stiff with icing sugar. Spoon into piping bag.

Drain blackcurrants and divide between pastry boats. Pipe on cream and decorate with toasted almonds.

Canadian cherry pie

Overall timing 1¼ hours

Freezing Not suitable

To serve 6

8 oz	Shortcrust pastry	225 g
2 lb	Fresh cherries *or*	900 g
2x15 oz	Cans of cherries	2x425 g
1 oz	Ground rice	25 g
2 oz	Caster sugar	50 g
1	Lemon	1
1	Egg white	1
	Caster sugar	

Preheat the oven to 450°F (230°C) Gas 8.

Roll out two-thirds of dough and use to line 7½ inch (19 cm) fluted loose-bottomed flan tin.

Stone cherries (drain first if canned) and put into saucepan with rice and sugar. Grate rind from lemon and squeeze out juice. Add both to pan and bring to the boil, stirring. Simmer for 2 minutes. Cool.

Spread cherry mixture in pastry case. Roll out remaining dough and lay over filling. Moisten edges and press together to seal. Brush with lightly beaten egg white and dredge with caster sugar.

Bake for 10 minutes, then reduce heat to 350°F (180°C) Gas 4. Bake for a further 40–45 minutes till top is golden.

Custard tart

Overall timing 1½ hours plus cooling

Freezing Not suitable

To serve 4–6

8 oz	Plain flour	225 g
2 oz	Lard	50 g
2 oz	Butter	50 g
2–3 tbsp	Water	2–3 x 15 ml
Filling		
1 pint	Milk	560 ml
1	Vanilla pod	1
	Strip of lemon rind	
4	Eggs	4
2 oz	Caster sugar	50 g
	Grated nutmeg	

Preheat the oven to 400°F (200°C) Gas 6.

Put the flour into a bowl and rub in the fat till the mixture resembles fine breadcrumbs. Gradually add the water and mix to a smooth dough.

Roll out the dough on a lightly floured surface and use to line a 9 inch (23 cm) flan tin or ring. Bake blind for 10 minutes. Remove from oven and reduce temperature to 350°F (180°C) Gas 4.

Put milk, vanilla pod and lemon rind into a pan and bring almost to the boil. Remove from heat and leave to infuse for 10 minutes. Remove vanilla pod and lemon rind.

Beat eggs and sugar in bowl. Pour in milk, stirring. Strain into flan case and sprinkle with nutmeg. Bake for 35 minutes or till just set. Cool.

Marmalade and ginger tart

Overall timing 1¼ hours

Freezing Not suitable

To serve 6–8

8 oz	Plain flour	225 g
1 teasp	Ground ginger	5 ml
4 oz	Butter	125 g
2 tbsp	Caster sugar	2x15 ml
1	Egg yolk	1
8 tbsp	Marmalade	8x15 ml

Sift flour and ginger into a bowl. Rub in the butter till the mixture resembles breadcrumbs. Add sugar and mix to a dough with the egg yolk and a little water. Knead lightly till smooth, then chill for 30 minutes.

Preheat the oven to 375°F (190°C) Gas 5.

Roll out about three-quarters of the dough on a floured surface and use to line a 9 inch (23 cm) pie plate or flan tin. Crimp the edges and prick base.

Spread a thick layer of marmalade over the tart base. Roll out the remaining dough and cut into strips with a pastry wheel. Make a lattice over the marmalade filling, pressing the joins to seal. Bake for about 40 minutes, till golden. Remove from tin and serve hot or cold with custard or ice cream.

Nectarine almond tart

Overall timing 50 minutes plus chilling

Freezing Suitable

To serve 4

8 oz	Plain flour	225 g
	Pinch of salt	
4 oz	Butter	125 g
2 oz	Caster sugar	50 g
1	Egg	1
Filling		
1 tbsp	Semolina	15 ml
1 tbsp	Ground almonds	15 ml
4 oz	Caster sugar	125 g
1¾ lb	Nectarines	800 g
½ oz	Split almonds	15 g

Sift the flour and salt into a bowl. Add butter, cut into flakes, sugar and egg and work into a dough. Chill for 30 minutes.

Preheat the oven to 425°F (220°C) Gas 7.

Roll out dough on a floured surface and use to line 9 inch (23 cm) loose-bottomed flan tin. Mix together the semolina, ground almonds and half the caster sugar. Sprinkle over the pastry.

Halve the nectarines and remove the stones. Arrange the fruit in the pastry case, cut sides down, and sprinkle with the remaining sugar and split almonds. Bake for 35–40 minutes.

Allow to cool slightly, then remove from tin and serve warm or cold with pouring cream.

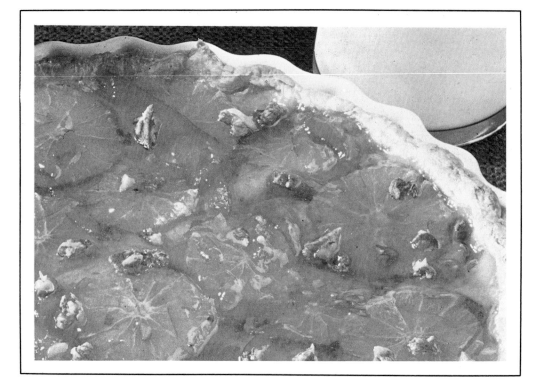

Orange lasagne flan

Overall timing 1½ hours

Freezing Suitable: reheat in 350°F (180°C) Gas 4 oven for 30 minutes

To serve 8

4 oz	Lasagne	125 g
7½ oz	Frozen puff pastry	212 g
3	Thin-skinned oranges	3
2 tbsp	Rum (optional)	2x15 ml
5 tbsp	Thin-cut marmalade	5x15 ml
1 tbsp	Chopped walnuts	15 ml
Confectioners' custard		
1 pint	Milk	560 ml
	Pinch of salt	
1	Vanilla pod	1
	Strip of lemon rind	
4 oz	Caster sugar	125 g
4	Medium eggs	4
1 oz	Plain flour	25 g

Cook lasagne in boiling salted water till tender. Drain and cool.

Meanwhile, thaw pastry and make confectioners' custard. Put milk, salt, vanilla and rind into pan and bring to the boil. Remove from heat and infuse for 10 minutes. Beat sugar, eggs and flour till smooth. Strain in milk, stirring. Return to pan and cook gently, stirring, till thick. Grate rind of one orange and stir into custard with rum, if used.

Preheat the oven to 375°F (190°C) Gas 5.

Roll out dough and use to line 9 inch (23 cm) flan dish. Spread with 2 tbsp (2x15 ml) marmalade. Cover with half custard, then the lasagne and remaining custard.

Peel and thinly slice remaining oranges. Arrange slices over flan to cover completely. Bake for 45 minutes.

Melt remaining marmalade and spoon over oranges to glaze. Sprinkle with walnuts and serve warm with pouring cream.

Iced strawberry tartlets

Overall timing 40 minutes

Freezing Not suitable

Makes 4

6 oz	Rich shortcrust pastry	175 g
4 oz	Gooseberry jam	125 g
2 tbsp	Sherry	2x15 ml
12 oz	Strawberries	350 g
1 pint	Vanilla ice cream or lemon sorbet	560 ml

Preheat the oven to 375°F (190°C) Gas 5. Put baking tray in oven to heat.

Divide dough into four. Put one-quarter into each of four 3 inch (7.5 cm) tartlet dishes and press into shape. Prick bottoms with a fork and place on heated baking tray. Bake for about 25 minutes till crisp and golden. Remove from the oven and leave to cool completely.

Meanwhile, put the jam and sherry into a saucepan and heat gently till melted. Sieve into a sauceboat and leave to cool.

Hull the strawberries. Cut a quarter of them in half lengthways and put the rest into a serving dish.

Arrange the tartlets on a serving dish. Put a scoop of ice cream or sorbet into each and decorate with halved strawberries. Serve immediately with remaining strawberries and gooseberry sauce.

Lime tart

Overall timing 50 minutes plus chilling

Freezing Suitable

To serve 8

6 oz	Shortcrust pastry	175 g
4 teasp	Powdered gelatine	4x5 ml
4 tbsp	Water	4x15 ml
4	Eggs	4
4 oz	Caster sugar	125 g
3	Limes	3
¼ pint	Carton of double cream	150 ml

Preheat the oven to 400°F (200°C) Gas 6.

Roll out dough on a lightly floured surface and use to line an 8 inch (20 cm) flan tin. Bake blind for 10 minutes, then remove beans and foil and bake for a further 10 minutes till golden. Allow to cool, then carefully remove from the tin.

To make the filling, dissolve the gelatine in the water. Separate eggs. Whisk the yolks and sugar together till pale and creamy. Grate rind from limes and squeeze out the juice. Stir two-thirds of the rind and all the juice into the egg mixture. Stir in the gelatine.

Whip cream till stiff. In another bowl, whisk the egg whites till stiff peaks form. Carefully fold cream, then whisked whites into lime mixture. Spoon into pastry case and fluff up the surface.

Sprinkle with the remaining grated lime rind and chill for at least 3 hours or overnight before serving.

Hot apple flan

Overall timing 1 hour

Freezing Not suitable

To serve 6

7 oz	Plain flour	200 g
	Pinch of salt	
1 tbsp	Icing sugar	15 ml
3½ oz	Butter	100 g
Filling		
1½ lb	Cooking apples	700 g
2 oz	Butter	50 g
4½ oz	Icing sugar	140 g
3 tbsp	Calvados or brandy	3x15 ml

Preheat the oven to 400°F (200°C) Gas 6.

To make pastry, sift flour, salt and sugar into a bowl. Add butter and rub in until mixture resembles fine breadcrumbs. Add enough water to mix to a firm dough. Knead lightly. Roll out dough and use to line an 8 inch (20 cm) flan dish. Bake blind for 20–25 minutes.

Meanwhile, make filling. Peel and core apples. Cut into quarters or eighths, depending on size. Melt butter in a saucepan, add apples and cook over a high heat for a few minutes till light brown. Add 4 oz (125 g) icing sugar and 1 tbsp (15 ml) Calvados or brandy. Cover and cook gently till apples are just tender.

Spoon apples and a little of the juice into the warm flan case. Sift over remaining icing sugar. Keep in a warm oven until needed.

Warm remaining Calvados or brandy in a ladle, then pour over apples. Light immediately and take flan to table while still flaming.

French cherry tart

Overall timing 1 hour plus chilling

Freezing Not suitable

To serve 8

8 oz	Plain flour	225 g
	Pinch of salt	
3½ oz	Icing sugar	100 g
4 oz	Butter	125 g
1	Lemon	1
1	Egg	1
Filling		
4 teasp	Dried breadcrumbs	4x5 ml
13½ oz	Jar of cherry pie filling	382 g
3	Eggs	3
3 oz	Caster sugar	75 g
1 tbsp	Cornflour	15 ml
	Ground cinnamon	
1 oz	Cream cheese	25 g

Put the flour, salt and icing sugar into a bowl. Rub in butter. Grate rind and squeeze juice from lemon. Add rind to bowl with egg and mix to a dough. Chill for 30 minutes.

Preheat the oven to 425°F (220°C) Gas 7.

Roll out dough and use to line 10 inch (25 cm) flan ring placed on baking tray. Bake blind for about 15 minutes.

Remove flan case from oven and reduce heat to 375°F (190°C) Gas 5. Sprinkle breadcrumbs over bottom of flan case. Spread cherry pie filling on top.

Separate eggs. Whisk egg yolks with 2 tbsp (2x15 ml) lemon juice, the caster sugar and cornflour until creamy. Beat in cinnamon and cream cheese until smooth.

Beat egg whites until soft peaks form. Fold into yolk mixture. Pour over cherries. Bake for 30–40 minutes. Carefully remove tart from ring and place on a serving dish. Dredge with more icing sugar and serve warm with cream or ice cream.

Linzertorte

Overall timing 50 minutes

Freezing Suitable

To serve 12

8 oz	Plain flour	225 g
$\frac{1}{2}$ teasp	Ground cinnamon	2.5 ml
5 oz	Butter	150 g
3 oz	Ground almonds	75 g
3 oz	Caster sugar	75 g
$\frac{1}{2}$	Lemon	$\frac{1}{2}$
2	Egg yolks	2
8 oz	Raspberry jam	225 g

Sift flour and cinnamon into a large bowl. Rub in butter. Stir in almonds and caster sugar. Grate rind from lemon and squeeze out juice. Add both to bowl with egg yolks and mix to a soft dough. Knead lightly, then chill for 1 hour.

Preheat the oven to 375°F (190°C) Gas 5.

Roll out two-thirds of the dough on a floured surface and use to line an 8 inch (20 cm) flan tin. Don't trim away excess dough.

Spread jam over the pastry case. Roll out remaining dough and cut into strips. Arrange in a lattice pattern across the jam. Fold dough edges in, crimping to make a decorative border.

Bake for 30–35 minutes. Leave to cool in tin. Serve with pouring cream.

Rhubarb and apple pie

Overall timing 2¼ hours plus cooling

Freezing Suitable

To serve 8

12 oz	Plain flour	350 g
½ teasp	Salt	2.5 ml
4 tbsp	Caster sugar	4x15 ml
4 oz	Butter	125 g
¼ pint	Water	150 ml
1	Egg	1
Filling		
2 lb	Rhubarb	900 g
1 lb	Cooking apples	450 g
8 oz	Granulated sugar	225 g
1 teasp	Ground ginger	5 ml
6 tbsp	Water	6x15 ml

Preheat the oven to 375°F (190°C) Gas 5.

Cut rhubarb into 1 inch (2.5 cm) lengths. Peel, core and slice apples. Put fruit into a saucepan with sugar, ginger and water and bring to the boil. Cover and simmer for 15 minutes till pulpy. Purée in a blender or rub through a sieve and leave to cool.

Sift flour and salt into a bowl and stir in sugar. Put butter and water into a pan and heat gently till butter melts. Bring to the boil, then pour into flour mixture and mix to a soft dough.

Quickly roll out two-thirds of dough and use to line a 7 inch (18 cm) springform cake tin. Pour fruit purée into pastry case. Roll out remaining dough and use to cover pie. Seal edges and crimp. Make a neat hole in centre. Decorate top with dough trimmings. Beat egg and brush over pie.

Bake for 1 hour till pastry is golden. Cool in the tin. Serve with pouring cream or ice cream.

Spicy rhubarb pie

Overall timing 1¾ hours

Freezing Not suitable

To serve 6–8

9 oz	Plain flour	250 g
	Pinch of salt	
¼ teasp	Mixed spice	1.25 ml
½ teasp	Ground cinnamon	2.5 ml
5 oz	Butter	150 g
2 tbsp	Caster sugar	2x15 ml
2 lb	Rhubarb	900 g
6 oz	Granulated sugar	175 g
1	Egg yolk	1

Sift flour, pinch of salt and spices into a bowl. Rub in the butter till the mixture resembles fine breadcrumbs. Stir in the caster sugar and enough water to make a soft but not sticky dough. Knead lightly till smooth, then chill for 30 minutes.

Meanwhile, trim the rhubarb and cut into 1 inch (2.5 cm) lengths. Put into a bowl with all but 1 tbsp (15 ml) of the granulated sugar and mix well.

Preheat the oven to 400°F (200°C) Gas 6. Place a baking tray on the shelf just above the centre to heat up.

Roll out half the dough on a floured surface and use to line a 9 inch (23 cm) pie plate. Brush the edge with water. Pile the rhubarb into the pie in a dome shape. Roll out remaining dough and cover the pie, sealing and crimping the edges.

Beat the egg yolk and brush over top of pie. Place pie on hot baking tray and bake for 20 minutes. Reduce the temperature to 350°F (180°C) Gas 4 and bake for a further 25 minutes till crisp and golden.

Remove from the oven, sprinkle remaining sugar over and serve immediately with cream or pouring custard.

Banana tart

Overall timing 1 hour 50 minutes

Freezing Not suitable

To serve 8

7 oz	Plain flour	200 g
½ teasp	Baking powder	2.5 ml
½ teasp	Salt	2.5 ml
3 tbsp	Caster sugar	3x15 ml
3½ oz	Butter	100 g
1	Medium egg	1
Filling		
3 oz	Seedless raisins *or*	75 g
2 oz	Stoned dates	50 g
2 tbsp	Rum	2x15 ml
4	Ripe bananas	4
2	Eggs	2
3 oz	Caster sugar	75 g
4 fl oz	Double cream	113 ml
2 oz	Split almonds	50 g

Sift flour, baking powder, salt and sugar into a bowl. Rub in butter. Add egg with a little water if necessary to bind to a dough. Chill for 1 hour.

Put raisins, or chopped dates, to steep in rum.

Preheat the oven to 400°F (200°C) Gas 6.

Roll out dough and use to line 9 inch (23 cm) fluted flan ring. Prick and bake blind for 10 minutes. Remove beans and paper, and bake for a further 5 minutes. Remove from oven.

Drain dried fruit, reserving rum. Peel bananas and cut in diagonal slices. Cover bottom of pastry case with the bananas and most of the dried fruit.

Whisk eggs and sugar together till pale and thick. Whip cream with reserved rum. Blend both mixtures together and pour over the fruit in pastry case. Scatter over almonds and reserved dried fruit.

Bake for 25 minutes until puffed, golden brown and set. Serve hot with single cream.

Sunburst peach tart

Overall timing 1 hour

Freezing Not suitable

To serve 6

3 oz	Butter	75 g
4 oz	Caster sugar	125 g
3	Eggs	3
5 oz	Plain flour	150 g
	Grated rind of 1 lemon	
14 oz	Can of sliced peaches	397 g
2 oz	Hazelnuts	50 g

Preheat the oven to 350°F (180°C) Gas 4.

Cream the butter and sugar together till pale and fluffy. Beat in the eggs one at a time, beating well between each addition. Fold in the sifted flour and lemon rind with a metal spoon. Pour the mixture into a greased and lined 8 inch (20 cm) springform tin and smooth the surface.

Drain the peaches thoroughly and arrange the slices in circles on the cake mixture. Sprinkle the chopped hazelnuts over. Bake for about 45 minutes.

Remove from the tin, place on a warmed serving dish and serve immediately with pouring custard or cream.

Plum tart

Overall timing 1¾ hours

Freezing Not suitable

To serve 6–8

12 oz	Self-raising flour	350 g
8 oz	Butter	225 g
3 tbsp	Caster sugar	3x15 ml
1	Egg	1
3–4 tbsp	Milk to mix	3–4x 15 ml
Filling		
1 pint	Milk	560 ml
1 teasp	Vanilla essence	5 ml
1½ lb	Ripe yellow plums	700 g
4	Egg yolks	4
6 oz	Caster sugar	175 g
3 oz	Plain flour	75 g

To make filling, put milk and vanilla essence into saucepan and bring to the boil. Remove from heat, cover and leave to infuse for 10 minutes.

Meanwhile halve and stone plums. Beat egg yolks with sugar till pale and thick. Beat in sifted flour, then gradually stir in milk. Pour back into saucepan and cook gently, stirring, till thick. Leave to cool.

Preheat the oven to 400°F (200°C) Gas 6.

Sift flour into a bowl and rub in 6 oz (175 g) butter. Stir in sugar, and add egg and enough milk to give a soft dough. Roll out and use to line greased 8 inch (20 cm) square deep cake tin, moulding it into the corners. Rest in refrigerator for 15 minutes.

Pour filling into pastry-lined tin and arrange plums on top, pressing them in lightly. Bake for 30 minutes.

Meanwhile, melt remaining butter in a saucepan. Remove tart from tin and place on a baking tray. Brush sides and top edge of pastry with butter and bake for a further 10 minutes till pastry is crisp and golden. Serve hot or cold.

Tarte Tatin

Overall timing 1¼ hours

Freezing Not suitable

To serve 8–10

7 oz	Frozen puff pastry	212 g
3 oz	Unsalted butter	75 g
3 oz	Caster sugar	75 g
7	Large dessert apples	7

Thaw the pastry. Preheat the oven to 425°F (220°C) Gas 7.

Cut the butter into pieces and put into a 9 inch (23 cm) round cake tin with the sugar. Peel and core the apples; cut six of them in half. Arrange the apple halves on end around the side of the tin and place the whole apple in the centre.

Place the tin over a low heat and heat till the butter melts. Increase the heat and cook, shaking the tin occasionally, till the sugar caramelizes and is golden. Remove from the heat. Brush a little water round the edge of the tin.

Roll out the dough on a floured surface to a 9 inch (23 cm) round and place over the apples. Press down lightly.

Bake for 25–30 minutes till the pastry is well risen and golden brown. Leave to cool in the tin for 5 minutes.

Run a knife round the edge of the tart and turn out on to a serving dish so that the caramelized apples are on top. Serve hot or cold with whipped cream or scoops of vanilla ice cream.

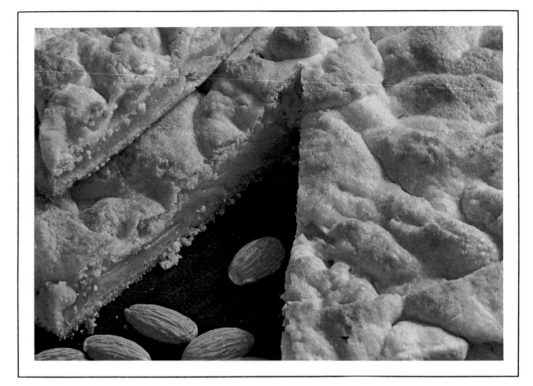

Almond marmalade tart

Overall timing 1¼ hours

Freezing Suitable

To serve 6–8

3½ oz	Butter	100 g
3½ oz	Caster sugar	100 g
1	Egg	1
4 oz	Ground almonds	125 g
5 oz	Self-raising flour	150 g
¼ teasp	Salt	1.25 ml
Filling		
12 oz	Cooking apples	350 g
	Juice of ½ lemon	
2 tbsp	Sugar	2x15 ml
6 tbsp	Fine-cut marmalade	6x15 ml
1 tbsp	Dried breadcrumbs	15 ml

Put butter, sugar and egg into a bowl and beat until light and fluffy. Add almonds, sifted flour and salt and mix to a soft, but not sticky dough. Chill for 30 minutes.

Meanwhile, peel and core apples. Slice thinly into a bowl and sprinkle with lemon juice. Stir in the sugar and marmalade and leave to stand till pastry is ready.

Preheat the oven to 400°F (200°C) Gas 6.

Put half the dough into a greased 8 inch (20 cm) sandwich tin and spread out to cover the bottom. Prick and sprinkle breadcrumbs over. Spread the apple mixture over and cover with small spoonfuls of remaining pastry.

Bake for about 35 minutes till golden. Remove from tin and serve hot or cold, cut into slices, with cream or custard.

Wholemeal bread

Overall timing 3 hours minimum

Freezing Suitable

Makes 2–4 loaves

1 tbsp	Brown sugar	15 ml
1½ pints	Lukewarm water	850 ml
1 oz	Dried yeast	25 g
3 lb	Wholemeal flour	1.4 kg
1 tbsp	Salt	15 ml
1 oz	Lard	25 g

Dissolve 1 teasp (5 ml) of the sugar in 9 fl oz (250 ml) of the warm water in a bowl. Sprinkle the dried yeast on top. Leave for about 10 minutes till frothy.

Mix flour, salt and the remaining sugar in a bowl. Rub in the lard, then add the yeast liquid and the rest of the water. Mix to scone-like dough. Knead the dough thoroughly till it feels firm and elastic and no longer sticky. This should take 5–10 minutes. Shape the dough into a ball and place in an oiled polythene bag. Leave to rise till doubled in size.

Turn the dough on to a board and knead again till firm. Divide into two or four and flatten each piece firmly with the knuckles to knock out air. Shape and place in loaf tins.

Brush the tops with a little salted water and put each tin into an oiled polythene bag. Leave to rise till the dough comes to just over the top of the tin and springs back when pressed with a floured finger – about 1 hour at room temperature.

Preheat the oven to 450°F (230°C) Gas 8. Bake the loaves for 30–40 minutes. Turn out to cool on a wire rack.

Brioche

Overall timing 1¼ hours plus proving

Freezing Suitable: shape dough and bake after thawing

Makes 1 large or 12 small

2 teasp	Caster sugar	2x5 ml
2 tbsp	Lukewarm water	2x15 ml
2 teasp	Dried yeast	2x5 ml
8 oz	Strong plain flour	225 g
	Salt	
2 oz	Butter	50 g
2	Eggs	2
	Milk for glazing	

Dissolve ½ teasp (2.5 ml) sugar in water and sprinkle yeast on top. Leave till frothy.

Sift flour, a pinch of salt and remaining sugar into a large bowl. Add yeast mixture, melted butter and eggs and mix to a soft dough. Knead till smooth and glossy. Leave to rise in a warm place till doubled in size.

Knock back dough and knead for 3–4 minutes till smooth. To make one large brioche, cut off one-quarter of the dough and shape both pieces into balls. Place large one in lightly greased 8 inch (20 cm) brioche tin and push a finger down through centre to base. Place smaller ball in indentation and press down lightly.

To make 12 small brioches, divide dough into 12 pieces and remove one-quarter from each. Shape all pieces into balls. Place each large ball in a 3 inch (7.5 cm) brioche tin, push a finger down through centre, then top with small balls, pressing down lightly. Leave to rise till doubled in size.

Preheat the oven to 450°F (230°C) Gas 8. Brush each brioche with milk and bake for 8–10 minutes (small) or 15–20 minutes (large) till well risen and golden. Serve warm.

Italian fruit bread

Overall timing 1½ hours plus proving

Freezing Suitable: reheat in 350°F (180°C) Gas 4 oven for 10 minutes

To serve 5

12 oz	Strong plain flour	350 g
4 teasp	Dried yeast	4x5 ml
2 oz	Caster sugar	50 g
¼ pint	Lukewarm milk	150 ml
¼ teasp	Salt	1.25 ml
2 oz	Pine nuts	50 g
2 oz	Candied peel	50 g
2 oz	Seedless raisins	50 g
2 oz	Butter	50 g
1	Egg	1
1 tbsp	Marsala	15 ml

Mix together 4 oz (125 g) flour, the yeast, 1 teasp (5 ml) sugar and the milk to a smooth batter. Leave till frothy.

Sift remaining flour and the salt into a large bowl. Add remaining sugar, the pine nuts, candied peel and raisins. Stir melted butter, beaten egg and Marsala into frothy batter, then add to fruit mixture. Mix to a soft dough. Turn out on to a lightly floured surface and knead till smooth and glossy. Cover with oiled polythene and leave to rise till doubled in size.

Knock back dough and knead till smooth. Shape into a smooth ball and place on greased baking tray. Leave to prove till doubled in size.

Preheat the oven to 400°F (200°C) Gas 6. Score a cross on top of the ball and bake for 10 minutes. Reduce the heat to 350°F (180°C) Gas 4 and bake for a further 25 minutes. Cool on a wire rack.

Caraway seed bread

Overall timing 1½ hours plus proving

Freezing Suitable: refresh in hot oven for 10 minutes

Makes 2 small or 1 large loaf

1 lb	Strong plain flour	450 g
1½ oz	Caster sugar	40 g
2 teasp	Dried yeast	2x5 ml
5 tbsp	Lukewarm water	5x15 ml
4 fl oz	Lukewarm milk	120 ml
1 teasp	Salt	5 ml
2 tbsp	Caraway seeds	2x15 ml
4 oz	Softened butter	125 g
2	Eggs	2
1 tbsp	Milk	15 ml

Mix together 4 oz (125 g) flour, 1 teasp (5 ml) sugar, the yeast, water and milk in a large bowl. Cover and leave in a warm place for about 20 minutes till frothy.

Mix remaining flour with salt, remaining sugar and caraway seeds. Add to yeast mixture with butter and beaten eggs. Mix well to a soft dough. Turn on to a lightly floured surface and knead till smooth and elastic. Cover and leave to rise until doubled in size.

Turn dough on to a lightly floured surface and knead till dough is firm again. Shape into two rolls about 6 inches (15 cm) long. Place on greased and floured baking tray. Make three cuts across top of each loaf. Brush with milk. Cover with polythene bag and leave to rise until loaves double in size.

Preheat the oven to 400°F (200°C) Gas 6. Bake the loaves for 30–35 minutes. Cool on a wire rack.

Milk buns

Overall timing About 3 hours

Freezing Suitable

Makes about 15

2 teasp	Dried yeast	2x5 ml
$\frac{1}{4}$ pint	Lukewarm milk	150 ml
9 oz	Plain flour	250 g
4 teasp	Caster sugar	4x5 ml
$\frac{1}{2}$ teasp	Salt	2.5 ml
$3\frac{1}{2}$ oz	Butter	100 g

Mix yeast, all but 2 tbsp (2x15 ml) milk, 2 oz (50 g) flour and 3 teasp (3x5 ml) sugar to make a batter. Leave till frothy.

Add rest of flour and salt to batter. Mix by hand to soft dough that leaves bowl clean. Knead till smooth and no longer sticky. Leave to rise for 1 hour in warm place.

Cut butter into small pieces. Make a hollow in dough and drop in a few pieces of butter. Knead or squeeze into dough. Continue adding butter in this way till dough becomes silky and smooth. Divide into egg-size pieces and shape into rolls. Place on greased baking tray. Lightly mark a cross on each. Leave to rise till doubled in size.

Preheat the oven to 375°F (190°C) Gas 5.

Heat remaining milk and sugar and brush over rolls. Bake for 30 minutes till golden brown. Cool on wire rack.

Fruit and nut bread

Overall timing 35 minutes plus rising

Freezing Suitable

Makes 1 loaf

7 fl oz	Lukewarm milk	200 ml
4 teasp	Dried yeast	4x5 ml
$2\frac{1}{2}$ oz	Caster sugar	65 g
1 lb	Strong plain flour	450 g
1 teasp	Salt	5 ml
4 oz	Butter	125 g
2 oz	Stoned prunes	50 g
2 oz	Dried figs	50 g
2 oz	Sultanas	50 g
4 oz	Mixed nuts	125 g
1	Egg	1
1 tbsp	Icing sugar	15 ml

Mix $\frac{1}{4}$ pint (150 ml) milk with yeast and 1 teasp (5 ml) sugar. Leave till frothy.

Sift flour and salt into a large bowl. Add yeast mixture, melted butter, remaining sugar, chopped fruit and nuts and remaining milk. Mix to a soft dough. Leave to rise till doubled in size.

Knead until smooth. Shape into a rectangle and place in 2 lb (900 g) loaf tin. Leave to prove until doubled in size.

Preheat the oven to 425°F (225°C) Gas 7. Brush top of loaf with lightly beaten egg and bake for 15 minutes. Cover top with grease-proof paper and reduce heat to 400°F (200°C) Gas 6. Bake for further 20–30 minutes. Dredge with icing sugar and serve warm.

Sesame bread

Overall timing 2 hours plus proving

Freezing Suitable

Makes 2 loaves

6	Saffron strands	6
¼ pint	Lukewarm milk	150 ml
4 fl oz	Lukewarm water	120 ml
1 tbsp	Dried yeast	15 ml
4 teasp	Caster sugar	4x5 ml
1 lb	Strong plain flour	450 g
2 oz	Butter	50 g
2	Eggs	2
½ teasp	Salt	2.5 ml
2 tbsp	Sesame seeds	2x15 ml

Mix together saffron, all but 2 tbsp (2x15 ml) milk, the water, yeast, 1 teasp (5 ml) sugar and 2 tbsp (2x15 ml) flour. Leave in a warm place till frothy.

Melt butter and cool, then beat into batter with one egg and the remaining milk and sugar. Sift remaining flour and the salt over batter and mix to a soft dough. Knead till smooth. Leave to rise till doubled in size.

Knock back the dough. Knead till smooth and divide into six pieces. Roll into sausages about 9 inches (23 cm) long. Moisten ends of sausages with beaten egg. Plait three together, pinching together at both ends to seal. Repeat with remaining three sausages and arrange on greased baking tray. Leave to rise till doubled in size.

Preheat the oven to 375°F (190°C) Gas 5. Brush plaits carefully with beaten egg, then sprinkle with sesame seeds. Bake for about 35 minutes. Cool on wire rack.

Quick cottage loaf

Overall timing 1½ hours

Freezing Suitable

Makes 1 loaf

1 oz	Fresh yeast	25 g
12 fl oz	Lukewarm water	350 ml
1 tablet	Vitamin C	25 mg
1¼ lb	Strong plain flour	600 g
2 teasp	Salt	2x5 ml
1 teasp	Sugar	5 ml
½ oz	Lard	15 g

Blend the fresh yeast with the warm water. Crush vitamin tablet and add to the yeast liquid.

Sift the flour, salt and sugar into a bowl and rub in lard. Add the yeast liquid and mix to a dough that leaves the bowl clean. Turn the dough on to a lightly floured surface and knead till smooth and elastic.

To shape dough into a cottage loaf, divide it into two pieces with one about a third bigger than the other. Shape both into rounds and place smaller one on top. Press handle of wooden spoon through centre of both pieces. Place on baking tray and cover with oiled polythene. Leave to rise for 40–50 minutes.

Preheat the oven to 450°F (230°C) Gas 8. Dust loaf with flour and bake for 30–35 minutes.

Soda bread

Overall timing 1 hour

Freezing Suitable: bake after thawing

Makes 1 loaf

1 lb	Strong white or white and wholemeal flour	450 g
1 teasp	Salt	5 ml
2 teasp	Bicarbonate of soda	2x5 ml
4 teasp	Cream of tartar	4x5 ml
1 oz	Fat	25 g
9 fl oz	Milk	250 ml

Preheat the oven to 425°F (220°C) Gas 7.

Sift the flour, salt, soda and cream of tartar into a bowl. Rub in the fat and add enough milk to make a soft dough. Knead for 1 minute, then shape into a ball and place on a greased baking tray. Mark with a cross, cutting almost to the base of the dough.

Bake for 40–50 minutes till well risen, lightly browned and firm underneath.

Spicy fruit bread

Overall timing 1½ hours plus proving

Freezing Suitable: reheat in 350°F (180°C) Gas 4 oven for 20 minutes

To serve 8

3 oz	Light soft brown sugar	75 g
¼ pint	Milk	150 ml
4 teasp	Dried yeast	4x5 ml
12 oz	Strong plain flour	350 g
½ teasp	Salt	2.5 ml
1 teasp	Ground cinnamon	5 ml
	Ground cloves	
3 oz	Softened butter	75 g
1	Egg	1
6 oz	Sultanas	175 g
2 oz	Currants	50 g

Dissolve ½ teasp (2.5 ml) sugar in all but 2 tbsp (2x15 ml) of the milk and sprinkle yeast on top. Leave in warm place till frothy.

Sift the flour, salt, cinnamon and a pinch of cloves into a large bowl. Add the yeast mixture, butter, egg, remaining sugar, the sultanas and currants. Mix to a soft dough. Knead the dough on a floured surface till glossy. Wrap in oiled polythene and leave to rise till doubled in size.

Turn the dough out on to a floured surface and knead till smooth. Shape into a thick sausage and place on a greased baking tray. Cover with oiled polythene and leave to prove till doubled in size.

Preheat the oven to 400°F (200°C) Gas 6. Brush the dough with the reserved milk and bake for about 40 minutes. Cool on a wire rack.

Cheese yeast cake

Overall timing 2½ hours

Freezing Suitable: reheat in 350°F (180°C) Gas 4 oven for 15–20 minutes, then add jam and almonds

To serve 16

8 oz	Plain flour	225 g
2 oz	Caster sugar	50 g
3 teasp	Dried yeast	3x5 ml
6 tbsp	Lukewarm milk	6x15 ml
1 oz	Softened butter	25 g
1	Egg	1
	Pinch of salt	
Topping		
2 oz	Butter	50 g
8 oz	Curd cheese	225 g
4 tbsp	Cold custard	4x15 ml
	Grated rind of 1 lemon	
1	Egg	1
4 oz	Caster sugar	125 g
1½ lb	Dessert apples	700 g
4 tbsp	Apricot jam	4x15 ml
2 oz	Flaked almonds	50 g

Mix together 2 oz (50 g) flour, 1 teasp (5 ml) sugar, yeast and milk. Leave till frothy.

Add remaining flour and sugar, the softened butter, egg and salt. Mix well to form a soft dough. Knead till smooth, then leave to rise for 30 minutes in a warm place.

Roll out dough and line bottom of greased 7x11 inch (18x28 cm) roasting tin.

Preheat oven to 400°F (200°C) Gas 6.

To make topping, melt butter and brush half over dough. Beat cheese with custard, lemon rind, egg and sugar. Spread evenly over dough. Peel, core and slice apples. Arrange on top of creamed mixture. Brush with remaining melted butter and bake for 45 minutes.

Remove cake from tin. Heat jam and spread over apples. Sprinkle with almonds and serve warm.

Danish pastries

Overall timing 2 hours including chilling

Freezing Suitable

Makes 15

1½ oz	Caster sugar	40 g
3 fl oz	Lukewarm milk	90 ml
1 teasp	Dried yeast	5 ml
9 oz	Plain flour	250 g
½ teasp	Salt	2.5 ml
6 oz	Butter	175 g
	Almond paste	
1	Egg	1
4 oz	Icing sugar	125 g

Dissolve 1 teasp (5 ml) sugar in milk and sprinkle yeast on top. Leave till frothy. Sift flour and salt into bowl, rub in ½ oz (15 g) butter and add rest of sugar and yeast mixture. Mix to a dough. Shape remaining butter into an oblong. Roll out dough into an oblong twice size of butter. Place butter in centre and wrap dough round.

Turn dough so folds are at sides. Roll into an oblong three times longer than it is wide. Fold bottom third up, top third down. Chill for 10 minutes. Repeat turning, rolling and chilling twice.

Roll out dough into oblong, 15x9 inches (38x23 cm), cut into 15 squares and shape as below:

Cockscombs: Put almond paste in centre of each and fold in half, sealing with beaten egg. Make cuts in folded edge, almost to cut edges; spread out in a fan shape. Envelopes: Put almond paste in centre of each and fold opposite corners to centre, securing tips with beaten egg. Windmills: Make diagonal cuts from each corner almost to centre. Place almond paste in centre and fold one corner of each triangle to it. Press firmly to secure. Arrange shapes on baking trays and prove for 20 minutes.

Preheat the oven to 425°F (220°C) Gas 7. Brush with beaten egg and bake for 18 minutes. Mix icing sugar with 2 tbsp (2x15 ml) water and trickle over hot pastries.

Bagels

Overall timing 1¼ hours plus proving and cooling

Freezing Suitable: refresh from frozen in 400°F (200°C) Gas 6 oven for 10 minutes

Makes 10

1 teasp	Caster sugar	5 ml
6 tbsp	Lukewarm water	6x15 ml
1 teasp	Dried yeast	5 ml
9 oz	Strong plain flour	250 g
1 teasp	Salt	5 ml
1	Egg	1
1 tbsp	Oil	15 ml
1	Egg yolk	1
1 teasp	Caraway seeds	5 ml
1 teasp	Poppy seeds	5 ml
1 teasp	Coarse salt	5 ml

Dissolve sugar in water and sprinkle yeast on top. Leave till frothy.

Sift flour and salt into a large bowl. Add egg, oil and yeast mixture. Mix to a soft dough. Knead till smooth and glossy. Leave to rise till doubled in size.

Knock back dough and knead till smooth. Divide into 10 equal portions and roll into sausage shapes about 7 inches (18 cm) long. Wrap sausage shapes round to make rings and pinch ends together to seal. Smooth joins by rocking dough on a floured surface. Arrange on a baking tray, cover with oiled polythene and leave to rise till almost doubled in bulk.

Preheat oven to 425°F (220°C) Gas 7.

Poach bagels, in batches, in boiling water for 2 minutes, turning them once. Remove from the pan with a draining spoon and arrange on a floured baking tray.

When all the bagels are ready, brush them with egg yolk. Sprinkle some with caraway seeds, some with poppy seeds and some with coarse salt. Bake for about 15 minutes till crisp and golden brown. Cool on a wire rack.

Chelsea buns

Overall timing 1 hour plus proving

Freezing Suitable

Makes 6

1 lb	Strong plain flour	450 g
7 tbsp	Caster sugar	7x15 ml
8 fl oz	Lukewarm milk	225 ml
4 teasp	Dried yeast	4x5 ml
4 oz	Butter	125 g
1	Egg	1
4 oz	Mixed dried fruit	125 g
1 teasp	Mixed spice	5 ml

Mix 4 oz (125 g) flour with 1 teasp (5 ml) sugar, 7 fl oz (200 ml) milk and the yeast to a smooth batter. Leave till frothy.

Sift remaining flour and 4 teasp (4x5 ml) sugar into a bowl and rub in 3 oz (75 g) butter. Add egg and yeast mixture and mix to a soft dough. Knead till smooth and glossy. Leave to rise till doubled in size.

Knock back dough and knead till smooth. Roll out to a 9 inch (23 cm) square. Brush remaining butter, melted, over dough. Mix all but 1 tbsp (15 ml) of remaining sugar with fruit and spice and sprinkle over dough. Roll up, then cut across into six thick slices. Arrange, cut sides up, in greased 9x6 inch (23x15 cm) roasting tin, leaving equal space between. Prove till slices join together.

Preheat oven to 375°F (190°C) Gas 5. Brush buns with remaining milk and sprinkle with remaining sugar. Bake for about 35 minutes till golden. Cool on wire rack.

Pretzels

Overall timing 1 hour plus proving

Freezing Suitable: reheat in 375°F (190°C) Gas 5 oven for 5–10 minutes

Makes about 30

½ teasp	Caster sugar	2.5 ml
7 fl oz	Lukewarm water	200 ml
2 teasp	Dried yeast	2x5 ml
10 oz	Strong plain flour	275 g
1 teasp	Salt	5 ml
1 teasp	Poppy seeds	5 ml
1 oz	Butter	25 g
2	Eggs	2
2 tbsp	Coarse salt	2x15 ml

Dissolve sugar in water and sprinkle yeast on top. Leave in warm place till frothy.

Sift flour and salt into a bowl and stir in poppy seeds, yeast mixture, melted butter and one egg. Mix to soft dough. Leave to rise till doubled in size.

Knead till smooth. Break off small pieces and tie into loose knots, tucking ends in. Arrange pretzels on greased baking trays. Leave to prove till doubled in size.

Preheat the oven to 400°F (200°C) Gas 6. Beat remaining egg and brush over pretzels. Sprinkle with coarse salt and bake for about 10 minutes till crisp and golden. Cool on wire rack.

Currant buns

Overall timing 2¼ hours

Freezing Suitable

Makes 12

1 lb	Strong plain flour	450 g
3 oz	Caster sugar	75 g
1 tbsp	Dried yeast	15 ml
11 fl oz	Lukewarm milk	325 ml
½ teasp	Salt	2.5 ml
1 teasp	Mixed spice	5 ml
4 oz	Currants	125 g
2 oz	Butter	50 g
1	Egg	1

Mix together 2 oz (50 g) flour, 1 teasp (5 ml) sugar, the yeast and ½ pint (300 ml) milk to a batter. Leave till frothy.

Sift remaining flour, salt and spice into a mixing bowl. Add currants, 2 oz (50 g) sugar, the yeast mixture, melted butter and egg. Mix to a soft dough. Knead till smooth and elastic. Leave to rise till doubled in size.

Knock back dough, then divide into 12 pieces. Knead each piece into a smooth bun. Place on baking trays, cover and leave to prove till doubled in size.

Preheat the oven to 375°F (190°C) Gas 5.

To make glaze, dissolve remaining sugar in rest of milk and brush lightly over the buns. Bake for 15–20 minutes. While still hot, brush with remaining glaze.

Jam doughnuts

Overall timing 3–3½ hours including rising

Freezing Suitable: reheat from frozen in 400°F (200°C) Gas 6 oven for 8 minutes

Makes 12

8 oz	Strong plain flour	225 g
2 teasp	Dried yeast	2x5 ml
5 tbsp	Caster sugar	5x15 ml
6 tbsp	Lukewarm milk	6x15 ml
¼ teasp	Salt	1.25 ml
1½ oz	Butter	40 g
1	Egg	1
	Oil for frying	
	Jam	

Mix together 2 oz (50 g) flour, the yeast, 2 teasp (2x5 ml) sugar and the milk to a batter. Leave till frothy.

Sift remaining flour and salt into bowl. Add yeast mixture, melted butter and beaten egg and mix to a soft dough. Knead till smooth and elastic. Leave to rise till doubled in size.

Knock back dough, divide into 12 and shape into balls. Leave to prove.

Heat the oil in a deep-fryer to 360°F (180°C). Press a deep hole in each dough ball and fill with about 1 teasp (5 ml) jam. Seal jam in well by pinching dough together. Deep fry for about 10 minutes. Drain on kitchen paper and roll in remaining sugar while still hot.

Lemon buns

Overall timing 1 hour plus cooling

Freezing Suitable: refresh in 400°F (200°C) Gas 6 oven for 10 minutes

Makes 12

2 oz	Caster sugar	50 g
5 tbsp	Lukewarm milk	5 x 15 ml
2 teasp	Dried yeast	2 x 5 ml
8 oz	Strong plain flour	225 g
	Salt	
	Grated rind of 2 lemons	
1	Egg	1
1	Egg yolk	1
2 oz	Butter	50 g

Dissolve $\frac{1}{2}$ teasp (2.5 ml) of the sugar in the milk and sprinkle the yeast on top. Leave in a warm place for 15 minutes till frothy.

Sift the flour and a pinch of salt into a bowl and stir in the remaining sugar and lemon rind. Add the yeast mixture, beaten egg and yolk and melted butter and mix to a stiff dough. Divide between greased 12-hole bun tray. Cover with oiled polythene and leave to rise in a warm place till doubled in size.

Preheat the oven to 375°F (190°C) Gas 5. Bake the buns for about 25 minutes till well risen. Cool on a wire rack.

Cherry and lemon loaf

Overall timing 1½ hours

Freezing Suitable

To serve 16

8 oz	Self-raising flour	225 g
	Pinch of salt	
4 oz	Butter	125 g
4 oz	Caster sugar	125 g
	Grated rind of 1 lemon	
1	Egg	1
4 fl oz	Milk	120 ml
4 oz	Glacé cherries	125 g

Preheat the oven to 350°F (180°C) Gas 4.

Sift all but 1 tbsp (15 ml) of flour and the salt into a bowl. Rub in butter until mixture resembles fine breadcrumbs. Stir in sugar and lemon rind. Make a well in centre and break in egg. Mix together, adding enough milk to give a soft consistency that won't drop unless flicked from the spoon. Coat cherries in reserved flour and fold into mixture.

Pour into greased and lined 2 lb (900 g) loaf tin and smooth surface. Bake for 45 minutes. Cover with greaseproof and bake for further 30 minutes. Cool on a wire rack.

Coffee ring cake

Overall timing 1½ hours

Freezing Suitable

To serve 16

5 oz	Butter	150 g
5 oz	Caster sugar	150 g
	Salt	
2	Large eggs	2
1	Orange	1
3 teasp	Instant coffee powder	3x5 ml
5 oz	Self-raising flour	150 g
¼ teasp	Ground cinnamon	1.25 ml
2 oz	Plain chocolate	50 g
Icing		
6 oz	Icing sugar	175 g
2 teasp	Instant coffee powder	2x5 ml
1 teasp	Cocoa	5 ml
2 tbsp	Hot water	2x15 ml
	Vanilla essence	

Preheat the oven to 325°F (170°C) Gas 3.

Cream butter with sugar and a pinch of salt till light and fluffy. Add eggs one at a time and beat well. Grate orange and add rind to bowl. Squeeze orange and mix 3 tbsp (3x15 ml) juice with the instant coffee. Sift flour and cinnamon and mix into the creamed mixture alternately with the orange/coffee mixture. Grate chocolate and fold in.

Spoon mixture into greased 8½ inch (22 cm) ring mould. Bake for 40–50 minutes. Cool on a wire rack.

To make the icing, sift icing sugar into bowl. Dissolve coffee and cocoa in hot water, then add to icing sugar with a few drops of vanilla essence and mix well. Pour over cooled cake and smooth surface with a knife.

Fatless sponge cake

Overall timing 1½ hours

Freezing Not suitable

To serve 8–10

4	Eggs	4
5 oz	Caster sugar	150 g
½ teasp	Vanilla essence	2.5 ml
2 oz	Plain flour	50 g
2 oz	Potato flour	50 g
1	Egg white	1

Preheat the oven to 350°F (180°C) Gas 4.

Separate eggs. Whisk the yolks with the sugar and vanilla essence in a bowl over a pan of hot water till mixture leaves a trail lasting 20 seconds when the beaters are lifted. Remove from the heat. Add the sifted flours and fold in with a wooden spatula or metal spoon.

Whisk egg whites till stiff. Add about one-quarter of the whites to the yolk mixture and stir in, then fold mixture into the remaining egg white with a metal spoon.

Turn mixture into greased and floured 9 inch (23 cm) fluted tin. Bake for 50 minutes to 1 hour or until top springs back when lightly pressed.

Tunisian fruit and nut cake

Overall timing 1¾ hours

Freezing Suitable

To serve 8

1 oz	Toasted hazelnuts	25 g
2 oz	Toasted pistachios	50 g
1	Orange	1
5	Eggs	5
8 oz	Caster sugar	225 g
4 oz	Dried breadcrumbs	125 g
2 oz	Plain flour	50 g
1 teasp	Baking powder	5 ml
½ teasp	Bicarbonate of soda	2.5 ml
½ teasp	Ground cinnamon	2.5 ml
4 oz	Sultanas	125 g

Preheat the oven to 350°F (180°C) Gas 4.

Chop the nuts finely. Finely grate rind from orange. Separate the eggs. Whisk the yolks with the sugar in a bowl over a pan of hot water till pale and thick.

Remove from the heat. Add orange rind, breadcrumbs, sifted flour, baking powder, bicarbonate of soda, cinnamon and nuts, and fold in with a metal spoon. Squeeze the orange and add 2 tbsp (2x15 ml) of the juice to the mixture with the sultanas. Whisk the egg whites till stiff but not dry and fold in carefully.

Pour mixture into greased and lined 9 inch (23 cm) springform tin. Bake for about 1 hour till firm and springy to the touch. Cool on a wire rack.

Whisky cake

Overall timing 2 hours plus cooling

Freezing Suitable

To serve 12

4 oz	Seedless raisins	125 g
4 tbsp	Whisky	4x15 ml
4 oz	Candied orange peel	125 g
	Grated rind of 1 orange	
6 oz	Butter	175 g
6 oz	Caster sugar	175 g
3	Eggs	3
4 oz	Plain flour	125 g
4 oz	Self-raising flour	125 g
¼ teasp	Ground cinnamon	1.25 ml

Preheat the oven to 350°F (180°C) Gas 4.

Soak the raisins in the whisky. Chop the candied peel and add to the raisins with the orange rind. Mix well and leave to soak for 10 minutes.

Cream the butter with the sugar till pale and fluffy. Beat the eggs and add, a little at a time, to the creamed mixture, beating well between each addition. Sift the flours and cinnamon over, add the fruit and soaking liquid and fold into the mixture with a metal spoon.

Spread the mixture in a greased and lined 8 inch (20 cm) round cake tin, smooth the surface and make a slight hollow in the centre. Bake for 1¼–1½ hours till a skewer inserted in the cake comes out clean. Allow to cool slightly in the tin, then transfer to a wire rack and leave to cool completely.

Moist date and ginger cake

Overall timing 1¼ hours

Freezing Suitable

To serve 12

8 oz	Stoned dates	225 g
1 teasp	Bicarbonate of soda	5 ml
¼ pint	Boiling water	150 ml
4 oz	Butter	125 g
4 oz	Soft dark brown sugar	125 g
2 tbsp	Black treacle	2x15 ml
1 tbsp	Golden syrup	15 ml
2	Eggs	2
8 oz	Self-raising flour	225 g
2 teasp	Ground ginger	2x5 ml
2 tbsp	Icing sugar	2x15 ml

Preheat the oven to 350°F (180°C) Gas 4.

Chop the dates and place in a small bowl. Sprinkle with bicarbonate of soda, then pour on the boiling water. Leave to cool.

Cream the butter with the sugar till light and fluffy. Beat in the black treacle and syrup, then the eggs, one at a time, beating well. Sift in the flour and ginger, and add the dates and soaking liquid. Stir till well blended.

Pour into a greased and lined 9 inch (23 cm) round cake tin. Bake for 50–60 minutes till the centre of the cake springs back when lightly pressed. Cool on a wire rack. Dredge with icing sugar before serving.

Sultana loaf cake

Overall timing 1½ hours

Freezing Suitable

To serve 16

8 oz	Self-raising flour	225 g
	Salt	
1 teasp	Ground ginger	5 ml
4 oz	Butter	125 g
2 oz	Caster sugar	50 g
6 oz	Sultanas	175 g
2 tbsp	Clear honey	2x15 ml
1	Egg	1
7 tbsp	Milk	7x15 ml

Preheat the oven to 350°F (180°C) Gas 4.

Sift the flour, a pinch of salt and the ginger into a large bowl. Rub in butter till the mixture resembles fine breadcrumbs. Stir in the sugar and sultanas. Make a well in the centre and add the honey, egg and half the milk. Mix together, adding the remaining milk if necessary to give a soft dropping consistency.

Spread the mixture in a greased and lined 2 lb (900 g) loaf tin and smooth the surface. Bake for 45 minutes. Cover the top lightly with foil and bake for a further 30 minutes till the loaf is springy when lightly pressed. Cool on a wire rack.

Marble ring cake

Overall timing 1½ hours

Freezing Suitable

To serve 10

4 oz	Butter	125 g
5 oz	Caster sugar	150 g
3	Eggs	3
7 oz	Self-raising flour	200 g
5 tbsp	Milk	5x15 ml
1 oz	Cocoa powder	25 g

Preheat the oven to 350°F (180°C) Gas 4.

Cream the butter with the sugar till mixture is pale and fluffy. Beat in the eggs, one at a time. Divide the mixture into two. Sift 4 oz (125 g) of the flour into one-half and fold in with 3 tbsp (3x15 ml) of the milk.

Sift the rest of the flour and the cocoa into the other half of the mixture and fold in with the remaining milk.

Spread a little of the plain mixture over the bottom and sides of a greased and floured 7½ inch (19 cm) ring mould. Carefully spread a thin layer of the chocolate mixture over the plain layer. Repeat the careful layering until both mixtures are used up.

Bake for 1 hour till well risen and firm to the touch. Cool cake slightly in the mould before turning out on to a wire rack to cool completely.

Swiss roll

Overall timing 30 minutes plus cooling

Freezing Suitable: fill after thawing

Makes 2

3	Large eggs	3
3 oz	Caster sugar	75 g
$\frac{1}{4}$ teasp	Vanilla essence	1.25 ml
3 oz	Plain flour	75 g
	Pinch of salt	
1 tbsp	Warm water	15 ml
4 tbsp	Jam	4x15 ml

Preheat the oven to 400°F (200°C) Gas 6.

Separate the eggs. Whisk yolks with the sugar and vanilla in a bowl over a pan of hot water till mixture forms trails when beaters are lifted. Remove from heat. Sift flour and fold into mixture.

Whisk the whites with salt till mixture forms soft peaks that curl downwards. Fold into yolk mixture with a metal spoon, then fold in warm water. Place mixture in greased and lined Swiss roll tin, spreading to sides. Bake for 12–15 minutes till sides of sponge shrink a little.

Turn out sponge on to sheet of greaseproof paper sprinkled with caster sugar. Carefully peel away paper from sponge. Trim edges of sponge with a sharp knife.

Working quickly, spread jam over sponge. With the help of the greaseproof, roll up sponge away from you. Place seam-side down on wire rack to cool.

Caramel ring cake

Overall timing 1¼ hours

Freezing Suitable: ice cake after thawing

To serve 12

4 oz	Butter	125 g
6 oz	Soft brown sugar	175 g
1 tbsp	Golden syrup	15 ml
2	Eggs	2
6 oz	Self-raising flour	175 g
1 teasp	Ground cinnamon	5 ml
	Pinch of salt	
¼ teasp	Bicarbonate of soda	1.25 ml
3 fl oz	Milk	90 ml
	Vanilla essence	
Icing		
1 oz	Butter	25 g
2 tbsp	Golden syrup	2x15 ml
1 tbsp	Milk	15 ml
1 teasp	Vanilla essence	5 ml
8 oz	Icing sugar	225 g
1 tbsp	Ground cinnamon	15 ml

Preheat oven to 350°F (180°C) Gas 4.

Cream butter with sugar; beat in eggs and syrup. Sift in flour, cinnamon and salt and beat well. Mix soda with milk and a few drops of vanilla essence and add to mixture. Place in a greased and floured 9½ inch (24 cm) ring tin and bake for 45–50 minutes. Cool on wire rack.

For the icing, heat butter and golden syrup in saucepan. Stir in milk and essence and remove from heat. Sift half of icing sugar and the cinnamon into saucepan and stir well. Stir in rest of sifted sugar.

Pour icing over cake and smooth with spatula dipped in hot water.

Chocolate ring cake

Overall timing 1½ hours plus cooling

Freezing Suitable: ice and decorate after thawing

To serve 15–20

4 oz	Butter	125 g
5 oz	Caster sugar	150 g
	Pinch of salt	
	Grated rind of 1 lemon	
4	Eggs	4
1 tbsp	Rum	15 ml
5 oz	Plain flour	150 g
2 oz	Cornflour	50 g
1 teasp	Baking powder	5 ml
Chocolate filling		
6 oz	Unsalted butter	175 g
2 oz	Icing sugar	50 g
2 tbsp	Cocoa powder	2x15 ml

Icing and decoration

8 oz	Cooking chocolate	225 g
½ oz	Butter	15 g
1 oz	Nuts	25 g
15–20	Glacé cherries	15–20

Preheat the oven to 350°F (180°C) Gas 4.

Cream butter with sugar, then beat in salt, grated rind, eggs and rum. Sift flour, cornflour and baking powder together and fold into creamed mixture. Spoon into greased 9 inch (23 cm) ring mould and bake for 55 minutes. Cool on a wire rack.

To make the filling, cream butter with sugar and cocoa powder. Cut cake into three or four thin layers and sandwich together with filling, saving some to decorate the top.

Melt chocolate and spread over cake. Melt butter and cook chopped nuts till golden. Sprinkle round the bottom edge of the chocolate. Pipe remaining chocolate filling in swirls on cake. Add cherry to each.

Cocoa Madeira cake

Overall timing 1 hour 20 minutes

Freezing Suitable

To serve 10

6 oz	Butter	175 g
6 oz	Caster sugar	175 g
3	Eggs	3
4 oz	Self-raising flour	125 g
2 oz	Cocoa powder	50 g
	Pinch of salt	
3 tbsp	Madeira	3x15 ml
2 tbsp	Milk	2x15 ml
2 oz	Walnuts	50 g

Preheat the oven to 350°F (180°C) Gas 4.

Cream the butter with the sugar till light and fluffy. Beat the eggs and add to creamed mixture a little at a time, beating well after each addition. Sift together the flour, cocoa and salt. Add to creamed mixture a little at a time, alternating with the Madeira and milk. When the mixture is smooth and will flick easily from the spoon, fold in half the chopped walnuts.

Put mixture into greased and lined 7 inch (18 cm) round cake tin and smooth top. Bake for 45 minutes. Sprinkle with remaining walnuts and bake for further 15–20 minutes till skewer inserted into cake comes out clean. Cool on a wire rack.

Honey spice loaf

Overall timing 1 hour 20 minutes

Freezing Suitable

To serve 16

4 oz	Caster sugar	125 g
5 tbsp	Water	5x15 ml
8 oz	Honey	225 g
8 oz	Rye flour	225 g
	Salt	
1½ teasp	Bicarbonate of soda	7.5 ml
¼ teasp	Ground cloves	1.25 ml
½ teasp	Ground cinnamon	2.5 ml
¼ teasp	Ground mace	1.25 ml
2 teasp	Ground aniseed	2x5 ml
4 tbsp	Ground almonds	4x15 ml
½ teasp	Almond essence	2.5 ml
4 oz	Glacé fruits	125 g

Preheat the oven to 325°F (170°C) Gas 3.

Put the sugar and water into a saucepan and heat gently till sugar is dissolved. Pour into a large bowl, add the honey and beat for 2 minutes. Sift the flour, a pinch of salt, the bicarbonate of soda and spices into the mixture. Add the almonds and essence and beat for 4–5 minutes.

Cut the glacé fruits into pieces and stir into the mixture. Spread in a greased and lined 2 lb (900 g) loaf tin and smooth the top. Bake for about 55 minutes till a skewer inserted in the centre comes out clean. Cool in the tin for 10 minutes, then turn out on to a wire rack and leave to cool completely. Cut into slices to serve.

Lemon and cardamom cake

Overall timing 1¼–1½ hours

Freezing Suitable

To serve 8

8 oz	Self-raising flour	225 g
1 teasp	Ground cardamom	5 ml
4 oz	Butter	125 g
4 oz	Caster sugar	125 g
1	Lemon	1
1	Egg	1
2 tbsp	Milk	2x15 ml
1 oz	Flaked almonds	25 g
½ teasp	Ground cinnamon	2.5 ml

Preheat the oven to 350°F (180°C) Gas 4.

Sift flour and cardamom into a large bowl. Rub in the butter till mixture resembles fine breadcrumbs. Stir in all but 1 teasp (5 ml) of the sugar. Grate the lemon rind and squeeze out the juice. Add both to bowl with the egg. Gradually mix ingredients, adding enough milk to give a soft consistency that won't drop unless flicked from the spoon.

Put mixture into greased and lined 7 inch (18 cm) round cake tin and smooth the surface. Mix together the almonds, cinnamon and reserved sugar and sprinkle over cake. Bake for 1–1¼ hours till cake comes away from the sides. Cool in tin for a few minutes, then turn out on to a wire rack and cool completely.

Lemon shortcake

Overall timing 1 hour

Freezing Suitable

To serve 8

1	Lemon	1
8 oz	Plain flour	225 g
	Salt	
3 oz	Caster sugar	75 g
3 oz	Butter	75 g
1	Egg	1

Preheat the oven to 375°F (190°C) Gas 5.

Grate the rind of the lemon and squeeze out the juice. Sift the flour and a pinch of salt into a mixing bowl and stir in the sugar. Add the melted butter, egg, grated lemon rind and 2 tbsp (2x15 ml) lemon juice. Mix well and knead lightly until the mixture is smooth.

Roll out on a floured surface to fit a greased 8 inch (20 cm) sandwich tin or flan ring. Bake for 20 minutes till golden. Cool in the tin.

Yogurt cake

Overall timing 2 hours

Freezing Suitable

To serve 10

5 oz	Carton of natural yogurt	141 g
10 oz	Caster sugar	275 g
10 oz	Plain flour	275 g
1 tbsp	Baking powder	15 ml
	Salt	
2	Eggs	2
5 tbsp	Corn oil	5x15 ml
2 tbsp	Rum	2x15 ml
1 tbsp	Icing sugar	15 ml

Preheat the oven to 350°F (180°C) Gas 4.

Pour the yogurt into a large bowl and beat in the sugar. Sift the flour and baking powder with a pinch of salt. Beat together the eggs, oil and rum and add to the yogurt alternately with the flour mixture, beating till smooth.

Pour the mixture into a greased and lined 7 inch (18 cm) round cake tin. Bake for $1\frac{3}{4}$ hours, covering the top lightly with foil after 45 minutes, till a skewer inserted in the centre comes out clean. Cool on a wire rack.

Sift the icing sugar over the cake and mark the top into 10 slices. Serve with cherry jam.

Gingerbread

Overall timing 1¼ hours

Freezing Suitable

Makes 9

8 oz	Plain flour	225 g
1 teasp	Bicarbonate of soda	5 ml
1½ teasp	Ground ginger	7.5 ml
2 oz	Black treacle	50 g
4 oz	Golden syrup	125 g
3 oz	Butter	75 g
2 oz	Soft brown sugar	50 g
2	Eggs	2
2 tbsp	Milk	2x15 ml

Preheat the oven to 325°F (170°C) Gas 3.

Sift flour, soda and ginger into a bowl. Place treacle and golden syrup in a saucepan with butter and brown sugar. Heat till melted.

Beat eggs and milk. Add with melted ingredients to dry ingredients. Mix to a thick batter. Pour into a greased and lined 7 inch (18 cm) square tin. Bake for 1 hour.

Golden fruit cake

Overall timing 2 hours

Freezing Suitable

To serve 8–10

4 oz	Butter	125 g
4 oz	Caster sugar	125 g
2	Eggs	2
8 oz	Self-raising flour	225 g
	Pinch of salt	
2 oz	Glacé cherries	50 g
3 oz	Sultanas	75 g
2 oz	Candied peel	50 g
1–2 tbsp	Water	1–2 x 15 ml

Preheat the oven to 400°F (200°C) Gas 6.

Cream butter with sugar till light and fluffy. Add the eggs, one at a time, beating between each addition. Stir in the flour, salt, fruit and peel. Mix well, then add enough water to make a soft, but not sticky, dough.

Pour mixture into greased and lined 1 lb (450 g) loaf tin. Bake for 30 minutes, then lower oven temperature to 350°F (180°C) Gas 4 and bake for a further 1 hour. Cover with a piece of foil if the top begins to turn brown too quickly. Cool on a wire rack.

Hazelnut and honey cake

Overall timing 1¼ hours

Freezing Suitable

To serve 8

6 oz	Butter	175 g
4 oz	Light brown sugar	125 g
4 tbsp	Clear honey	4x15 ml
2	Whole eggs	2
2	Egg yolks	2
8 oz	Wholemeal self-raising flour	225 g
	Pinch of salt	
4 oz	Toasted hazelnuts	125 g
4 tbsp	Milk	4x15 ml

Preheat the oven to 350°F (180°C) Gas 4.

Cream the butter with the sugar and honey, then beat in the whole eggs and yolks. Fold in sifted flour, salt and chopped hazelnuts alternately with the milk.

Put mixture into a greased and lined 7 inch (18 cm) round cake tin. Bake for 1 hour until springy to the touch. Cool on wire rack. Coat with a fudgy icing if a more elaborate cake is desired.

Nutty honey cake

Overall timing 1 hour

Freezing Not suitable

To serve 8–10

6 oz	Butter	175 g
3 oz	Clear honey	75 g
5 oz	Plain flour	150 g
5 oz	Wholemeal flour	150 g
Filling		
4 oz	Mixed nuts	125 g
2 oz	Sultanas	50 g
1 teasp	Ground cinnamon	5 ml
	Clear honey	

Preheat the oven to 350°F (180°C) Gas 4.

Cream butter with honey till light and fluffy. Mix in sifted flours to make a dough. Roll out half dough on a floured surface and press into greased and lined 7 inch (18 cm) round tin.

Chop nuts and mix with sultanas and cinnamon. Bind with honey. Spread filling over dough in tin.

Roll out remaining dough and cover filling. Press edges to seal. Bake for 30–40 minutes till golden. Cool in the tin.

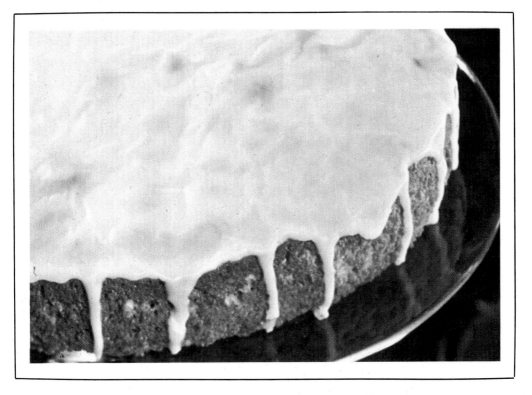

Orange and almond sponge

Overall timing 1 hour plus cooling

Freezing Suitable: ice after thawing

To serve 10

1	Large orange	1
5	Eggs	5
5 oz	Caster sugar	150 g
3½ oz	Self-raising flour	100 g
	Pinch of salt	
¼ teasp	Ground ginger	1.25 ml
½ teasp	Ground cinnamon	2.5 ml
5 oz	Ground almonds	150 g
	Almond essence	
5 oz	Icing sugar	150 g
1 tbsp	Curaçao	15 ml

Preheat the oven to 400°F (200°C) Gas 6.

Grate the rind from the orange and squeeze out the juice. Separate the eggs. Whisk egg yolks with the sugar till the mixture is pale and thick. Sift the flour, salt and spices over the mixture and add the ground almonds, three drops of essence, orange rind and 3 tbsp (3x15 ml) of the orange juice. Fold in gently.

Whisk the egg whites till stiff and fold into the mixture with a metal spoon. Carefully pour mixture into a greased and lined 9 inch (23 cm) cake tin and smooth the surface. Bake for about 35 minutes till springy to the touch. Cool on a wire rack.

Sift the icing sugar into a bowl and add the Curaçao and 1 tbsp (15 ml) of the remaining orange juice to make an icing that will coat the back of the spoon. Pour the icing on to the top of the cake. Lift the wire rack and tap it several times on the working surface so that the icing flows over the cake and trickles down the sides. Leave to set.

Praline-topped lemon cake

Overall timing 1½ hours

Freezing Suitable

To serve 8

4 oz	Butter	125 g
5 oz	Caster sugar	150 g
4	Eggs	4
5 oz	Plain flour	150 g
3 oz	Cornflour	75 g
2 teasp	Baking powder	2x5 ml
2 tbsp	Grated lemon rind	2x15 ml
2 oz	Almonds	50 g
Buttercream		
5 oz	Butter	150 g
5 oz	Icing sugar	150 g
1	Egg yolk	1
2 tbsp	Lemon juice	2x15 ml

Preheat the oven to 350°F (180°C) Gas 4.

Cream butter with 4 oz (125 g) sugar till light and fluffy. Separate eggs and beat egg yolks into creamed mixture. Sift flour, cornflour and baking powder together and fold into creamed mixture with lemon rind. Whisk egg whites till stiff and fold in.

Pour into greased and lined 8 inch (20 cm) cake tin and smooth surface. Bake for 50–60 minutes till top springs back when lightly pressed. Cool on wire rack.

Melt remaining sugar with 1 teasp (5 ml) water in a heavy-based saucepan. Boil until caramelized to a pale golden colour. Add chopped almonds and mix well. Spread on to a greased baking tray. Allow to cool and set hard, then break praline into tiny pieces with a rolling-pin.

To make buttercream, cream butter with sifted icing sugar till soft, then beat in egg yolk and lemon juice.

Cut cake into three layers and sandwich together with most of buttercream. Spread remainder on top and lightly press in praline.

Fresh cherry cake

Overall timing 1½ hours

Freezing Suitable

To serve 8

6	Digestive biscuits	6
1¾ lb	Fresh cherries	750 g
3 oz	Ground almonds	75 g
9 oz	Caster sugar	250 g
½ teasp	Ground cinnamon	2.5 ml
5	Eggs	5
2 tbsp	Kirsch	2x15 ml
1	Lemon	1
4 oz	Plain flour	125 g

Preheat the oven to 350°F (180°C) Gas 4.

Crush the biscuits and sprinkle over the bottom and sides of an oiled 10 inch (25 cm) cake tin.

Stone cherries. Arrange over the bottom of the coated cake tin.

Mix together the almonds, 2 oz (50 g) of the sugar and the cinnamon. Separate the eggs. Beat together the egg yolks, remaining sugar, Kirsch and grated rind and juice of the lemon. Stir in the almond mixture, then fold in the flour lightly. Whisk the egg whites till stiff and fold into the cake mixture using a metal spoon.

Spread the cake mixture over the cherries. Bake for 1 hour 10 minutes. Cool on a wire rack. Dredge with icing sugar before serving.

Spicy slab cake

Overall timing 1¼ hours

Freezing Suitable

To serve 12

10 oz	Butter	275 g
10 oz	Caster sugar	275 g
5	Eggs	5
10 oz	Self-raising flour	275 g
1 teasp	Ground ginger	5 ml
1 teasp	Ground cinnamon	5 ml
1 teasp	Grated nutmeg	5 ml
¼ teasp	Ground cloves	1.25 ml
8 oz	Stoned dates	225 g
4 oz	Walnuts	125 g
3 tbsp	Milk	3 x 15 ml

Preheat the oven to 350°F (180°C) Gas 4.

Cream the butter with the sugar till pale and fluffy. Beat the eggs lightly with a fork, then gradually beat into the creamed mixture. Sift the flour and spices into the bowl, add the chopped dates and walnuts and fold in with a metal spoon, adding the milk to give a soft dropping consistency.

Spread the mixture in a greased and lined 12x9 inch (30x23 cm) tin and smooth the top. Bake for about 45 minutes till firm and a skewer inserted in centre comes out clean. Cool on a wire rack. Cut into squares to serve.

Queen of Sheba cake

Overall timing 2 hours plus cooling

Freezing Suitable

To serve 8

10 oz	Plain chocolate	275 g
6	Eggs	6
9 oz	Butter	250 g
9 oz	Honey	250 g
5 oz	Plain flour	150 g
1 tbsp	Oil	15 ml
4 oz	Hazelnuts	125 g
4 oz	Split almonds	125 g
1 tbsp	Chocolate vermicelli	15 ml
3 tbsp	Icing sugar	3x15 ml

Preheat the oven to 350°F (180°C) Gas 4.

Gently melt 9 oz (250 g) of the chocolate. Separate the eggs. Cream the butter with the honey, then beat in the chocolate and egg yolks. Add sifted flour, oil and chopped nuts and beat well. Whisk the egg whites till stiff and fold into the mixture.

Turn into a greased and lined 9 inch (23 cm) cake tin. Bake for 1½ hours.

Meanwhile, make curls from remaining chocolate: melt chocolate in saucepan and pour on to oiled marble slab or Formica surface. When chocolate has almost set but is not hard, scrape off thin slivers or curls with a knife. Chill.

Cool cake on a wire rack.

Sprinkle chocolate vermicelli over cake, then sift icing sugar around edge. Arrange the chocolate curls in the centre.

Sachertorte

Overall timing 1½ hours plus cooling

Freezing Not suitable

To serve 8

4 oz	Plain chocolate	125 g
4 oz	Unsalted butter	125 g
6 oz	Caster sugar	175 g
5	Eggs	5
3 oz	Ground almonds	75 g
4 tbsp	Self-raising flour	4x15 ml
½ pint	Carton of double or whipping cream	268 ml
	Hazelnuts	
Icing		
8 oz	Plain chocolate	225 g
4 oz	Butter	125 g

Preheat the oven to 400°F (200°C) Gas 6.

Melt chocolate with butter till smooth. Beat in the sugar. Separate eggs and gradually add yolks to chocolate mixture, beating well. Whisk egg whites till stiff. Gently fold whites into chocolate mixture, followed by ground almonds and flour. Divide mixture between two greased 8 inch (20 cm) sandwich tins and smooth top. Bake for 20–25 minutes. Cool on a wire rack.

Whip half cream till thick and use to sandwich together the cooled cakes.

To make icing, melt chocolate with butter in a bowl placed over a pan of hot water. Leave to cool for 20–30 minutes until of a coating consistency, then spread over top and sides of cake. Whip remaining cream and pipe large swirls around the edge of the cake. Decorate each swirl with a hazelnut.

Special honey sponge

Overall timing 35 minutes plus cooling

Freezing Suitable: fill and decorate after thawing

To serve 8

7 oz	Self-raising flour	200 g
1 oz	Cornflour	25 g
½ teasp	Baking powder	2.5 ml
3 oz	Icing sugar	75 g
4 oz	Butter	125 g
4 oz	Caster sugar	125 g
1 tbsp	Clear honey	15 ml
2	Large eggs	2
4 fl oz	Milk	120 ml
3 oz	Nuts	75 g
Filling and decoration		
2 oz	Butter	50 g
4 oz	Icing sugar	125 g
1 tbsp	Clear honey	15 ml
1 tbsp	Warm water	15 ml
2 oz	Blanched almonds and walnuts	50 g
4 fl oz	Carton of double cream	113 ml

Preheat the oven to 350°F (180°C) Gas 4.

Sift flour, cornflour, baking powder and icing sugar together. Cream butter with caster sugar and honey. Beat in eggs, then fold in flour mixture alternately with milk. Stir in chopped nuts. Divide between two greased 7 inch (18 cm) sandwich tins. Bake for 20 minutes. Cool on wire rack.

To make the filling, cream butter with icing sugar, honey and water. Spread on one cake, sprinkle with most of the chopped nuts, then place second cake on top. Whip cream until stiff. Spoon into piping bag fitted with large star nozzle and pipe decorative swirls around top of cake. Decorate with rest of nuts.

Italian nut and honey cake

Overall timing 1 hour

Freezing Not suitable

To serve 10

6 oz	Almonds	175 g
4 oz	Walnuts	125 g
8 oz	Chopped mixed peel	225 g
¼ teasp	Ground allspice	1.25 ml
½ teasp	Ground cinnamon	2.5 ml
1 teasp	Ground coriander	5 ml
5 oz	Plain flour	150 g
4 oz	Icing sugar	125 g
1 tbsp	Water	15 ml
5 oz	Clear honey	150 g

Preheat the oven to 425°F (220°C) Gas 7.

Spread the nuts on a baking tray and toast in the oven till golden. Remove from oven and roughly chop. Reduce oven temperature to 375°F (190°C) Gas 5.

Add chopped mixed peel, spices and flour to nuts and mix well together.

Reserve 1 tbsp (15 ml) of the icing sugar and put the rest in a heavy-based pan with the water and honey. Stir constantly over a low heat until bubbles appear on the surface. Remove from heat immediately. Gradually stir nut and fruit mixture into the syrup.

Turn into 8 inch (20 cm) loose-bottomed flan tin lined with rice paper and smooth surface with a wet knife blade. Sprinkle with reserved icing sugar. Bake for about 30 minutes. Mark into 10 portions and leave to cool in tin before cutting.

Mocha gâteau

Overall timing 1¼ hours

Freezing Suitable

To serve 12

2 teasp	Instant coffee	2x5 ml
4	Large eggs	4
4 oz	Caster sugar	125 g
4 oz	Plain flour	125 g
2 oz	Butter	50 g
2 oz	Milk chocolate flake	50 g
Filling and topping		
1 tbsp	Cornflour	15 ml
¼ pint	Milk	150 ml
3 tbsp	Caster sugar	3x15 ml
1 tbsp	Instant coffee	15 ml
1	Egg yolk	1
6 oz	Butter	175 g
3 oz	Icing sugar	75 g

Preheat the oven to 375°F (190°C) Gas 5.

Dissolve coffee in 1 tbsp (15 ml) water in large bowl over pan of hot water. Add eggs, sugar and pinch of salt and whisk till very thick. Remove bowl from pan. Sift flour and fold in alternately with melted butter. Pour into greased and lined 8 inch (20 cm) cake tin. Bake for 40 minutes. Cool on a wire rack.

To make filling, place cornflour in small saucepan and blend in milk. Add sugar and coffee and bring to the boil, stirring. Simmer for 2–3 minutes, stirring constantly. Remove from heat and cool slightly, then add egg yolk and beat well. Cook over gentle heat for 2 minutes, then remove from heat and leave to cool.

Beat butter with sifted icing sugar. Add cooled custard and beat to a smooth creamy consistency.

Cut sponge into two layers and sandwich back together with one-third of filling. Coat cake with remainder and decorate with crumbled flake.

Pear refrigerator cake

Overall timing 45 minutes plus 4 hours
chilling

Freezing Not suitable

To serve 6

1 pint	Water	560 ml
2 tbsp	Lemon juice	2x15 ml
3 oz	Granulated sugar	75 g
1	Vanilla pod	1
4	Large firm pears	4
4 oz	Softened butter	125 g
3 oz	Icing sugar	75 g
2 oz	Ground almonds	50 g
7 oz	Nice biscuits	200 g
2 tbsp	Kirsch	2x15 ml
2 oz	Chocolate cake covering	50 g
2 tbsp	Single cream	2x15 ml

Put water, lemon juice, granulated sugar and
vanilla pod into a saucepan and heat gently,
stirring till sugar dissolves. Bring to the boil.
Peel, core and quarter pears and add to the
syrup. Simmer gently for 10 minutes till transparent. Remove from the heat and leave to
cool in the syrup.

Cream butter with sifted icing sugar and
ground almonds. Crush biscuits and add to
mixture with the Kirsch.

Lift pears out of syrup and drain on kitchen
paper. Reserve syrup. Thinly slice pears and
fold into creamed mixture. Spoon into a 2 lb
(900 g) loaf tin lined with foil. Smooth top,
fold foil in over cake and put a weight on top.
Chill for at least 4 hours.

Melt chocolate in a bowl over a pan of hot
water. Remove from the heat and stir in 2 tbsp
(2x15 ml) pear syrup and the cream.

Remove cake from tin and place on a serving
dish. Spread warm chocolate icing over and
leave to set.

Refrigerator coffee cake

Overall timing 1½ hours

Freezing Suitable

To serve 12

6 oz	Butter	175 g
6 oz	Caster sugar	175 g
1 teasp	Vanilla essence	5 ml
3	Eggs	3
8 oz	Self-raising flour	225 g
	Pinch of salt	
4 tbsp	Milk	4x15 ml
12	Sugar coffee beans	12
1 oz	Flaked almonds	25 g
Coffee cream		
4	Eggs	4
10 oz	Granulated sugar	275 g
14 oz	Butter	400 g
2 tbsp	Coffee essence	2x15 ml

Preheat the oven to 350°F (180°C) Gas 4.

Cream butter with sugar till light and fluffy. Beat in vanilla essence and eggs. Sift flour and salt and add to mixture alternately with milk. Pour into greased and lined 2 lb (900 g) loaf tin. Bake for 35 minutes. Cool on a wire rack.

Lightly beat eggs in a saucepan. Add sugar and heat very gently till sugar has dissolved. Remove from heat and allow to cool, stirring occasionally. Cream butter, then gradually beat in cold egg mixture and coffee essence.

Cut the sponge cake into three layers and sandwich back together with some of the cream. Place cake on a piece of foil on a plate and coat top and sides with cream, saving a little for decoration. Chill for at least 1 hour till cream is firm.

Slide cake off foil onto plate. Mark with ridges, using a fork. Decorate with remaining cream, coffee beans and almonds.

Battenberg cake

Overall timing 1½ hours plus cooling

Freezing Suitable: add almond paste after thawing

To serve 10

8 oz	Butter	225 g
8 oz	Caster sugar	225 g
4	Eggs	4
8 oz	Self-raising flour	225 g
4 tbsp	Milk	4x15 ml
	Red food colouring	
3 tbsp	Apricot jam	3x15 ml
8 oz	Almond paste	225 g

Preheat the oven to 375°F (190°C) Gas 5. Grease and line Swiss roll tin, making pleat in paper down centre to divide in half lengthways.

Cream butter with sugar. Beat in eggs. Sift flour and fold into creamed mixture with milk. Spread half mixture into one side of tin. Add a few drops of food colouring to remaining mixture and spread into other half of tin. Bake for about 45 minutes.

Cut each cake in half lengthways. Warm jam and use to stick cake pieces together in chequerboard pattern. Spread jam over cake. Sprinkle caster sugar over working surface, roll out almond paste and wrap round cake. Crimp edges and make diamond pattern on top using a sharp knife.

Coffee cream torte

Overall timing 1½ hours plus chilling

Freezing Suitable: add cream after thawing

To serve 12

2 teasp	Instant coffee powder	2x5 ml
4	Large eggs	4
5 oz	Caster sugar	150 g
	Pinch of salt	
4 oz	Plain flour	125 g
2 oz	Butter	50 g
¼ pint	Strong black coffee	150 ml
2 tbsp	Rum or Tia Maria	2x15 ml
½ pint	Double cream	284 ml
1 oz	Icing sugar	25 g
12	Chocolate truffles	12

Preheat the oven to 375°F (190°C) Gas 5.

Dissolve coffee in 1 tbsp (15 ml) water in a bowl placed over a pan of hot water. Add eggs, 4 oz (125 g) sugar and salt and whisk till thick. Remove bowl from pan. Sift flour and fold in alternately with melted butter. Pour into greased and lined 8 inch (20 cm) cake tin and bake for 40 minutes.

Dissolve remaining sugar in black coffee and stir in rum or Tia Maria. Spoon over cake, then cool and chill.

Whip cream with icing sugar till stiff. Turn out cake on to serving plate. Spread over half cream. Decorate with remaining cream and truffles.

Banana and walnut gâteau

Overall timing 1 hour plus cooling

Freezing Not suitable

To serve 8–10

4	Large eggs	4
6 oz	Caster sugar	175 g
2 tbsp	Warm water	2x15 ml
4 oz	Plain flour	125 g
1 teasp	Baking powder	5 ml
2 tbsp	Milk	2x15 ml
2 oz	Butter	50 g
½ pint	Carton of double cream	284 ml
5	Large bananas	5
	Chopped walnuts	
	Walnut halves	

Preheat the oven to 375°F (190°C) Gas 5.

Separate eggs. Beat yolks with sugar and water till light and fluffy. Sift flour with baking powder and add to yolk mixture alternately with milk. Melt butter and add.

Whisk egg whites till stiff and fold into mixture. Spoon into a greased and lined 8 inch (20 cm) round deep cake tin. Bake for 30–35 minutes. Cool on a wire rack.

Whip the cream till thick. Peel and slice the bananas.

Cut the cake into three layers. Sandwich back together with most of the cream and banana slices and the chopped walnuts. Decorate the top with the rest of the cream and bananas and walnut halves. Serve immediately.

Chocolate log

Overall timing 40 minutes plus chilling

Freezing Not suitable

To serve 10–12

2	Eggs	2
1½ oz	Caster sugar	40 g
1 oz	Plain flour	25 g
1 oz	Cornflour	25 g
1 oz	Chopped pistachio nuts or angelica	25 g
Filling and icing		
3½ oz	Softened butter	100 g
7 oz	Icing sugar	200 g
7 oz	Plain chocolate cake covering	200 g
2 tbsp	Rum or brandy (optional)	2x15 ml

Preheat the oven to 400°F (200°C) Gas 6.

Separate eggs. Beat whites in a bowl with sugar till stiff peaks form. Beat yolks till pale, then fold into whites. Sift flour and cornflour into mixture and fold in gently. Spread mixture evenly in greased and lined 13½x9½ inch (34x24 cm) Swiss roll tin and bake for 10 minutes till lightly golden. Turn cake out on to tea-towel. Carefully peel off paper and roll up cake enclosing towel. Cool.

Cream butter with sugar. Melt chocolate and beat into creamed mixture with rum or brandy, if using.

Unroll cake and spread with half chocolate mixture. Roll up and place on a serving plate, seam underneath. Cover cake with remaining chocolate mixture. Make marks in chocolate icing with a fork so that it looks like bark. Sprinkle log with chopped pistachio nuts or angelica and chill before serving.

Christening cake

Overall timing 3 hours plus overnight chilling

Freezing Suitable: fill and ice after thawing

To serve 30

12	Eggs	12
12 oz	Caster sugar	350 g
14 oz	Plain flour	400 g
2 oz	Butter	50 g
4 oz	Ground almonds	125 g
1 lb	Sugared almonds	450 g
	Silver balls	
Filling		
5	Egg yolks	5
9 oz	Granulated sugar	250 g
5 tbsp	Water	5x15 ml
12 oz	Unsalted butter	350 g
Icing		
1 lb	Icing sugar	450 g
2	Egg whites	2

Preheat the oven to 375°F (190°C) Gas 5.

Make cake mixture in two batches. Beat half eggs and sugar till thick and pale. Sift half flour and fold into egg mixture with half melted butter and almonds. Pour into greased and lined sandwich tins, one 6 inch (15 cm) and one 10 inch (25 cm). Bake for 15–20 minutes for small cake and 30 minutes for large cake. Cool on a wire rack. Make second batch and bake in 7 inch (18 cm) tin and 9 inch (22 cm) tin, allowing 30–35 minutes.

To make filling, put egg yolks into a bowl and whisk well. Dissolve sugar in water in a saucepan. Boil for 2–3 minutes, without allowing it to colour. Pour hot syrup on to egg yolks, beating continuously. Cool, then gradually work in softened butter. Use to sandwich cake layers together and to secure cakes on top of each other, largest on bottom. Chill overnight.

To make icing, sift icing sugar into a large bowl, add egg whites and beat well. Add 1–2 tbsp (1–2x15 ml) hot water to give a coating consistency. Coat the entire cake with icing. Place on a serving dish. Decorate with sugared almonds and silver balls.

Christmas cake

Overall timing Cake: 2–2¼ hours. Icing: 30 minutes plus 24 hours standing

Freezing Not suitable

1¼ lb	Mixed dried fruit	600 g
2 oz	Candied peel	50 g
6 oz	Dark brown sugar	175 g
3 tbsp	Golden syrup	3 x 15 ml
4 oz	Butter	125 g
6 oz	Self-raising flour	175 g
6 oz	Plain flour	175 g
2 teasp	Bicarbonate of soda	2 x 5 ml
2 teasp	Mixed spice	2 x 5 ml
2	Large eggs	2
3 tbsp	Apricot jam	3 x 15 ml
12 oz	Almond paste	350 g
2	Egg whites	2
1 lb	Icing sugar	450 g
2 teasp	Lemon juice	2 x 5 ml
1 teasp	Glycerine	5 ml

Put fruit in saucepan with peel, sugar, syrup, butter and 8 fl oz (220 ml) water. Bring to the boil, then simmer for 3 minutes. Turn into a bowl and cool.

Preheat the oven to 325°F (170°C) Gas 3. Sift flours, soda and spice three times, then add to fruit mixture. Beat in eggs. Place in greased and lined 8 inch (20 cm) cake tin, making a slight depression in centre. Bake for about 1½–2 hours or till skewer inserted in centre comes out clean. Cool in tin.

To decorate cake, brush top and sides with warmed apricot jam. Roll out almond paste and use to cover top and sides. Smooth all seams.

Whisk egg whites to a fairly stiff foam. Gradually beat in sifted icing sugar and lemon juice. When icing forms little peaks when lifted up with a knife blade, mix in glycerine. Cover bowl and leave for 24 hours.

Beat icing gently. Spread over cake, flicking up into peaks with a knife blade. Leave to set for a week before cutting.

Frosted walnut cake

Overall timing 1¼ hours plus cooling

Freezing Suitable: fill and ice after thawing

To serve 10

6 oz	White vegetable fat	175 g
12 oz	Caster sugar	350 g
½ teasp	Vanilla essence	2.5 ml
9 oz	Plain flour	250 g
1 tbsp	Baking powder	15 ml
7 fl oz	Milk	200 ml
4	Egg whites	4
Frosting		
1 lb	Cube sugar	450 g
¼ teasp	Cream of tartar	1.25 ml
2	Egg whites	2
½ teasp	Vanilla essence	2.5 ml
2 oz	Chopped walnuts	50 g
10	Walnut halves	10

Preheat the oven to 350°F (180°C) Gas 4.

Cream fat with sugar and vanilla essence till fluffy. Sift flour, baking powder and a pinch of salt together and fold into creamed mixture alternately with milk. Whisk egg whites till stiff and fold in. Divide between three greased and lined 8 inch (20 cm) sandwich tins. Bake for 30–35 minutes. Cool on a wire rack.

To make frosting, put sugar, cream of tartar and 6 fl oz (170 ml) water in a saucepan and stir over a low heat till sugar dissolves. Stop stirring and bring to the boil. Boil to a temperature of 240°F (116°C).

Meanwhile, whisk egg whites till stiff. Pour syrup in a thin stream on to whites, whisking constantly till frosting stands in soft peaks. Whisk in vanilla essence. Fold chopped walnuts into one-quarter of frosting and use to sandwich cakes together. Spread remaining frosting over cake and decorate with walnut halves.

Chocolate pistachio gâteau

Overall timing 1 hour plus chilling

Freezing Not suitable

To serve 10

12 oz	Plain flour	350 g
	Pinch of salt	
9 oz	Butter	250 g
5 oz	Sugar	150 g
2	Egg yolks	2
Filling		
4 oz	Shelled pistachios	125 g
4	Egg whites	4
7 oz	Caster sugar	200 g
4 oz	Ground almonds	125 g
	Grated rind of $\frac{1}{2}$ lemon	
1 tbsp	Rum	15 ml
2 oz	Milk chocolate	50 g

Sift the flour and salt into a bowl and rub in the fat till the mixture resembles fine breadcrumbs. Stir in the sugar and egg yolks and mix to a soft dough. Chill for 30 minutes.

Preheat the oven to 400°F (200°C) Gas 6.

Divide the dough in half. Roll out and use to line two 9 inch (23 cm) sponge tins. Prick bottoms and bake blind for 15 minutes. Cool on a wire rack.

Reserve a few pistachios for decoration; finely chop the rest. Whisk the egg whites till soft peaks form. Gradually whisk in the sugar till the mixture is stiff and glossy. Fold the chopped nuts into the meringue with the ground almonds, grated lemon rind and rum. Spoon into the pastry cases. Place one pastry cake on a baking tray and invert the other on top. Return to the oven and bake for a further 15 minutes. Cool on a wire rack.

Melt the chocolate in a bowl over a pan of hot water. Spread over the top of the cake with a palette knife. Cut the reserved pistachios in half and arrange in a circle around the edge of the cake.

Brownies

Overall timing 45 minutes plus cooling

Freezing Suitable

Makes 30

4 oz	Plain dessert chocolate	125 g
4 oz	Unsalted butter	125 g
1 teasp	Vanilla essence	5 ml
4	Eggs	4
½ teasp	Salt	2.5 ml
14 oz	Caster sugar	400 g
4 oz	Plain flour	125 g
4 oz	Walnuts	125 g

Preheat the oven to 350°F (180°C) Gas 4.

Put chocolate into a bowl with the butter and vanilla essence and place over a pan of simmering water. Stir till melted, then remove bowl from pan and cool.

Whisk eggs and salt till pale and fluffy. Sprinkle the sugar on top and continue whisking till evenly mixed. Fold in the chocolate mixture with a metal spoon, then fold in the sifted flour and coarsely chopped nuts.

Pour into a greased and lined 9x13 inch (23x33 cm) tin and smooth the top. Bake for about 25 minutes till firm. Cool in the tin, then cut into squares. If serving as a dessert top the brownies with whipped cream.

Iced marzipan biscuits

Overall timing 1½ hours plus cooling

Freezing Not suitable

Makes 30

14 oz	Plain flour	400 g
7 oz	Caster sugar	200 g
	Pinch of salt	
1	Large egg	1
7 oz	Butter	200 g
Filling and icing		
8 oz	Marzipan	225 g
5½ oz	Icing sugar	165 g
1 tbsp	Rum	15 ml
	Lemon or almond essence	
4 oz	Apricot jam	125 g
2 tbsp	Water	2x15 ml

Sift flour, sugar and salt into a bowl. Add egg and butter, cut into small pieces. Quickly knead together to form a smooth dough. Chill for 30 minutes.

Preheat the oven to 350°F (180°C) Gas 4.

Roll out dough to ¼ inch (6 mm) thickness. Cut out small shapes with a pastry cutter and place on a greased baking tray. Bake for 15 minutes.

Meanwhile, knead marzipan, 2 oz (50 g) icing sugar, rum and a few drops of essence together. Roll out to ⅛ inch (3 mm) thickness on a board dusted with icing sugar. Cut out shapes using the same cutter as for the pastry.

Remove pastry shapes from oven and immediately spread thickly with jam. Sandwich a piece of marzipan between two hot biscuits. Work quickly – the hot biscuits and jam need to adhere to the marzipan. Lift off baking trays and place on wire rack.

To make icing, mix together remaining icing sugar, a little almond essence and water and use to coat the warm biscuits. Leave to dry and cool.

Date squares

Overall timing 1 hour

Freezing Suitable

Makes 12

1 lb	Stoned dates	450 g
3 tbsp	Water	3 x 15 ml
1 tbsp	Lemon juice	15 ml
7 oz	Self-raising flour	200 g
1 oz	Bran	25 g
4 oz	Butter	125 g
3 oz	Caster sugar	75 g
1	Egg	1
1 tbsp	Milk	15 ml

Preheat the oven to 350°F (180°C) Gas 4.

Chop dates and place in saucepan with water and lemon juice. Cook, stirring, till mixture is like a paste – about 5 minutes. Leave to cool.

Place flour and bran in mixing bowl. Rub in butter till mixture resembles breadcrumbs. Add 2 oz (50 g) of the sugar. Separate egg. Add yolk and milk to dough and knead till smooth.

Divide dough in half. Press one half over bottom of greased 9 inch (23 cm) square cake tin. Spread with date mixture. Roll out rest of dough and place on dates.

Lightly whisk egg white with a fork. Brush over top and sprinkle with remaining caster sugar. Bake for 30–35 minutes. Cut into squares while hot and leave in tin to cool before serving.

Duchesses

Overall timing 2 hours

Freezing Not suitable

Makes 12

2	Egg whites	2
4 oz	Caster sugar	125 g
2 oz	Ground hazelnuts	50 g
1 oz	Toasted hazelnuts	25 g
2 oz	Plain chocolate	50 g

Preheat the oven to 250°F (130°C) Gas ½.

Whisk the egg whites with half the sugar till stiff. Carefully fold in the ground nuts, then the remaining sugar. Spoon the mixture into a piping bag fitted with a plain wide nozzle. Pipe 1 inch (2.5 cm) wide fingers about 3 inches (7.5 cm) long on to a baking tray lined with rice paper. Sprinkle with chopped toasted hazelnuts and bake for 1½ hours.

Cut paper round fingers with a sharp knife, then remove from tray.

Melt the chocolate. Spread rice-papered sides of half the fingers with chocolate and join to remaining fingers. Leave to set.

Honey galettes

Overall timing 40 minutes plus chilling

Freezing Suitable: refresh in 375°F (190°C) Gas 5 oven for 5 minutes

Makes 8

6 oz	Self-raising flour	175 g
3½ oz	Butter	100 g
2 oz	Thick honey	50 g
1 tbsp	Caster sugar	15 ml
1	Lemon	1
1	Egg	1
	Granulated sugar	

Preheat the oven to 375°F (190°C) Gas 5.

Sift the flour into a mixing bowl. Make a well in the centre and add the softened butter, honey and caster sugar. Grate the rind from the lemon and add to the bowl with 1 tbsp (15 ml) of the juice. Separate the egg and add the yolk to the bowl. Mix well together with a wooden spoon until the mixture forms a ball and leaves the sides of the bowl clean. Chill for 30 minutes.

Divide mixture into eight and roll out each piece on a lightly floured surface to a round about ½ inch (12.5 mm) thick. Place on baking trays.

Whisk egg white lightly and brush over biscuits. Sprinkle each biscuit with 1–2 tbsp (1–2x15 ml) granulated sugar. Bake for about 15 minutes, then remove from trays and cool on wire rack.

Crunchy nut biscuits

Overall timing 1¼ hours

Freezing Suitable

Makes about 24

8 oz	Shelled hazelnuts	225 g
6 oz	Caster sugar	175 g
¼ teasp	Ground cinnamon	1.25 ml
4	Egg whites	4
	Pinch of cream of tartar	
¼ teasp	Vanilla essence	1.25 ml

Preheat oven to 300°F (150°C) Gas 2. Grease and flour baking trays.

Spread shelled nuts on grill pan and toast on all sides till golden brown. Roughly chop nuts and put in a bowl with sugar and cinnamon.

In another bowl, whisk egg whites with cream of tartar and vanilla essence till very stiff. Gently fold in nut mixture. Scrape the egg/nut mixture into a greased heavy-based frying pan and cook over a very low heat for about 15 minutes, turning mixture constantly with a wooden spoon, until it is pale brown.

Put spoonfuls of the mixture on prepared baking trays, about 1 inch (2.5 cm) apart. Bake for about 30 minutes, then reduce temperature to 250°F (130°C) Gas ½ and bake for a further 10 minutes until the biscuits are crisp.

Coconut macaroons

Overall timing 1¼ hours

Freezing Not suitable

Makes 15

4 oz	Desiccated coconut	125 g
1 teasp	Vanilla essence	5 ml
	Salt	
¼	Can of condensed milk	¼
2	Egg whites	2
½ teasp	Cream of tartar	2.5 ml

Preheat the oven to 300°F (150°C) Gas 2.

Place coconut, vanilla and a good pinch of salt in mixing bowl. Add condensed milk and mix to firm paste. Whisk egg whites and cream of tartar till stiff, then fold into paste.

Heap small spoonfuls of mixture on to baking tray lined with rice paper, leaving spreading space. Bake for 45 minutes. Turn off oven and leave inside for 15 minutes.

Choc-topped cookies

Overall timing 1 hour

Freezing Not suitable

Makes 55–60

2 oz	Stoned dates	50 g
2 oz	Seedless raisins	50 g
5 oz	Ground hazelnuts	150 g
3 oz	Milk chocolate	75 g
3 oz	Cornflour	75 g
3	Egg whites	3
	Salt	
8 oz	Caster sugar	225 g
4 oz	Plain chocolate cake covering	125 g

Preheat the oven to 350°F (180°C) Gas 4.

Coarsely chop dates and mix with raisins, hazelnuts, grated milk chocolate and cornflour. Beat egg whites with pinch of salt till stiff, then gradually beat in sugar. Fold in chocolate mixture.

With a teaspoon, place small portions on baking trays lined with rice paper, leaving spreading space. Bake for 35 minutes. Cool, then cut paper around biscuits.

Melt plain chocolate and brush over top and sides of biscuits. Leave to set before serving.

Lemon refrigerator cookies

Overall timing 20 minutes plus overnight chilling

Freezing Suitable: bake after thawing

Makes 48

8 oz	Plain flour	225 g
1 teasp	Baking powder	5 ml
4 oz	Butter	125 g
3 oz	Caster sugar	75 g
	Grated rind of 2 lemons	
½ teasp	Ground cinnamon	2.5 ml
1	Egg	1

Sift flour and baking powder into a bowl. Rub in butter till mixture resembles fine bread-crumbs. Add sugar, lemon rind and cinnamon, then beat the egg and mix well into the dough.

Shape the mixture into one or two sausage shapes about 1½ inches (4 cm) in diameter. Wrap in foil, twisting the ends to seal. Chill overnight.

Preheat the oven to 375°F (190°C) Gas 5.

Remove dough from foil wrapper and thinly slice. Place slices on greased baking trays. Bake for 10–12 minutes, till golden. Cool on wire rack.

Lemon spice squares

Overall timing 1½ hours

Freezing Suitable

Makes 9

4 oz	Butter	125 g
4 oz	Caster sugar	125 g
	Grated rind of 1 lemon	
2	Eggs	2
2 oz	Chopped candied lemon peel	50 g
4 oz	Plain flour	125 g
2 oz	Ground almonds	50 g
½ teasp	Ground cinnamon	2.5 ml
½ teasp	Ground cloves	2.5 ml
1½ teasp	Baking powder	7.5 ml
2 tbsp	Lemon juice	2 x 15 ml

Preheat the oven to 325°F (170°C) Gas 3.

Cream butter with sugar till light and fluffy. Add lemon rind and beat in the eggs. Stir in the candied lemon peel. Sift together the flour, spices and baking powder and fold into mixture, followed by the almonds and lemon juice.

Turn the mixture into a greased and lined 7 inch (18 cm) square cake tin and smooth the surface. Bake for 1 hour till top springs back when lightly pressed. Cool on a wire rack. Cut into squares to serve.

Shortbread fingers

Overall timing 1½ hours plus cooling

Freezing Not suitable

Makes 6

12 oz	Butter	350 g
4 oz	Caster sugar	125 g
8 oz	Plain flour	225 g
8 oz	Self-raising flour	225 g
¼ teasp	Salt	1.25 ml

Preheat the oven to 275°F (140°C) Gas 1.

Cream the butter with the sugar till pale and fluffy. Sift the two flours and salt together and work into the creamed mixture to make a dough.

Turn dough on to a floured surface and press out to a thick rectangle. Make decorative notches down the long sides by pinching with the fingers. Place on a baking tray and prick all over with a fork. Mark lines for the fingers.

Bake for 1 hour. Cool, then break into fingers on the marked lines. Dredge with extra caster sugar.

Scones

Overall timing 20 minutes

Freezing Not suitable

Makes 8

8 oz	Plain flour	225 g
3 teasp	Baking powder	3x5 ml
	Pinch of salt	
2 oz	Butter	50 g
2 tbsp	Caster sugar	2x15 ml
¼ pint	Milk	150 ml
	Milk or egg for glazing	

Preheat the oven to 450°F (230°C) Gas 8.

Sift flour, baking powder and salt into a mixing bowl. Rub in butter. Add sugar and milk and mix to a soft dough.

Roll out quickly to ½ inch (12.5 mm) thickness on a lightly floured board. Lightly flour scone cutter and cut out scones. Place on lightly floured baking tray and glaze tops with top of the milk or lightly beaten egg. Bake for 10 minutes. Wrap in tea-towel till ready to serve.

Variation

Peel, core and grate 1 dessert apple and scatter over rolled-out dough. Fold in half and press firmly together. Cut and bake as above.

Madeleines with cinnamon

Overall timing 50 minutes plus chilling

Freezing Suitable: bake after thawing

Makes 16

6 oz	Plain flour	175 g
3 oz	Butter	75 g
1 tbsp	Caster sugar	15 ml
1	Egg yolk	1
Filling		
4 oz	Butter	125 g
4 oz	Caster sugar	125 g
2	Eggs	2
2 oz	Ground almonds	50 g
$\frac{1}{4}$ teasp	Almond essence	1.25 ml
4 oz	Self-raising flour	125 g
1 teasp	Ground cinnamon	5 ml
	Milk to mix	
	Apricot jam	
1 tbsp	Icing sugar	15 ml

Sift flour into a bowl and rub in fat. Stir in sugar, egg yolk and enough water to bind to a soft dough. Roll out to $\frac{1}{4}$ inch (6 mm) thickness and use to line two madeleine sheets. Trim the edges and chill for 30 minutes. Preheat the oven to 375°F (190°C) Gas 5.

To make filling, cream butter with all but 1 tbsp (15 ml) caster sugar. Gradually beat in eggs, then mix in almonds and almond essence. Sift in flour and cinnamon and fold in with enough milk to give a soft dropping consistency.

Put $\frac{1}{2}$ teasp (2.5 ml) jam into each pastry case, then spoon filling into each case. Bake for 15–20 minutes till the filling is golden and springs back when lightly pressed. Cool on a wire rack.

Mix icing sugar and remaining caster sugar together and sift over tartlets before serving.

Sponge fingers

Overall timing 30 minutes

Freezing Suitable

Makes 16

4	Eggs	4
4 oz	Caster sugar	125 g
1 oz	Cornflour	25 g
3 oz	Plain flour	75 g
	Icing sugar	

Preheat the oven to 375°F (190°C) Gas 5.

Separate the eggs. Whisk whites in a bowl with 2 tbsp (2x15 ml) of the caster sugar till soft peaks form. In another bowl, beat egg yolks with remaining caster sugar. Fold yolks into whites carefully, then gradually fold in the sifted flours.

Put mixture into a piping bag fitted with a plain wide nozzle and pipe fingers 3–4 inches (7.5–10 cm) long on to greased and floured baking trays, spacing them well apart. Dust lightly with sifted icing sugar and bake for 12 minutes. Cool on wire rack.

Spicy raisin biscuits

Overall timing 1 hour plus chilling

Freezing Not suitable

Makes 40

8 oz	Butter	225 g
8 oz	Caster sugar	225 g
1	Egg	1
2 tbsp	Rum	2x15 ml
8 oz	Seedless raisins	225 g
12 oz	Self-raising flour	350 g
	Salt	
½ teasp	Ground cloves	2.5 ml
1 teasp	Ground ginger	5 ml
1	Egg white	1

Cream butter with all but 1 tbsp (15 ml) sugar till pale and fluffy. Gradually beat in egg and rum. Stir in raisins. Sift flour, pinch of salt and spices into mixture and mix to a soft dough. Chill for 30 minutes.

Preheat the oven to 350°F (180°C) Gas 4.

Roll out dough on a floured surface till ¼ inch (6 mm) thick. Stamp out rounds with pastry cutter. Arrange on greased baking trays.

Beat egg white and remaining sugar together till frothy and brush over biscuits. Bake for about 15 minutes till pale golden. Cool on the trays for 3–4 minutes till firm, then transfer to a wire rack and leave to cool completely.

Spicy sweet fritters

Overall timing 45 minutes

Freezing Not suitable

Makes 20

9 oz	Plain flour	250 g
½ teasp	Ground ginger	2.5 ml
½ teasp	Ground allspice	2.5 ml
½ teasp	Ground mace	2.5 ml
	Salt	
4 oz	Icing sugar	125 g
3	Egg yolks	3
1 tbsp	Orange-flower water	15 ml
3½ oz	Butter	100 g
	Grated rind of 1 lemon	
	Oil for deep frying	

Sift flour, spices, pinch of salt and 3 oz (75 g) icing sugar into a bowl. Mix egg yolks and flower water with 2 tbsp (2x15 ml) cold water. Add to bowl with butter and rind. Mix to a soft dough.

Roll out dough till ¼ inch (6 mm) thick. Cut out fancy shapes with pastry cutters.

Heat oil in a deep-fryer to 340°F (170°C). Fry biscuits, a few at a time, for about 5 minutes till golden. Drain on kitchen paper. Sift the remaining icing sugar over.

Golden arcs

Overall timing 30 minutes

Freezing Not suitable

Makes 30

8 oz	Fine cornmeal	225 g
6 oz	Plain flour	175 g
2 teasp	Ground cardamom	2x5 ml
½ teasp	Ground coriander	2.5 ml
4 oz	Caster sugar	125 g
¼ teasp	Vanilla essence	1.25 ml
8 oz	Butter	225 g
4	Egg yolks	4

Preheat the oven to 400°F (200°C) Gas 6.

Sift the cornmeal, flour and spices into a bowl and stir in the sugar. Add the vanilla, butter and egg yolks and mix to a soft dough.

Put the mixture into a piping bag fitted with a star nozzle and pipe in 3 inch (7.5 cm) lengths on to a greased and floured baking tray. Bake for about 15 minutes till golden. Remove from the oven and allow to cool for 5 minutes. Transfer to a wire rack and leave to cool completely.

Orange liqueur biscuits

Overall timing 45 minutes plus chilling

Freezing Suitable: cut out and bake after thawing

Makes 36

2	Hard-boiled egg yolks	2
8 oz	Plain flour	225 g
4 oz	Caster sugar	125 g
	Salt	
	Ground cinnamon	
4 oz	Butter	125 g
2 tbsp	Orange liqueur	2x15 ml

Push egg yolks through a sieve into a mixing bowl. Sift in the flour and mix well. Make a well in centre and add sugar and a pinch each of salt and cinnamon.

Cut the butter into pieces and work into the mixture, a little at a time. Work in the liqueur and roll paste into a ball. Lightly dust with flour and leave in a cool place (not the refrigerator) for at least 1 hour.

Preheat the oven to 375°F (190°C) Gas 5.

Roll out the paste thinly and stamp out shapes with fancy pastry cutters. Place biscuits on a greased and lined baking tray and bake for 10–15 minutes, till light golden. Remove biscuits carefully from paper and cool on a wire rack.

Rhine biscuits

Overall timing 45 minutes plus chilling

Freezing Not suitable

Makes 30

9 oz	Plain flour	250 g
1 teasp	Ground cinnamon	5 ml
½ teasp	Ground cloves	2.5 ml
6 oz	Butter	175 g
4 oz	Caster sugar	125 g
	Grated rind of 1 lemon	
1	Egg	1
5 tbsp	Milk	5 x 15 ml

Sift the flour and spices into a bowl. Add the butter and rub in till the mixture resembles fine breadcrumbs. Stir in the sugar and lemon rind. Add the egg and enough milk to make a stiff dough. Knead lightly and chill for 1 hour.

Preheat the oven to 350°F (180°C) Gas 4.

Roll out the dough on a floured board till ¼ inch (6 mm) thick, then cut out shapes with a pastry cutter. Arrange on a greased and floured baking tray. Bake for 15–20 minutes till golden. Remove from the oven and leave to cool for 3 minutes. Transfer to a wire rack and leave to cool completely.

Almond crescents

Overall timing 30 minutes plus cooling

Freezing Suitable: bake from frozen, allowing 20–25 minutes

Makes 20

5 oz	Blanched almonds	150 g
2 oz	Caster sugar	50 g
	A few drops of vanilla essence	
1	Egg white	1
1 oz	Plain flour	25 g
1	Egg	1
1 oz	Flaked almonds	25 g
2 tbsp	Milk sweetened with icing sugar	2x15 ml

Preheat the oven to 400°F (200°C) Gas 6.

Mix chopped almonds with caster sugar and vanilla essence. Moisten with egg white until evenly combined. Add flour and gather mixture together with fingertips. Divide into "nut-sized" pieces. With lightly floured hands, roll into small cigar shapes with pointed ends. Brush each one with beaten egg and sprinkle with flaked almonds. Bend into a crescent shape.

Place on a greased baking tray and brush lightly with any remaining egg. Bake for about 10–15 minutes till evenly coloured. Remove from oven and brush immediately with sweetened milk. Using a palette knife or egg slice, carefully loosen crescents and transfer to wire rack to cool.

Macaroons

Overall timing 2½ hours

Freezing Not suitable

Makes 55

4	Egg whites	4
12 oz	Caster sugar	350 g
11 oz	Ground almonds	300 g
	Grated rind of 1 orange	
	Grated rind of 1 lemon	
	Pinch of salt	
1 teasp	Ground cinnamon	5 ml
½ teasp	Ground cardamom	2.5 ml

Preheat the oven to 275°F (140°C) Gas 1.

Whisk the egg whites till stiff. Gradually whisk in the caster sugar, a spoonful at a time. Fold in the almonds, orange and lemon rind, salt and spices.

Place heaped teaspoonfuls of mixture on baking trays lined with rice paper. Put on the middle and lower shelves of the oven and leave to dry for 1½–2 hours. Halfway through, swap trays round.

Cool on baking trays. Break paper from around each macaroon.

Pastries

Pastry horns

Overall timing 4½ hours

Freezing Suitable: shape and bake after thawing

Makes 6

9 oz	Plain flour	250 g
	Pinch of salt	
8 oz	Butter	225 g
4 fl oz	Cold water	120 ml
1	Egg	1
	Caster sugar	
	Whipped cream	
	Jam	

Sift flour and salt into a bowl. Rub in half the butter, then add water and mix to a dough. Chill for 1 hour. Chill remaining butter.

Place chilled butter between two sheets of greaseproof paper and roll out to a 5x3 inch (13x8 cm) rectangle.

Roll out dough on floured surface to 10x8 inch (25x20 cm) rectangle. Put butter in centre. Fold down top third over butter, then fold up bottom third. Turn so that folds are to the side. Roll out to 5x14 inch (13x36 cm) rectangle and fold again as before. Chill for 15 minutes.

Repeat the rolling, turning and folding four more times, chilling between each process.

Preheat the oven to 425°F (220°C) Gas 7.

Roll out dough to ⅛ inch (3 mm) thick. Trim to a 15x6 inch (38x15 cm) rectangle, then cut into six 1 inch (2.5 cm) strips. Glaze the strips with beaten egg, then wrap them, glazed side out, round six pastry horn moulds, starting at the point and overlapping the dough slightly.

Place on a baking tray and dredge with caster sugar. Bake for 10 minutes till crisp and golden. Slide off the moulds and cool.

Fill the horns with cream and jam.

Soured cream pastries

Overall timing 10 minutes plus chilling

Freezing Not suitable

Makes 20

12 oz	Plain flour	350 g
6 oz	Butter	175 g
1	Egg yolk	1
¼ pint	Carton of soured cream	150 ml
Filling		
8 oz	Cream cheese	225 g
2 oz	Caster sugar	50 g
2 oz	Sultanas	50 g

Sift flour into a bowl and rub in the butter till the mixture resembles fine breadcrumbs. Add the egg yolk and soured cream and mix with a palette knife to make a soft dough. Chill for 1 hour.

Mix together the cream cheese, sugar and sultanas.

Preheat the oven to 400°F (200°C) Gas 6.

Roll out the dough and cut out 40 rounds with a fluted 2 inch (5 cm) cutter. Put a spoonful of the filling on to half the rounds, then cover with the remaining rounds and press the edges together to seal. Arrange on a baking sheet and bake for 25 minutes till golden brown.

Mille feuilles

Overall timing 40 minutes plus cooling

Freezing Not suitable

Makes 6

7½ oz	Frozen puff pastry	212 g
1 pint	Milk	560 ml
	Pinch of salt	
1	Vanilla pod	1
	Strip of lemon rind	
4 oz	Caster sugar	125 g
4	Medium eggs	4
1 oz	Plain flour	25 g
2 tbsp	Rum	2x15 ml
	Icing sugar	

Thaw pastry. Preheat the oven to 425°F (220°C) Gas 7.

Put the milk, salt, vanilla pod and lemon rind into a saucepan and bring to the boil. Remove from the heat and infuse for 10 minutes.

Beat together the sugar, eggs and flour in a bowl till smooth. Gradually strain the milk into the bowl, stirring, then pour the mixture back into the saucepan. Bring to the boil, stirring, and simmer till thick. Stir in the rum. Remove from the heat. Cover with damp greaseproof paper and cool.

Halve dough and roll out into two rectangles, 12x4 inches (30x10 cm). Trim edges and knock up. Place on dampened baking trays. Mark one rectangle into six 2 inch (5 cm) slices with a sharp, pointed knife. Bake for about 10 minutes till well risen and golden. Allow to cool.

Place unmarked pastry rectangle on a board and spread with custard. Place marked pastry rectangle on top and dredge well with icing sugar. Cut into slices along marked lines. Eat same day.

Baklava

Overall timing 1½ hours

Freezing Suitable

Makes 8

4 oz	Unsalted butter	125 g
1 lb	Ready-made phyllo pastry	450 g
8 oz	Walnuts, almonds or pistachios	225 g
2 tbsp	Caster sugar	2x15 ml
½ teasp	Ground cinnamon	2.5 ml
Syrup		
4 oz	Clear honey	125 g
¼ pint	Water	150 ml
2 tbsp	Lemon juice	2x15 ml

Preheat the oven to 425°F (220°C) Gas 7.

Melt the butter in a small saucepan and brush a little over the bottom and sides of a 10x8 inch (25x20 cm) roasting tin.

Layer half the pastry sheets in the tin, brushing liberally with butter between each sheet, and folding in the edges so that sheets fit the tin. Keep rest of the pastry covered to prevent it drying out.

Mix together the chopped nuts, sugar and cinnamon and spread over pastry. Cover with remaining pastry layers, brushing each with butter. Brush the top layer well with any remaining butter.

Cut through the top two layers of pastry with a sharp knife to divide into four widthways, then cut each quarter in half diagonally so you have eight triangles. Bake for 15 minutes, then reduce heat to 350°F (180°C) Gas 4 and bake for a further 25–30 minutes till well risen and golden.

Meanwhile, make the syrup. Melt the honey in the water and add the lemon juice. Allow to cool.

Remove baklava from oven, pour cold syrup over and leave to cool in tin. Cut along the marked lines to serve.

Irish apple turnovers

Overall timing 2 hours including refrigeration

Freezing Suitable: refresh in 350°F (180°C) Gas 4 oven for 10–15 minutes

Makes 20 small or 12 large

9 oz	Plain flour	250 g
2 teasp	Baking powder	2x5 ml
5 oz	Caster sugar	150 g
5 oz	Butter	150 g
2 tbsp	Cold water	2x15 ml
1 lb	Cox's Orange Pippins	450 g
1 tbsp	Apricot jam	15 ml
2 tbsp	Mixed dried fruit	2x15 ml
	Icing sugar	

Sift flour, baking powder and sugar into a bowl and make a well in the centre. Cut the softened butter into small pieces and put round the edge. Add water and knead to make a smooth dough. Chill for 1 hour.

Preheat the oven to 350°F (180°C) Gas 4.

Core apples. Place them on a baking tray and bake for 20 minutes till tender. Peel them, then mash and mix with the apricot jam and dried fruit.

Increase the oven temperature to 400°F (200°C) Gas 6.

Roll out dough on a lightly floured board to ⅛ inch (3 mm) thickness. Cut out rounds or squares. Spoon a little apple mixture into the centre of each dough shape. Moisten edges with water, fold the dough over to form a half moon, triangle or rectangle, and press edges well together. Place on a greased baking tray.

Bake for 15–20 minutes. Dredge with icing sugar and serve warm with whipped cream or vanilla ice cream.

Jam puffs

Overall timing 20 minutes plus thawing

Freezing Not suitable

Makes 12

7½ oz	Frozen puff pastry	212 g
1	Egg	1
5 tbsp	Jam	5x15 ml

Thaw pastry. Preheat the oven to 425°F (220°C) Gas 7.

Roll out dough to ¼ inch (6 mm) thickness. Cut into 2 inch (5 cm) rounds with a pastry cutter. Mark the centres with a small cutter or a bottle lid. Do not cut through.

Place on a dampened baking tray and brush with beaten egg. Bake for about 10 minutes till well risen and golden. Cool on a wire rack.

Remove centres and put a heaped teaspoon of jam in each. Use centres of pastry as lids, if liked. Serve warm.

Palmiers

Overall timing 1½ hours plus chilling

Freezing Suitable: shape and bake after thawing

Makes 12–16

8 oz	Plain flour	225 g
½ teasp	Salt	2.5 ml
6 oz	Butter	175 g
2 teasp	Lemon juice	2x5 ml
¼ pint	Cold water	150 ml
	Caster sugar	

Sift flour and salt into a bowl and rub in 1½ oz (40 g) butter. Mix in lemon juice and enough water to make a soft but not sticky dough. Knead till smooth.

Roll out dough on floured surface to 15x5 inch (38x13 cm) rectangle. Divide remaining butter into three and cut into small pieces. Dot one-third of butter over top two-thirds of dough. Fold up bottom third, then fold top third over it. Press edges to seal and turn dough so folds are to the side.

Repeat rolling out, adding another third of fat and folding, then chill for 15 minutes.

Repeat process again, using rest of butter, and chill for 15 minutes.

Preheat the oven to 425°F (220°C) Gas 7.

Roll out dough to ¼ inch (6mm) thick. Sprinkle with caster sugar. Fold the long sides in to meet at the centre and sprinkle again with sugar. Fold the long sides in again to make four layers. Cut across folds to make ½ inch (12.5 mm) slices.

Arrange slices on dampened baking tray and flatten slightly. Bake for 6 minutes on each side. Serve warm.

Almond tartlets

Overall timing 1 hour plus cooling

Freezing Suitable: ice and decorate after thawing

Makes 12

14 oz	Shortcrust pastry	400 g
4	Eggs	4
3½ oz	Caster sugar	100 g
4 oz	Ground almonds	125 g
Decoration		
5 oz	Icing sugar	150 g
1 tbsp	Milk	15 ml
1 tbsp	Lemon juice	15 ml
12	Glacé cherries	12
	Angelica leaves	

Preheat the oven to 400°F (200°C) Gas 6.

Roll out the dough and use to line 12 tartlet tins. Bake blind for 10 minutes, then remove from oven.

Separate the eggs. Add sugar to yolks and whisk together till pale and thick. Fold in ground almonds. In another bowl, whisk egg whites till stiff, then fold into almond mixture.

Fill pastry cases with almond mixture. Place on a baking tray and bake for 15–20 minutes till centre is firm and springy. Leave to cool.

Sift the icing sugar into a bowl and beat in milk and lemon juice till smooth. Spread over tartlets. Decorate with whole glacé cherries and angelica leaves and leave till set.

Mince pies

Overall timing 30 minutes

Freezing Suitable: bake from frozen in 425°F (220°C) Gas 7 oven for 20–30 minutes

Makes 15–20

8 oz	Shortcrust pastry	225 g
8 oz	Mincemeat	225 g
3 tbsp	Brandy	3x15 ml
6 tbsp	Milk	6x15 ml
2 tbsp	Caster sugar	2x15 ml

Preheat the oven to 400°F (200°C) Gas 6.

Roll out the dough on a floured surface. Stamp out 20 rounds with a 2½ inch (6.5 cm) cutter, then 20 rounds with a 2 inch (5 cm) cutter. Press the larger rounds into a greased 20-hole bun tray.

Mix the mincemeat and brandy in a small bowl and divide between the pastry cases. Dip small dough rounds in the milk, then place one on each pie. Using a fork, press the edges together firmly to seal.

Sprinkle the caster sugar over the top. Bake for about 20 minutes till golden. Serve hot or cold.

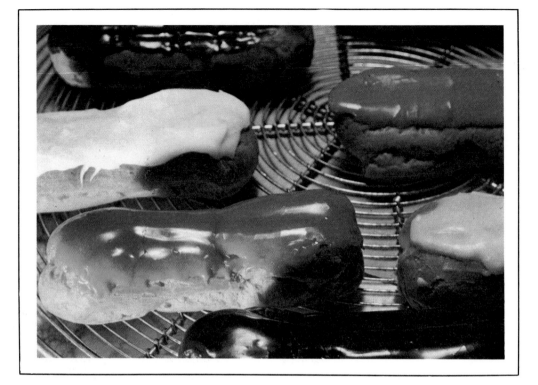

Eclairs

Overall timing 1½ hours

Freezing Suitable: bake from frozen

Makes 16

4 oz	Choux paste	125 g
½ pint	Whipping cream	300 ml
2 tbsp	Caster sugar	2x15 ml
4 oz	Icing sugar	125 g
2 teasp	Drinking chocolate	2x5 ml
1–2 tbsp	Hot water	1–2x 15 ml

Preheat the oven to 425°F (220°C) Gas 7.

Spoon paste into piping bag fitted with ½ inch (12.5 mm) plain nozzle and pipe fingers, about 3 inches (7.5 cm) long, on greased baking trays. Leave plenty of space between fingers so they have room to expand during baking. Bake for about 30 minutes till golden and crisp. Transfer to a wire rack. Make a slit down side of each éclair to allow steam to escape and leave to cool.

Whip cream with sugar until just thick and holding soft peaks. Spoon cream into cooled éclairs and return to wire rack placed over greaseproof paper.

Mix icing sugar with drinking chocolate and hot water. The glacé icing should be thick enough to coat the back of a spoon. If too thick, add a little more water; if too runny, add more icing sugar. Dip top of one éclair at a time into icing. Leave on wire rack till icing is set. Eat the same day.

Index